RAIL ATLAS OF BRITAIN

Compiled by **S. K. Baker**

Oxford Publishing Co. Oxford

Oxford Publishing Co.

First Edition 1977
(SBN 86093 009 2)
Second Edition 1978
(SBN 86093 046 7)
Third Edition 1980
(SBN 86093 106 4)

Maps for Third Edition produced by
Katerprint Co. Ltd., Cowley, Oxford.

Printed and Bound in the
City of Oxford

Published by
Oxford Publishing Co.
8 The Roundway
Headington, Oxford

PREFACE TO FIRST EDITION

The inspiration for this atlas was two-fold; firstly a feeling of total bewilderment by 'Llans' and 'Abers' on first visiting South Wales four years ago, and secondly a wall railway map drawn by a friend, Martin Bairstow. Since then, at university, there has been steady progress in drawing the rail network throughout Great Britain. The author feels sure that this atlas as it has finally evolved will be useful to all with an interest in railways, whether professional or enthusiast. The emphasis is on the current network since it is felt that this information is not published elsewhere.

Throughout, the main aim has been to show clearly, using expanded sheets where necessary, the railways of this country, including the whole of London Transport and light railways. Passenger lines are distinguished by colour according to operating company and all freight-only lines are depicted in red. The criterion for a British Rail passenger line has been taken as at least one advertised passenger train per day in each direction. On passenger routes, to assist the traveller, single and multiple track sections, with crossing loops on single lines have been shown. Symbols are used to identify both major centres of rail freight, such as collieries and power stations, and railway installations such as locomotive depots and works. Secondary information, for example junction names and significant tunnels, with lengths if greater than one mile, has been added in areas where clarity would not be significantly affected.

The author would like to express his thanks to members of the Oxford University Railway Society and to Nigel Bird, Chris Hammond and Richard Warson in particular for help in compiling and correcting the maps. His cousin, Dr Tony McCann deserves special thanks for removing much of the tedium by computer sorting the index, as do Oxford City Libraries for providing excellent reference facilities.

June 1977

PREFACE TO THIRD EDITION

This expanded third edition of the Rail Atlas of Britain includes the many recent alterations in the rail network since the last edition and also incorporates several new features, notably three maps of the railways of Northern Ireland. Much more detail is shown, for example, customer names and tunnels over 100 yards long. To permit this without loss of clarity, seven new insets and four larger scale maps are added.

The author would like to thank those friends who have helped him to collect material for this new edition, and also everyone who has written to him, expressing their appreciation of the Atlas, and supplying much useful information.

Stuart K. Baker

Sheffield, South Yorks.
September 1980

CONTENTS

	Page
Preface to 1st and 3rd Editions	(i)
Key to symbols and codes used on maps	(ii)
Diagram showing incidence of maps	(iii)
Maps	1–88
Index to Passenger Stations	89–106
Index to B.R. Depots and Stabling Points	107
Index to Freight Terminals and Yards	108–115
Index to Minor Railways	115
Index to B.R.E.L. Works	115

Publisher's Note

Although situations are constantly changing on the railways of Britain every effort has been made by the author to ensure complete accuracy of the maps in the book at the time of going to press.

We must also state that the availability of information regarding all lines and track beds in Britain is not a source of permission to walk on British Rail property or explore closed lines.

KEY TO ATLAS

		Surface	Tunnel	Tube
British Rail — Passenger Also Northern Ireland and Isle of Man Railways	Multiple Track			
	Single Track			
London Transport *(Line indicated by code)* Also Greater Glasgow and Tyne & Wear	Multiple Track	C	C	C
	Single Track	C	C	C
Preserved & Minor Passenger Railways	Multiple Track			
	Single Track			
Freight only lines — *(British Rail & Others)*	No Single/ Multiple Distinction			

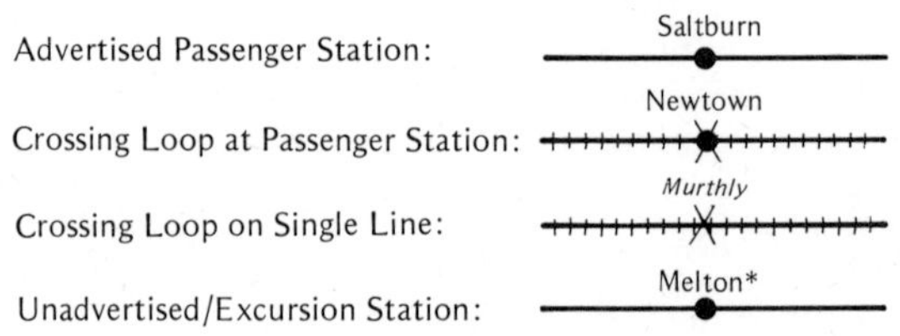

Advertised Passenger Station:
Saltburn
Crossing Loop at Passenger Station:
Newtown
Crossing Loop on Single Line:
Murthly
Unadvertised/Excursion Station:
Melton*

			LM ER
Major Power Signalboxes	PRESTON	B.R. Region Breaks	
Carriage Sidings	C.S.	Colliery *(including opencast site)*	
Freight/Marshalling Yard	TINSLEY	Power Station	
Freightliner Terminal	FLT	Oil Refinery	
National Carriers Depot	NCL	Oil Terminal	
Locomotive Depot/Stabling Point	BS	Cement Works or Terminal	
British Rail Engineering Ltd.	BREL	Quarry	
Junction Names	*Haughley Junc.*	Other Freight Terminal	

DIAGRAM OF MAPS

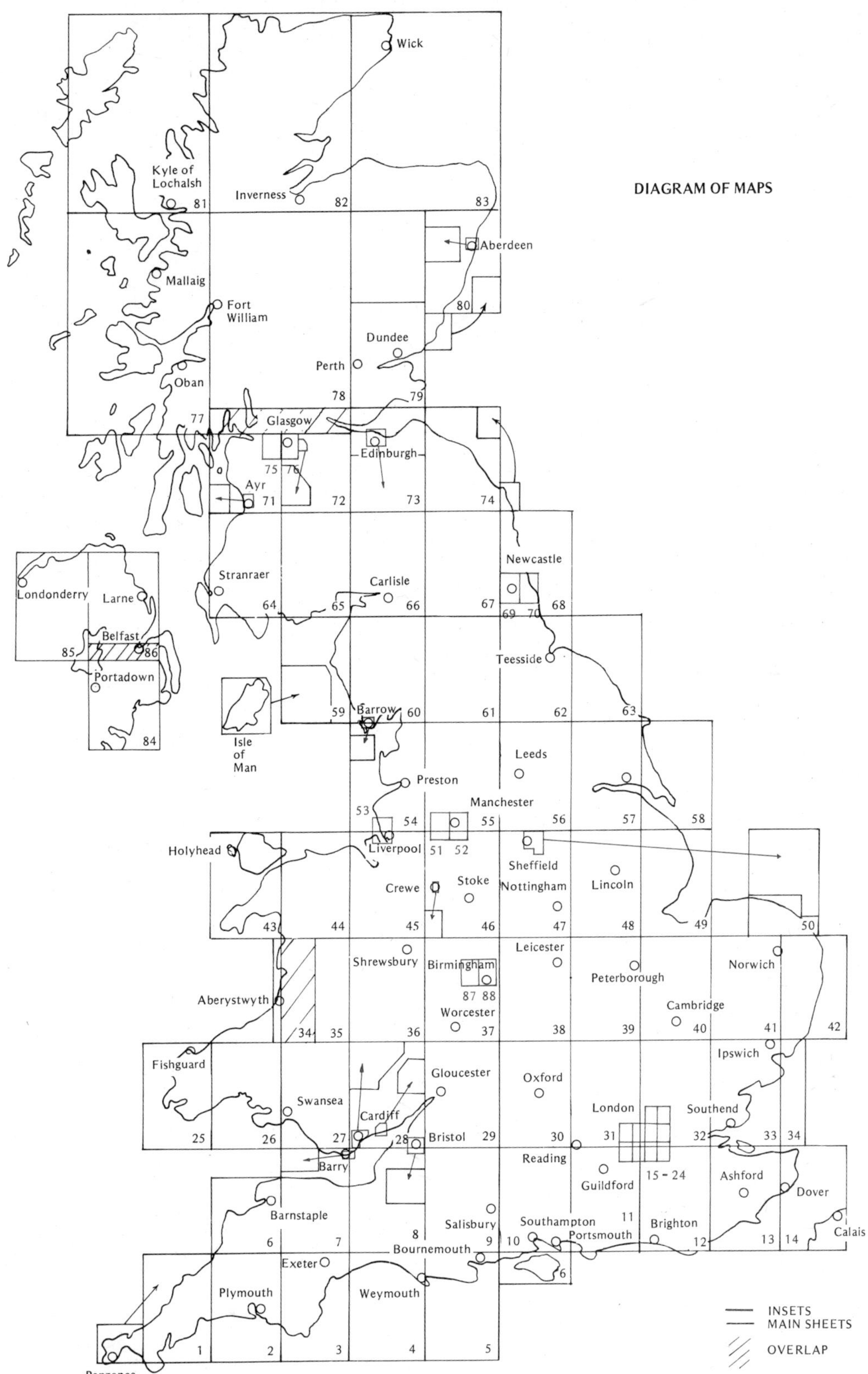
Wick
Kyle of Lochalsh
Inverness
81
82
83
Aberdeen
Mallaig
Fort William
80
Dundee
Perth
Oban
78
79
77
Glasgow
Edinburgh
75
76
Ayr
71
72
73
74
Newcastle
Stranraer
Carlisle
Londonderry
Larne
64
65
66
67
68
69
70
Belfast
85
86
Portadown
84
Teesside
Isle of Man
59
Barrow
60
61
62
63
Leeds
Preston
Manchester
53
54
55
56
57
58
Holyhead
Liverpool
51
52
Sheffield
Crewe
Stoke
Nottingham
Lincoln
43
44
45
46
47
48
49
50
Leicester
Shrewsbury
Birmingham
Peterborough
Norwich
87
88
Aberystwyth
Worcester
Cambridge
34
35
36
37
38
39
40
41
42
Ipswich
Fishguard
Gloucester
Oxford
Swansea
London
Southend
Cardiff
25
26
27
28
Bristol
29
30
31
32
33
34
Barry
Reading
Guildford
15 - 24
Ashford
Dover
Barnstaple
Salisbury
Southampton
11
Brighton
Calais
6
7
8
9
10
Portsmouth
12
13
14
Bournemouth
Exeter
6
Plymouth
Weymouth
1
2
3
4
5
Penzance
INSETS
MAIN SHEETS
OVERLAP

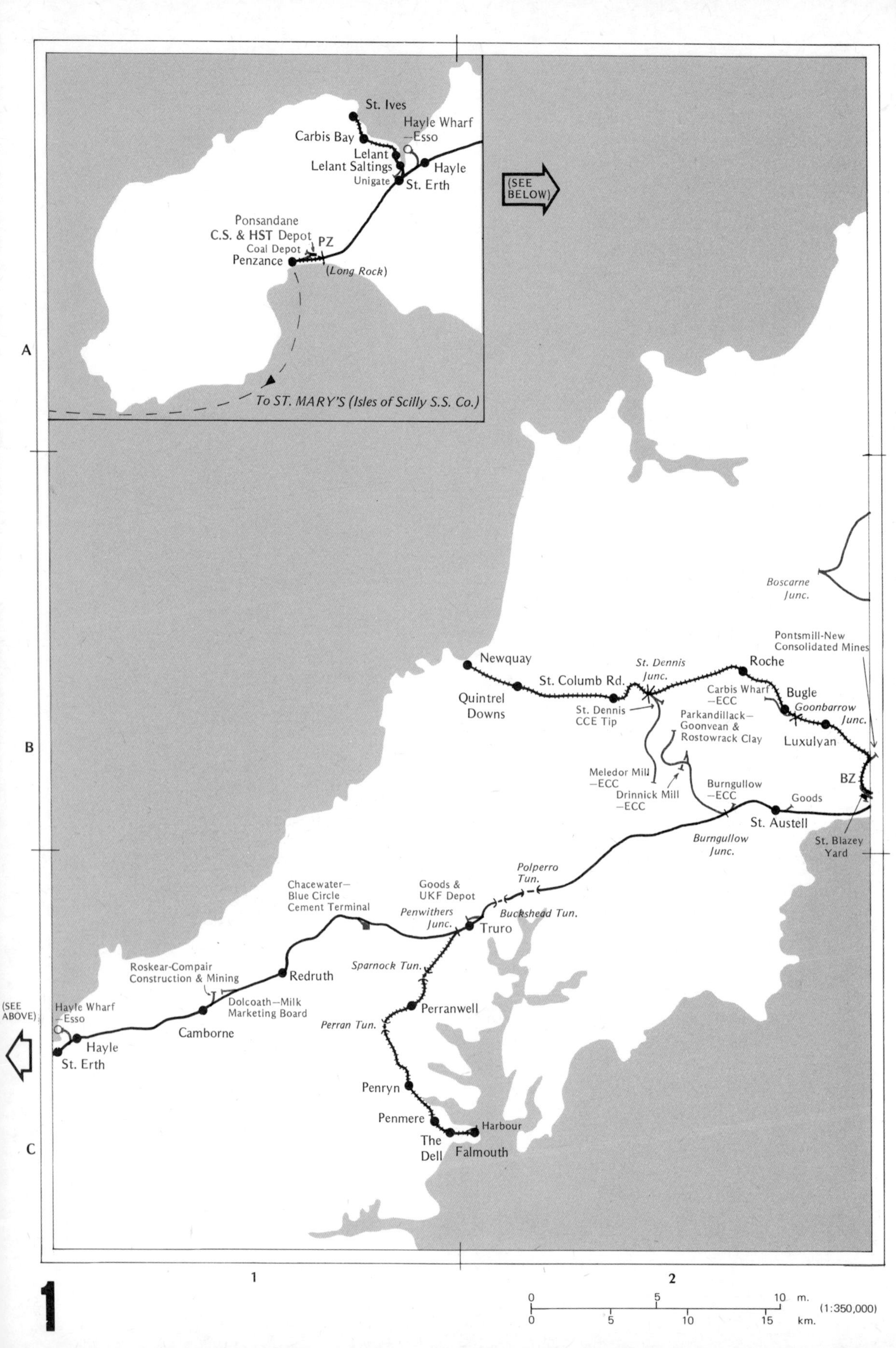
St. Ives
Carbis Bay
Hayle Wharf
—Esso
Lelant
Lelant Saltings
Hayle
Unigate
St. Erth
(SEE BELOW)
Ponsandane
C.S. & HST Depot
PZ
Coal Depot
Penzance
(Long Rock)
To ST. MARY'S (Isles of Scilly S.S. Co.)
A
B
C
Boscarne Junc.
Pontsmill-New Consolidated Mines
Newquay
St. Columb Rd.
St. Dennis Junc.
Roche
Quintrel Downs
St. Dennis CCE Tip
Carbis Wharf —ECC
Bugle
Goonbarrow Junc.
Parkandillack— Goonvean & Rostowrack Clay
Luxulyan
Meledor Mill —ECC
Drinnick Mill —ECC
Burngullow —ECC
Goods
BZ
St. Austell
Burngullow Junc.
St. Blazey Yard
Polperro Tun.
Chacewater— Blue Circle Cement Terminal
Goods & UKF Depot
Buckshead Tun.
Penwithers Junc.
Truro
Sparnock Tun.
Roskear-Compair Construction & Mining
Redruth
Dolcoath—Milk Marketing Board
Perranwell
(SEE ABOVE)
Hayle Wharf —Esso
Camborne
Perran Tun.
Hayle
St. Erth
Penryn
Penmere
Harbour
The Dell
Falmouth
1
2
0 5 10 m.
0 5 10 15 km.
(1:350,000)

1

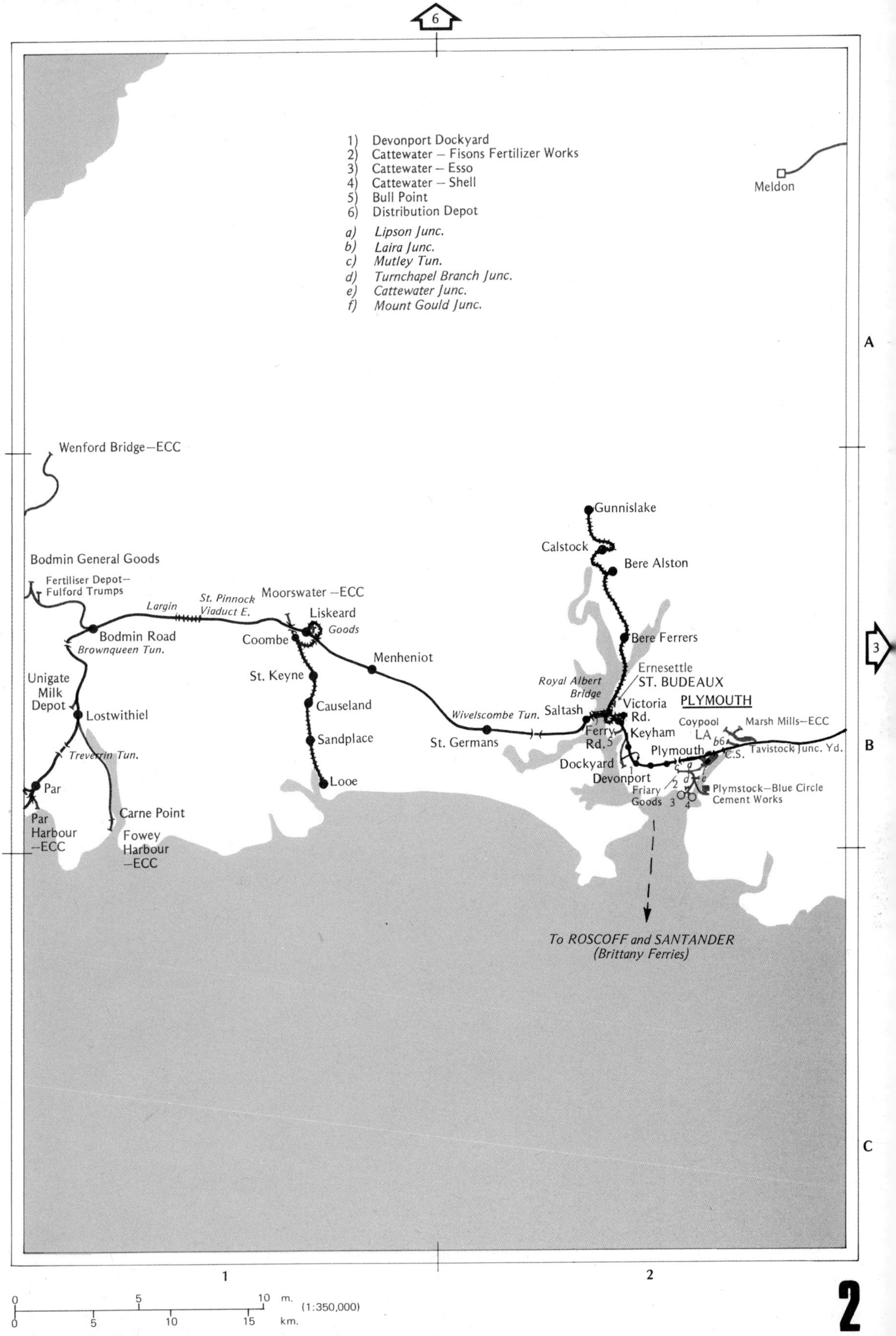

6

1) Devonport Dockyard
2) Cattewater – Fisons Fertilizer Works
3) Cattewater – Esso
4) Cattewater – Shell
5) Bull Point
6) Distribution Depot

a) Lipson Junc.
b) Laira Junc.
c) Mutley Tun.
d) Turnchapel Branch Junc.
e) Cattewater Junc.
f) Mount Gould Junc.

Meldon

A

Wenford Bridge–ECC

Gunnislake
Calstock
Bere Alston
Bodmin General Goods
Fertiliser Depot–
Fulford Trumps
Largin
St. Pinnock Viaduct E.
Moorswater –ECC
Liskeard
Goods
Coombe
Bodmin Road
Brownqueen Tun.
Bere Ferrers
Menheniot
St. Keyne
Unigate Milk Depot
Ernesettle
Royal Albert Bridge
ST. BUDEAUX
Causeland
Lostwithiel
Victoria Rd.
PLYMOUTH
Wivelscombe Tun.
Saltash
Ferry Rd.
Coypool
Marsh Mills–ECC
Sandplace
St. Germans
Keyham
LA
Tavistock Junc. Yd.
C.S.
Plymouth
Treverrin Tun.
Dockyard
Looe
Devonport
Par
Friary Goods
Plymstock–Blue Circle Cement Works
Carne Point
Par Harbour –ECC
Fowey Harbour –ECC

B

To ROSCOFF and SANTANDER
(Brittany Ferries)

C

3

1 2

0 5 10 m. (1:350,000)
0 5 10 15 km.

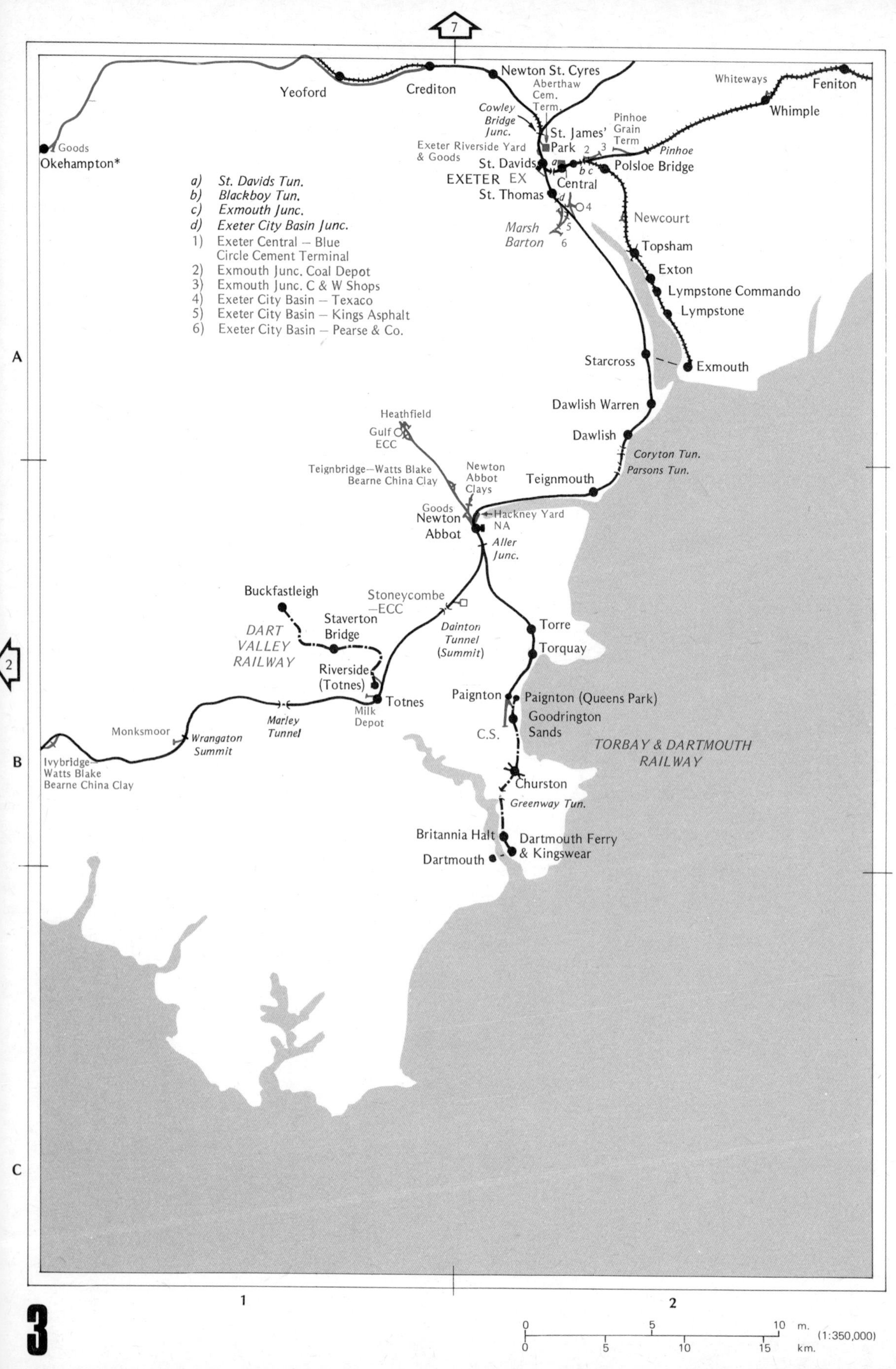

7
Newton St. Cyres
Yeoford
Crediton
Okehampton*
Goods
Abertham Cem. Term.
Cowley Bridge Junc.
St. James' Park
Exeter Riverside Yard & Goods
St. Davids
EXETER
EX
Central
St. Thomas
Whiteways
Feniton
Whimple
Pinhoe Grain Term
Pinhoe
Polsloe Bridge
Marsh Barton
Newcourt
Topsham
Exton
Lympstone Commando
Lympstone
Exmouth
a) St. Davids Tun.
b) Blackboy Tun.
c) Exmouth Junc.
d) Exeter City Basin Junc.
1) Exeter Central – Blue Circle Cement Terminal
2) Exmouth Junc. Coal Depot
3) Exmouth Junc. C & W Shops
4) Exeter City Basin – Texaco
5) Exeter City Basin – Kings Asphalt
6) Exeter City Basin – Pearse & Co.
Starcross
Dawlish Warren
Dawlish
Coryton Tun.
Parsons Tun.
Heathfield
Gulf ECC
Teignbridge–Watts Blake Bearne China Clay
Newton Abbot Clays
Teignmouth
Goods
Newton Abbot
Hackney Yard NA
Aller Junc.
Buckfastleigh
Stoneycombe –ECC
Staverton Bridge
DART VALLEY RAILWAY
Dainton Tunnel (Summit)
Riverside (Totnes)
Torre
Torquay
Totnes
Milk Depot
Paignton
Paignton (Queens Park)
Goodrington Sands
C.S.
Monksmoor
Wrangaton Summit
Marley Tunnel
Ivybridge–Watts Blake Bearne China Clay
TORBAY & DARTMOUTH RAILWAY
Churston
Greenway Tun.
Britannia Halt
Dartmouth Ferry & Kingswear
Dartmouth
2
A
B
C
1
2
0 5 10 m.
0 5 10 15 km.
(1:350,000)

8
Axminster
Maiden Newton
Colyton
Colyford
SEATON TRAMWAY (2′ 9″)
Axmouth
Seaton
A
5
B
C
1
2
0
5
10
m.
(1:350,000)
0
5
10
15
km.

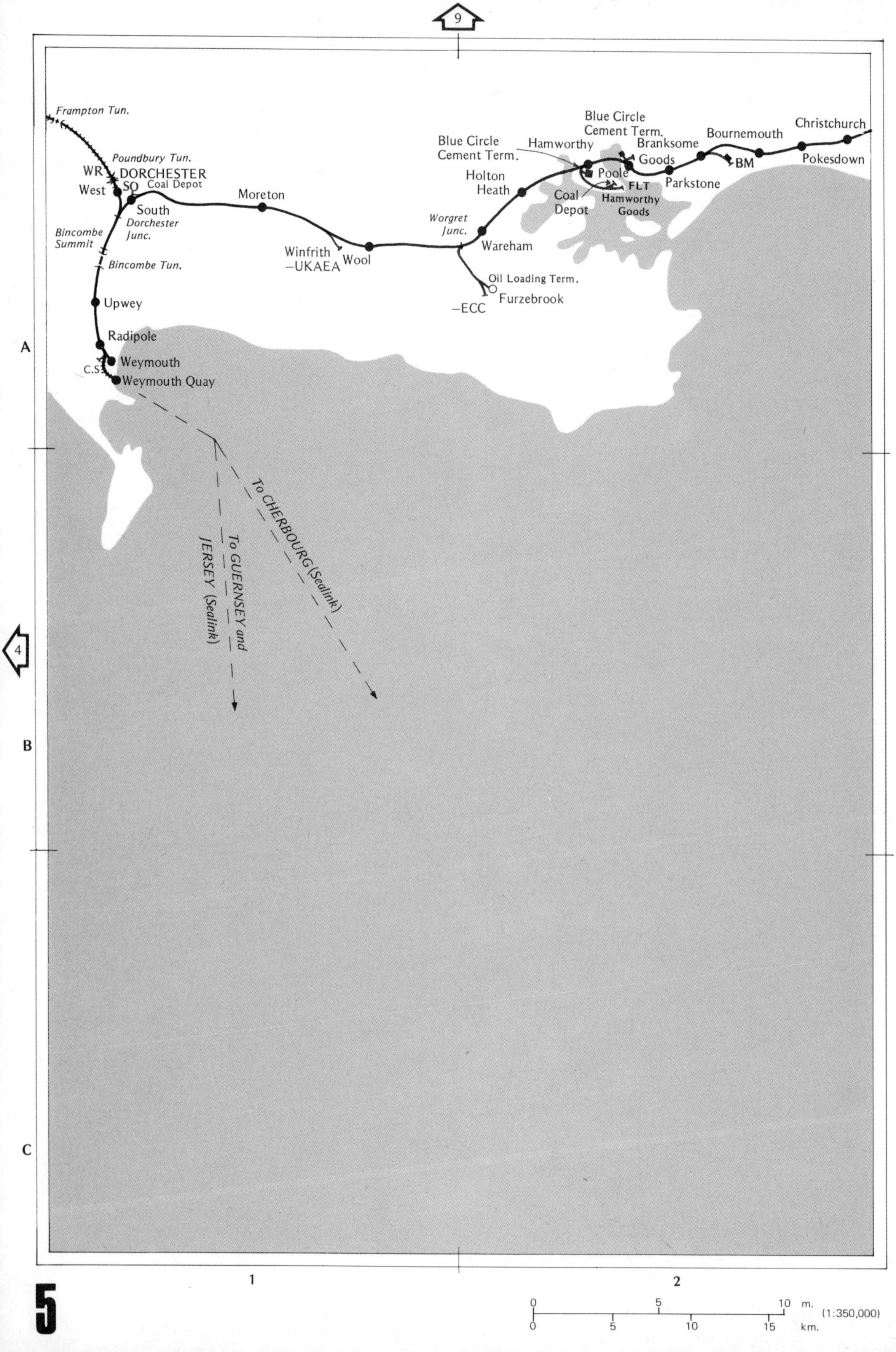

9
Frampton Tun.
Poundbury Tun.
WR
DORCHESTER
West
SO
Coal Depot
South
Dorchester Junc.
Bincombe Summit
Bincombe Tun.
Upwey
Radipole
Weymouth
C.S.
Weymouth Quay
Moreton
Winfrith
–UKAEA
Wool
Worgret Junc.
Wareham
Oil Loading Term.
Furzebrook
–ECC
Holton Heath
Blue Circle Cement Term.
Hamworthy
Blue Circle Cement Term.
Poole
Coal Depot
FLT
Hamworthy Goods
Branksome
Goods
Parkstone
Bournemouth
BM
Christchurch
Pokesdown
To CHERBOURG (Sealink)
To GUERNSEY and JERSEY (Sealink)
4
A
B
C
1
2
0 5 10 m.
0 5 10 15 km.
(1:350,000)

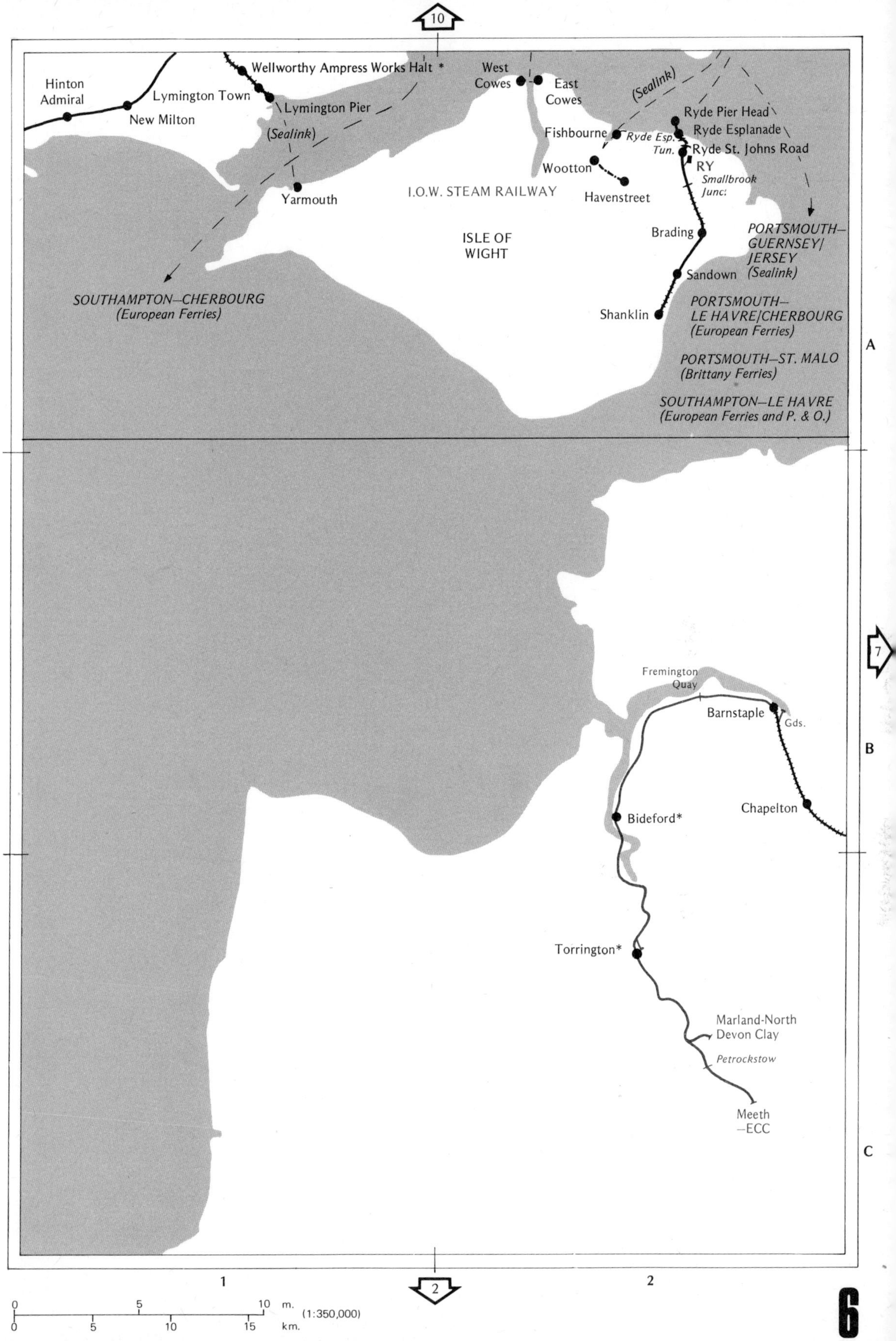

10
Hinton
Admiral
New Milton
Lymington Town
Wellworthy Ampress Works Halt *
Lymington Pier
(Sealink)
Yarmouth
West
Cowes
East
Cowes
(Sealink)
Fishbourne
Wootton
Havenstreet
I.O.W. STEAM RAILWAY
Ryde Pier Head
Ryde Esplanade
Ryde Esp.
Tun.
Ryde St. Johns Road
RY
Smallbrook
Junc.
Brading
Sandown
Shanklin
ISLE OF
WIGHT
SOUTHAMPTON—CHERBOURG
(European Ferries)
PORTSMOUTH—
GUERNSEY/
JERSEY
(Sealink)
PORTSMOUTH—
LE HAVRE/CHERBOURG
(European Ferries)
PORTSMOUTH—ST. MALO
(Brittany Ferries)
SOUTHAMPTON—LE HAVRE
(European Ferries and P. & O.)
A
7
Fremington
Quay
Barnstaple
Gds.
B
Chapelton
Bideford*
Torrington*
Marland-North
Devon Clay
Petrockstow
Meeth
—ECC
C
1
2
2
0 5 10 m.
(1:350,000)
0 5 10 15 km.

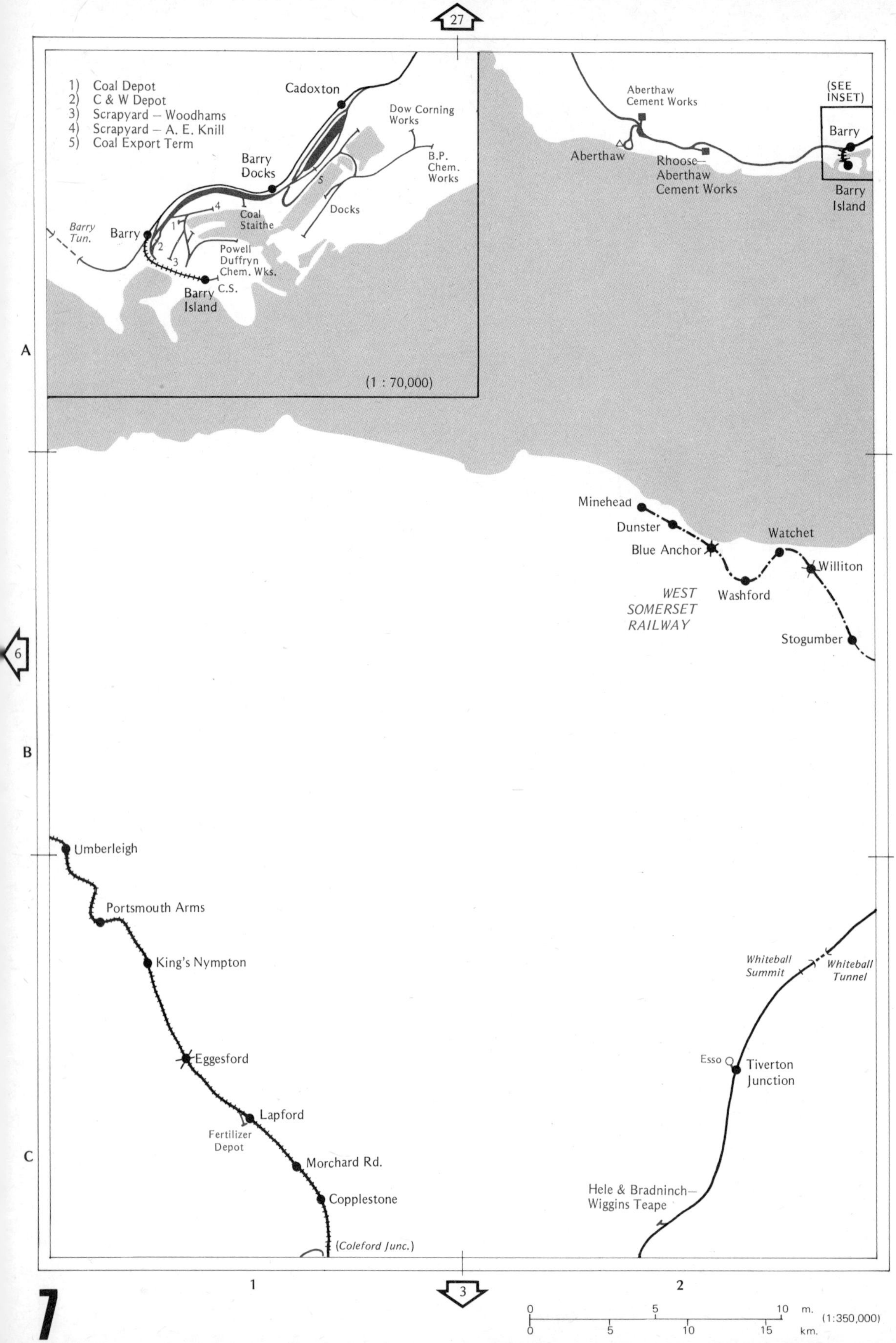

27

1) Coal Depot
2) C & W Depot
3) Scrapyard – Woodhams
4) Scrapyard – A. E. Knill
5) Coal Export Term

Cadoxton
Dow Corning Works
B.P. Chem. Works
Barry Docks
Docks
Coal Staithe
Barry Tun.
Barry
Powell Duffryn Chem. Wks.
C.S.
Barry Island
(1 : 70,000)

Aberthaw Cement Works
Aberthaw
Rhoose–Aberthaw Cement Works
(SEE INSET)
Barry
Barry Island

A

Minehead
Dunster
Blue Anchor
Watchet
Williton
Washford
WEST SOMERSET RAILWAY
Stogumber

6

B

Umberleigh
Portsmouth Arms
King's Nympton
Eggesford
Lapford
Fertilizer Depot
Morchard Rd.
Copplestone
(Coleford Junc.)

Whiteball Summit
Whiteball Tunnel
Esso
Tiverton Junction
Hele & Bradninch–Wiggins Teape

C

1
3
2

0 5 10 m.
0 5 10 15 km.
(1:350,000)

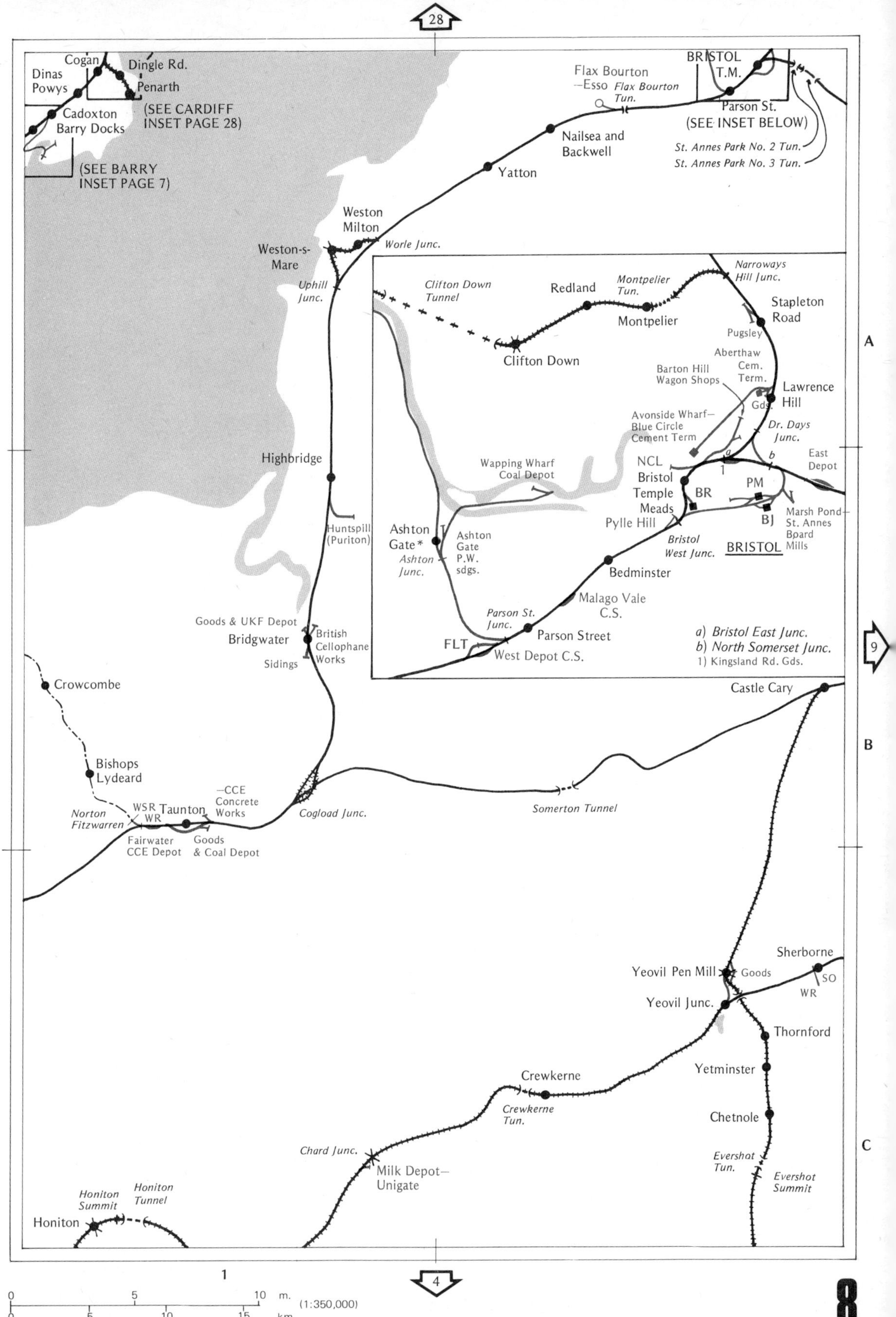

28

Cogan
Dinas Powys
Dingle Rd.
Penarth
Cadoxton
Barry Docks
(SEE CARDIFF INSET PAGE 28)
(SEE BARRY INSET PAGE 7)

Flax Bourton —Esso
Flax Bourton Tun.
BRISTOL T.M.
Parson St.
(SEE INSET BELOW)
St. Annes Park No. 2 Tun.
St. Annes Park No. 3 Tun.
Nailsea and Backwell
Yatton
Weston Milton
Weston-s-Mare
Worle Junc.
Uphill Junc.
Highbridge
Huntspill (Puriton)
Goods & UKF Depot
Bridgwater
British Cellophane Works
Sidings
Crowcombe
Bishops Lydeard
Norton Fitzwarren
WSR
WR
Taunton
—CCE Concrete Works
Fairwater CCE Depot
Goods & Coal Depot
Cogload Junc.
Somerton Tunnel
Castle Cary

Clifton Down Tunnel
Clifton Down
Redland
Montpelier Tun.
Montpelier
Narroways Hill Junc.
Stapleton Road
Pugsley
Aberthaw Cem. Term.
Barton Hill Wagon Shops
Lawrence Hill
Gds.
Avonside Wharf—Blue Circle Cement Term
Dr. Days Junc.
East Depot
a
b
1
NCL
Bristol Temple Meads
BR
PM
BJ
Marsh Pond—St. Annes Board Mills
Wapping Wharf Coal Depot
Ashton Gate*
Ashton Gate P.W. sdgs.
Ashton Junc.
Pylle Hill
Bristol West Junc.
BRISTOL
Bedminster
Malago Vale C.S.
Parson St. Junc.
Parson Street
FLT
West Depot C.S.

a) Bristol East Junc.
b) North Somerset Junc.
1) Kingsland Rd. Gds.

A
B
C
9

Sherborne
SO
WR
Yeovil Pen Mill
Goods
Yeovil Junc.
Thornford
Yetminster
Chetnole
Evershot Tun.
Evershot Summit
Crewkerne
Crewkerne Tun.
Chard Junc.
Milk Depot—Unigate
Honiton
Honiton Summit
Honiton Tunnel

1
4

0 5 10 m.
0 5 10 15 km.
(1:350,000)

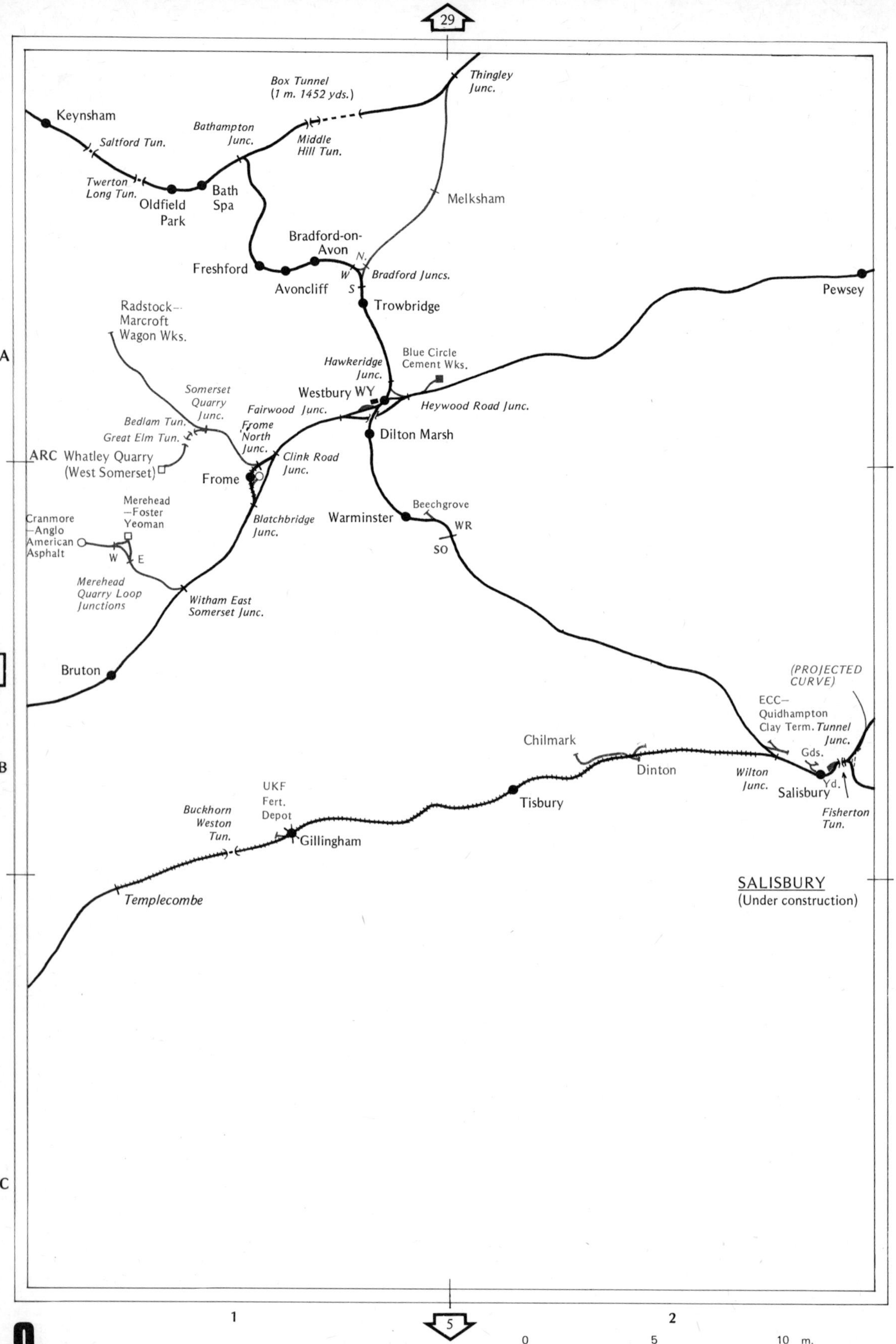

29

Box Tunnel
(1 m. 1452 yds.)
Thingley
Junc.
Keynsham
Saltford Tun.
Bathampton
Junc.
Middle
Hill Tun.
Twerton
Long Tun.
Oldfield
Park
Bath
Spa
Melksham
Bradford-on-
Avon
N
Freshford
W
Bradford Juncs.
Avoncliff
S
Trowbridge
Pewsey
Radstock–
Marcroft
Wagon Wks.
A
Hawkeridge
Junc.
Blue Circle
Cement Wks.
Somerset
Quarry
Junc.
Westbury WY
Fairwood Junc.
Heywood Road Junc.
Bedlam Tun.
Frome
North
Junc.
Dilton Marsh
Great Elm Tun.
ARC Whatley Quarry
(West Somerset)
Clink Road
Junc.
Frome
Merehead
–Foster
Yeoman
Beechgrove
Cranmore
–Anglo
American
Asphalt
Blatchbridge
Junc.
Warminster
WR
W
E
SO
Merehead
Quarry Loop
Junctions
Witham East
Somerset Junc.
8
Bruton
(PROJECTED
CURVE)
ECC–
Quidhampton
Clay Term.
Tunnel
Junc.
Chilmark
Gds.
B
Dinton
Wilton
Junc.
Yd.
Salisbury
UKF
Fert.
Depot
Tisbury
Buckhorn
Weston
Tun.
Fisherton
Tun.
Gillingham
SALISBURY
(Under construction)
Templecombe
C
1
2
5
0 5 10 m.
0 5 10 15 km.
(1:350,000)

9

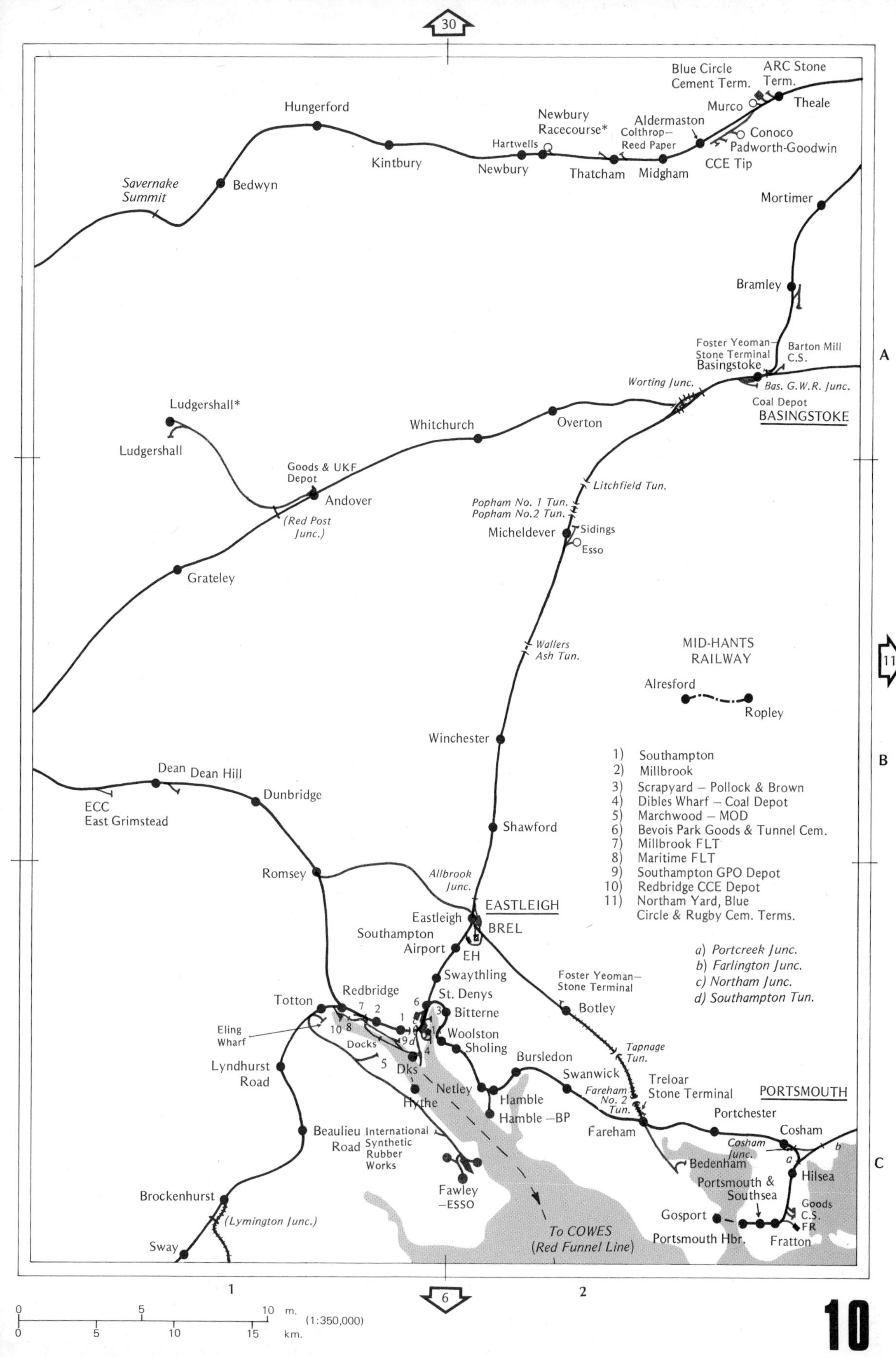

30
Hungerford
Kintbury
Newbury
Newbury Racecourse*
Hartwells
Thatcham
Colthrop– Reed Paper
Midgham
Aldermaston
CCE Tip
Padworth-Goodwin
Conoco
Murco
Blue Circle Cement Term.
ARC Stone Term.
Theale
Savernake Summit
Bedwyn
Mortimer
Bramley
Foster Yeoman– Stone Terminal
Basingstoke
Barton Mill C.S.
Bas. G.W.R. Junc.
Coal Depot
BASINGSTOKE
Worting Junc.
Overton
Whitchurch
Ludgershall*
Ludgershall
Goods & UKF Depot
Andover
(Red Post Junc.)
Grateley
Litchfield Tun.
Popham No. 1 Tun.
Popham No.2 Tun.
Sidings
Micheldever
Esso
Wallers Ash Tun.
MID-HANTS RAILWAY
Alresford
Ropley
11
Winchester
Dean
Dean Hill
ECC East Grimstead
Dunbridge
Shawford
Romsey
Allbrook Junc.
EASTLEIGH
Eastleigh
BREL
Southampton Airport
EH
Swaythling
St. Denys
Bitterne
Woolston
Sholing
Redbridge
Totton
Eling Wharf
Docks
Dks
Lyndhurst Road
Netley
Hythe
Hamble
Hamble –BP
Bursledon
Swanwick
Foster Yeoman– Stone Terminal
Botley
Tapnage Tun.
Fareham No. 2 Tun.
Treloar Stone Terminal
Fareham
PORTSMOUTH
Portchester
Cosham
Cosham Junc.
Bedenham
Hilsea
Portsmouth & Southsea
Goods C.S.
FR
Gosport
Portsmouth Hbr.
Fratton
Beaulieu Road
International Synthetic Rubber Works
Fawley –ESSO
To COWES (Red Funnel Line)
Brockenhurst
(Lymington Junc.)
Sway
1) Southampton
2) Millbrook
3) Scrapyard – Pollock & Brown
4) Dibles Wharf – Coal Depot
5) Marchwood – MOD
6) Bevois Park Goods & Tunnel Cem.
7) Millbrook FLT
8) Maritime FLT
9) Southampton GPO Depot
10) Redbridge CCE Depot
11) Northam Yard, Blue Circle & Rugby Cem. Terms.
a) Portcreek Junc.
b) Farlington Junc.
c) Northam Junc.
d) Southampton Tun.
A
B
C
1
2
6
0 5 10 m.
0 5 10 15 km.
(1:350,000)

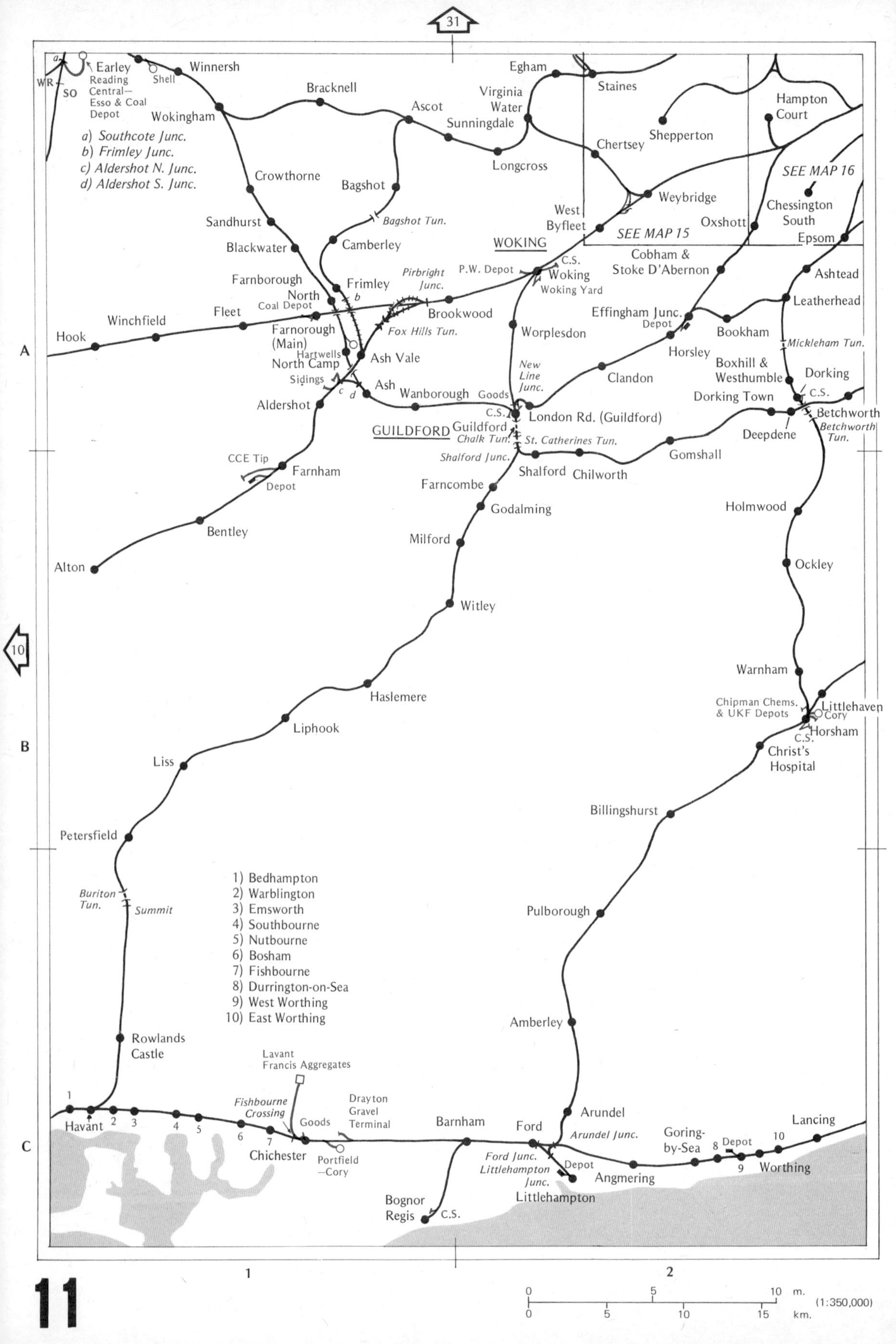

31
10
a) Southcote Junc.
b) Frimley Junc.
c) Aldershot N. Junc.
d) Aldershot S. Junc.
Earley
Reading Central—Esso & Coal Depot
Shell
WR
SO
Winnersh
Wokingham
Bracknell
Ascot
Egham
Virginia Water
Sunningdale
Staines
Longcross
Chertsey
Shepperton
Hampton Court
SEE MAP 16
Crowthorne
Bagshot
Bagshot Tun.
Sandhurst
Blackwater
Camberley
Weybridge
West Byfleet
SEE MAP 15
Oxshott
Chessington South
Epsom
WOKING
C.S.
Woking
Woking Yard
P.W. Depot
Pirbright Junc.
Farnborough North
Frimley
Coal Depot
Fleet
Winchfield
Hook
Brookwood
Fox Hills Tun.
Farnorough (Main)
Hartwells
North Camp
Sidings
Ash Vale
Ash
Aldershot
Wanborough
Goods
Worplesdon
New Line Junc.
Cobham & Stoke D'Abernon
Effingham Junc.
Depot
Horsley
Bookham
Clandon
Ashtead
Leatherhead
Mickleham Tun.
Boxhill & Westhumble
Dorking
Dorking Town
C.S.
Deepdene
Betchworth
Betchworth Tun.
C.S.
London Rd. (Guildford)
GUILDFORD
Guildford
Chalk Tun.
St. Catherines Tun.
Shalford Junc.
Shalford
Chilworth
Gomshall
CCE Tip
Farnham
Depot
Farncombe
Godalming
Bentley
Milford
Alton
Holmwood
Ockley
Witley
Haslemere
Liphook
Liss
Warnham
Chipman Chems. & UKF Depots
Littlehaven
Cory
Horsham
C.S.
Christ's Hospital
Billingshurst
Petersfield
Buriton Tun.
Summit
1) Bedhampton
2) Warblington
3) Emsworth
4) Southbourne
5) Nutbourne
6) Bosham
7) Fishbourne
8) Durrington-on-Sea
9) West Worthing
10) East Worthing
Pulborough
Amberley
Rowlands Castle
Lavant Francis Aggregates
Arundel
Havant
Fishbourne Crossing
Goods
Drayton Gravel Terminal
Barnham
Ford
Arundel Junc.
Goring-by-Sea
Depot
Lancing
Chichester
Portfield —Cory
Ford Junc.
Littlehampton Junc.
Depot
Angmering
Worthing
Bognor Regis
C.S.
Littlehampton
A
B
C
1
2
0 5 10 m.
0 5 10 15 km.
(1:350,000)

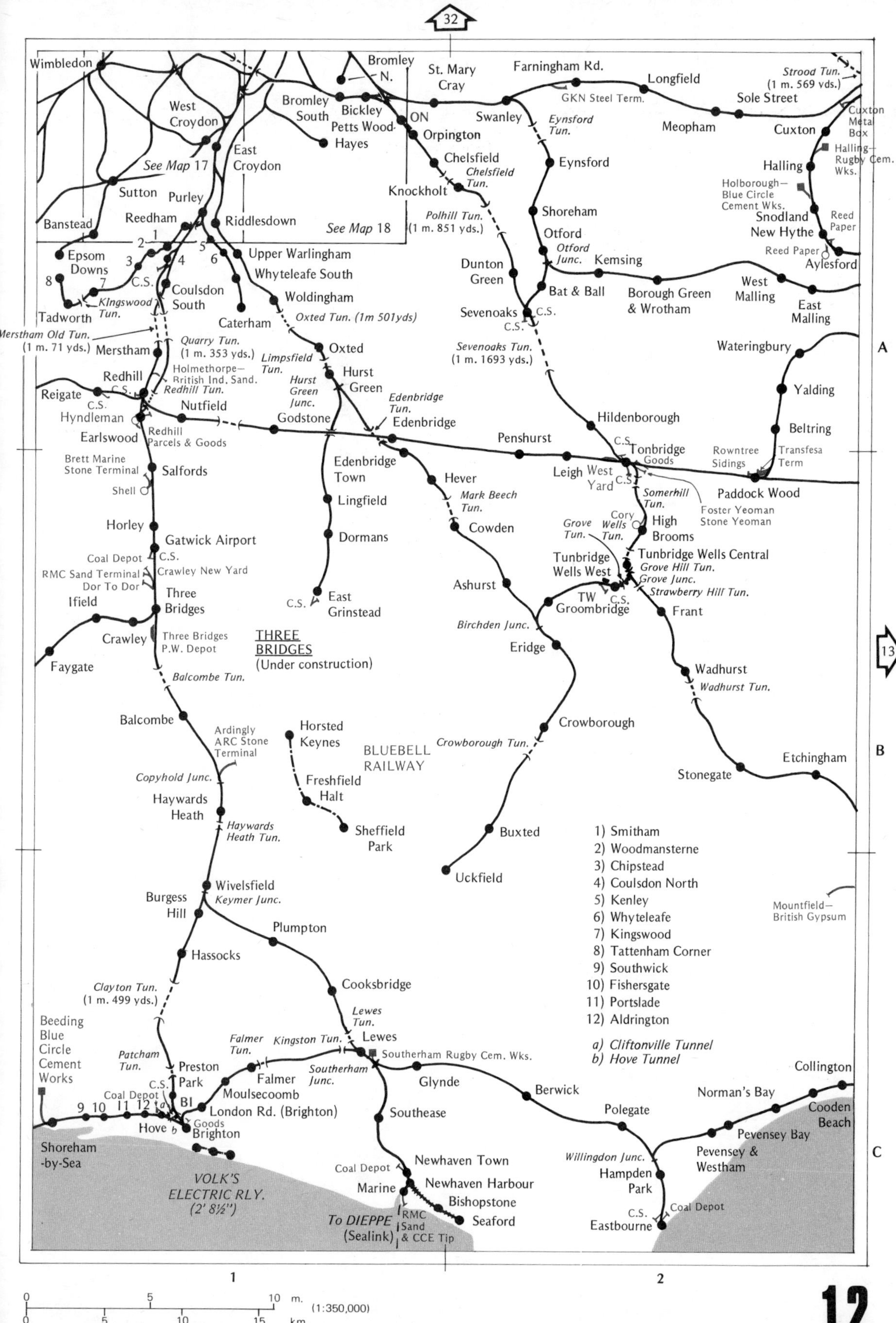
32
Wimbledon
West Croydon
East Croydon
See Map 17
Bromley South
Bromley N.
Bickley
Petts Wood
Hayes
ON
Orpington
St. Mary Cray
Farningham Rd.
GKN Steel Term.
Longfield
Sole Street
Strood Tun. (1 m. 569 yds.)
Cuxton Metal Box
Cuxton
Meopham
Swanley
Eynsford Tun.
Eynsford
Halling—Rugby Cem. Wks.
Halling
Holborough—Blue Circle Cement Wks.
Snodland
Reed Paper
New Hythe
Reed Paper
Aylesford
Chelsfield
Chelsfield Tun.
Knockholt
Polhill Tun. (1 m. 851 yds.)
Shoreham
Otford
Otford Junc.
Kemsing
Sutton
Purley
Banstead
Reedham
Riddlesdown
See Map 18
Upper Warlingham
Whyteleafe South
Epsom Downs
C.S.
Coulsdon South
Kingswood Tun.
Tadworth
Caterham
Woldingham
Oxted Tun. (1m 501yds)
Dunton Green
Bat & Ball
Borough Green & Wrotham
West Malling
East Malling
Sevenoaks
C.S.
Merstham Old Tun. (1 m. 71 yds.)
Merstham
Quarry Tun. (1 m. 353 yds.)
Limpsfield Tun.
Oxted
Sevenoaks Tun. (1 m. 1693 yds.)
Wateringbury
A
Redhill
Holmethorpe—British Ind. Sand.
Redhill Tun.
Hurst Green
Hurst Green Junc.
Edenbridge Tun.
Yalding
Reigate
C.S.
Hyndleman
Nutfield
Godstone
Edenbridge
Hildenborough
Beltring
Earlswood
Redhill Parcels & Goods
Penshurst
C.S.
Tonbridge Goods
Rowntree Sidings
Transfesa Term
Brett Marine Stone Terminal
Salfords
Edenbridge Town
Hever
Leigh
West Yard
C.S.
Paddock Wood
Shell
Lingfield
Mark Beech Tun.
Somerhill Tun.
Foster Yeoman Stone Yeoman
Horley
Gatwick Airport
Dormans
Cowden
Grove Tun.
Cory
Wells Tun.
High Brooms
Coal Depot
C.S.
Crawley New Yard
RMC Sand Terminal
Dor To Dor
Tunbridge Wells West
Tunbridge Wells Central
Grove Hill Tun.
Grove Junc.
Strawberry Hill Tun.
Three Bridges
Ifield
C.S.
East Grinstead
Ashurst
TW
C.S.
Groombridge
Frant
Crawley
Three Bridges P.W. Depot
THREE BRIDGES (Under construction)
Birchden Junc.
Eridge
13
Faygate
Balcombe Tun.
Wadhurst
Wadhurst Tun.
Balcombe
Ardingly ARC Stone Terminal
Horsted Keynes
BLUEBELL RAILWAY
Crowborough Tun.
Crowborough
B
Copyhold Junc.
Freshfield Halt
Stonegate
Etchingham
Haywards Heath
Haywards Heath Tun.
Sheffield Park
Buxted
Uckfield
Wivelsfield
Keymer Junc.
Burgess Hill
Plumpton
Hassocks
Mountfield—British Gypsum
1) Smitham
2) Woodmansterne
3) Chipstead
4) Coulsdon North
5) Kenley
6) Whyteleafe
7) Kingswood
8) Tattenham Corner
9) Southwick
10) Fishersgate
11) Portslade
12) Aldrington
a) Cliftonville Tunnel
b) Hove Tunnel
Cooksbridge
Clayton Tun. (1 m. 499 yds.)
Beeding Blue Circle Cement Works
Lewes Tun.
Lewes
Falmer Tun.
Kingston Tun.
Southerham Rugby Cem. Wks.
Patcham Tun.
Preston Park
Southerham Junc.
Falmer
Glynde
Berwick
Collington
C.S.
Coal Depot
Moulsecoomb
BI
London Rd. (Brighton)
Norman's Bay
Southease
Polegate
Cooden Beach
Hove
Goods
Brighton
Pevensey Bay
Shoreham -by-Sea
Pevensey & Westham
Willingdon Junc.
C
Coal Depot
Newhaven Town
Newhaven Harbour
VOLK'S ELECTRIC RLY. (2' 8½")
Marine
Bishopstone
Hampden Park
RMC Sand & CCE Tip
Seaford
To DIEPPE (Sealink)
C.S.
Coal Depot
Eastbourne
1
2
0 5 10 m.
0 5 10 15 km.
(1:350,000)

33

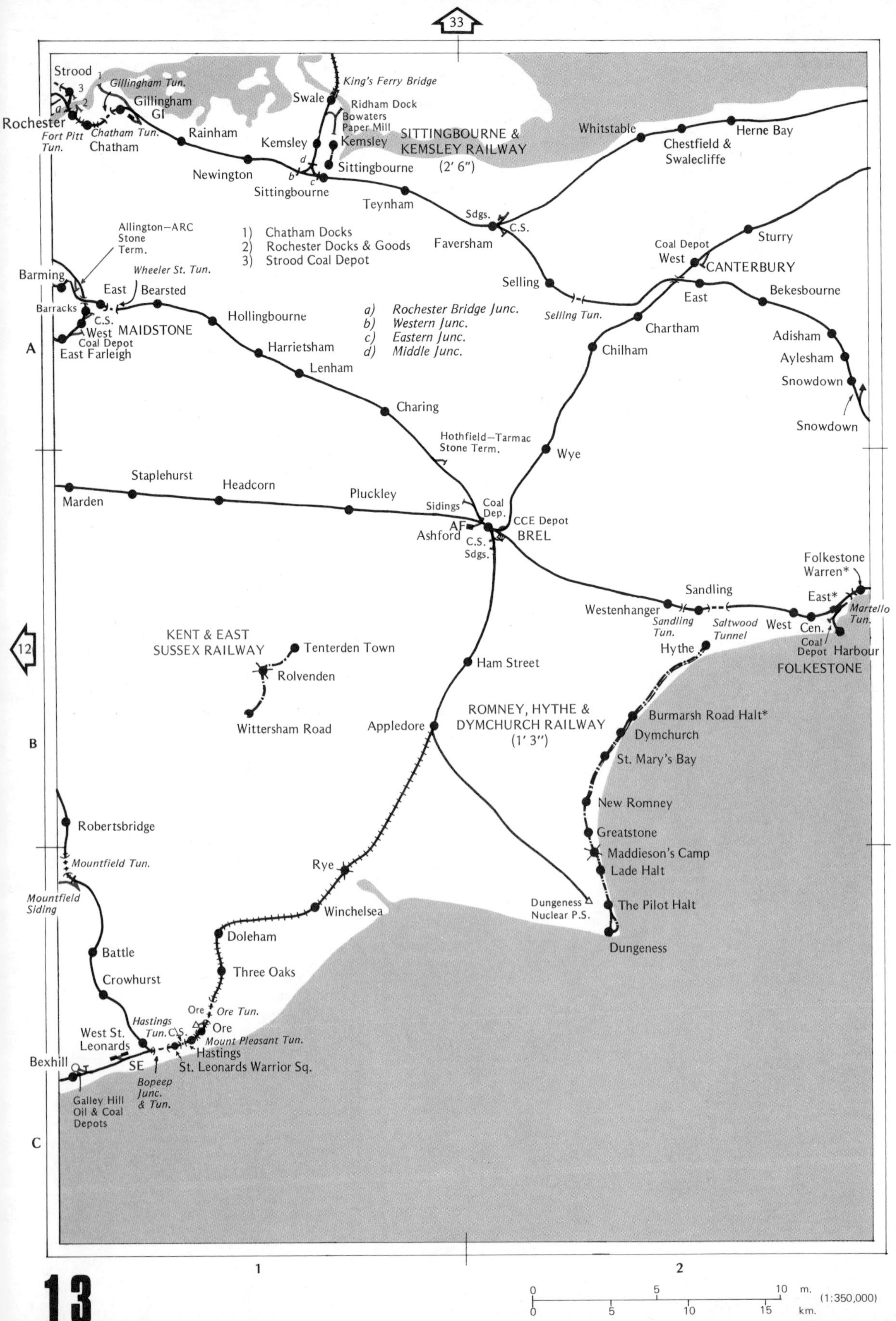
Strood
Rochester
Fort Pitt Tun.
Gillingham Tun.
Gillingham
GI
Chatham Tun.
Chatham
Rainham
Newington
Sittingbourne
Swale
King's Ferry Bridge
Ridham Dock
Bowaters Paper Mill
Kemsley
Kemsley
Sittingbourne
SITTINGBOURNE & KEMSLEY RAILWAY
(2' 6")
Whitstable
Chestfield & Swalecliffe
Herne Bay
Teynham
Sdgs.
C.S.
Faversham
Selling
Selling Tun.
Coal Depot
West
CANTERBURY
East
Sturry
Bekesbourne
Chartham
Chilham
Adisham
Aylesham
Snowdown
Snowdown
1) Chatham Docks
2) Rochester Docks & Goods
3) Strood Coal Depot
a) Rochester Bridge Junc.
b) Western Junc.
c) Eastern Junc.
d) Middle Junc.
Allington—ARC Stone Term.
Barming
Wheeler St. Tun.
East
Bearsted
Barracks
C.S.
West
MAIDSTONE
Coal Depot
East Farleigh
Hollingbourne
Harrietsham
Lenham
Charing
Hothfield—Tarmac Stone Term.
Wye
Staplehurst
Headcorn
Pluckley
Marden
Sidings
Coal Dep.
AF
Ashford
CCE Depot
BREL
C.S.
Sdgs.
Folkestone Warren*
East*
Martello Tun.
Sandling
Westenhanger
Sandling Tun.
Saltwood Tunnel
West
Cen.
Coal Depot
Harbour
FOLKESTONE
Hythe
KENT & EAST SUSSEX RAILWAY
Tenterden Town
Rolvenden
Wittersham Road
Ham Street
Appledore
ROMNEY, HYTHE & DYMCHURCH RAILWAY
(1' 3")
Burmarsh Road Halt*
Dymchurch
St. Mary's Bay
New Romney
Greatstone
Maddieson's Camp
Lade Halt
The Pilot Halt
Dungeness
Dungeness Nuclear P.S.
Robertsbridge
Mountfield Tun.
Mountfield Siding
Rye
Winchelsea
Doleham
Three Oaks
Battle
Crowhurst
Ore
Ore Tun.
Ore
Hastings Tun.
C.S.
Mount Pleasant Tun.
West St. Leonards
Hastings
St. Leonards Warrior Sq.
Bexhill
SE
Bopeep Junc. & Tun.
Galley Hill Oil & Coal Depots
A
B
C
1
2
0 5 10 m.
0 5 10 15 km.
(1:350,000)

12

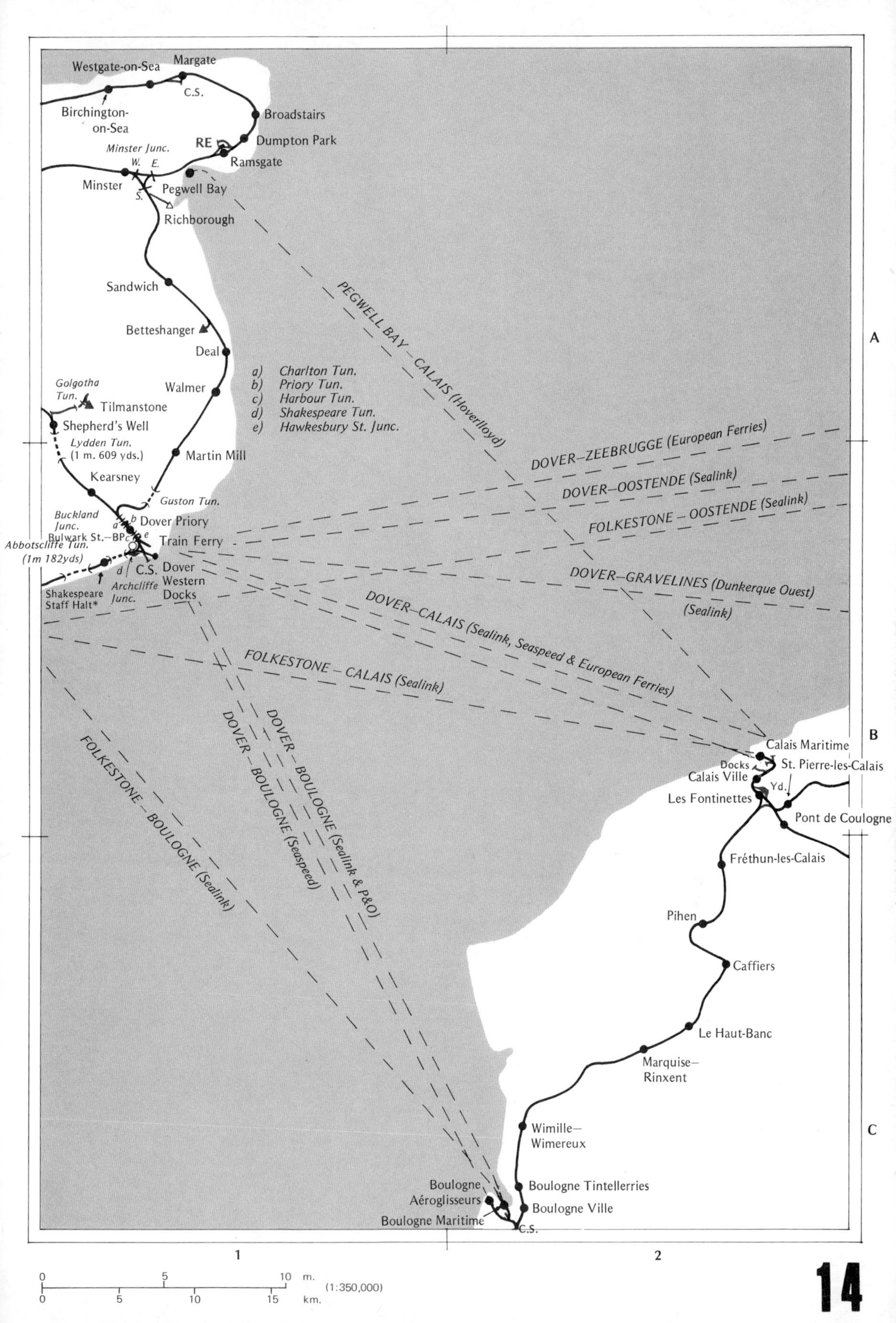

Westgate-on-Sea
Margate
C.S.
Birchington-on-Sea
Broadstairs
RE
Dumpton Park
Minster Junc.
W.
E.
Ramsgate
Minster
S.
Pegwell Bay
Richborough
Sandwich
Betteshanger
Deal
a) Charlton Tun.
b) Priory Tun.
c) Harbour Tun.
d) Shakespeare Tun.
e) Hawkesbury St. Junc.
Golgotha Tun.
Tilmanstone
Walmer
Shepherd's Well
Lydden Tun. (1 m. 609 yds.)
Martin Mill
Kearsney
Guston Tun.
Buckland Junc.
Dover Priory
Bulwark St.–BP
Train Ferry
Abbotscliffe Tun. (1m 182yds)
C.S.
Dover Western Docks
Archcliffe Junc.
Shakespeare Staff Halt*
PEGWELL BAY – CALAIS (Hoverlloyd)
DOVER–ZEEBRUGGE (European Ferries)
DOVER–OOSTENDE (Sealink)
FOLKESTONE – OOSTENDE (Sealink)
DOVER–GRAVELINES (Dunkerque Ouest) (Sealink)
DOVER–CALAIS (Sealink, Seaspeed & European Ferries)
FOLKESTONE – CALAIS (Sealink)
DOVER – BOULOGNE (Sealink & P&O)
DOVER – BOULOGNE (Seaspeed)
FOLKESTONE – BOULOGNE (Sealink)
Calais Maritime
Docks
St. Pierre-les-Calais
Calais Ville
Yd.
Les Fontinettes
Pont de Coulogne
Fréthun-les-Calais
Pihen
Caffiers
Le Haut-Banc
Marquise–Rinxent
Wimille–Wimereux
Boulogne Aéroglisseurs
Boulogne Tintellerries
Boulogne Ville
Boulogne Maritime
C.S.
A
B
C
1
2
0 5 10 m.
0 5 10 15 km.
(1:350,000)

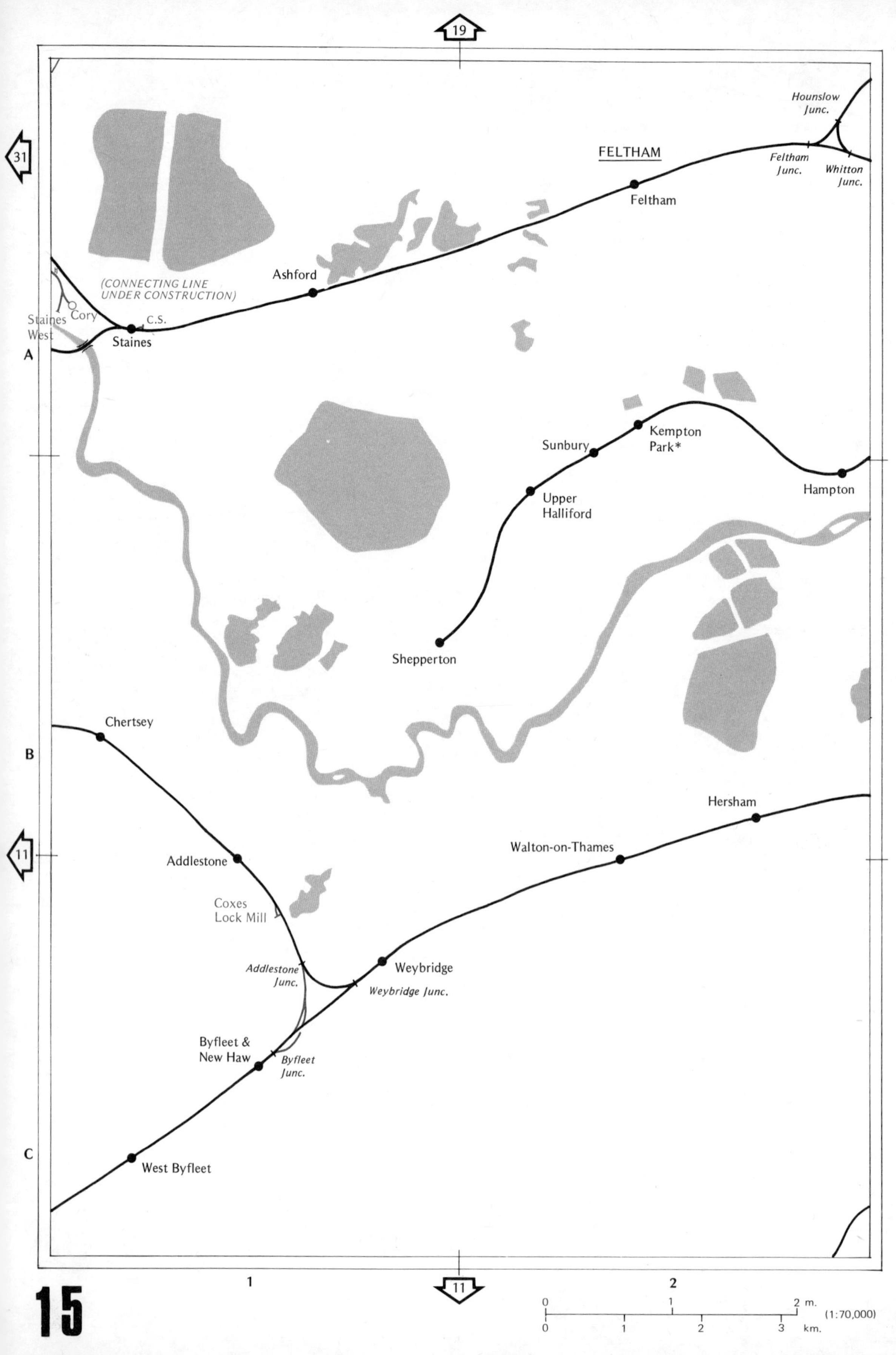
19
31
11
11
Hounslow Junc.
FELTHAM
Feltham Junc.
Whitton Junc.
Feltham
Ashford
(CONNECTING LINE UNDER CONSTRUCTION)
Cory
C.S.
Staines West
Staines
A
Kempton Park*
Sunbury
Upper Halliford
Hampton
Shepperton
Chertsey
B
Hersham
Walton-on-Thames
Addlestone
Coxes Lock Mill
Addlestone Junc.
Weybridge
Weybridge Junc.
Byfleet & New Haw
Byfleet Junc.
C
West Byfleet
1
2
0 1 2 m.
0 1 2 3 km.
(1:70,000)

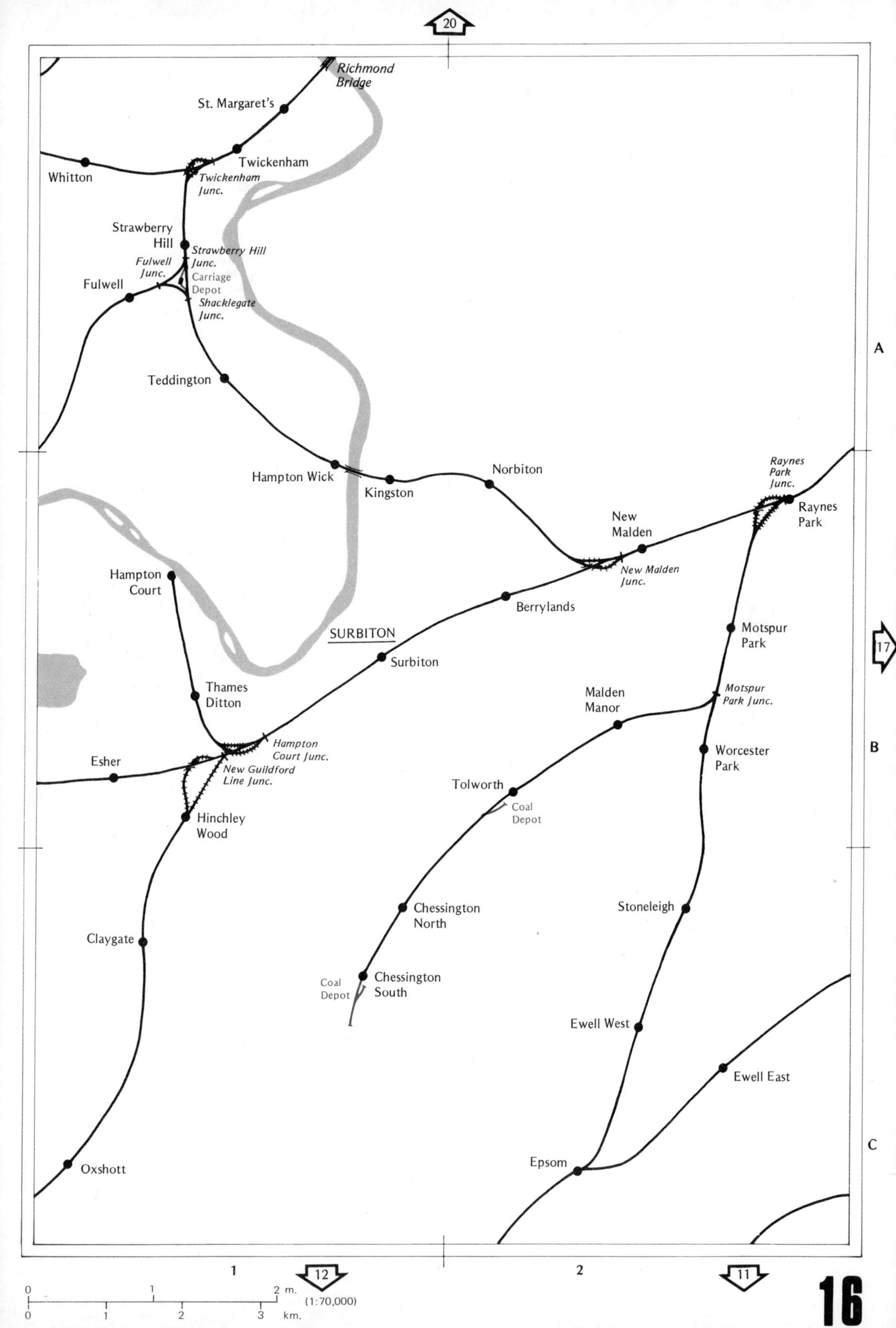
20
Richmond Bridge
St. Margaret's
Twickenham
Whitton
Twickenham Junc.
Strawberry Hill
Strawberry Hill Junc.
Fulwell Junc.
Carriage Depot
Fulwell
Shacklegate Junc.
A
Teddington
Hampton Wick
Kingston
Norbiton
Raynes Park Junc.
Raynes Park
New Malden
New Malden Junc.
Hampton Court
Berrylands
Motspur Park
17
SURBITON
Surbiton
Thames Ditton
Malden Manor
Motspur Park Junc.
Hampton Court Junc.
Worcester Park
B
Esher
New Guildford Line Junc.
Tolworth
Coal Depot
Hinchley Wood
Chessington North
Stoneleigh
Claygate
Chessington South
Coal Depot
Ewell West
Ewell East
C
Epsom
Oxshott
1
12
2
11
0
1
2 m.
(1:70,000)
0
1
2
3
km.

21

D
East Putney Tun.
Southfields
D
WD
Wimbledon Park
Wimbledon Staff Halt*
Earlsfield
Wandsworth Common
Clapham South
Balham
Balham Junc.
N
Tooting Bec
Tooting Broadway
E.M.U. Depot
Streatham Hill
Leigham Court (Streatham Hill Tun.)
Leigham Junc.
Leigham Tun.
Herne Hill N. Junc.
Herne Hill
S. Junc.
North Dulwich
Knight's Hill Tunnel
Tulse Hill
West Dulwich
West Norwood Junc.
West Norwood
Sydenham Hill
Penge Tunnel (1 m. 381 yds)
Streatham Tun.
Streatham
Streatham Junc.
Streatham Junc. North
Streatham Junc. S.
Streatham Common
Streatham Common Junc.
Gipsy Hill
Crystal Palace Tun.
Crystal Palace

A

Wimbledon
Haydons Road
Tooting
Collier's Wood
Wimbledon Goods
South Wimbledon
Merton Park
Morden Road
Wimbledon Chase
N
Norbury
Bromley Junc.
South Merton
Morden
Thornton Heath
Norwood Junction
Goods Depot
Tennison Rd. Stabling Point
Coal Depot
Norwood Fork Junc.
Norwood Yard
Woodside Junc.
Depot
Morden South
Mitcham
Mitcham North Junc.
Mitcham Junction
Mitcham South Junc.
Beddington Lane
Selhurst Emergency Spur Junc.
Selhurst
SU
Selhurst Junc.
Gloucester Rd. Junc.
Gloryhole Junc.
St. James Junc.
St. Helier

16

Windmill Bridge Junc.
West Croydon
Depot
Addiscombe
Bingham Road

B

Croydon 'B'
Waddon Marsh
Hackbridge
Sutton Common
East Croydon
Woodside Tun.
Parkhill Tun.
Combe Lane Tun.
Carshalton
West Sutton
Waddon
Coombe Road
South Croydon
South Croydon Junc.
Sutton Junc.
Sutton
Cory
Selsdon
Selsdon Junc.
Sutton Wimbledon Line Junc.
Wallington
Carshalton Beeches
Cheam
Purley Oaks
Sanderstead
Belmont
Purley
Caterham Line Junc.
Coal Depot & Stone Terminal —Brett Marine

C

Reedham
Riddlesdown
Chipstead Line Junc.
Riddlesdown Tunnel
Kenley
Banstead

12

1 2

17

B	BAKERLOO	M	METROPOLITAN
C	CENTRAL	M(EL)	METROPOLITAN (East London)
O	CIRCLE	N	NORTHERN
D	DISTRICT	P	PICCADILLY
J	JUBILEE	V	VICTORIA

0 1 2 m.
0 1 2 3 km.
(1:70,000)

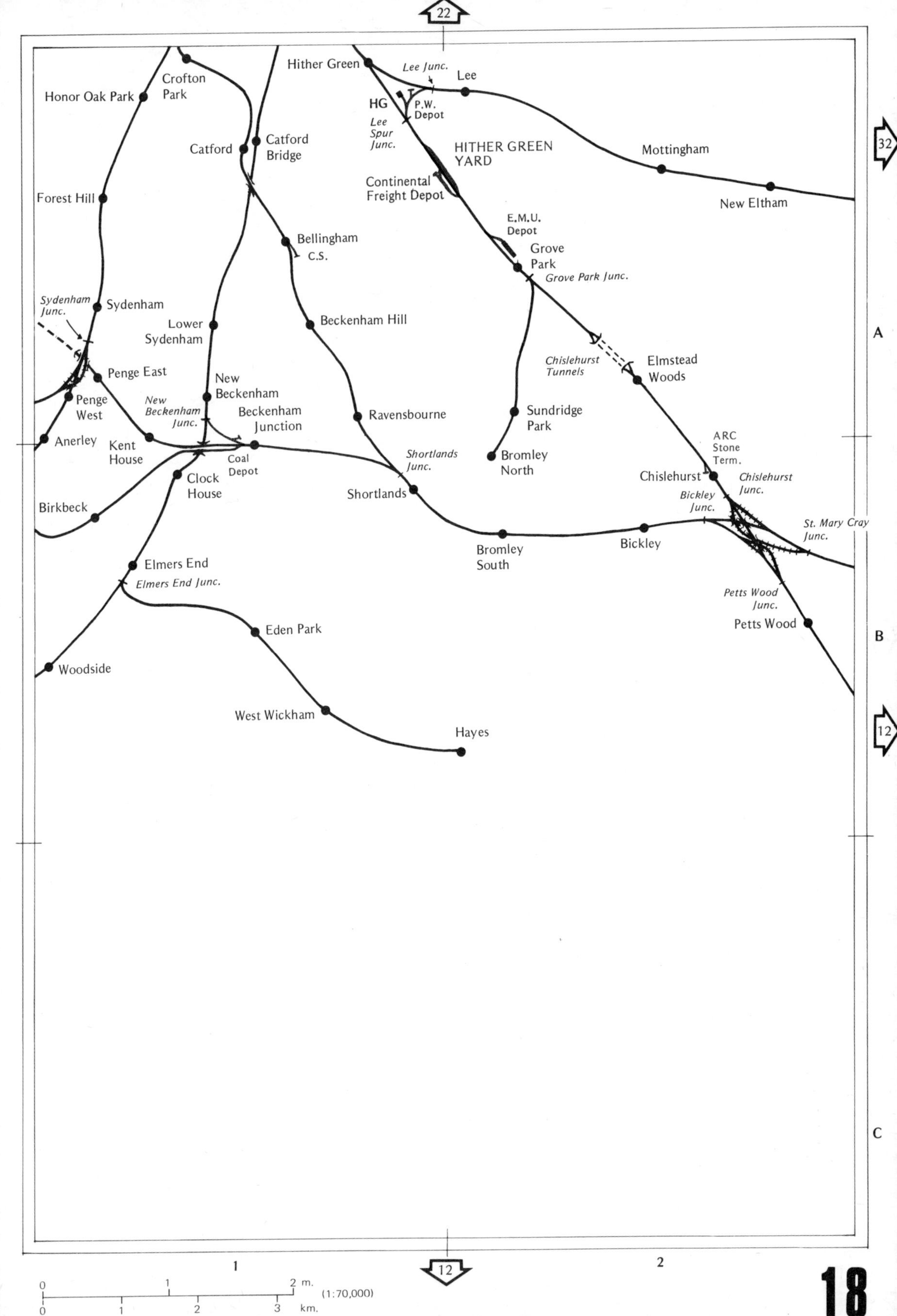
22
Hither Green
Lee Junc.
Lee
HG
P.W. Depot
Lee Spur Junc.
HITHER GREEN YARD
Continental Freight Depot
Mottingham
New Eltham
32
Honor Oak Park
Crofton Park
Catford
Catford Bridge
Forest Hill
Bellingham
C.S.
E.M.U. Depot
Grove Park
Grove Park Junc.
Sydenham Junc.
Sydenham
Lower Sydenham
Beckenham Hill
Chislehurst Tunnels
Elmstead Woods
A
Penge East
Penge West
New Beckenham
New Beckenham Junc.
Beckenham Junction
Ravensbourne
Sundridge Park
Anerley
Kent House
Coal Depot
Shortlands Junc.
Bromley North
ARC Stone Term.
Clock House
Shortlands
Chislehurst
Chislehurst Junc.
Bickley Junc.
Birkbeck
St. Mary Cray Junc.
Bromley South
Bickley
Elmers End
Elmers End Junc.
Petts Wood Junc.
Eden Park
Petts Wood
B
Woodside
West Wickham
12
Hayes
C
1
12
2
0 1 2 m.
(1:70,000)
0 1 2 3 km.

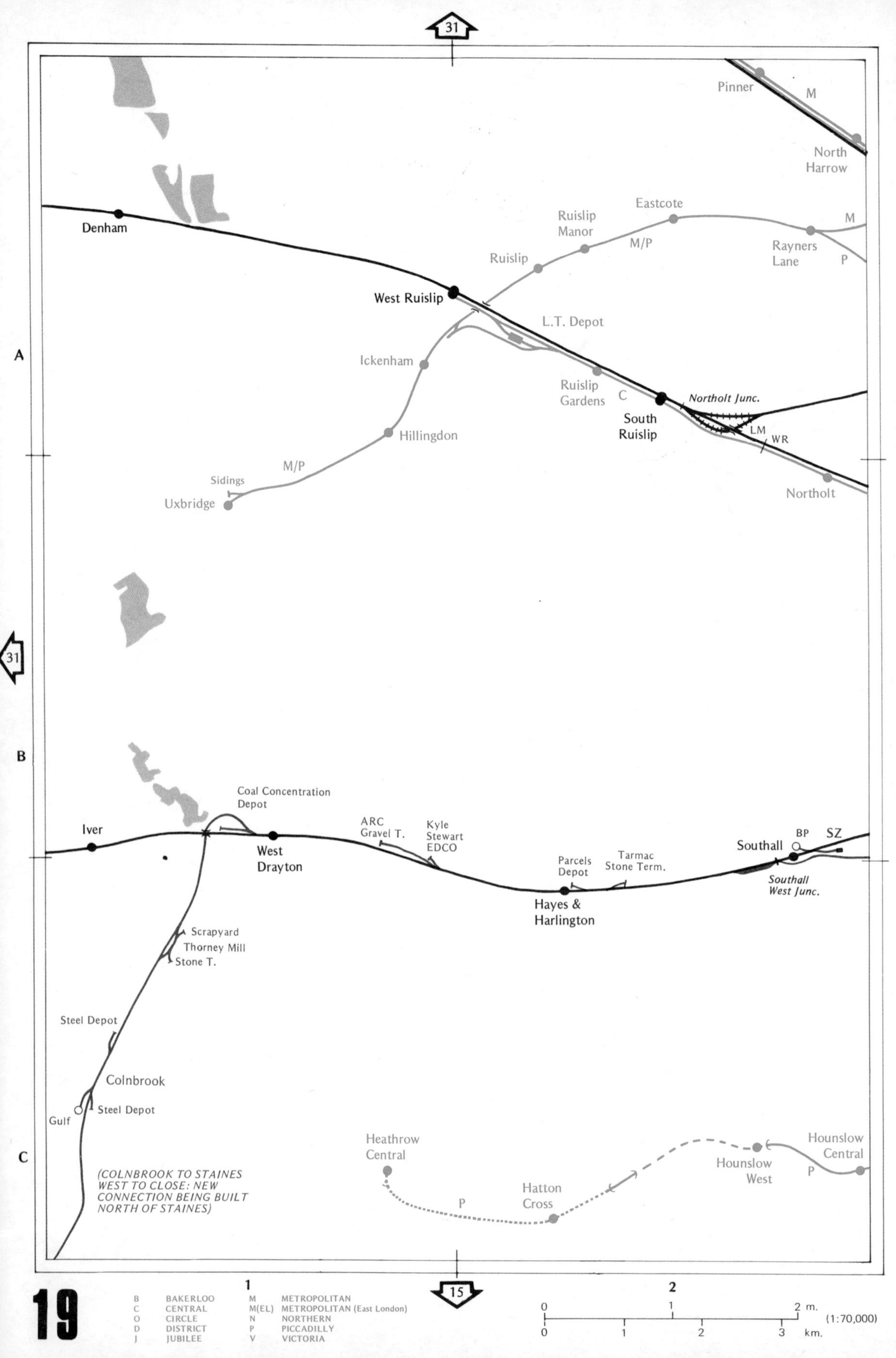
31
Pinner
M
North
Harrow
Denham
Eastcote
Ruislip
Manor
M
M/P
Rayners
Lane
Ruislip
P
West Ruislip
L.T. Depot
A
Ickenham
Ruislip
Gardens
C
Northolt Junc.
South
Ruislip
Hillingdon
LM
WR
M/P
Sidings
Northolt
Uxbridge
31
B
Coal Concentration
Depot
ARC
Gravel T.
Kyle
Stewart
EDCO
Iver
BP
SZ
Southall
West
Drayton
Parcels
Depot
Tarmac
Stone Term.
Southall
West Junc.
Hayes &
Harlington
Scrapyard
Thorney Mill
Stone T.
Steel Depot
Colnbrook
Steel Depot
Gulf
Heathrow
Central
Hounslow
Central
Hounslow
West
C
P
(COLNBROOK TO STAINES
WEST TO CLOSE: NEW
CONNECTION BEING BUILT
NORTH OF STAINES)
Hatton
Cross
P
15
1
2
B BAKERLOO
C CENTRAL
O CIRCLE
D DISTRICT
J JUBILEE
M METROPOLITAN
M(EL) METROPOLITAN (East London)
N NORTHERN
P PICCADILLY
V VICTORIA
0 1 2 m.
0 1 2 3 km.
(1:70,000)

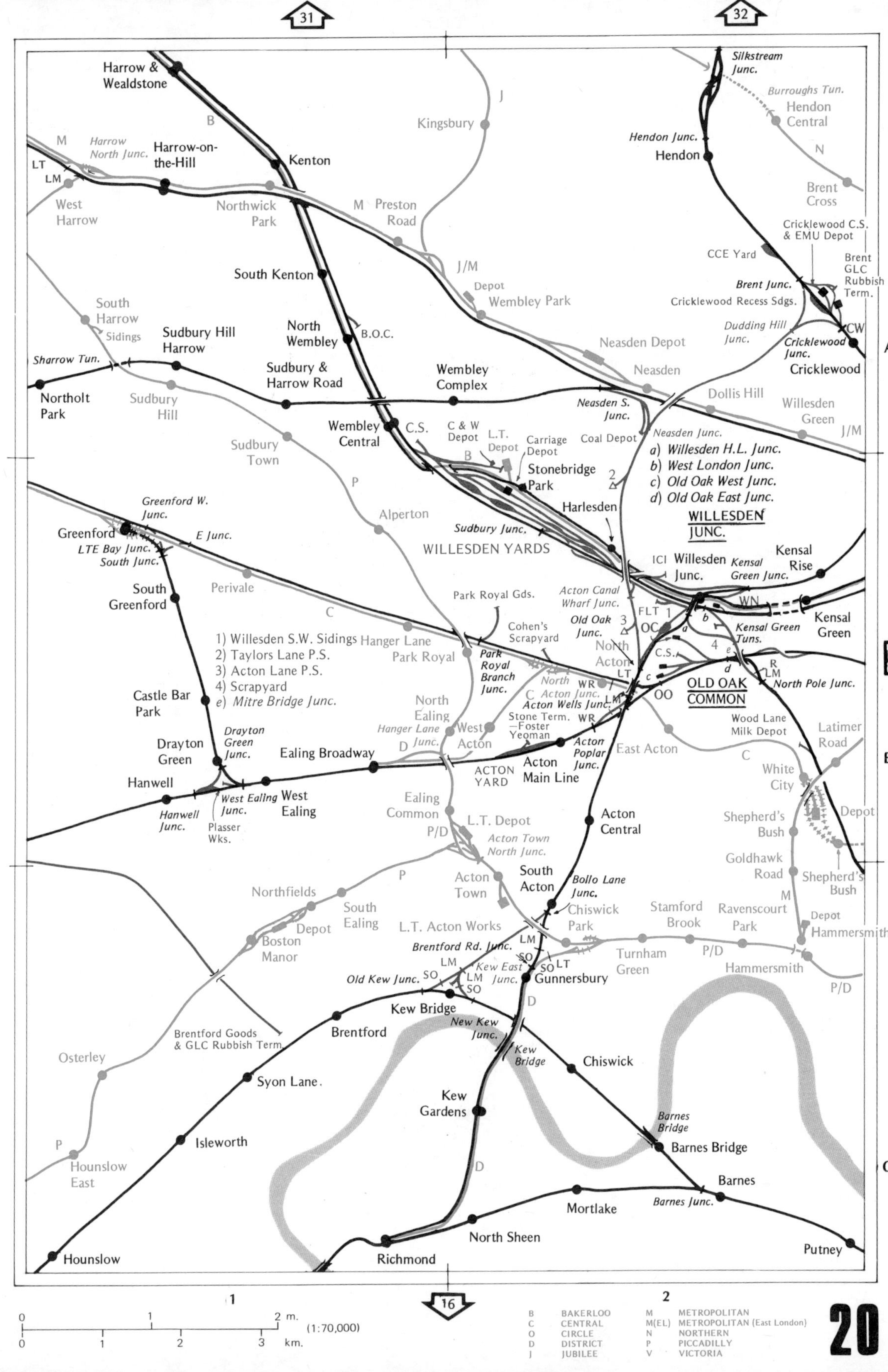
31
32
Harrow & Wealdstone
Silkstream Junc.
Burroughs Tun.
Hendon Central
Kingsbury
J
B
M
Harrow North Junc.
Harrow-on-the-Hill
LT
LM
Kenton
Hendon Junc.
Hendon
N
West Harrow
Northwick Park
M
Preston Road
Brent Cross
Cricklewood C.S. & EMU Depot
CCE Yard
Brent GLC Rubbish Term.
South Kenton
J/M
Depot
Wembley Park
Brent Junc.
Cricklewood Recess Sdgs.
South Harrow
Sidings
Sudbury Hill Harrow
North Wembley
B.O.C.
Dudding Hill Junc.
CW
Neasden Depot
Cricklewood Junc.
Cricklewood
A
Sharrow Tun.
Sudbury & Harrow Road
Wembley Complex
Neasden
Northolt Park
Sudbury Hill
Dollis Hill
Willesden Green
Neasden S. Junc.
Wembley Central
C.S.
C & W Depot
L.T. Depot
Carriage Depot
Coal Depot
Neasden Junc.
J/M
Sudbury Town
B
Stonebridge Park
a) Willesden H.L. Junc.
b) West London Junc.
c) Old Oak West Junc.
d) Old Oak East Junc.
P
2
Harlesden
WILLESDEN JUNC.
Greenford W. Junc.
Alperton
Sudbury Junc.
Greenford
E Junc.
LTE Bay Junc.
South Junc.
WILLESDEN YARDS
ICI
Willesden Junc.
Kensal Green Junc.
Kensal Rise
South Greenford
Perivale
Park Royal Gds.
Acton Canal Wharf Junc.
FLT
1
WN
Kensal Green
C
Old Oak Junc.
3
OC
Kensal Green Tuns.
1) Willesden S.W. Sidings
2) Taylors Lane P.S.
3) Acton Lane P.S.
4) Scrapyard
e) Mitre Bridge Junc.
Hanger Lane
Park Royal
Cohen's Scrapyard
North Acton
4
C.S.
21
Park Royal Branch Junc.
LT
R
LM
North Pole Junc.
OLD OAK COMMON
North Acton Junc.
WR
Castle Bar Park
North Ealing
Acton Wells Junc.
LM
OO
Stone Term. —Foster Yeoman
WR
Wood Lane Milk Depot
Latimer Road
Drayton Green Junc.
Hanger Lane Junc.
West Acton
Drayton Green
D
Acton Poplar Junc.
East Acton
C
Ealing Broadway
B
ACTON YARD
Acton Main Line
White City
Hanwell
West Ealing Junc.
West Ealing
Ealing Common
Shepherd's Bush
Depot
Hanwell Junc.
Plasser Wks.
L.T. Depot
Acton Central
P/D
Acton Town North Junc.
Goldhawk Road
P
Acton Town
South Acton
Shepherd's Bush
Northfields
Bollo Lane Junc.
M
South Ealing
Chiswick Park
Stamford Brook
Ravenscourt Park
Depot
Depot
L.T. Acton Works
Hammersmith
Boston Manor
LM
Brentford Rd. Junc.
Turnham Green
P/D
SO
Hammersmith
LM
Kew East Junc.
SO
LT
P/D
Old Kew Junc.
SO
LM
SO
Gunnersbury
D
Kew Bridge
Brentford Goods & GLC Rubbish Term.
New Kew Junc.
Brentford
Osterley
Kew Bridge
Chiswick
Syon Lane
Kew Gardens
Isleworth
Barnes Bridge
Barnes Bridge
P
Hounslow East
D
C
Barnes
Mortlake
Barnes Junc.
North Sheen
Putney
Hounslow
Richmond
16
1
2
0
1
2 m.
(1:70,000)
0
1
2
3
km.
B BAKERLOO
C CENTRAL
O CIRCLE
D DISTRICT
J JUBILEE
M METROPOLITAN
M(EL) METROPOLITAN (East London)
N NORTHERN
P PICCADILLY
V VICTORIA

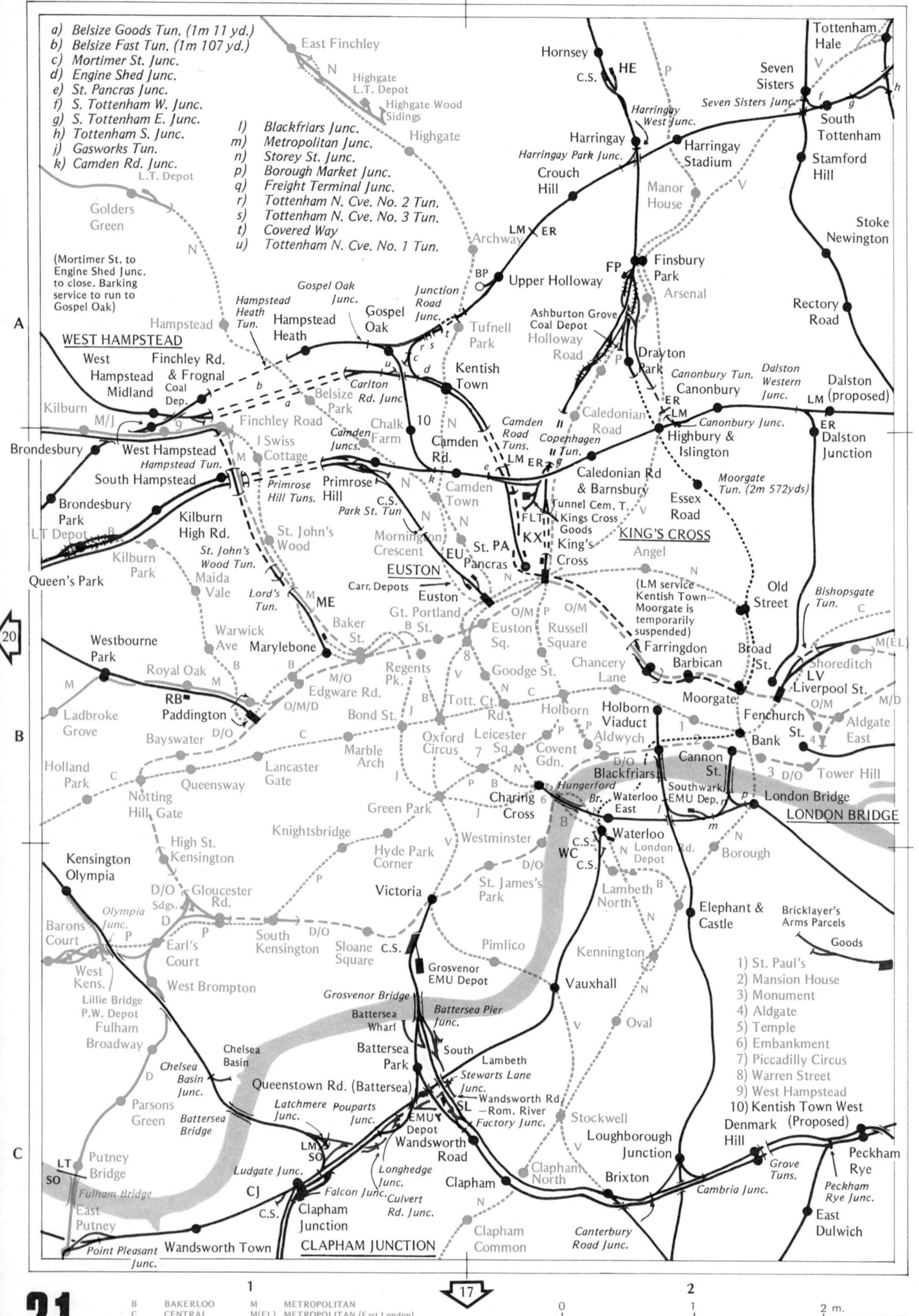
23
a) Belsize Goods Tun. (1m 11 yd.)
b) Belsize Fast Tun. (1m 107 yd.)
c) Mortimer St. Junc.
d) Engine Shed Junc.
e) St. Pancras Junc.
f) S. Tottenham W. Junc.
g) S. Tottenham E. Junc.
h) Tottenham S. Junc.
j) Gasworks Tun.
k) Camden Rd. Junc.
l) Blackfriars Junc.
m) Metropolitan Junc.
n) Storey St. Junc.
p) Borough Market Junc.
q) Freight Terminal Junc.
r) Tottenham N. Cve. No. 2 Tun.
s) Tottenham N. Cve. No. 3 Tun.
t) Covered Way
u) Tottenham N. Cve. No. 1 Tun.
(Mortimer St. to Engine Shed Junc. to close. Barking service to run to Gospel Oak)
East Finchley
Highgate L.T. Depot
Highgate Wood Sidings
Highgate
L.T. Depot
Golders Green
Hornsey
C.S.
HE
Harringay West Junc.
Harringay
Harringay Park Junc.
Harringay Stadium
Crouch Hill
Manor House
Tottenham Hale
Seven Sisters
Seven Sisters Junc.
South Tottenham
Stamford Hill
Stoke Newington
Rectory Road
Archway
LM ER
BP
Upper Holloway
FP
Finsbury Park
Arsenal
Ashburton Grove Coal Depot
Holloway Road
Tufnell Park
Drayton Park
Canonbury Tun.
Canonbury
Dalston Western Junc.
Dalston (proposed)
Dalston Junction
Canonbury Junc.
Highbury & Islington
Caledonian Road
Caledonian Rd & Barnsbury
Essex Road
Moorgate Tun. (2m 572yds)
Gospel Oak Junc.
Junction Road Junc.
Hampstead Heath Tun.
Hampstead Heath
Gospel Oak
Hampstead
WEST HAMPSTEAD
West Hampstead Midland
Finchley Rd. & Frognal
Coal Dep.
Kentish Town
Carlton Rd. Junc
Belsize Park
Kilburn
M/J
Brondesbury
West Hampstead
Hampstead Tun.
Finchley Road
Swiss Cottage
Chalk Farm
Camden Juncs.
Camden Rd.
Camden Road Tuns.
Copenhagen Tun.
South Hampstead
Primrose Hill Tuns.
Primrose Hill
C.S. Park St. Tun
Camden Town
Tunnel Cem. T.
Kings Cross Goods
FLT
KX
King's Cross
KING'S CROSS
Brondesbury Park
Kilburn High Rd.
LT Depot
Kilburn Park
St. John's Wood
St. John's Wood Tun.
Maida Vale
Queen's Park
Lord's Tun.
ME
Mornington Crescent
EUSTON
EU
St. PA Pancras
Carr. Depots
Euston
Angel
(LM service Kentish Town–Moorgate is temporarily suspended)
Old Street
Bishopsgate Tun.
Baker St.
Gt. Portland St.
Euston Sq.
Russell Square
Farringdon
Barbican
Broad St.
Westbourne Park
Warwick Ave
Marylebone
Royal Oak
RB
Paddington
Edgware Rd.
Regents Pk.
Goodge St.
Chancery Lane
Moorgate
Shoreditch
LV
Liverpool St.
Ladbroke Grove
Bayswater
Bond St.
Oxford Circus
Tott. Ct. Rd.
Holborn
Holborn Viaduct
Aldwych
Fenchurch St.
Aldgate East
Bank
Holland Park
Lancaster Gate
Marble Arch
Leicester Sq.
Covent Gdn.
Blackfriars
Cannon St.
Tower Hill
Notting Hill Gate
Queensway
Green Park
Charing Cross
Hungerford Br.
Waterloo East
Southwark EMU Dep.
London Bridge
LONDON BRIDGE
Knightsbridge
Westminster
C.S.
WC
Waterloo
London Rd. Depot
Borough
Kensington Olympia
High St. Kensington
Hyde Park Corner
St. James's Park
Lambeth North
Gloucester Rd.
D/O Sdgs.
Victoria
Elephant & Castle
Bricklayer's Arms Parcels
Goods
Olympia Junc.
Barons Court
Earl's Court
South Kensington
Sloane Square
C.S.
Pimlico
Kennington
West Kens.
West Brompton
Grosvenor EMU Depot
Vauxhall
Lillie Bridge P.W. Depot
Fulham Broadway
Grosvenor Bridge
Battersea Wharf
Battersea Pier Junc.
Oval
Chelsea Basin
Battersea Park
South Lambeth
Stewarts Lane Junc.
Chelsea Basin Junc.
Queenstown Rd. (Battersea)
SL
Wandsworth Rd.—Rom. River Factory Junc.
Parsons Green
Battersea Bridge
Latchmere Junc.
Pouparts Junc.
EMU Depot
Wandsworth Road
Stockwell
Loughborough Junction
Denmark Hill
Peckham Rye
Peckham Rye Junc.
Grove Tuns.
LM SO
Putney Bridge
LT
SO
Fulham Bridge
East Putney
Ludgate Junc.
Longhedge Junc.
CJ
Falcon Junc.
Culvert Rd. Junc.
Clapham Junction
C.S.
Clapham
Clapham North
Brixton
Cambria Junc.
East Dulwich
Clapham Common
Canterbury Road Junc.
Point Pleasant Junc.
Wandsworth Town
CLAPHAM JUNCTION
1) St. Paul's
2) Mansion House
3) Monument
4) Aldgate
5) Temple
6) Embankment
7) Piccadilly Circus
8) Warren Street
9) West Hampstead
10) Kentish Town West (Proposed)
A
B
C
20
17
1
2

B	BAKERLOO	M	METROPOLITAN
C	CENTRAL	M(EL)	METROPOLITAN (East London)
O	CIRCLE	N	NORTHERN
D	DISTRICT	P	PICCADILLY
J	JUBILEE	V	VICTORIA

0 1 2 m.
0 1 2 3 km.
(1:70,000)

24

Black Horse Rd.
Wood St.
V
V
C
St. James Street
Walthamstow Central
Walthamstow Queen's Rd.
Snaresbrook
Barkingside
C
Newbury Park
Wanstead
Redbridge
Gants Hill
Copper Mill Junc.
Leyton Midland Road
Leytonstone
Clapton Junc.
Parcels
Lea Bridge
TEMPLE MILLS YARD
Leytonstone High Rd.
IL
Clapton
Clapton Tun.
Ilford
C.S.
C.S.
Ilford—Unigate Milk Depot
Leyton
A
Queens Road Tun.
BREL
Wanstead Park
Forest Gate Junc.
Manor Park
Woodgrange Park
Hackney Downs N. Junc.
Stratford FLT
Loughton Branch Junc. Sth.
SR
Hackney Downs
Hackney Wick
High Meads Junc.
Forest Gate
Woodgrange Park Junc.
Hackney Central
Lea Junc.
LIFT
g
SF
Maryland
EM
Barking Stn. Junc.
East Ham
Barking
C.S.
D
Victoria Park Junc.
Channelsea Sidings
h
d
Stratford
M/D
London Fields
a
b
c
Stratford Southern Junc.
Upton Park
Barking Tilbury Line Junc. West
Thornton Fields C.S.
Rugby Cem. Term.
Carless
Barking Tilbury Line Junc. East
Stratford Market Goods
Upton Park Coal Depot
Bow Goods
Steel Stockholders
Plaistow
Cambridge Heath
C
Steetley Chem. Wks.
a) Carpenters Rd. N. Junc.
b) Carpenters Rd. S. Junc.
c) Stratford Western Junc.
d) Stratford Central Junc.
e) Bricklayers Arms Junc.
f) South Bermondsey Junc.
g) Channelsea S. Junc.
h) Channelsea N. Junc.
Mile End—Tarmac Stone Term.
Bow Junc.
Bethnal Green
C
Bow Rd.
LT
M/D
West Ham
Bethnal Green E. Junc.
ER
Plaistow & West Ham Coal Depot
32
Bethnal Green
M/D
Mile End
Gas Factory Junc.
Bromley-by-Bow
Abbey Mills Junc.
Stepney Green
Canning Town
Whitechapel
West Ham—Cohens Scrapyard
M(EL)
Custom House Victoria Dock
(Reversing Spur)
Stepney East
B
Poplar Cen. Junc.
Silvertown Tun.
Shadwell
Poplar Docks
Bow Creek (Thames Wharf)
Crossfields Glass
Silvertown
Wapping
North Woolwich
(Silvertown Tramway)
T.W. Ward Scrapyard
Rotherhithe
(Woolwich Free Ferry)
Angerstein Wharf
M(EL)
Thames Metal (Scrapyard)
Foster Yeoman Stone Term.
Dock St. St. Tun.
Coleman St. Tun.
Calderwood St. Tun.
Cross St. Tun.
Goods
Southwark Park Junc.
Surrey Docks
Mount St. Tun.
Plumstead
Charlton Tun.
Woolwich Dockyard
George IV Tun.
Woolwich Arsenal
C.S.
Surrey Canal Junc.
Surrey Canal Junc.
Charlton
f
Westcombe Park
North Kent West Junc.
e
Charlton Junc.
South Bermondsey
North Kent East Junc.
Greenwich College Tun.
CCE Works
Angerstein Junc.
Maze Hill
L.T. Depot
Deptford
New Cross Gate C.S.
St. James Sdgs.
New Cross
Greenwich
Blackheath Tunnel
Queens Road Peckham
New Cross Gate
Tanners Hill Junc.
St. John's
Lewisham Vale Junc.
Lewisham
Blackheath Junc.
C
Nunhead
Kidbrooke Tun.
Kidbrooke
Nunhead Junc.
Brockley
Parks Bridge Junc.
Courthill Loop Junc. North
Blackheath
Falconwood
Eltham Well Hall
Ladywell Junc.
Courthill Loop Junc. South
Eltham Park
Ladywell

1 2

18

0 1 2 m.
0 1 2 3 km.
(1:70,000)

B	BAKERLOO	M	METROPOLITAN
C	CENTRAL	M(EL)	METROPOLITAN (East London)
O	CIRCLE	N	NORTHERN
D	DISTRICT	P	PICCADILLY
J	JUBILEE	V	VICTORIA

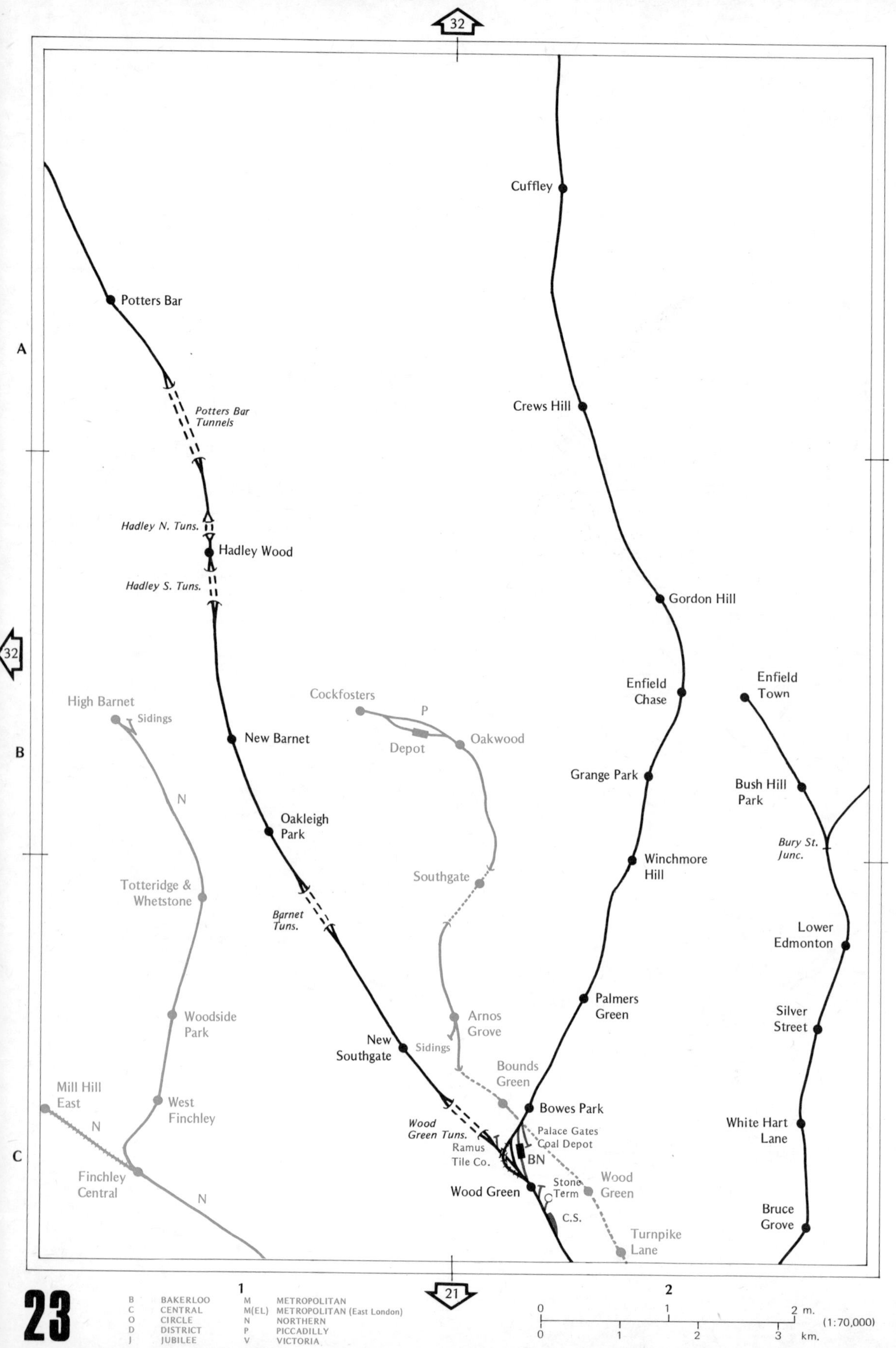
32
32
A
B
C
Potters Bar
Potters Bar Tunnels
Hadley N. Tuns.
Hadley Wood
Hadley S. Tuns.
New Barnet
Oakleigh Park
Barnet Tuns.
New Southgate
Wood Green Tuns.
Ramus Tile Co.
Wood Green
Cuffley
Crews Hill
Gordon Hill
Enfield Chase
Grange Park
Winchmore Hill
Palmers Green
Bowes Park
Palace Gates Coal Depot
BN
Stone Term
C.S.
Enfield Town
Bush Hill Park
Bury St. Junc.
Lower Edmonton
Silver Street
White Hart Lane
Bruce Grove
High Barnet
Sidings
N
Totteridge & Whetstone
Woodside Park
West Finchley
Mill Hill East
N
Finchley Central
N
Cockfosters
P
Depot
Oakwood
Southgate
Arnos Grove
Sidings
Bounds Green
Wood Green
Turnpike Lane
21
1
2

B	BAKERLOO	M	METROPOLITAN
C	CENTRAL	M(EL)	METROPOLITAN (East London)
O	CIRCLE	N	NORTHERN
D	DISTRICT	P	PICCADILLY
J	JUBILEE	V	VICTORIA

0 1 2 m.
0 1 2 3 km.
(1:70,000)

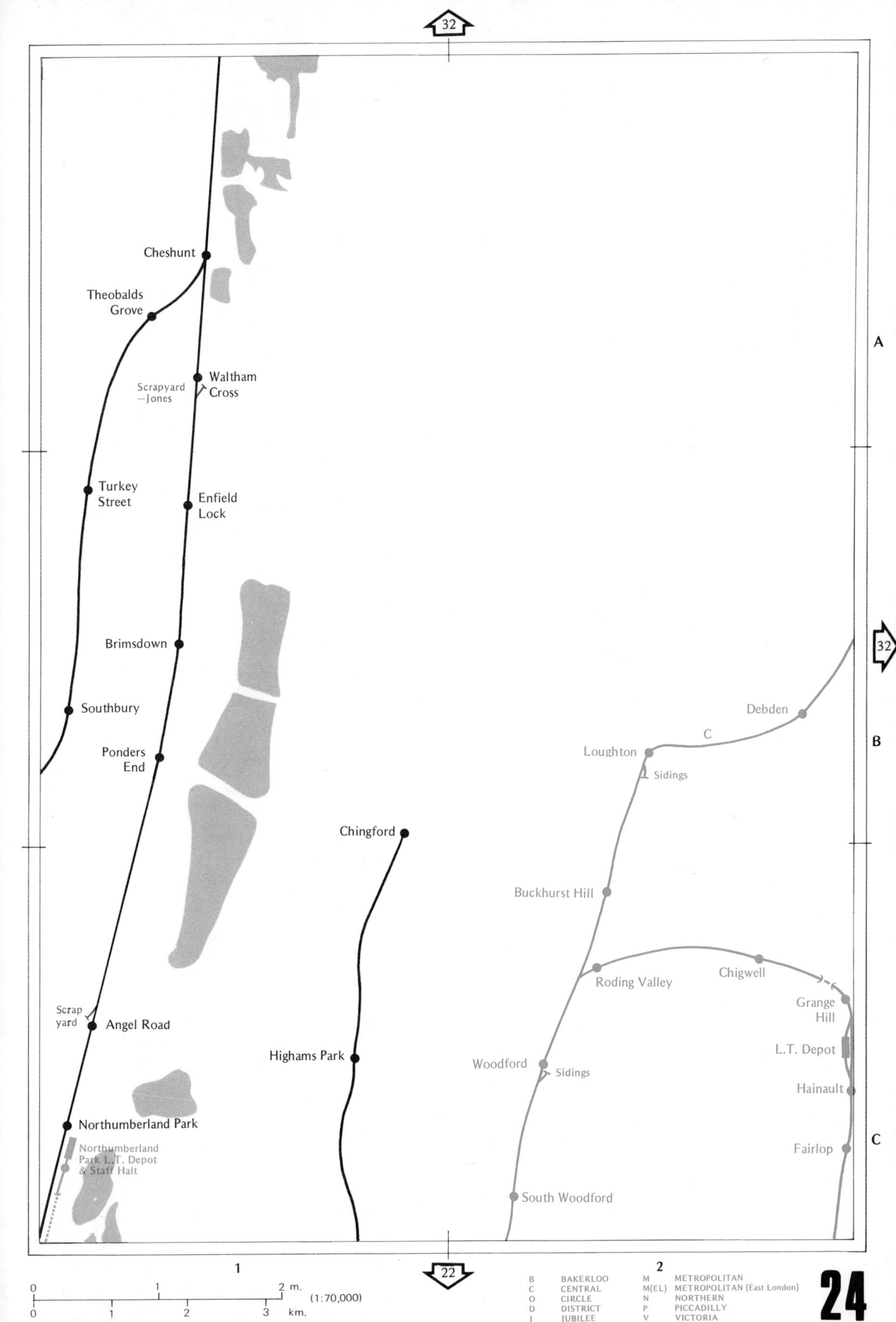
32
Cheshunt
Theobalds
Grove
Waltham
Cross
Scrapyard
—Jones
Turkey
Street
Enfield
Lock
Brimsdown
Southbury
Ponders
End
Chingford
Scrap
yard
Angel Road
Highams Park
Northumberland Park
Northumberland
Park L.T. Depot
& Staff Halt
Debden
C
Loughton
Sidings
Buckhurst Hill
Roding Valley
Chigwell
Grange
Hill
L.T. Depot
Woodford
Sidings
Hainault
Fairlop
South Woodford
A
B
C
32
22
1
2
0
1
2 m.
(1:70,000)
0
1
2
3
km.
B BAKERLOO
C CENTRAL
O CIRCLE
D DISTRICT
J JUBILEE
M METROPOLITAN
M(EL) METROPOLITAN (East London)
N NORTHERN
P PICCADILLY
V VICTORIA

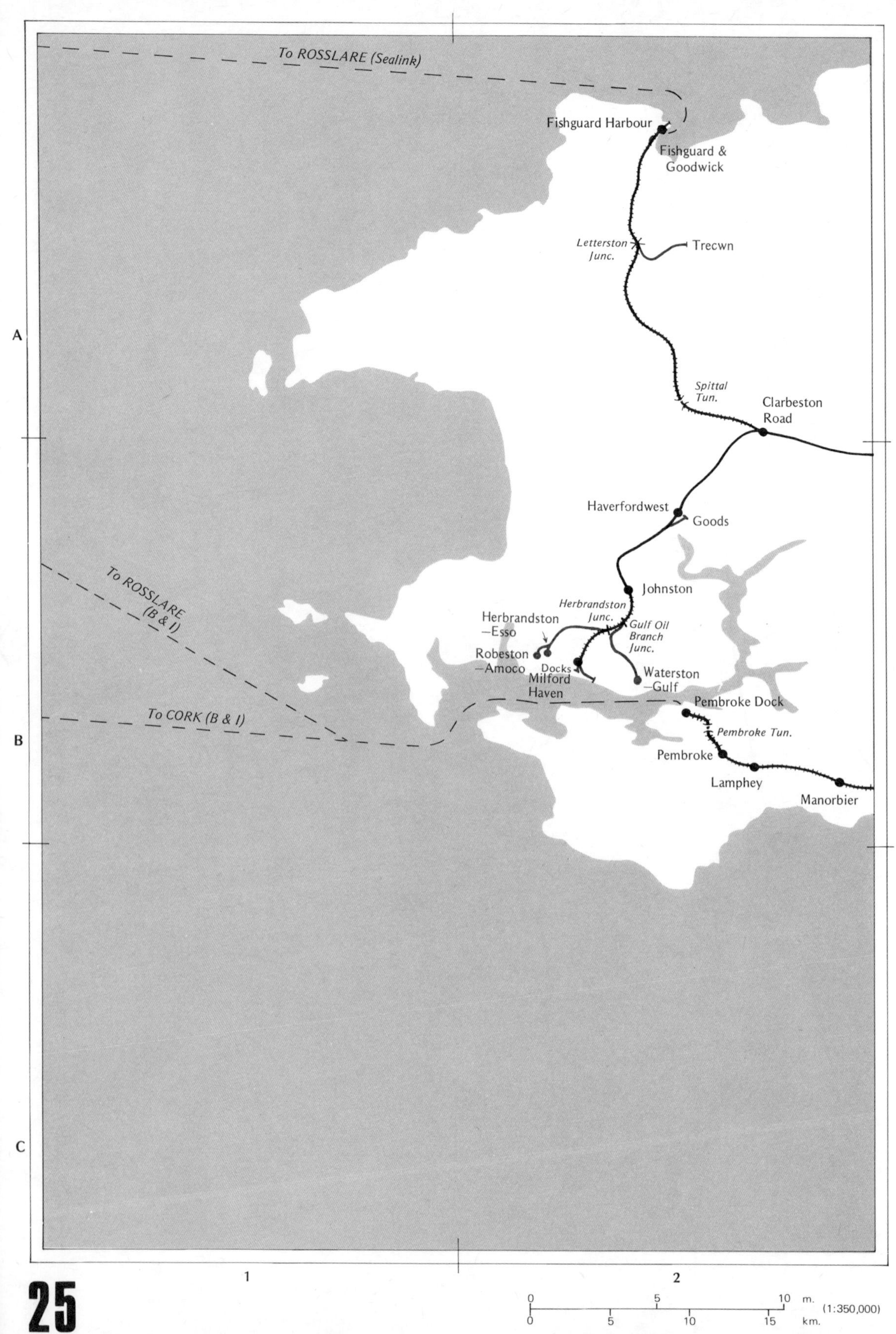

To ROSSLARE (Sealink)
Fishguard Harbour
Fishguard &
Goodwick
Letterston
Junc.
Trecwn
A
Spittal
Tun.
Clarbeston
Road
Haverfordwest
Goods
To ROSSLARE
(B & I)
Johnston
Herbrandston
Junc.
Herbrandston
–Esso
Gulf Oil
Branch
Junc.
Robeston
–Amoco
Docks
Milford
Haven
Waterston
–Gulf
Pembroke Dock
To CORK (B & I)
Pembroke Tun.
B
Pembroke
Lamphey
Manorbier
C
1
2
0 5 10 m.
0 5 10 15 km.
(1:350,000)

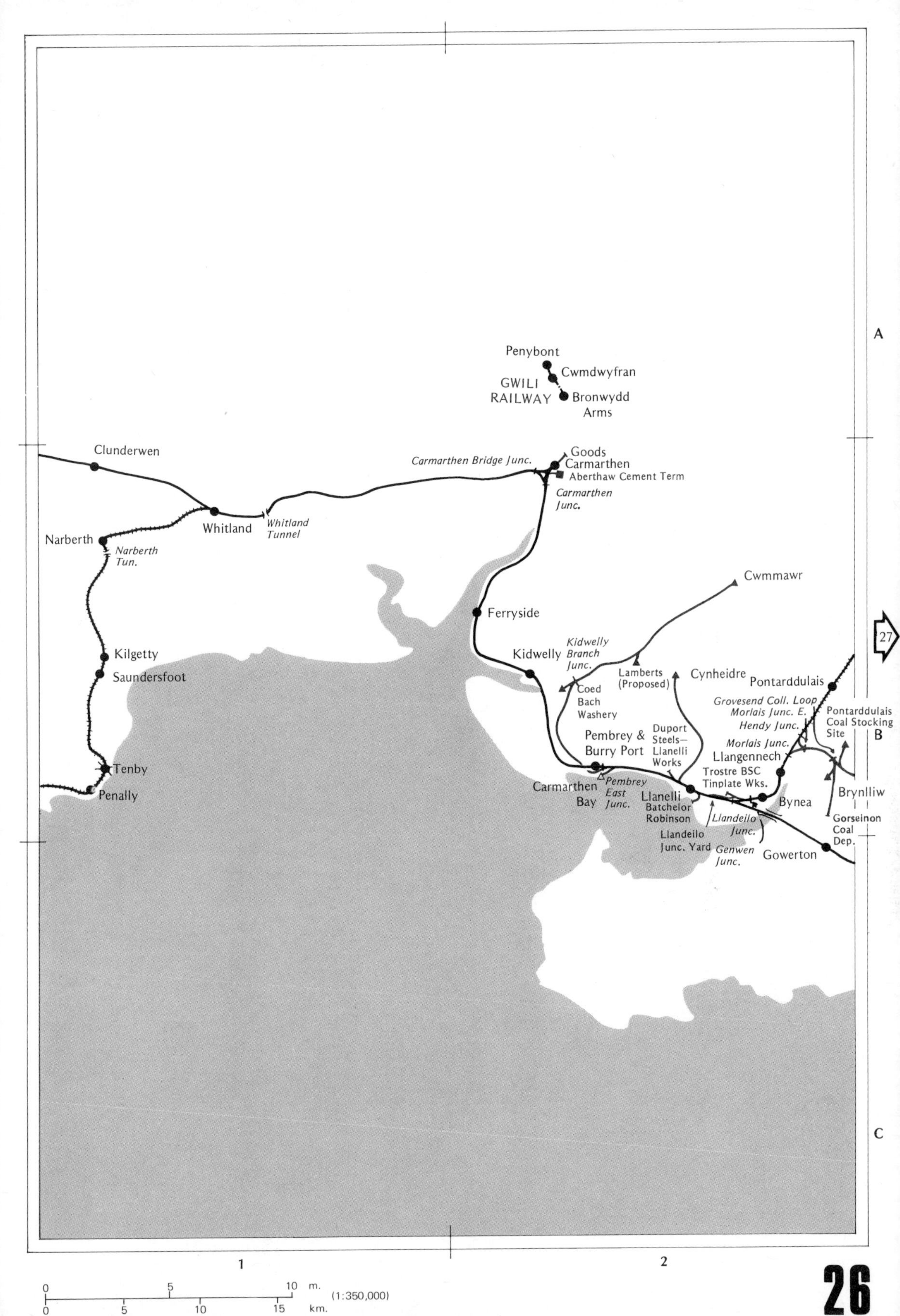

A
B
C
1
2
27
Penybont
Cwmdwyfran
GWILI
RAILWAY
Bronwydd
Arms
Clunderwen
Goods
Carmarthen Bridge Junc.
Carmarthen
Aberthaw Cement Term
Carmarthen
Junc.
Whitland
Whitland
Tunnel
Narberth
Narberth
Tun.
Cwmmawr
Ferryside
Kidwelly
Branch
Junc.
Kidwelly
Kilgetty
Saundersfoot
Lamberts
(Proposed)
Cynheidre
Pontarddulais
Coed
Bach
Washery
Grovesend Coll. Loop
Morlais Junc. E.
Hendy Junc.
Pontarddulais
Coal Stocking
Site
Pembrey &
Burry Port
Duport
Steels—
Llanelli
Works
Morlais Junc.
Llangennech
Tenby
Trostre BSC
Tinplate Wks.
Penally
Carmarthen
Bay
Pembrey
East
Junc.
Llanelli
Batchelor
Robinson
Bynea
Brynlliw
Llandeilo
Junc.
Gorseinon
Coal
Dep.
Llandeilo
Junc. Yard
Genwen
Junc.
Gowerton
0 5 10 m.
0 5 10 15 km.
(1:350,000)

35

1) Pontlottyn
2) Merthyr Vale
3) Quaker's Yard
4) Merthyr Vale
5) Danygraig FLT
6) Port Tennant – Wagon Repairs
7) Swansea Burrows Sidings
8) Swansea East Coal Depot
9) Penallta Junc. Tip

a) Jersey Marine North Junc.
b) Dynevor Junc.
c) Jersey Marine South Junc.
d) Landore Junc.

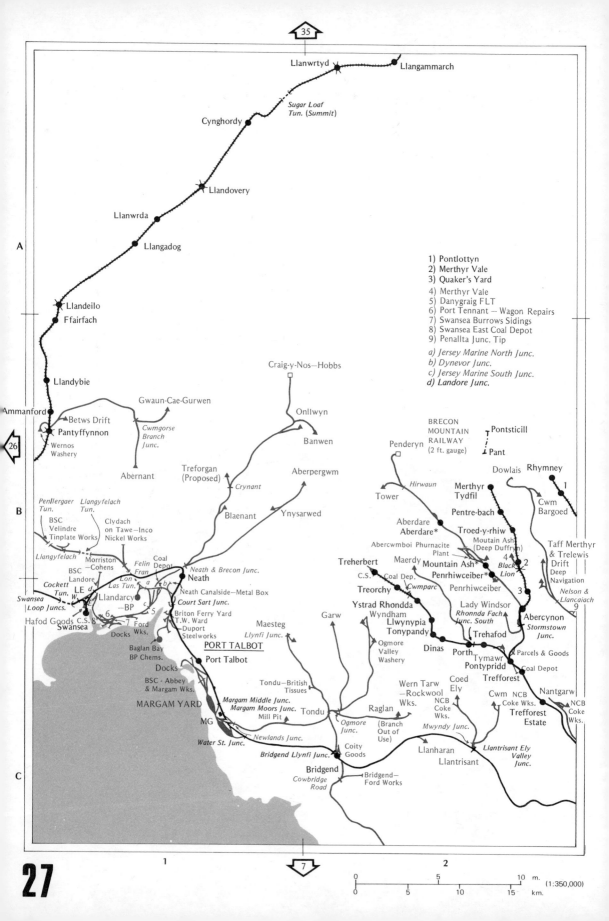

Llanwrtyd
Llangammarch
Sugar Loaf Tun. (Summit)
Cynghordy
Llandovery
Llanwrda
Llangadog
Llandeilo
Ffairfach
Llandybie
Ammanford
Betws Drift
Pantyffynnon
Wernos Washery
Gwaun-Cae-Gurwen
Cwmgorse Branch Junc.
Abernant
Craig-y-Nos–Hobbs
Onllwyn
Banwen
Treforgan (Proposed)
Crynant
Blaenant
Aberpergwm
Ynysarwed
Penllergaer Tun.
Llangyfelach Tun.
BSC Velindre Tinplate Works
Clydach on Tawe–Inco Nickel Works
Llangyfelach
Morriston –Cohens
BSC Landore
Felin Fran
Coal Depot
Neath & Brecon Junc.
Neath
Cockett Tun.
LE
Lon Las Tun.
Llandarcy –BP
Neath Canalside–Metal Box
Court Sart Junc.
Swansea Loop Juncs.
Hafod Goods
C.S.
Swansea
Docks
Ford Wks.
Briton Ferry Yard
T.W. Ward
Duport Steelworks
Baglan Bay BP Chems.
PORT TALBOT
Port Talbot
Docks
BSC - Abbey & Margam Wks.
MARGAM YARD
MG
Margam Middle Junc.
Margam Moors Junc.
Mill Pit
Water St. Junc.
Newlands Junc.
Bridgend Llynfi Junc.
Maesteg
Llynfi Junc.
Tondu–British Tissues
Tondu
Garw
Ogmore Junc.
Wyndham
Ogmore Valley Washery
Raglan
(Branch Out of Use)
Coity Goods
Bridgend
Cowbridge Road
Bridgend– Ford Works
Wern Tarw –Rockwool Wks.
Llanharan
Llantrisant
Coed Ely
NCB Coke Wks.
Mwyndy Junc.
Llantrisant Ely Valley Junc.
Cwm
NCB Coke Wks.
Trefforest Estate
Trefforest
Nantgarw
NCB Coke Wks.
BRECON MOUNTAIN RAILWAY (2 ft. gauge)
Pontsticill
Pant
Penderyn
Hirwaun
Tower
Aberdare
Aberdare*
Dowlais
Rhymney
Merthyr Tydfil
Pentre-bach
Troed-y-rhiw
Cwm Bargoed
Abercwmboi Phurnacite Plant
Moutain Ash (Deep Duffryn)
Maerdy
Mountain Ash*
Penrhiwceiber*
Black Lion
Penrhiwceiber
Taff Merthyr & Trelewis Drift
Deep Navigation
Nelson & Llancaiach
Treherbert
C.S.
Coal Dep.
Cwmparc
Treorchy
Ystrad Rhondda
Llwynypia
Tonypandy
Dinas
Lady Windsor
Rhondda Fach Junc. South
Trehafod
Abercynon
Stormstown Junc.
Porth
Tymawr
Pontypridd
Parcels & Goods
Coal Depot

A
B
C
1
2

26

7

0 5 10 m.
0 5 10 15 km.
(1:350,000)

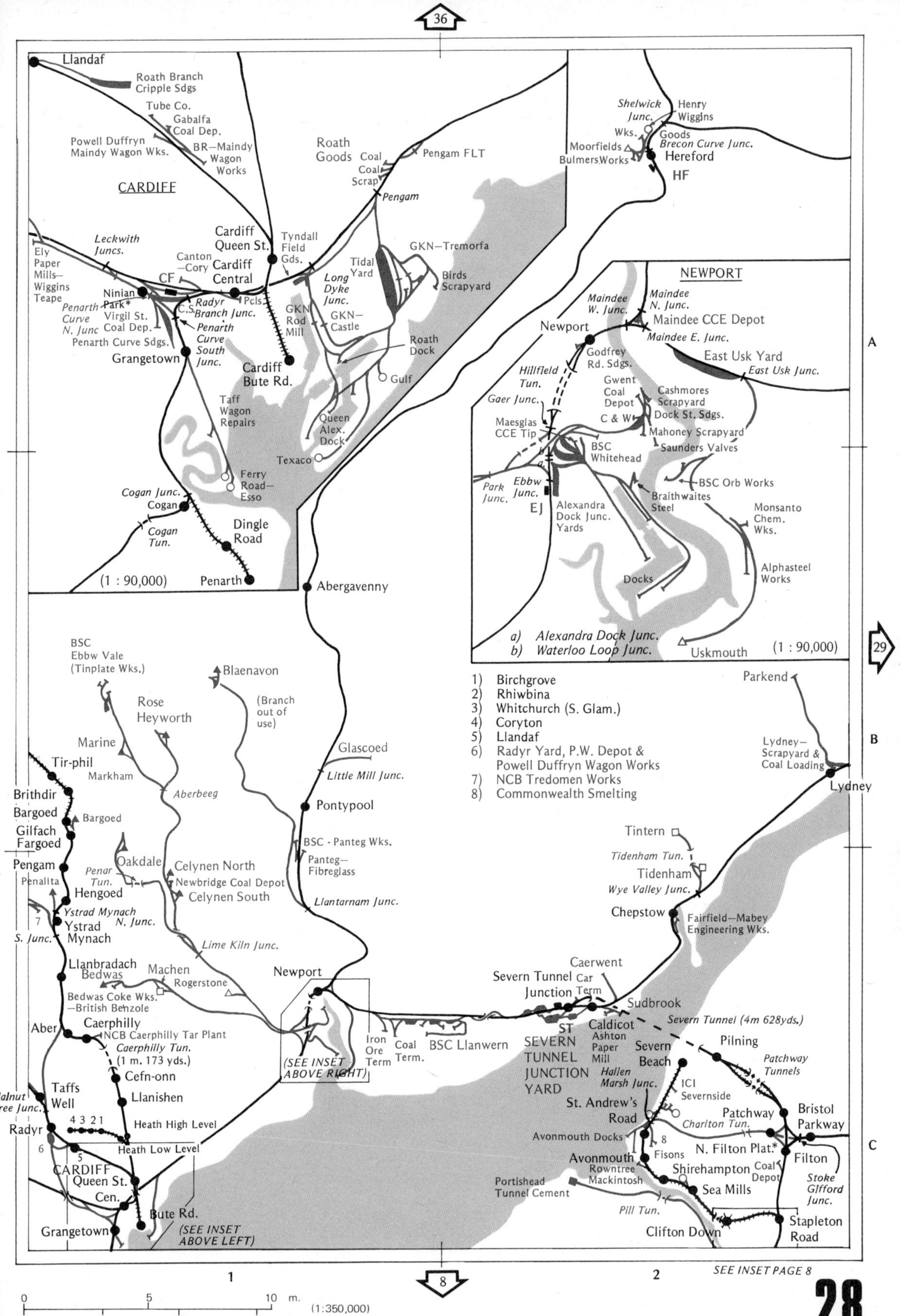

36

CARDIFF

Llandaf
Roath Branch Cripple Sdgs
Tube Co.
Gabalfa Coal Dep.
Powell Duffryn Maindy Wagon Wks.
BR—Maindy Wagon Works
Roath Goods
Coal
Coal
Scrap
Pengam FLT
Pengam
Leckwith Juncs.
Ely Paper Mills—Wiggins Teape
Canton —Cory
Cardiff Queen St.
Cardiff Central
Tyndall Field Gds.
CF
Ninian Park*
Penarth Curve N. Junc
Virgil St. Coal Dep.
C.S.
Radyr Branch Junc.
Pcls.
Penarth Curve South Junc.
Penarth Curve Sdgs.
Grangetown
Cardiff Bute Rd.
Long Dyke Junc.
Tidal Yard
GKN—Tremorfa
Birds Scrapyard
GKN Rod Mill
GKN—Castle
Roath Dock
Gulf
Queen Alex. Dock
Texaco
Taff Wagon Repairs
Ferry Road—Esso
Cogan Junc.
Cogan
Cogan Tun.
Dingle Road
Penarth
(1 : 90,000)

Shelwick Junc.
Henry Wiggins
Wks.
Goods
Brecon Curve Junc.
Moorfields
Bulmers Works
Hereford
HF

NEWPORT

Maindee W. Junc.
Maindee N. Junc.
Maindee CCE Depot
Maindee E. Junc.
Newport
East Usk Yard
East Usk Junc.
Godfrey Rd. Sdgs.
Hillfield Tun.
Gaer Junc.
Gwent Coal Depot
Cashmores Scrapyard
Dock St. Sdgs.
C & W
Maesglas CCE Tip
Mahoney Scrapyard
Saunders Valves
BSC Whitehead
BSC Orb Works
Park Junc.
Ebbw Junc.
EJ
Alexandra Dock Junc. Yards
Braithwaites Steel
Monsanto Chem. Wks.
Alphasteel Works
Docks
a) *Alexandra Dock Junc.*
b) *Waterloo Loop Junc.*
Uskmouth
(1 : 90,000)

29

1) Birchgrove
2) Rhiwbina
3) Whitchurch (S. Glam.)
4) Coryton
5) Llandaf
6) Radyr Yard, P.W. Depot & Powell Duffryn Wagon Works
7) NCB Tredomen Works
8) Commonwealth Smelting

Abergavenny
BSC Ebbw Vale (Tinplate Wks.)
Blaenavon
(Branch out of use)
Rose Heyworth
Marine
Markham
Glascoed
Little Mill Junc.
Tir-phil
Brithdir
Bargoed
Bargoed
Gilfach Fargoed
Aberbeeg
Pontypool
Pengam
Penalita
Oakdale
Penar Tun.
Celynen North
Newbridge Coal Depot
Celynen South
BSC - Panteg Wks.
Panteg—Fibreglass
Hengoed
Ystrad Mynach N. Junc.
7
S. Junc.
Ystrad Mynach
Llantarnam Junc.
Lime Kiln Junc.
Llanbradach
Bedwas
Machen
Rogerstone
Bedwas Coke Wks. —British Benzole
Newport
Aber
Caerphilly
NCB Caerphilly Tar Plant
Caerphilly Tun. (1 m. 173 yds.)
Cefn-onn
Llanishen
Taffs Well
Walnut Tree Junc.
Radyr
4 3 2 1
Heath High Level
6
5
Heath Low Level
CARDIFF Queen St.
Cen.
Grangetown
Bute Rd.
(SEE INSET ABOVE LEFT)
(SEE INSET ABOVE RIGHT)
Iron Ore Term
Coal Term.
BSC Llanwern

Parkend
Lydney—Scrapyard & Coal Loading
Lydney
Tintern
Tidenham Tun.
Tidenham
Wye Valley Junc.
Chepstow
Fairfield—Mabey Engineering Wks.
Caerwent
Severn Tunnel Junction
Car Term
Sudbrook
Severn Tunnel (4m 628yds.)
ST
SEVERN TUNNEL JUNCTION YARD
Caldicot
Ashton Paper Mill
Severn Beach
Pilning
Patchway Tunnels
Hallen Marsh Junc.
ICI Severnside
St. Andrew's Road
Patchway
Bristol Parkway
Charlton Tun.
Avonmouth Docks
8
Fisons
N. Filton Plat.*
Filton
Avonmouth
Rowntree Mackintosh
Shirehampton
Coal Depot
Stoke Gifford Junc.
Portishead Tunnel Cement
Sea Mills
Pill Tun.
Clifton Down
Stapleton Road

A
B
C
1
2
SEE INSET PAGE 8

8

0 5 10 m.
0 5 10 15 km.
(1:350,000)

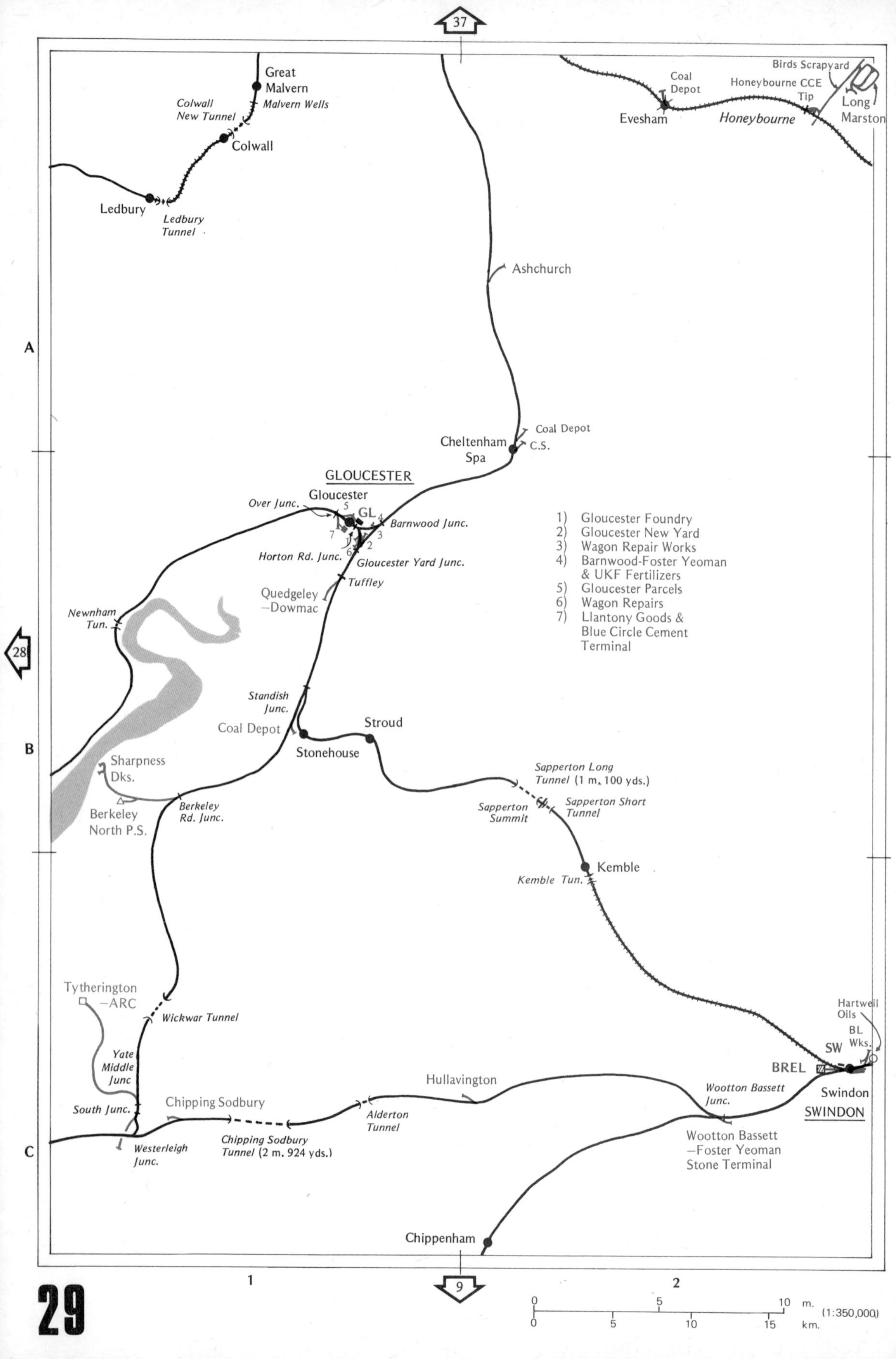
37
Great
Malvern
Colwall
New Tunnel
Malvern Wells
Colwall
Ledbury
Ledbury
Tunnel
Coal
Depot
Evesham
Honeybourne
Birds Scrapyard
Honeybourne CCE
Tip
Long
Marston
Ashchurch
A
Coal Depot
Cheltenham
Spa
C.S.
GLOUCESTER
Gloucester
Over Junc.
GL
Barnwood Junc.
Horton Rd. Junc.
Gloucester Yard Junc.
Tuffley
Quedgeley
–Dowmac
1) Gloucester Foundry
2) Gloucester New Yard
3) Wagon Repair Works
4) Barnwood-Foster Yeoman & UKF Fertilizers
5) Gloucester Parcels
6) Wagon Repairs
7) Llantony Goods & Blue Circle Cement Terminal
Newnham
Tun.
28
Standish
Junc.
Coal Depot
Stroud
Stonehouse
B
Sharpness
Dks.
Berkeley
North P.S.
Berkeley
Rd. Junc.
Sapperton Long
Tunnel (1 m. 100 yds.)
Sapperton
Summit
Sapperton Short
Tunnel
Kemble
Kemble Tun.
Tytherington
–ARC
Wickwar Tunnel
Yate
Middle
Junc
South Junc.
Chipping Sodbury
Westerleigh
Junc.
Chipping Sodbury
Tunnel (2 m. 924 yds.)
Alderton
Tunnel
Hullavington
Wootton Bassett
Junc.
Wootton Bassett
–Foster Yeoman
Stone Terminal
Hartwell
Oils
BL
Wks.
SW
BREL
Swindon
SWINDON
C
Chippenham
1
9
2
0 5 10 m.
0 5 10 15 km.
(1:350,000)

38

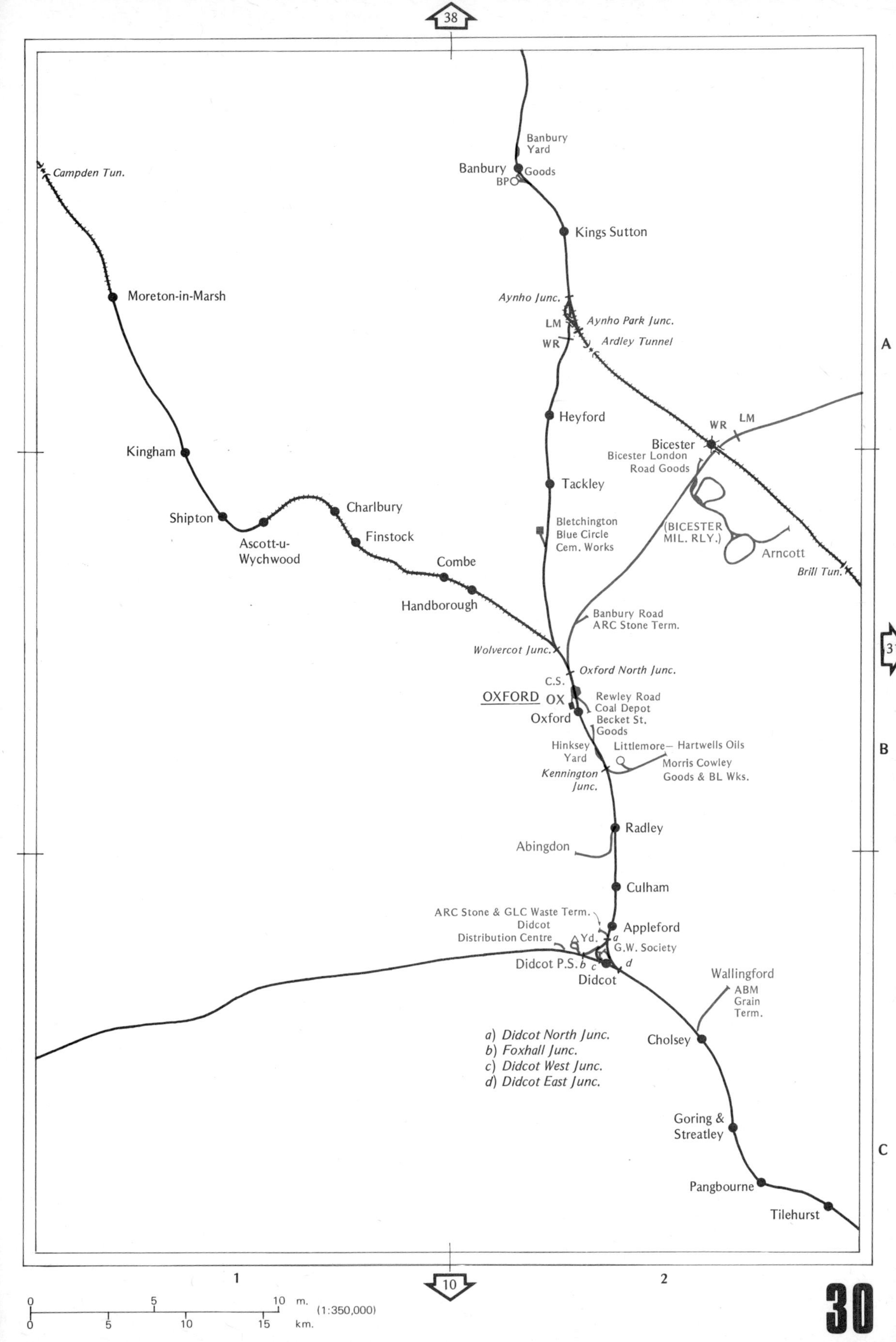

Campden Tun.
Moreton-in-Marsh
Kingham
Shipton
Ascott-u-
Wychwood
Charlbury
Finstock
Combe
Handborough
Wolvercot Junc.
Banbury Yard
Banbury
Goods
BP
Kings Sutton
Aynho Junc.
LM
Aynho Park Junc.
WR
Ardley Tunnel
Heyford
Tackley
Bletchington
Blue Circle
Cem. Works
WR
LM
Bicester
Bicester London
Road Goods
(BICESTER
MIL. RLY.)
Arncott
Brill Tun.
Banbury Road
ARC Stone Term.
Oxford North Junc.
C.S.
OXFORD
OX
Oxford
Rewley Road
Coal Depot
Becket St.
Goods
Hinksey
Yard
Littlemore— Hartwells Oils
Morris Cowley
Goods & BL Wks.
Kennington
Junc.
Radley
Abingdon
Culham
ARC Stone & GLC Waste Term.
Didcot
Distribution Centre
Yd.
Appleford
a
G.W. Society
Didcot P.S.
b
c
d
Didcot
Wallingford
ABM
Grain
Term.
Cholsey
a) Didcot North Junc.
b) Foxhall Junc.
c) Didcot West Junc.
d) Didcot East Junc.
Goring &
Streatley
Pangbourne
Tilehurst
A
B
C
1
2
0 5 10 m.
0 5 10 15 km.
(1:350,000)

31

10

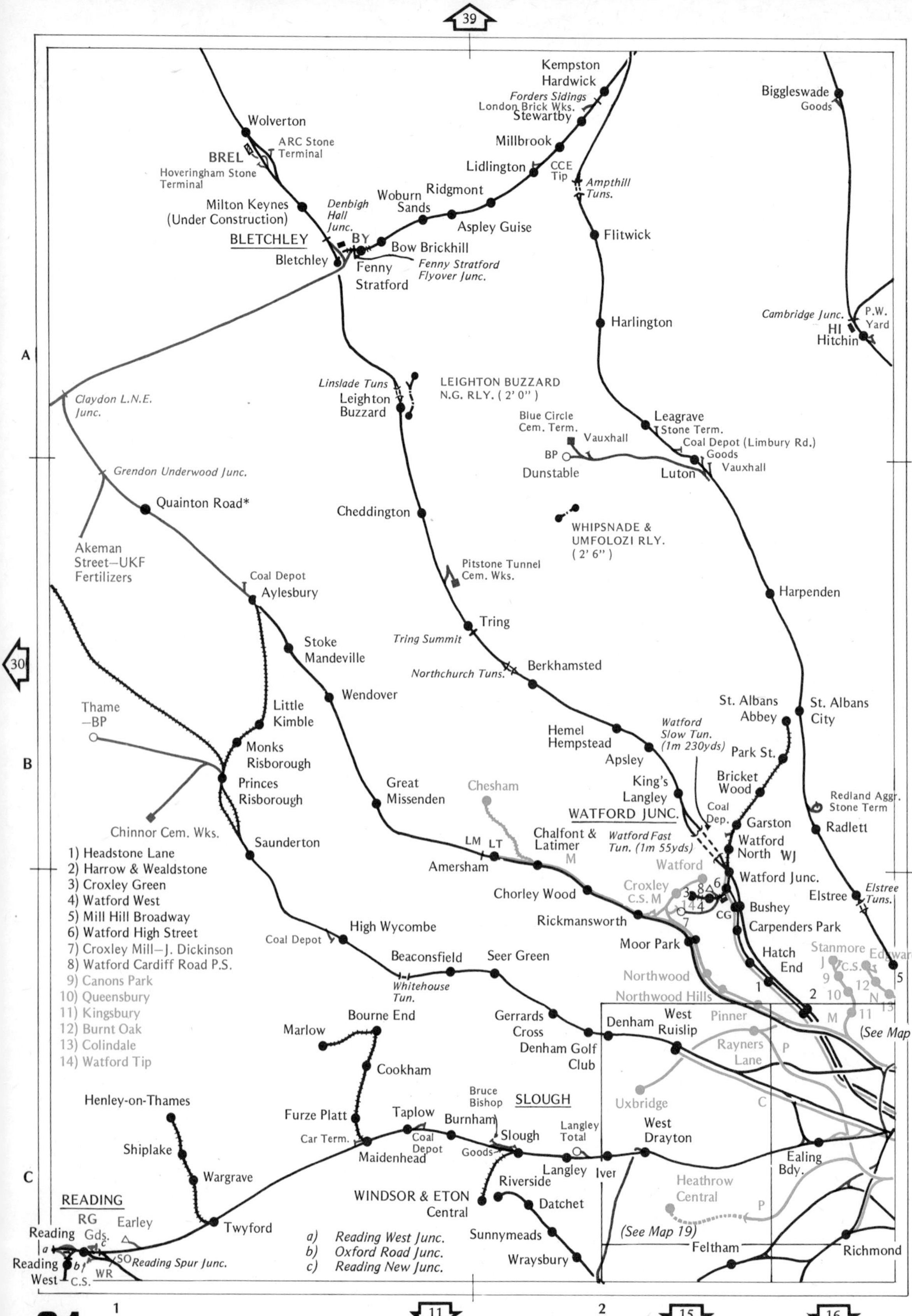

39

Kempston Hardwick
Forders Sidings
London Brick Wks.
Stewartby
Biggleswade
Goods
Wolverton
ARC Stone Terminal
BREL
Hoveringham Stone Terminal
Millbrook
Lidlington
CCE Tip
Ampthill Tuns.
Milton Keynes (Under Construction)
Denbigh Hall Junc.
Woburn Sands
Ridgmont
Aspley Guise
BLETCHLEY
BY
Bletchley
Bow Brickhill
Fenny Stratford
Fenny Stratford Flyover Junc.
Flitwick
Harlington
Cambridge Junc.
HI
Hitchin
P.W. Yard
A
Claydon L.N.E. Junc.
Linslade Tuns
Leighton Buzzard
LEIGHTON BUZZARD N.G. RLY. (2' 0")
Blue Circle Cem. Term.
Leagrave
Stone Term.
Coal Depot (Limbury Rd.)
Goods
Vauxhall
BP
Dunstable
Luton
Vauxhall
Grendon Underwood Junc.
Quainton Road*
Cheddington
WHIPSNADE & UMFOLOZI RLY. (2' 6")
Akeman Street—UKF Fertilizers
Pitstone Tunnel Cem. Wks.
Coal Depot
Aylesbury
Harpenden
Tring
Tring Summit
Stoke Mandeville

30

Northchurch Tuns.
Berkhamsted
Wendover
Thame —BP
Little Kimble
St. Albans Abbey
St. Albans City
Hemel Hempstead
Watford Slow Tun. (1m 230yds)
Apsley
Park St.
B
Monks Risborough
Princes Risborough
Great Missenden
Chesham
King's Langley
Bricket Wood
Redland Aggr. Stone Term
Coal Dep.
Garston
Radlett
WATFORD JUNC.
Chalfont & Latimer
Watford Fast Tun. (1m 55yds)
Watford North
WJ
Chinnor Cem. Wks.
Saunderton
LM
LT
M
Amersham
Watford
Watford Junc.
Croxley C.S. M
Elstree
Elstree Tuns.
Chorley Wood
Bushey
CG
Rickmansworth
Carpenders Park
Coal Depot
High Wycombe
Moor Park
Hatch End
Stanmore
J
C.S.
Edgware
Beaconsfield
Seer Green
Whitehouse Tun.
Northwood
Northwood Hills
N
Bourne End
Gerrards Cross
Denham
West Ruislip
Pinner
M
(See Map 20)
Marlow
Denham Golf Club
Rayners Lane
P
Cookham
Uxbridge
C
Bruce Bishop
SLOUGH
Henley-on-Thames
Furze Platt
Taplow
Burnham
Langley Total
West Drayton
Car Term.
Coal Depot
Slough
Shiplake
Maidenhead
Goods
Ealing Bdy.
Langley
Iver
Riverside
Heathrow Central
Wargrave
C
WINDSOR & ETON Central
Datchet
P
READING
RG
Earley
Twyford
(See Map 19)
Reading
Gds.
Sunnymeads
Feltham
Richmond
Reading West
C.S.
SO
WR
Reading Spur Junc.
Wraysbury

1) Headstone Lane
2) Harrow & Wealdstone
3) Croxley Green
4) Watford West
5) Mill Hill Broadway
6) Watford High Street
7) Croxley Mill—J. Dickinson
8) Watford Cardiff Road P.S.
9) Canons Park
10) Queensbury
11) Kingsbury
12) Burnt Oak
13) Colindale
14) Watford Tip

a) Reading West Junc.
b) Oxford Road Junc.
c) Reading New Junc.

1 2

B	BAKERLOO	M	METROPOLITAN
C	CENTRAL	M(EL)	METROPOLITAN (East London)
O	CIRCLE	N	NORTHERN
D	DISTRICT	P	PICCADILLY
J	JUBILEE	V	VICTORIA

11 15 16

0 5 10 m.
0 5 10 15 km.
(1:350,000)

a) *Crayford 'A' Junc.*
b) *Crayford 'B' Junc.*
c) *Tilbury E. Junc.*
d) *Crayford Creek Junc.*
e) *Perry St. Fork Junc.*
f) *Slade Green Junc.*
g) *Tilbury W. Junc.*
h) *Tilbury S. Junc.*
j) *Greenhithe Tun.*
k) *West Thurrock Junc.*

1) Willesden Junc.
2) Finsbury Park
3) Stratford
4) Clapham Junction
5) Lewisham
6) London Bridge
7) Victoria
8) Upminster Bridge
9) Hornchurch
10) Elm Park
11) Dagenham East
12) Dagenham Heathway
13) Becontree
14) Upney
15) Seven Kings
16) Goodmayes
17) Bexleyheath
18) Crayford
19) Albany Park
20) Stone Crossing
21) Greenhithe
22) Swanscombe
23) Northfleet
24) Hoo Staff Halt*
25) Northfleet – Blue Circle
26) Shell Chemicals
27) Swanscombe – Blue Circle
28) Thames Matex Works
29) West Thurrock Pr. & Gamble
30) Blue Circle Terminal

(EPPING TO ONGAR IS PROPOSED FOR CLOSURE BY LT)

0 5 10 m. (1:350,000)
0 5 10 15 km.

B	BAKERLOO	M	METROPOLITAN
C	CENTRAL	M(EL)	METROPOLITAN (East London)
O	CIRCLE	N	NORTHERN
D	DISTRICT	P	PICCADILLY
J	JUBILEE	V	VICTORIA

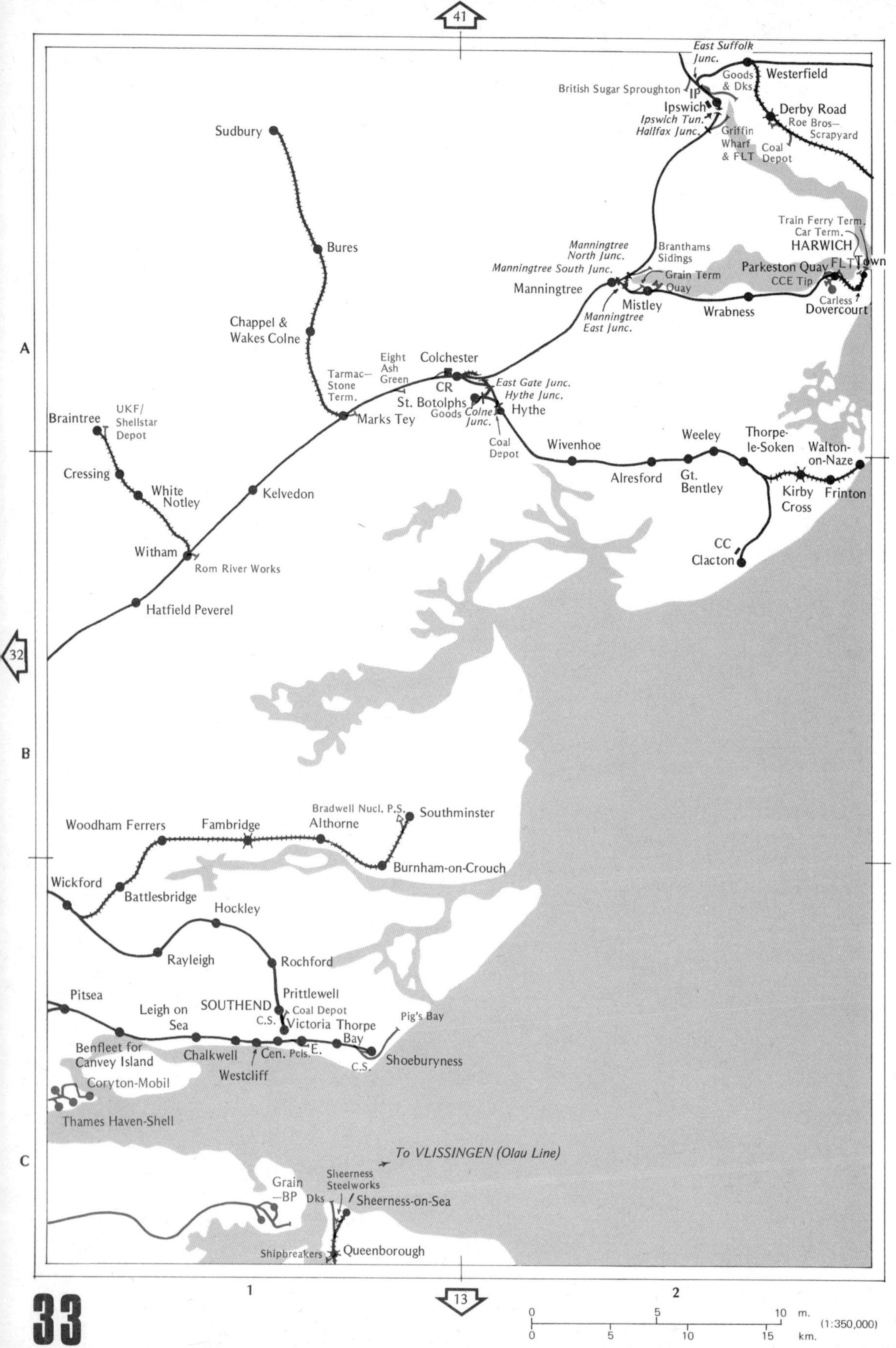

41
East Suffolk Junc.
Westerfield
Goods & Dks.
British Sugar Sproughton
IP
Ipswich
Ipswich Tun.
Halifax Junc.
Derby Road
Roe Bros—Scrapyard
Griffin Wharf & FLT
Coal Depot
Sudbury
Train Ferry Term.
Car Term.
HARWICH
Bures
Manningtree North Junc.
Branthams Sidings
Manningtree South Junc.
Grain Term Quay
Parkeston Quay
FLT
Town
CCE Tip
Manningtree
Mistley
Wrabness
Carless
Dovercourt
Chappel & Wakes Colne
Manningtree East Junc.
A
Eight Ash Green
Colchester
Tarmac—Stone Term.
CR
East Gate Junc.
Hythe Junc.
St. Botolphs
Goods
Colne Junc.
Hythe
Braintree
UKF/Shellstar Depot
Marks Tey
Coal Depot
Wivenhoe
Weeley
Thorpe-le-Soken
Walton-on-Naze
Cressing
Alresford
Gt. Bentley
Kirby Cross
Frinton
White Notley
Kelvedon
Witham
Rom River Works
CC
Clacton
Hatfield Peverel
32
B
Bradwell Nucl. P.S.
Southminster
Woodham Ferrers
Fambridge
Althorne
Burnham-on-Crouch
Wickford
Battlesbridge
Hockley
Rayleigh
Rochford
Pitsea
Prittlewell
Leigh on Sea
SOUTHEND
Coal Depot
C.S.
Victoria
Thorpe Bay
Pig's Bay
Benfleet for Canvey Island
Chalkwell
Cen.
Pcls.
E.
C.S.
Shoeburyness
Westcliff
Coryton-Mobil
Thames Haven-Shell
C
To VLISSINGEN (Olau Line)
Sheerness Steelworks
Grain —BP
Dks
Sheerness-on-Sea
Shipbreakers
Queenborough
1
13
2
0 5 10 m.
0 5 10 15 km.
(1:350,000)

42
44

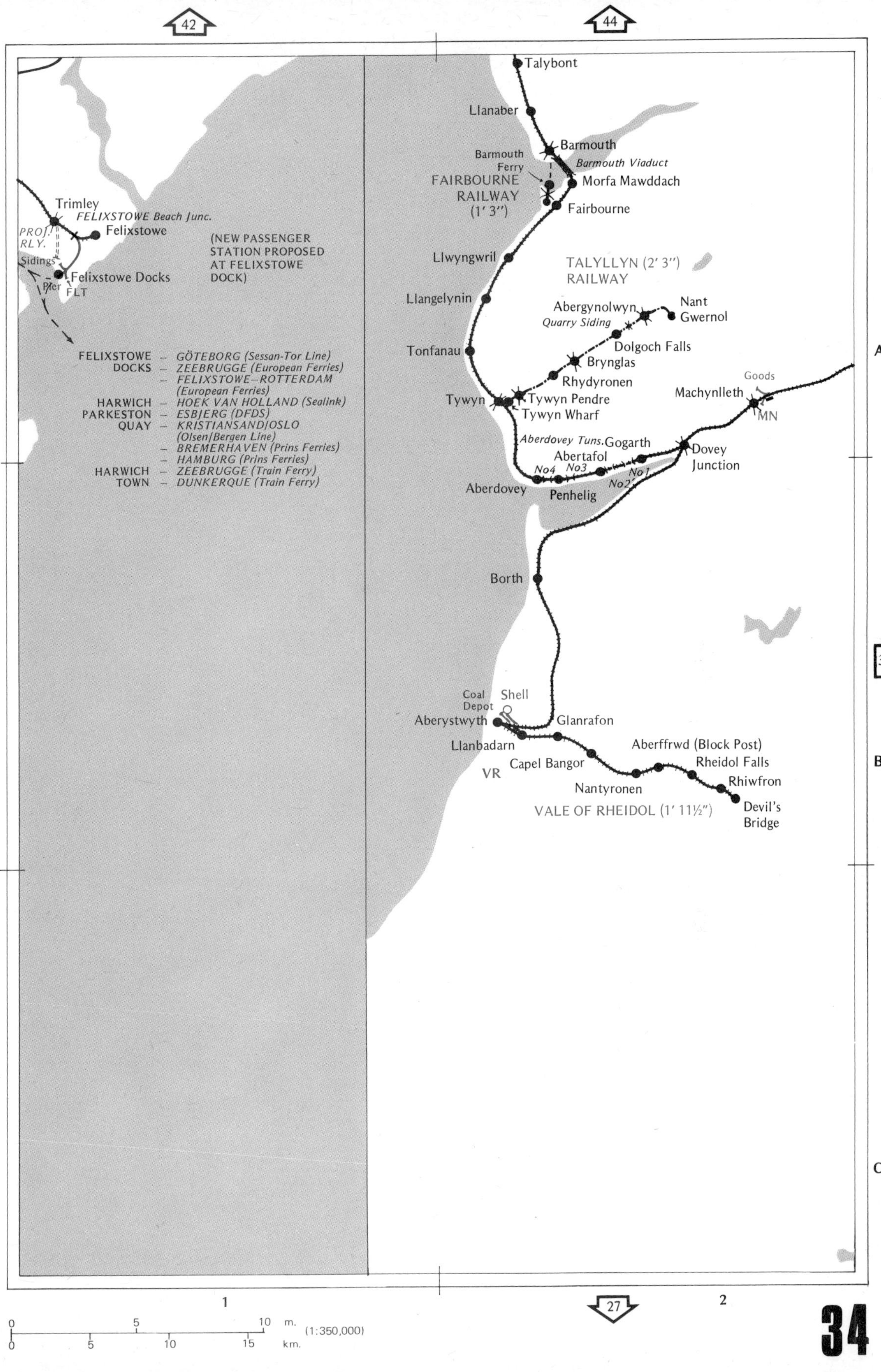
Trimley
FELIXSTOWE Beach Junc.
Felixstowe
PROJ. RLY.
Sidings
Felixstowe Docks
Pier
FLT
(NEW PASSENGER STATION PROPOSED AT FELIXSTOWE DOCK)
FELIXSTOWE DOCKS – GÖTEBORG (Sessan-Tor Line)
– ZEEBRUGGE (European Ferries)
– FELIXSTOWE–ROTTERDAM (European Ferries)
HARWICH PARKESTON QUAY – HOEK VAN HOLLAND (Sealink)
– ESBJERG (DFDS)
– KRISTIANSAND/OSLO (Olsen/Bergen Line)
– BREMERHAVEN (Prins Ferries)
– HAMBURG (Prins Ferries)
HARWICH TOWN – ZEEBRUGGE (Train Ferry)
– DUNKERQUE (Train Ferry)
Talybont
Llanaber
Barmouth
Barmouth Ferry
Barmouth Viaduct
Morfa Mawddach
FAIRBOURNE RAILWAY (1′ 3″)
Fairbourne
Llwyngwril
TALYLLYN (2′ 3″) RAILWAY
Llangelynin
Abergynolwyn
Nant Gwernol
Quarry Siding
Dolgoch Falls
Tonfanau
Brynglas
Rhydyronen
Goods
Machynlleth
MN
Tywyn
Tywyn Pendre
Tywyn Wharf
Aberdovey Tuns.
Gogarth
Dovey Junction
Abertafol
No4
No3
No1
No2
Aberdovey
Penhelig
Borth
Coal Depot
Shell
Aberystwyth
Glanrafon
Llanbadarn
Capel Bangor
Aberffrwd (Block Post)
Rheidol Falls
Rhiwfron
VR
Nantyronen
VALE OF RHEIDOL (1′ 11½″)
Devil's Bridge
A
B
C
1
2
0 5 10 m.
0 5 10 15 km.
(1:350,000)

35
27

44
Barmouth
Barmouth Viaduct
Morfa Mawddach
Fairbourne
TALYLLYN
RAILWAY
(2′ 3″)
Abergynolwyn
Nant Gwernol
Quarry Siding
Dolgoch Falls
Bryncrug
Rhydyronen
A
Cemmes Road
Goods
Machynlleth
MN
Talerddig (Summit)
Heniarth
Llanfair Caereinion
Abertafol
Aberdovey Tuns.
Gogarth
No. 3
No. 1
No. 2
Dovey Junction
No. 4
Penhelig
Caersws
Newtown
Coal
Depot
Borth
34
Glanrafon
Aberffrwd
(Block Post)
Capel
Bangor
Rheidol Falls
Rhiwfron
Nantyronen
Devil's Bridge
B
VALE OF RHEIDOL
(1′ 11½″)
Pen-y-Bont
Llandrindod
C
Builth Road
Garth
Cilmeri
1
27
2
0 5 10 m.
0 5 10 15 km.
(1:350,000)

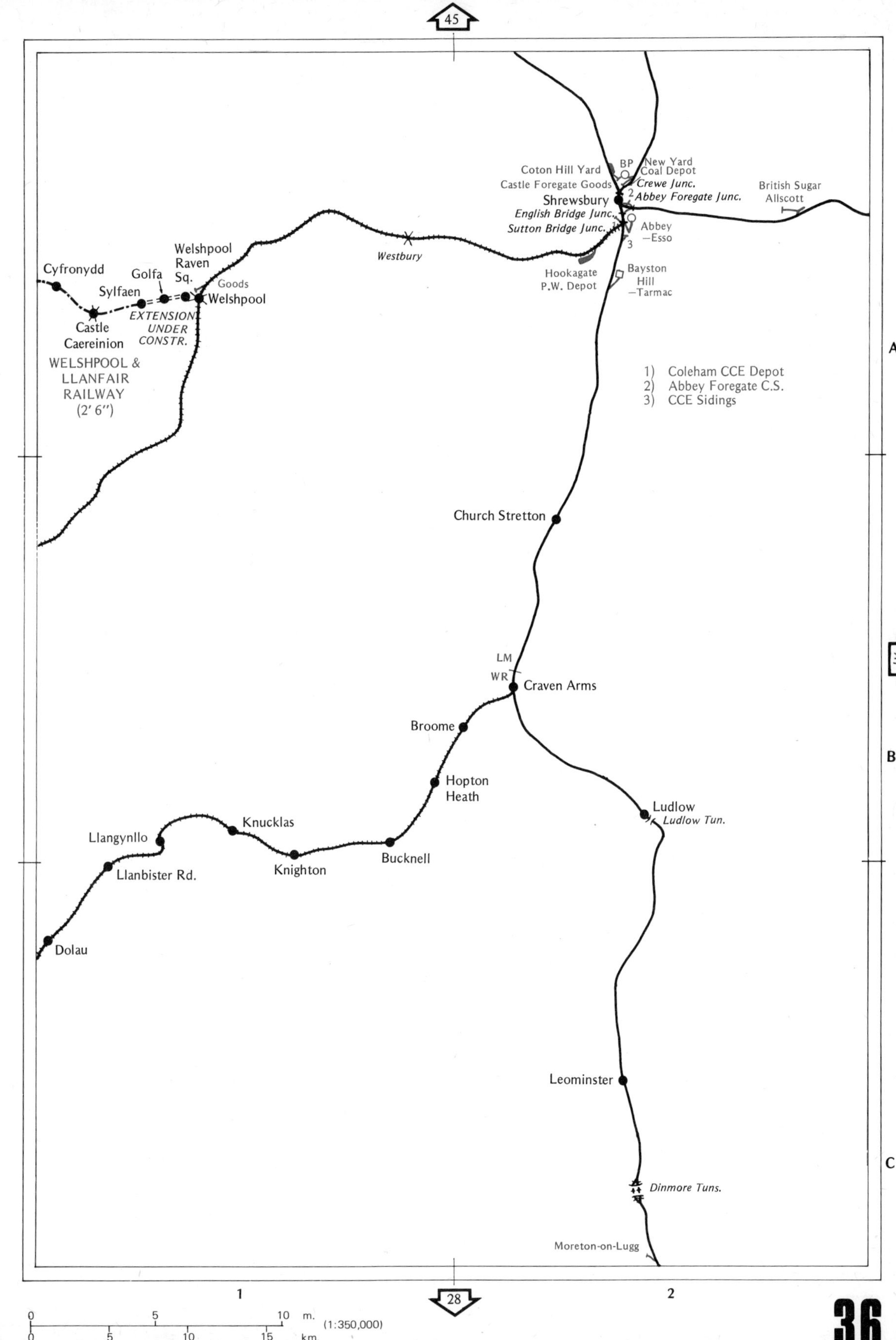

45
Coton Hill Yard
BP
New Yard
Coal Depot
Castle Foregate Goods
Crewe Junc.
Abbey Foregate Junc.
Shrewsbury
English Bridge Junc.
Sutton Bridge Junc.
Abbey
—Esso
British Sugar
Allscott
Hookagate
P.W. Depot
Bayston
Hill
—Tarmac
Westbury
Welshpool
Raven
Sq.
Goods
Welshpool
Cyfronydd
Golfa
Sylfaen
Castle
Caereinion
EXTENSION
UNDER
CONSTR.
WELSHPOOL &
LLANFAIR
RAILWAY
(2′ 6″)
1) Coleham CCE Depot
2) Abbey Foregate C.S.
3) CCE Sidings
Church Stretton
LM
WR
Craven Arms
Broome
Hopton
Heath
Ludlow
Ludlow Tun.
Knucklas
Llangynllo
Llanbister Rd.
Knighton
Bucknell
Dolau
Leominster
Dinmore Tuns.
Moreton-on-Lugg
37
A
B
C
1
2
28
0 5 10 m.
0 5 10 15 km.
(1:350,000)

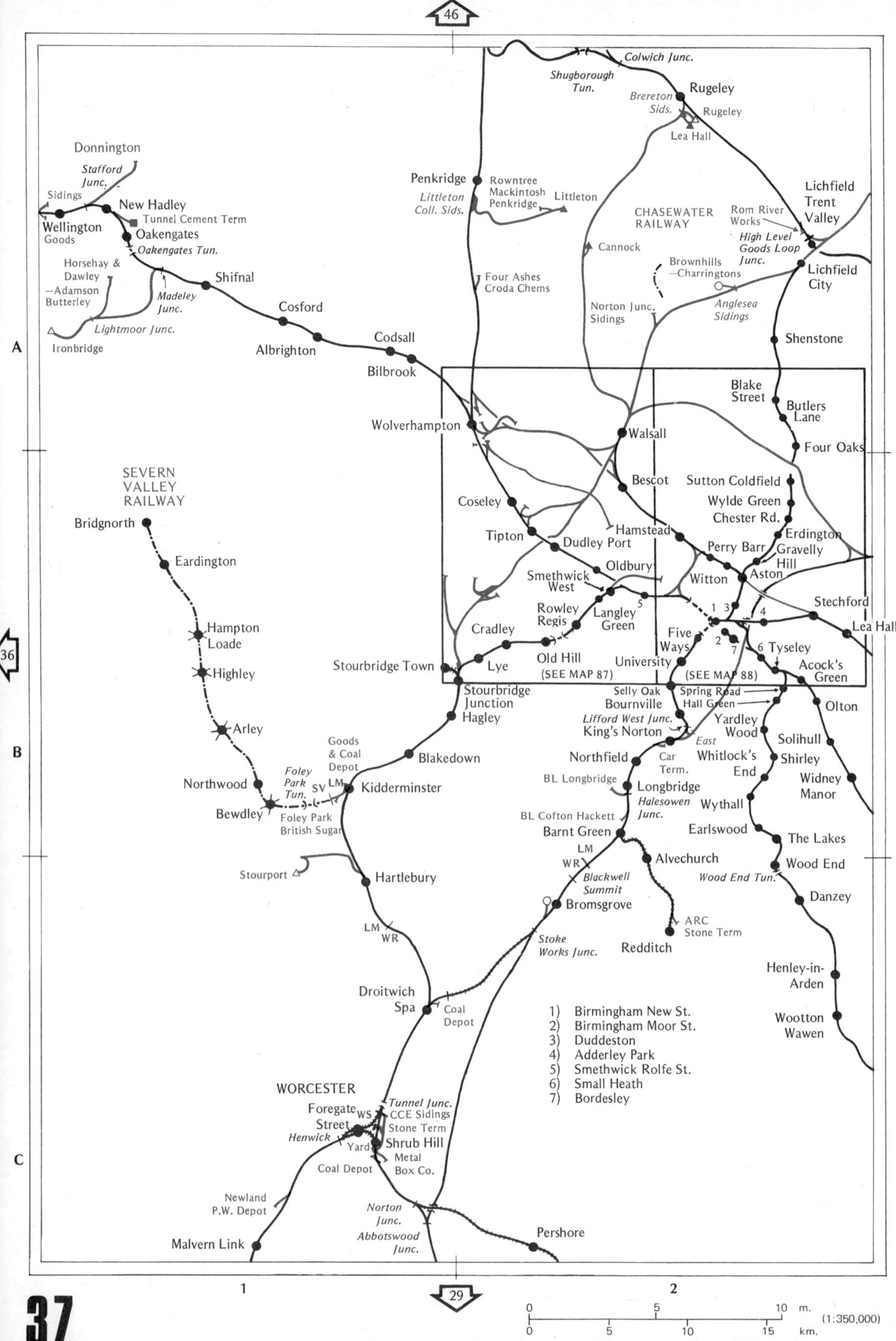

46
Colwich Junc.
Shugborough Tun.
Rugeley
Brereton Sids.
Rugeley
Lea Hall
Donnington
Stafford Junc.
Sidings
New Hadley
Tunnel Cement Term
Wellington Goods
Oakengates
Oakengates Tun.
Penkridge
Littleton Coll. Sids.
Rowntree Mackintosh Penkridge
Littleton
CHASEWATER RAILWAY
Rom River Works
Lichfield Trent Valley
High Level Goods Loop Junc.
Lichfield City
Cannock
Brownhills —Charringtons
Anglesea Sidings
Norton Junc. Sidings
Horsehay & Dawley —Adamson Butterley
Madeley Junc.
Shifnal
Cosford
Four Ashes Croda Chems
Lightmoor Junc.
Ironbridge
Albrighton
Codsall
Bilbrook
Shenstone
Blake Street
Butlers Lane
Wolverhampton
Walsall
Four Oaks
SEVERN VALLEY RAILWAY
Bescot
Sutton Coldfield
Wylde Green
Chester Rd.
Coseley
Bridgnorth
Tipton
Dudley Port
Hamstead
Erdington
Perry Barr
Gravelly Hill
Eardington
Oldbury
Smethwick West
Witton
Aston
Rowley Regis
Langley Green
Stechford
Hampton Loade
Cradley
Five Ways
Lea Hall
Tyseley
Acock's Green
Highley
Stourbridge Town
Lye
Old Hill
(SEE MAP 87)
University
(SEE MAP 88)
Stourbridge Junction
Hagley
Selly Oak
Bournville
Spring Road
Hall Green
Olton
Lifford West Junc.
King's Norton
Yardley Wood
Arley
East
Solihull
Goods & Coal Depot
Blakedown
Northfield
Car Term.
Whitlock's End
Shirley
Foley Park Tun.
Northwood
SV
LM
Kidderminster
BL Longbridge
Longbridge
Widney Manor
Bewdley
Foley Park British Sugar
Halesowen Junc.
Wythall
BL Cofton Hackett
Barnt Green
Earlswood
LM
WR
Alvechurch
The Lakes
Stourport
Hartlebury
Blackwell Summit
Wood End
Wood End Tun.
Bromsgrove
Danzey
LM
WR
ARC Stone Term
Stoke Works Junc.
Redditch
Henley-in-Arden
Droitwich Spa
Coal Depot
Wootton Wawen
1) Birmingham New St.
2) Birmingham Moor St.
3) Duddeston
4) Adderley Park
5) Smethwick Rolfe St.
6) Small Heath
7) Bordesley
WORCESTER
Tunnel Junc.
Foregate Street
WS
CCE Sidings
Stone Term
Henwick
Yard
Shrub Hill
Metal Box Co.
Coal Depot
Newland P.W. Depot
Norton Junc.
Abbotswood Junc.
Pershore
Malvern Link
A
B
C
1
2
36
29
0 5 10 m.
0 5 10 15 km.
(1:350,000)

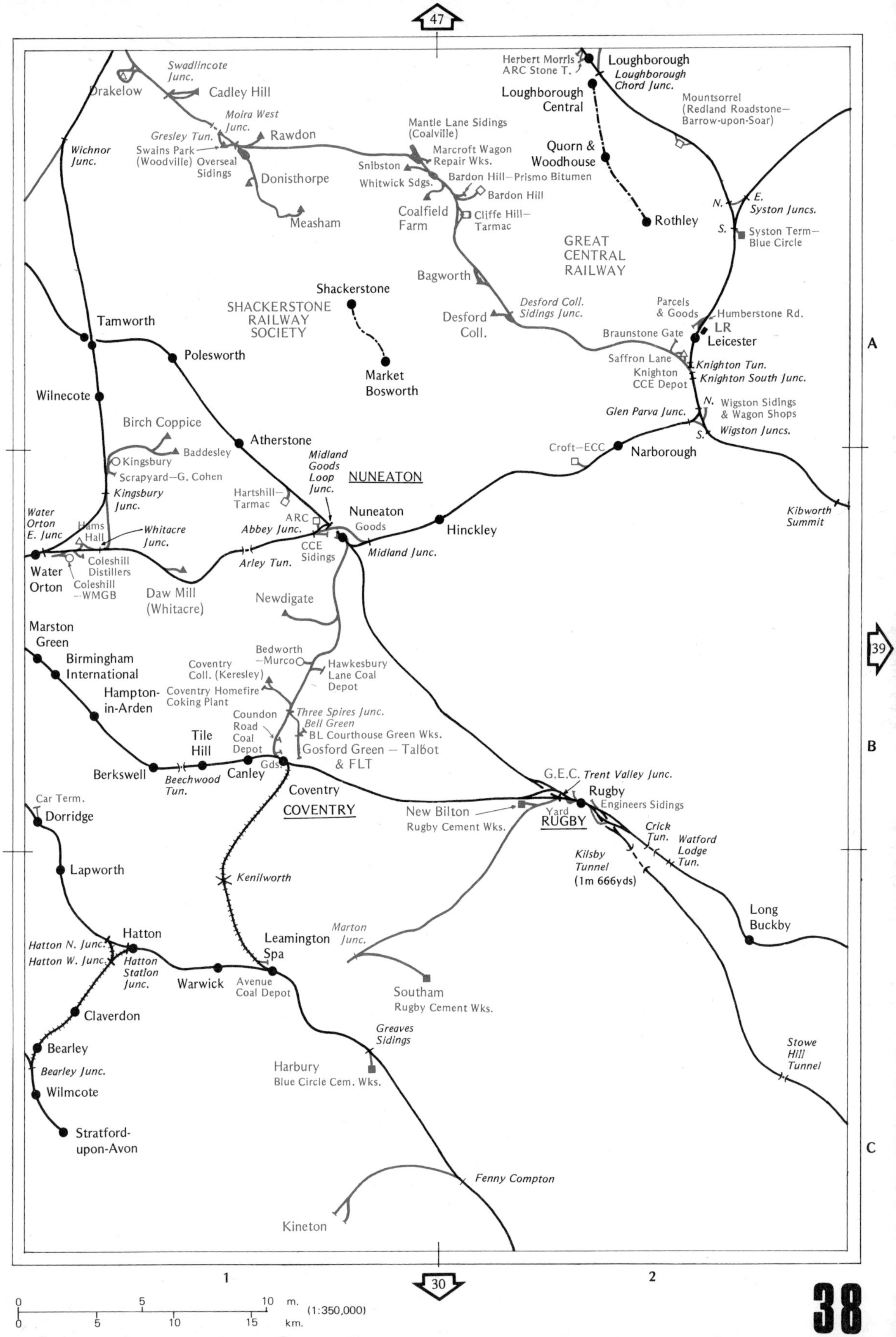

47

Swadlincote Junc.
Drakelow
Cadley Hill
Moira West Junc.
Gresley Tun.
Rawdon
Wichnor Junc.
Swains Park (Woodville)
Overseal Sidings
Donisthorpe
Measham
Herbert Morris
ARC Stone T.
Loughborough
Loughborough Chord Junc.
Loughborough Central
Mountsorrel (Redland Roadstone—Barrow-upon-Soar)
Mantle Lane Sidings (Coalville)
Marcroft Wagon Repair Wks.
Snibston
Whitwick Sdgs.
Bardon Hill—Prismo Bitumen
Bardon Hill
Coalfield Farm
Cliffe Hill—Tarmac
Quorn & Woodhouse
Rothley
GREAT CENTRAL RAILWAY
N. E. Syston Juncs.
S.
Syston Term—Blue Circle
Bagworth
Shackerstone
SHACKERSTONE RAILWAY SOCIETY
Desford Coll.
Desford Coll. Sidings Junc.
Parcels & Goods
Humberstone Rd.
LR
Leicester
Braunstone Gate
Saffron Lane
Knighton Tun.
Knighton South Junc.
Knighton CCE Depot
Tamworth
Polesworth
Market Bosworth
Wilnecote
Glen Parva Junc.
N. Wigston Sidings & Wagon Shops
Wigston Juncs.
S.
Birch Coppice
Baddesley
Kingsbury
Scrapyard—G. Cohen
Atherstone
Midland Goods Loop Junc.
NUNEATON
Croft—ECC
Narborough
Kingsbury Junc.
Hartshill—Tarmac
Water Orton E. Junc
Hams Hall
Whitacre Junc.
ARC
Abbey Junc.
Nuneaton
Goods
CCE Sidings
Midland Junc.
Hinckley
Kibworth Summit
Water Orton
Coleshill Distillers
Coleshill—WMGB
Arley Tun.
Daw Mill (Whitacre)
Newdigate
Marston Green
Birmingham International
Hampton-in-Arden
Bedworth—Murco
Coventry Coll. (Keresley)
Hawkesbury Lane Coal Depot
Coventry Homefire Coking Plant
Coundon Road Coal Depot
Three Spires Junc.
Bell Green
BL Courthouse Green Wks.
Gosford Green — Talbot & FLT
Tile Hill
Berkswell
Beechwood Tun.
Canley
Gds.
Coventry
COVENTRY
G.E.C.
Trent Valley Junc.
Rugby
Engineers Sidings
Yard
RUGBY
New Bilton
Rugby Cement Wks.
Car Term.
Dorridge
Crick Tun.
Watford Lodge Tun.
Kilsby Tunnel (1m 666yds)
Lapworth
Kenilworth
Long Buckby
Hatton
Hatton N. Junc.
Hatton W. Junc.
Hatton Station Junc.
Leamington Spa
Marton Junc.
Warwick
Avenue Coal Depot
Southam
Rugby Cement Wks.
Claverdon
Bearley
Bearley Junc.
Wilmcote
Greaves Sidings
Harbury
Blue Circle Cem. Wks.
Stowe Hill Tunnel
Stratford-upon-Avon
Fenny Compton
Kineton

A
B
C
1
2
39
30

0 5 10 m.
0 5 10 15 km.
(1:350,000)

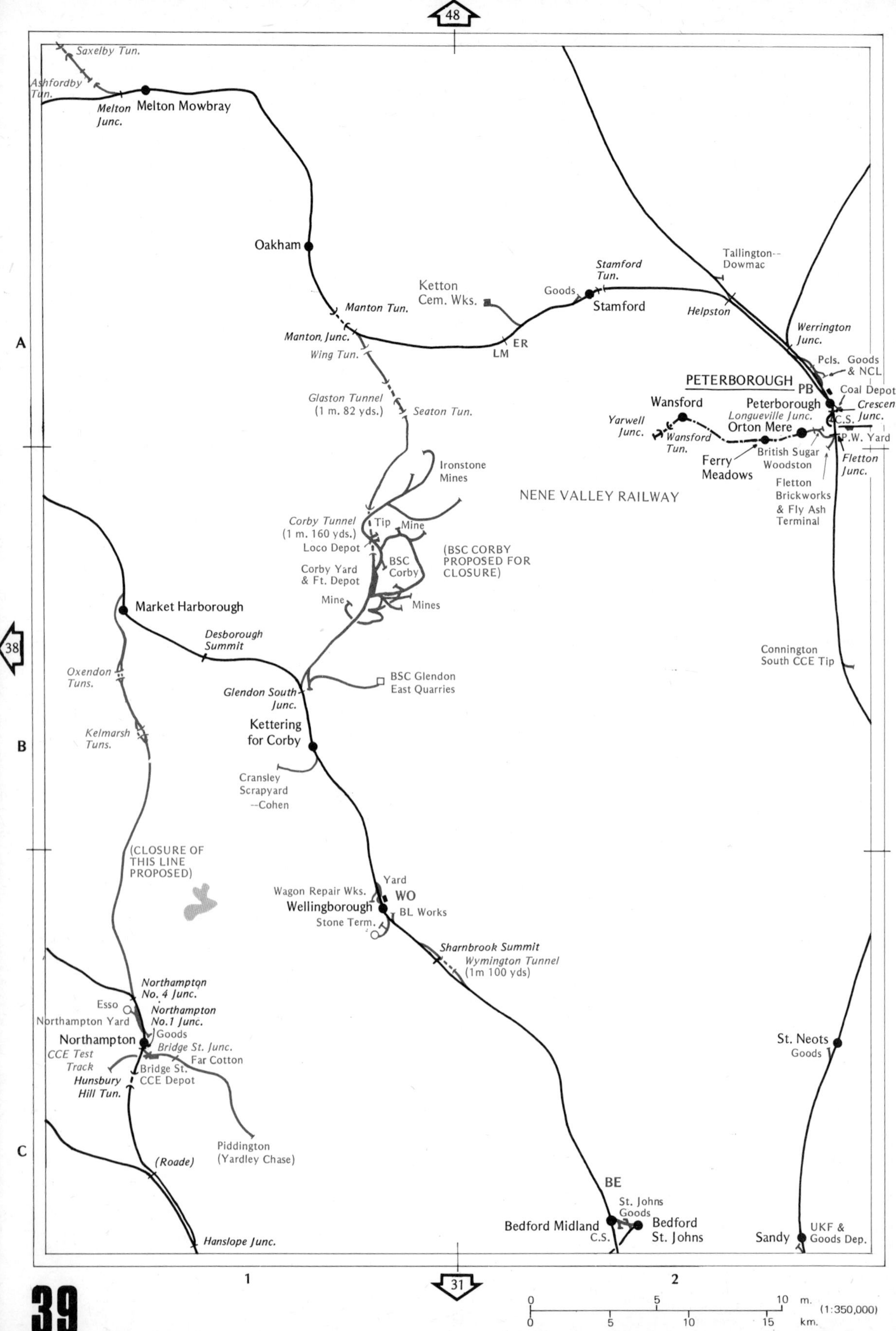
48
Saxelby Tun.
Ashfordby Tun.
Melton Junc.
Melton Mowbray
Oakham
Manton Tun.
Manton Junc.
Wing Tun.
Glaston Tunnel (1 m. 82 yds.)
Seaton Tun.
Ketton Cem. Wks.
Goods
Stamford Tun.
Stamford
ER
LM
Tallington--Dowmac
Helpston
Werrington Junc.
Pcls.
Goods & NCL
PETERBOROUGH
PB
Coal Depot
Peterborough
Crescent Junc.
Longueville Junc.
C.S.
P.W. Yard
Wansford
Yarwell Junc.
Wansford Tun.
Orton Mere
British Sugar Woodston
Ferry Meadows
Fletton Junc.
Fletton Brickworks & Fly Ash Terminal
NENE VALLEY RAILWAY
Ironstone Mines
Corby Tunnel (1 m. 160 yds.)
Tip
Mine
Loco Depot
BSC Corby
(BSC CORBY PROPOSED FOR CLOSURE)
Corby Yard & Ft. Depot
Mine
Mines
Market Harborough
Desborough Summit
38
Oxendon Tuns.
Glendon South Junc.
BSC Glendon East Quarries
Kelmarsh Tuns.
Kettering for Corby
Cransley Scrapyard --Cohen
Connington South CCE Tip
(CLOSURE OF THIS LINE PROPOSED)
Yard
Wagon Repair Wks.
WO
Wellingborough
BL Works
Stone Term.
Sharnbrook Summit
Wymington Tunnel (1m 100 yds)
Northampton No. 4 Junc.
Esso
Northampton No.1 Junc.
Northampton Yard
Goods
Northampton
Bridge St. Junc.
CCE Test Track
Far Cotton
Bridge St. CCE Depot
Hunsbury Hill Tun.
Piddington (Yardley Chase)
(Roade)
Hanslope Junc.
St. Neots
Goods
BE
St. Johns Goods
Bedford Midland
C.S.
Bedford St. Johns
Sandy
UKF & Goods Dep.
A
B
C
1
2
31
0 5 10 m.
0 5 10 15 km.
(1:350,000)

49

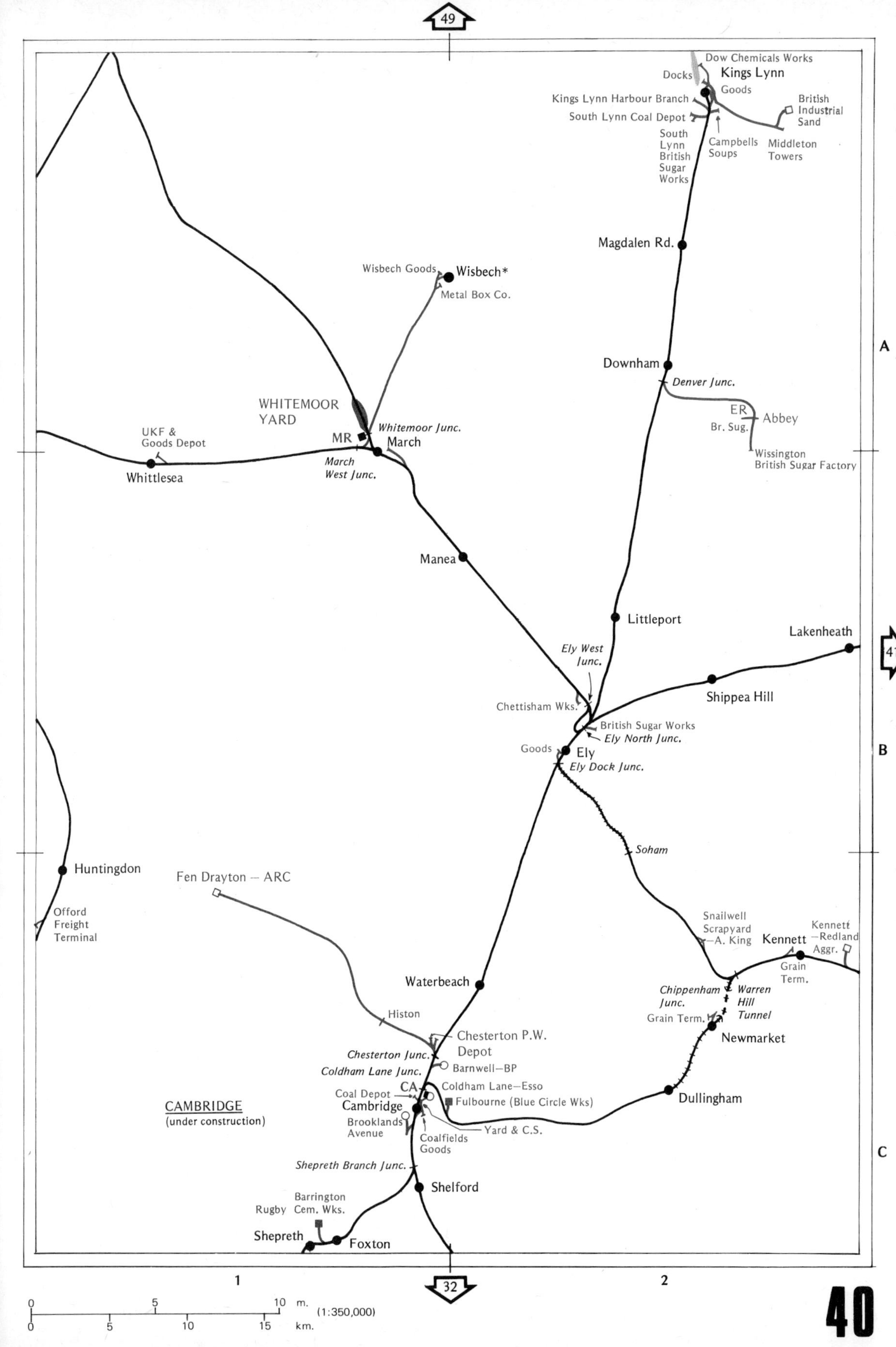
Dow Chemicals Works
Docks
Kings Lynn
Goods
Kings Lynn Harbour Branch
South Lynn Coal Depot
British Industrial Sand
South Lynn British Sugar Works
Campbells Soups
Middleton Towers
Magdalen Rd.
Wisbech Goods
Wisbech*
Metal Box Co.
A
Downham
Denver Junc.
WHITEMOOR YARD
ER
Abbey
Br. Sug.
UKF & Goods Depot
MR
Whitemoor Junc.
March
Wissington British Sugar Factory
Whittlesea
March West Junc.
Manea
Littleport
Lakenheath
Ely West Junc.
Shippea Hill
Chettisham Wks.
British Sugar Works
Ely North Junc.
Goods
Ely
B
Ely Dock Junc.
Soham
Huntingdon
Fen Drayton — ARC
Offord Freight Terminal
Snailwell Scrapyard —A. King
Kennett
Kennett —Redland Aggr.
Grain Term.
Waterbeach
Chippenham Junc.
Warren Hill Tunnel
Grain Term.
Histon
Newmarket
Chesterton P.W. Depot
Chesterton Junc.
Barnwell—BP
Coldham Lane Junc.
CA
Coldham Lane—Esso
Coal Depot
Dullingham
CAMBRIDGE (under construction)
Cambridge
Fulbourne (Blue Circle Wks)
Brooklands Avenue
Yard & C.S.
Coalfields Goods
C
Shepreth Branch Junc.
Shelford
Barrington Cem. Wks.
Rugby
Shepreth
Foxton
1
2
0 5 10 m.
0 5 10 15 km.
(1:350,000)

41

32

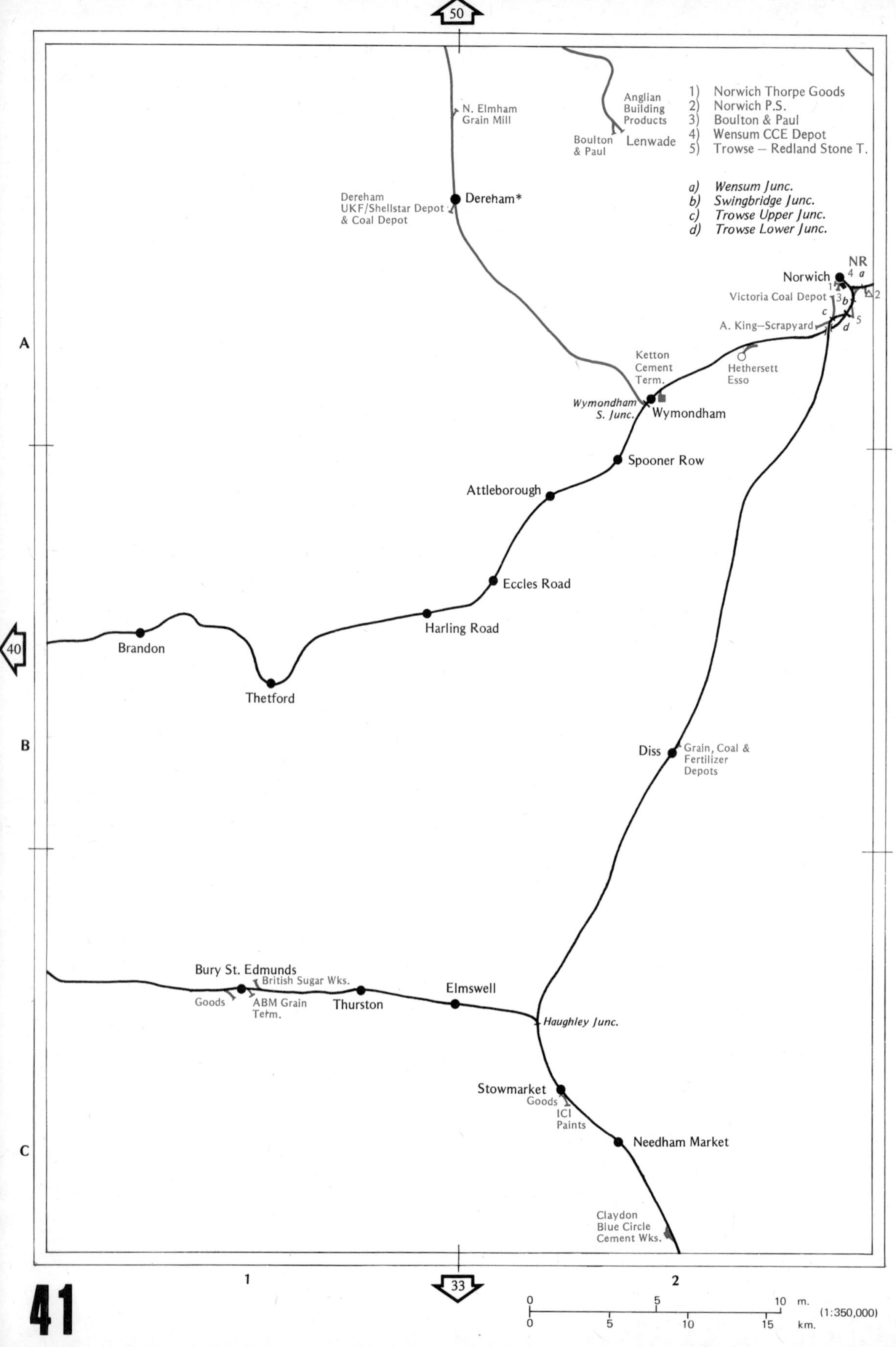
50
N. Elmham
Grain Mill
Anglian
Building
Products
Boulton
& Paul
Lenwade
1) Norwich Thorpe Goods
2) Norwich P.S.
3) Boulton & Paul
4) Wensum CCE Depot
5) Trowse – Redland Stone T.
a) Wensum Junc.
b) Swingbridge Junc.
c) Trowse Upper Junc.
d) Trowse Lower Junc.
Dereham
UKF/Shellstar Depot
& Coal Depot
Dereham*
NR
Norwich
Victoria Coal Depot
A. King–Scrapyard
A
Ketton
Cement
Term.
Hethersett
Esso
Wymondham
S. Junc.
Wymondham
Spooner Row
Attleborough
Eccles Road
Harling Road
40
Brandon
Thetford
B
Diss
Grain, Coal &
Fertilizer
Depots
Bury St. Edmunds
British Sugar Wks.
Goods
ABM Grain
Term.
Thurston
Elmswell
Haughley Junc.
Stowmarket
Goods
ICI
Paints
Needham Market
C
Claydon
Blue Circle
Cement Wks.
1
33
2
0 5 10 m.
0 5 10 15 km.
(1:350,000)

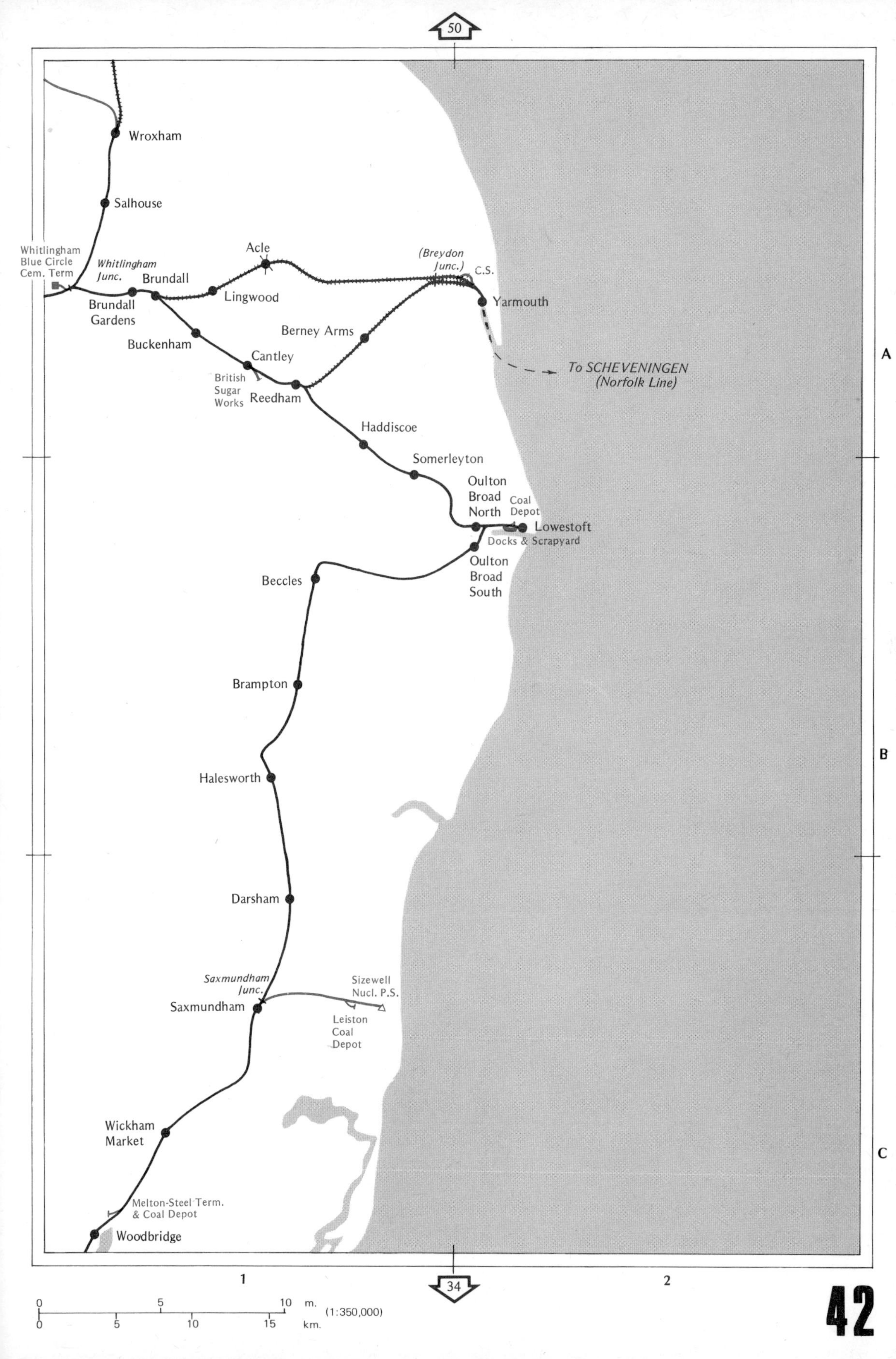
50
Wroxham
Salhouse
Whitlingham
Blue Circle
Cem. Term
Whitlingham
Junc.
Acle
Brundall
Lingwood
(Breydon
Junc.)
C.S.
Yarmouth
Brundall
Gardens
Berney Arms
Buckenham
Cantley
British
Sugar
Works
Reedham
To SCHEVENINGEN
(Norfolk Line)
A
Haddiscoe
Somerleyton
Oulton
Broad
North
Coal
Depot
Lowestoft
Docks & Scrapyard
Oulton
Broad
South
Beccles
Brampton
B
Halesworth
Darsham
Saxmundham
Junc.
Saxmundham
Sizewell
Nucl. P.S.
Leiston
Coal
Depot
Wickham
Market
C
Melton-Steel Term.
& Coal Depot
Woodbridge
1
34
2
0 5 10 m.
0 5 10 15 km.
(1:350,000)

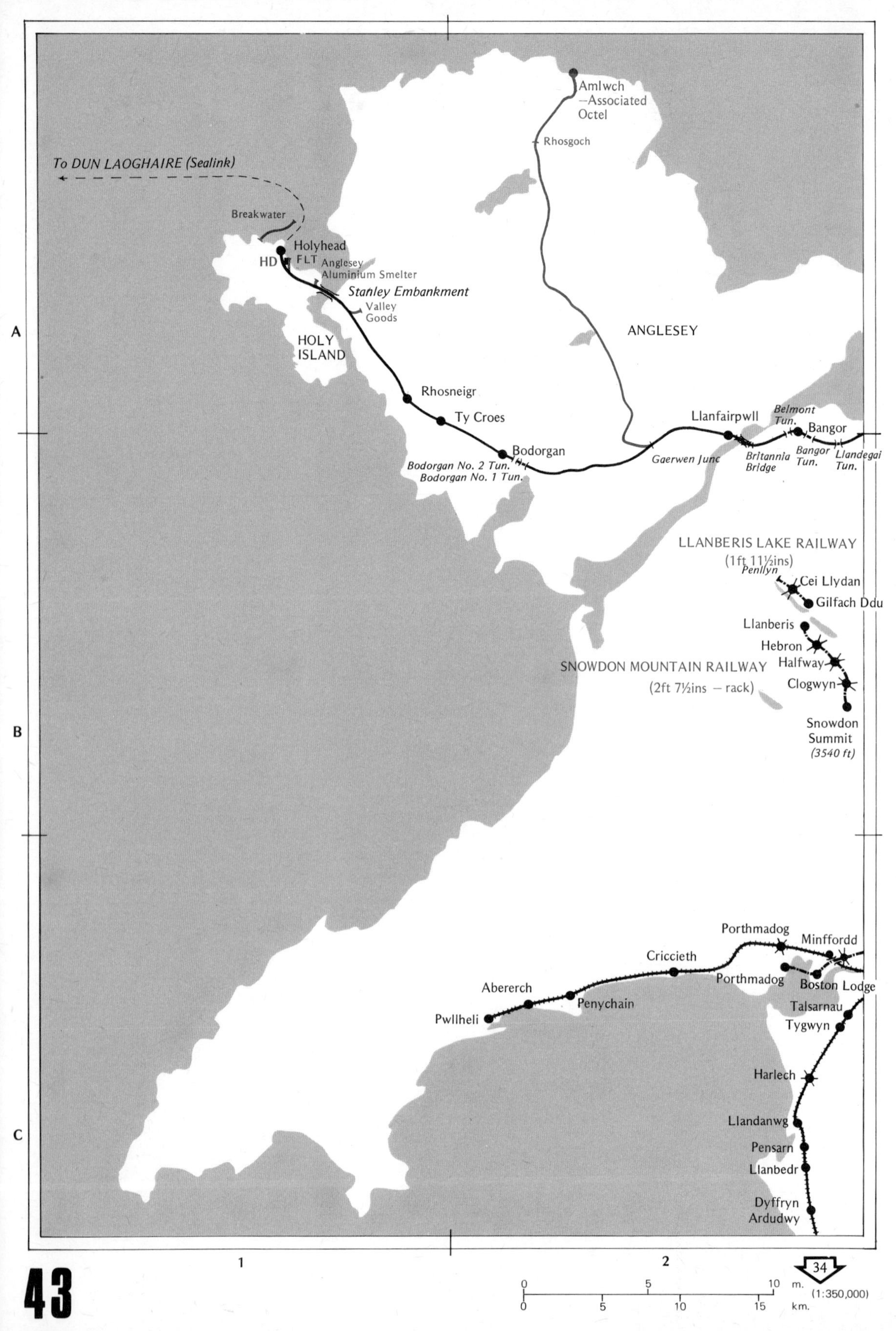
To DUN LAOGHAIRE (Sealink)
Amlwch
—Associated
Octel
Rhosgoch
Breakwater
Holyhead
HD
FLT
Anglesey
Aluminium Smelter
Stanley Embankment
Valley
Goods
HOLY
ISLAND
ANGLESEY
Rhosneigr
Ty Croes
Bodorgan
Bodorgan No. 2 Tun.
Bodorgan No. 1 Tun.
Gaerwen Junc
Llanfairpwll
Britannia
Bridge
Belmont
Tun.
Bangor
Bangor
Tun.
Llandegai
Tun.
LLANBERIS LAKE RAILWAY
(1ft 11½ins)
Penllyn
Cei Llydan
Gilfach Ddu
Llanberis
Hebron
Halfway
SNOWDON MOUNTAIN RAILWAY
(2ft 7½ins — rack)
Clogwyn
Snowdon
Summit
(3540 ft)
Porthmadog
Minffordd
Criccieth
Porthmadog
Boston Lodge
Abererch
Penychain
Pwllheli
Talsarnau
Tygwyn
Harlech
Llandanwg
Pensarn
Llanbedr
Dyffryn
Ardudwy
A
B
C
1
2
34
0 5 10 m.
0 5 10 15 km.
(1:350,000)

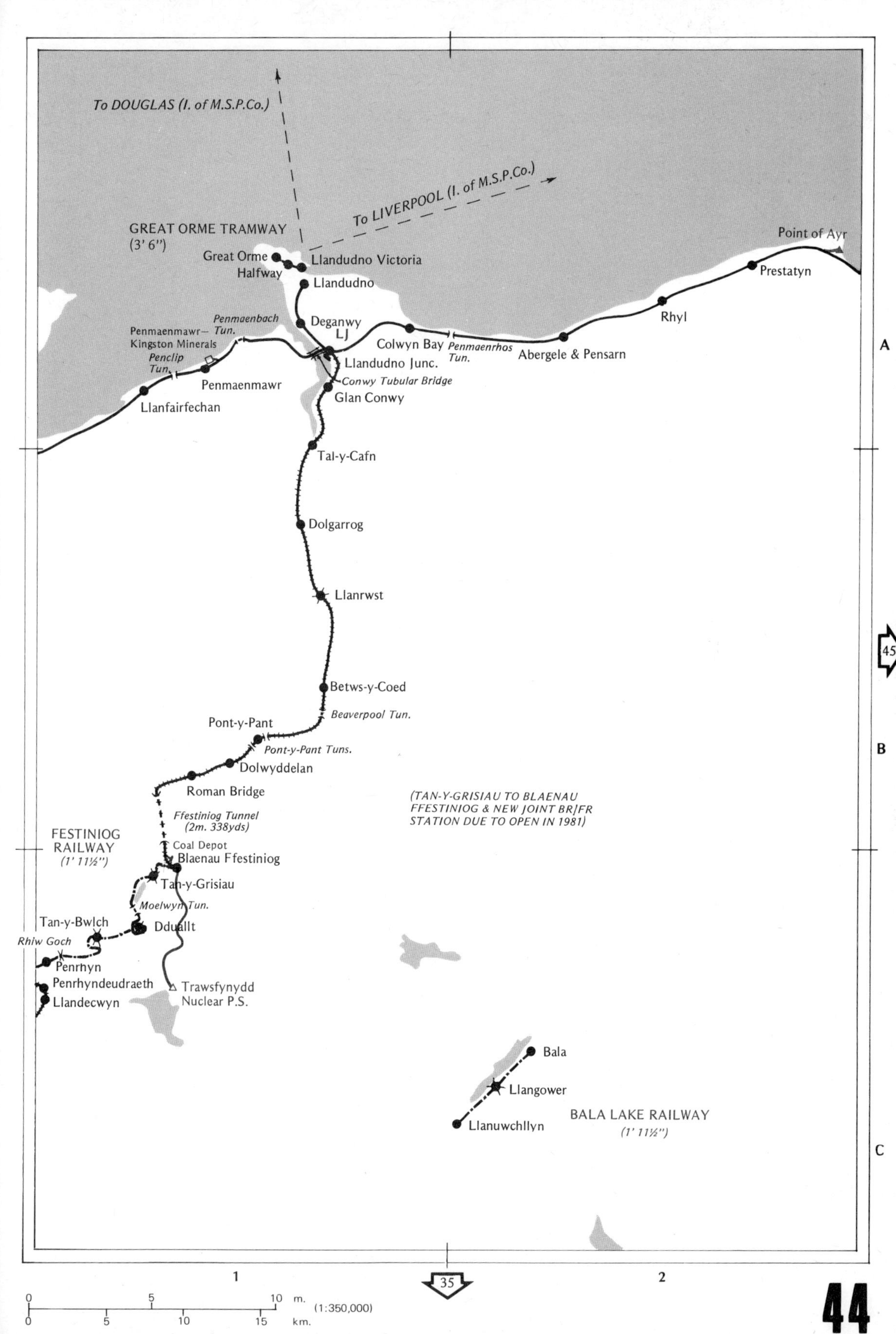
To DOUGLAS (I. of M.S.P.Co.)
To LIVERPOOL (I. of M.S.P.Co.)
GREAT ORME TRAMWAY
(3' 6")
Great Orme
Halfway
Llandudno Victoria
Llandudno
Point of Ayr
Prestatyn
Rhyl
Deganwy
LJ
Colwyn Bay
Penmaenrhos Tun.
Abergele & Pensarn
Penmaenbach Tun.
Penmaenmawr– Kingston Minerals
Penclip Tun.
Penmaenmawr
Llanfairfechan
Llandudno Junc.
Conwy Tubular Bridge
Glan Conwy
Tal-y-Cafn
Dolgarrog
Llanrwst
Betws-y-Coed
Beaverpool Tun.
Pont-y-Pant
Pont-y-Pant Tuns.
Dolwyddelan
Roman Bridge
Ffestiniog Tunnel
(2m. 338yds)
(TAN-Y-GRISIAU TO BLAENAU FFESTINIOG & NEW JOINT BR/FR STATION DUE TO OPEN IN 1981)
FESTINIOG RAILWAY
(1' 11½")
Coal Depot
Blaenau Ffestiniog
Tan-y-Grisiau
Moelwyn Tun.
Tan-y-Bwlch
Dduallt
Rhiw Goch
Penrhyn
Penrhyndeudraeth
Llandecwyn
Trawsfynydd Nuclear P.S.
Bala
Llangower
Llanuwchllyn
BALA LAKE RAILWAY
(1' 11½")
A
B
C
1
2
0 5 10 m.
0 5 10 15 km.
(1:350,000)
45
35

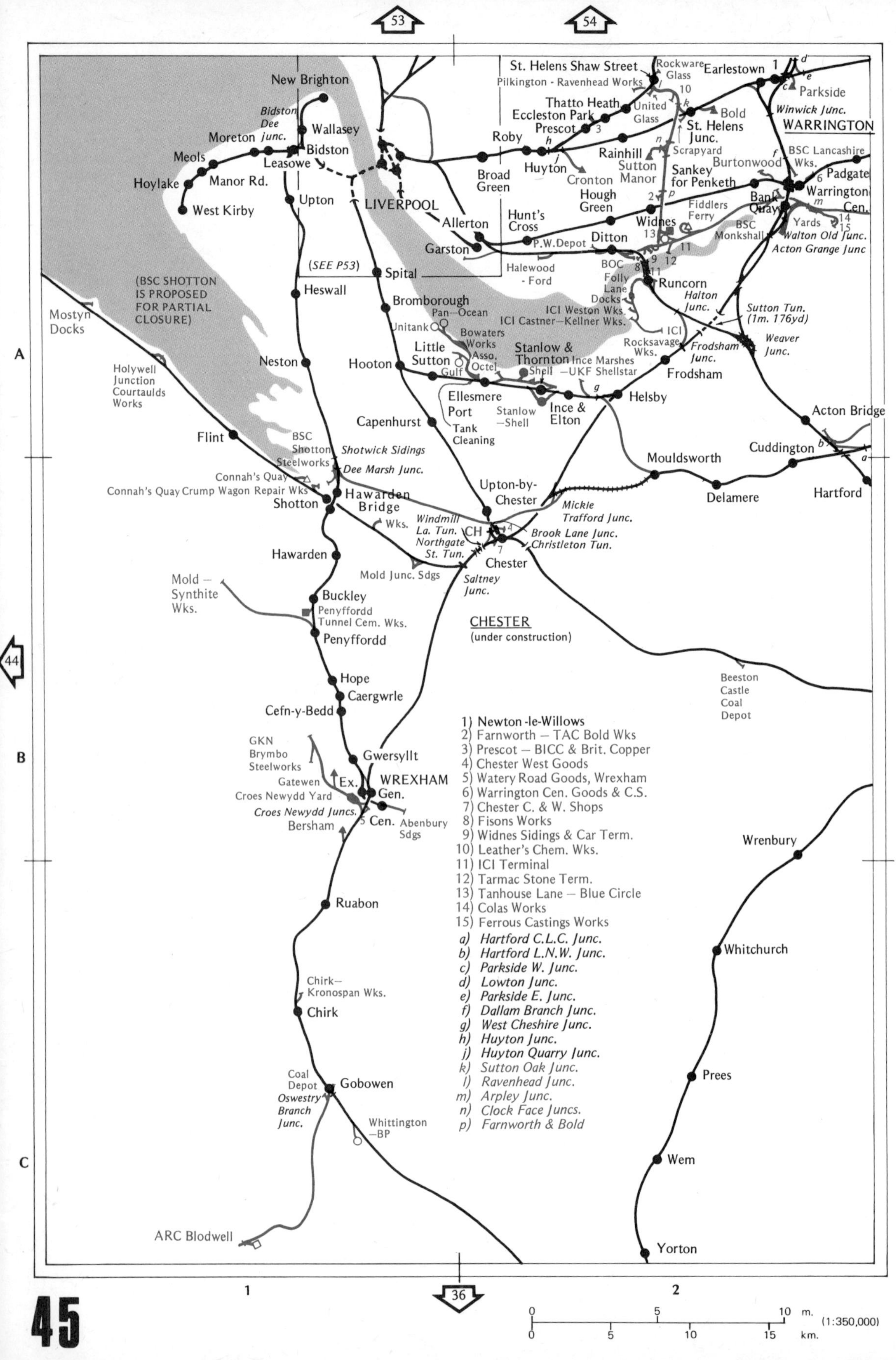

53
54
44
36
St. Helens Shaw Street
Pilkington - Ravenhead Works
Rockware Glass
Earlestown
Parkside
Winwick Junc.
WARRINGTON
New Brighton
Bidston Dee Junc.
Wallasey
Moreton
Meols
Bidston
Leasowe
Hoylake
Manor Rd.
West Kirby
Upton
LIVERPOOL
Thatto Heath
Eccleston Park
Prescot
United Glass
Bold
St. Helens Junc.
Roby
Huyton
Broad Green
Rainhill
Cronton
Sutton Manor
Scrapyard
Sankey for Penketh
Burtonwood
BSC Lancashire Wks.
Padgate
Warrington Bank Quay
Warrington Cen.
Hough Green
Fiddlers Ferry
Yards
Allerton
Hunt's Cross
Widnes
BSC Monkshall
Walton Old Junc.
Acton Grange Junc
Garston
P.W. Depot
Ditton
(SEE P53)
Spital
Halewood - Ford
BOC
Folly Lane Docks
Runcorn
Halton Junc.
Heswall
(BSC SHOTTON IS PROPOSED FOR PARTIAL CLOSURE)
Bromborough
Pan—Ocean
Unitank
ICI Weston Wks.
ICI Castner—Kellner Wks.
Sutton Tun. (1m. 176yd)
Mostyn Docks
Bowaters Works
Asso. Octel
Little Sutton
Gulf
ICI Rocksavage Wks.
Weaver Junc.
Frodsham Junc.
Neston
Hooton
Stanlow & Thornton
Ince Marshes
Shell
—UKF Shellstar
Frodsham
Holywell Junction Courtaulds Works
Ellesmere Port
Stanlow —Shell
Ince & Elton
Helsby
Capenhurst
Tank Cleaning
Acton Bridge
Flint
BSC Shotton Steelworks
Shotwick Sidings
Dee Marsh Junc.
Mouldsworth
Cuddington
Connah's Quay
Connah's Quay Crump Wagon Repair Wks
Shotton
Hawarden Bridge
Upton-by-Chester
Mickle Trafford Junc.
Delamere
Hartford
Wks.
Windmill La. Tun.
Northgate St. Tun.
CH
Brook Lane Junc.
Christleton Tun.
Hawarden
Chester
Mold Junc. Sdgs
Saltney Junc.
Mold — Synthite Wks.
Buckley
Penyffordd Tunnel Cem. Wks.
CHESTER
(under construction)
Penyffordd
Hope
Caergwrle
Beeston Castle Coal Depot
Cefn-y-Bedd
GKN Brymbo Steelworks
Gwersyllt
Gatewen
Ex.
WREXHAM
Gen.
Croes Newydd Yard
Croes Newydd Juncs.
Cen.
Abenbury Sdgs
Bersham
1) Newton-le-Willows
2) Farnworth — TAC Bold Wks
3) Prescot — BICC & Brit. Copper
4) Chester West Goods
5) Watery Road Goods, Wrexham
6) Warrington Cen. Goods & C.S.
7) Chester C. & W. Shops
8) Fisons Works
9) Widnes Sidings & Car Term.
10) Leather's Chem. Wks.
11) ICI Terminal
12) Tarmac Stone Term.
13) Tanhouse Lane — Blue Circle
14) Colas Works
15) Ferrous Castings Works
a) Hartford C.L.C. Junc.
b) Hartford L.N.W. Junc.
c) Parkside W. Junc.
d) Lowton Junc.
e) Parkside E. Junc.
f) Dallam Branch Junc.
g) West Cheshire Junc.
h) Huyton Junc.
j) Huyton Quarry Junc.
k) Sutton Oak Junc.
l) Ravenhead Junc.
m) Arpley Junc.
n) Clock Face Juncs.
p) Farnworth & Bold
Wrenbury
Ruabon
Whitchurch
Chirk—Kronospan Wks.
Chirk
Coal Depot
Gobowen
Oswestry Branch Junc.
Whittington —BP
Prees
Wem
ARC Blodwell
Yorton
A
B
C
1
2
0 5 10 m.
0 5 10 15 km.
(1:350,000)

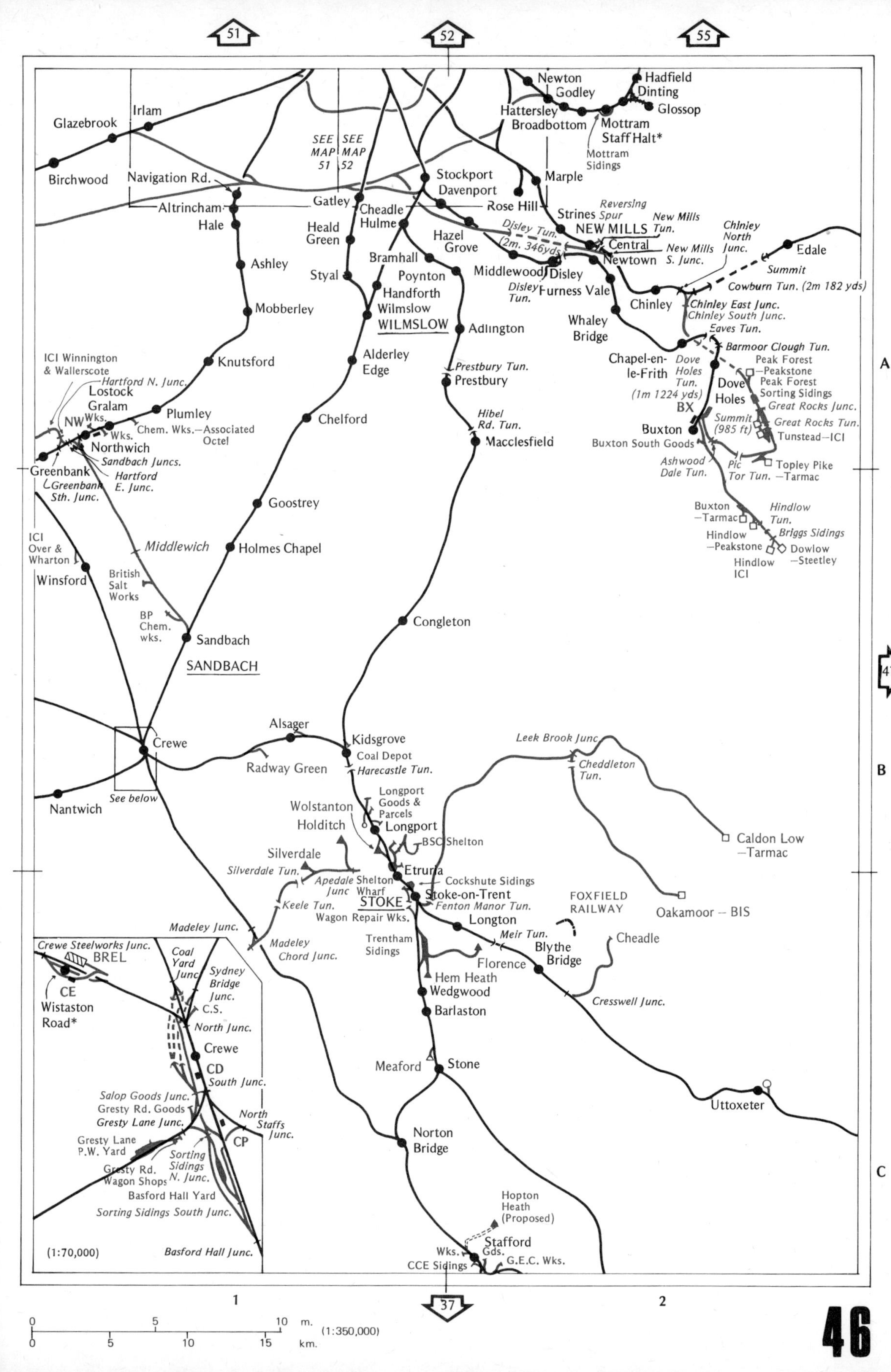
51
52
55
Glazebrook
Irlam
Birchwood
Navigation Rd.
Altrincham
Hale
Ashley
Mobberley
Knutsford
SEE MAP 51
SEE MAP 52
Gatley
Heald Green
Styal
Cheadle Hulme
Stockport
Davenport
Bramhall
Poynton
Hazel Grove
Handforth
Wilmslow
WILMSLOW
Adlington
Alderley Edge
Chelford
Goostrey
Holmes Chapel
Prestbury Tun.
Prestbury
Hibel Rd. Tun.
Macclesfield
Newton
Godley
Hattersley
Broadbottom
Hadfield
Dinting
Glossop
Mottram Staff Halt*
Mottram Sidings
Marple
Rose Hill
Strines
Reversing Spur
New Mills Tun.
NEW MILLS
Central
Newtown
New Mills S. Junc.
Disley Tun. (2m. 346yds)
Middlewood
Disley
Disley Tun.
Furness Vale
Whaley Bridge
Chinley
Chinley North Junc.
Edale
Summit
Cowburn Tun. (2m 182 yds)
Chinley East Junc.
Chinley South Junc.
Eaves Tun.
Barmoor Clough Tun.
Chapel-en-le-Frith
Dove Holes Tun. (1m 1224 yds)
Dove Holes
Peak Forest —Peakstone
Peak Forest Sorting Sidings
Great Rocks Junc.
Great Rocks Tun.
Summit (985 ft)
BX
Buxton
Buxton South Goods
Tunstead—ICI
Ashwood Dale Tun.
Pic Tor Tun.
Topley Pike —Tarmac
Buxton —Tarmac
Hindlow Tun.
Briggs Sidings
Hindlow —Peakstone
Dowlow —Steetley
Hindlow ICI
ICI Winnington & Wallerscote
Hartford N. Junc.
Lostock Gralam
NW
Wks.
Wks.
Northwich
Plumley
Chem. Wks.—Associated Octel
Sandbach Juncs.
Hartford E. Junc.
Greenbank
Greenbank Sth. Junc.
ICI Over & Wharton
Winsford
Middlewich
British Salt Works
BP Chem. wks.
Sandbach
SANDBACH
Congleton
Crewe
See below
Nantwich
Alsager
Radway Green
Kidsgrove
Coal Depot
Harecastle Tun.
Longport Goods & Parcels
Wolstanton
Holditch
Longport
BSC Shelton
Silverdale
Silverdale Tun.
Apedale Junc
Shelton Wharf
Etruria
Cockshute Sidings
Keele Tun.
STOKE
Stoke-on-Trent
Fenton Manor Tun.
Wagon Repair Wks.
Longton
Madeley Junc.
Madeley Chord Junc.
Trentham Sidings
Meir Tun.
Florence
Blythe Bridge
Hem Heath
Wedgwood
Barlaston
Meaford
Stone
Norton Bridge
Leek Brook Junc.
Cheddleton Tun.
Caldon Low —Tarmac
FOXFIELD RAILWAY
Oakamoor — BIS
Cheadle
Cresswell Junc.
Uttoxeter
Hopton Heath (Proposed)
Stafford
Wks.
Gds.
CCE Sidings
G.E.C. Wks.
Crewe Steelworks Junc.
BREL
CE
Wistaston Road*
Coal Yard Junc.
Sydney Bridge Junc.
C.S.
North Junc.
Crewe
CD
South Junc.
Salop Goods Junc.
Gresty Rd. Goods
Gresty Lane Junc.
North Staffs Junc.
Gresty Lane P.W. Yard
CP
Sorting Sidings N. Junc.
Gresty Rd. Wagon Shops
Basford Hall Yard
Sorting Sidings South Junc.
(1:70,000)
Basford Hall Junc.
47
37
A
B
C
1
2
0 5 10 m.
0 5 10 15 km.
(1:350,000)

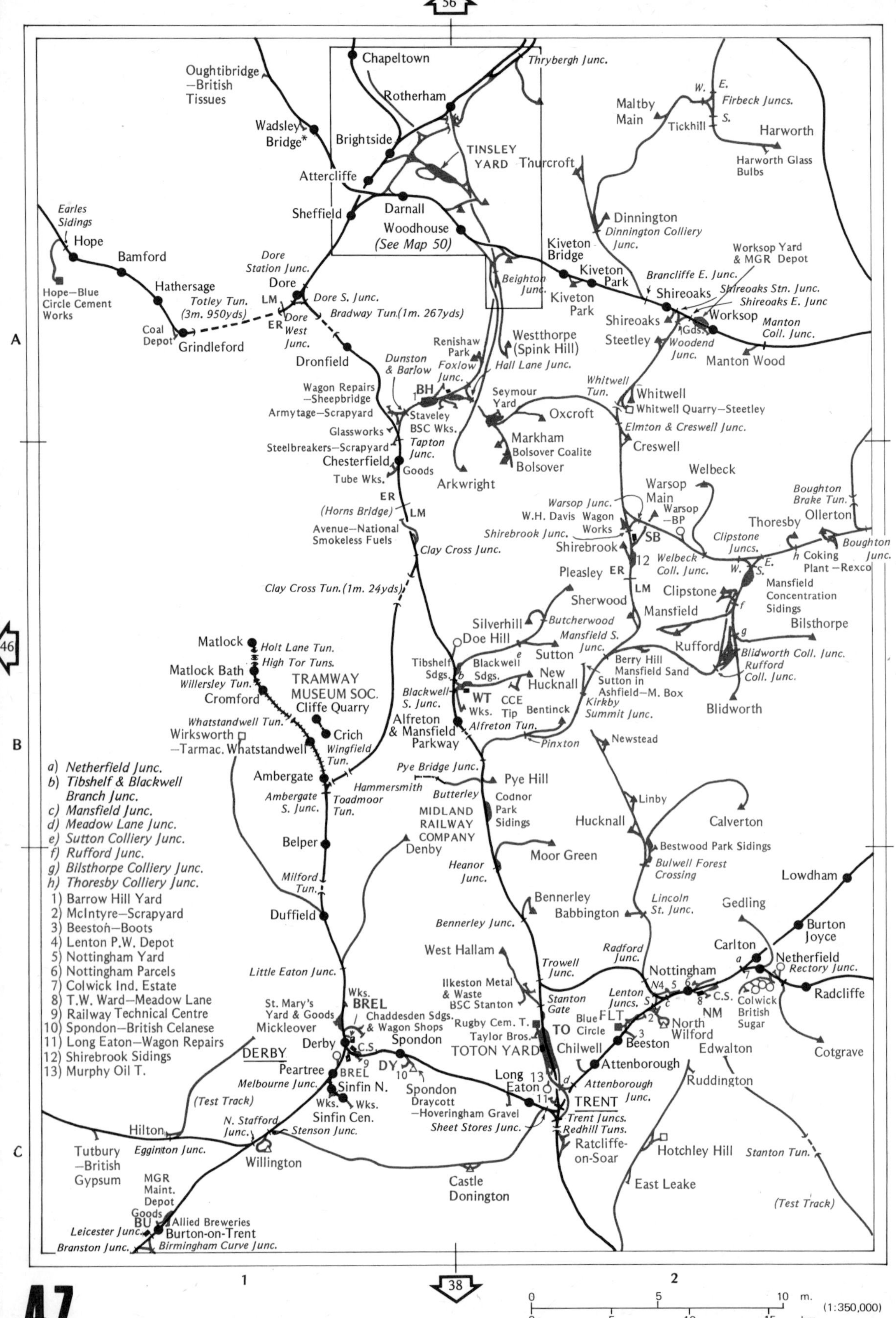

56
46
38
A
B
C
1
2
Chapeltown
Thrybergh Junc.
Oughtibridge
—British
Tissues
Rotherham
Maltby
Main
W.
E.
Firbeck Juncs.
S.
Tickhill
Harworth
Harworth Glass
Bulbs
Wadsley
Bridge*
Brightside
TINSLEY
YARD
Thurcroft
Attercliffe
Darnall
Sheffield
Woodhouse
(See Map 50)
Dinnington
Dinnington Colliery
Junc.
Earles
Sidings
Hope
Bamford
Hathersage
Hope—Blue
Circle Cement
Works
Dore
Station Junc.
Dore
Kiveton
Bridge
Kiveton
Park
Beighton
Junc.
Kiveton
Park
Worksop Yard
& MGR Depot
Brancliffe E. Junc.
Shireoaks
Shireoaks Stn. Junc.
Shireoaks E. Junc
Totley Tun.
(3m. 950yds)
LM
ER
Dore S. Junc.
Dore
West
Junc.
Bradway Tun.(1m. 267yds)
Coal
Depot
Grindleford
Dronfield
Shireoaks
Worksop
Gds.
Manton
Coll. Junc.
Steetley
Woodend
Junc.
Manton Wood
Renishaw
Park
Westthorpe
(Spink Hill)
Dunston
& Barlow
Foxlow
Junc.
Hall Lane Junc.
Wagon Repairs
—Sheepbridge
BH
1
Seymour
Yard
Whitwell
Tun.
Whitwell
Whitwell Quarry—Steetley
Armytage—Scrapyard
Staveley
BSC Wks.
Oxcroft
Elmton & Creswell Junc.
Glassworks
Markham
Bolsover Coalite
Bolsover
Creswell
Steelbreakers—Scrapyard
Tapton
Junc.
Chesterfield
Goods
Tube Wks.
Arkwright
Welbeck
Warsop
Main
Boughton
Brake Tun.
ER
(Horns Bridge)
LM
Warsop Junc.
W.H. Davis Wagon
Works
Warsop
—BP
Thoresby
Ollerton
Avenue—National
Smokeless Fuels
Shirebrook Junc.
SB
Clipstone
Juncs.
Boughton
Junc.
Clay Cross Junc.
Shirebrook
12
Welbeck
Coll. Junc.
h
Coking
Plant —Rexco
Pleasley
ER
W.
S.
E.
Mansfield
Concentration
Sidings
Clay Cross Tun. (1m. 24yds)
LM
Clipstone
Sherwood
Mansfield
f
Bilsthorpe
Silverhill
Butcherwood
Mansfield S.
Junc.
g
Matlock
Holt Lane Tun.
Doe Hill
Rufford
High Tor Tuns.
e
Sutton
Bildworth Coll. Junc.
Tibshelf
Sdgs.
Blackwell
Sdgs.
New
Hucknall
Berry Hill
Mansfield Sand
Rufford
Coll. Junc.
Matlock Bath
Willersley Tun.
TRAMWAY
MUSEUM SOC.
b
Sutton in
Ashfield—M. Box
Cromford
Cliffe Quarry
Blackwell
S. Junc.
WT
Wks.
CCE
Tip
Bentinck
Kirkby
Summit Junc.
Blidworth
Whatstandwell Tun.
Alfreton
& Mansfield
Parkway
Alfreton Tun.
Crich
Wirksworth
—Tarmac.
Whatstandwell
Wingfield
Tun.
Pinxton
Newstead
a) Netherfield Junc.
b) Tibshelf & Blackwell
Branch Junc.
c) Mansfield Junc.
d) Meadow Lane Junc.
e) Sutton Colliery Junc.
f) Rufford Junc.
g) Bilsthorpe Colliery Junc.
h) Thoresby Colliery Junc.
1) Barrow Hill Yard
2) McIntyre—Scrapyard
3) Beeston—Boots
4) Lenton P.W. Depot
5) Nottingham Yard
6) Nottingham Parcels
7) Colwick Ind. Estate
8) T.W. Ward—Meadow Lane
9) Railway Technical Centre
10) Spondon—British Celanese
11) Long Eaton—Wagon Repairs
12) Shirebrook Sidings
13) Murphy Oil T.
Pye Bridge Junc.
Ambergate
Pye Hill
Hammersmith
Linby
Ambergate
S. Junc.
Toadmoor
Tun.
Butterley
Codnor
Park
Sidings
MIDLAND
RAILWAY
COMPANY
Hucknall
Calverton
Belper
Denby
Moor Green
Bestwood Park Sidings
Heanor
Junc.
Bulwell Forest
Crossing
Lowdham
Milford
Tun.
Bennerley
Lincoln
St. Junc.
Gedling
Babbington
Duffield
Burton
Joyce
Bennerley Junc.
Carlton
Radford
Junc.
West Hallam
Netherfield
a
Rectory Junc.
Trowell
Junc.
Nottingham
Little Eaton Junc.
N4
5
6
7
Radcliffe
Ilkeston Metal
& Waste
BSC Stanton
Lenton
Juncs.
S.
c
8
C.S.
Wks.
BREL
St. Mary's
Yard & Goods
Stanton
Gate
NM
Colwick
British
Sugar
Chaddesden Sdgs.
& Wagon Shops
Blue
Circle
FLT
2
North
Wilford
Mickleover
Rugby Cem. T.
Taylor Bros.
TO
3
Beeston
Edwalton
Cotgrave
Derby
Spondon
DERBY
C.S.
TOTON YARD
Chilwell
Peartree
BREL
9
DY
Attenborough
Long
Eaton
13
Ruddington
Melbourne Junc.
Sinfin N.
10
d
Attenborough
Junc.
Spondon
Draycott
—Hoveringham Gravel
11
TRENT
Wks.
Wks.
(Test Track)
Sinfin Cen.
Trent Juncs.
N. Stafford
Junc.
Stenson Junc.
Sheet Stores Junc.
Redhill Tuns.
Hilton
Ratcliffe-
on-Soar
Hotchley Hill
Stanton Tun.
Tutbury
—British
Gypsum
Egginton Junc.
Willington
MGR
Maint.
Depot
Castle
Donington
East Leake
Goods
BU
Allied Breweries
(Test Track)
Leicester Junc.
Burton-on-Trent
Branston Junc.
Birmingham Curve Junc.
0
5
10 m.
0
5
10
15 km.
(1:350,000)

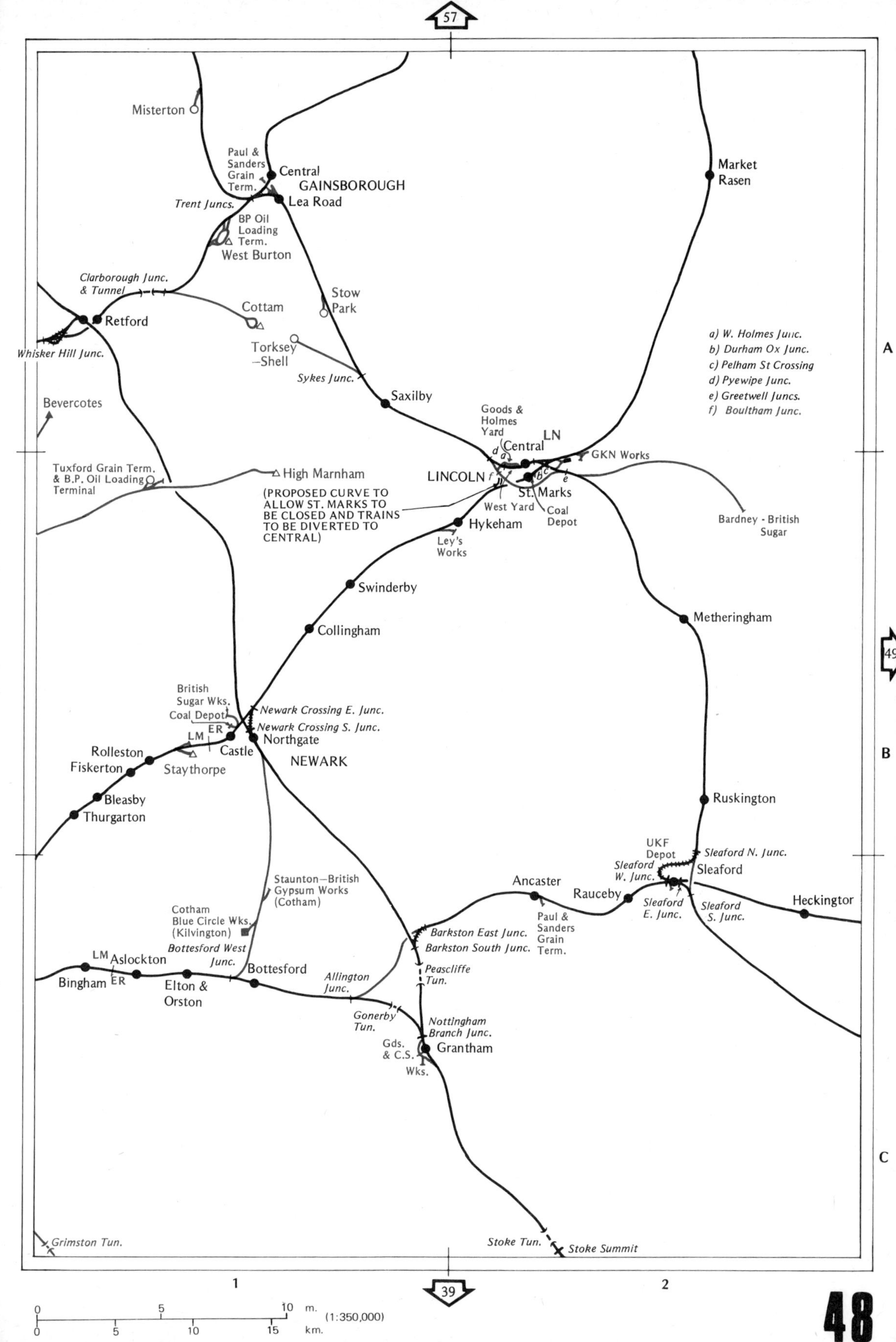
57
Misterton
Paul &
Sanders
Grain
Term.
Central
GAINSBOROUGH
Lea Road
Trent Juncs.
BP Oil
Loading
Term.
West Burton
Market
Rasen
Clarborough Junc.
& Tunnel
Retford
Cottam
Stow
Park
Whisker Hill Junc.
Torksey
—Shell
Sykes Junc.
a) W. Holmes Junc.
b) Durham Ox Junc.
c) Pelham St Crossing
d) Pyewipe Junc.
e) Greetwell Juncs.
f) Boultham Junc.
A
Bevercotes
Saxilby
Goods &
Holmes
Yard
Central
LN
GKN Works
Tuxford Grain Term.
& B.P. Oil Loading
Terminal
High Marnham
LINCOLN
St. Marks
West Yard
Coal
Depot
(PROPOSED CURVE TO
ALLOW ST. MARKS TO
BE CLOSED AND TRAINS
TO BE DIVERTED TO
CENTRAL)
Hykeham
Ley's
Works
Bardney - British
Sugar
Swinderby
Collingham
Metheringham
49
British
Sugar Wks.
Coal Depot
Newark Crossing E. Junc.
Newark Crossing S. Junc.
ER
LM
Castle
Northgate
NEWARK
Rolleston
Fiskerton
Staythorpe
B
Bleasby
Thurgarton
Ruskington
UKF
Depot
Sleaford N. Junc.
Sleaford W. Junc.
Sleaford
Ancaster
Rauceby
Heckington
Sleaford E. Junc.
Sleaford S. Junc.
Staunton—British
Gypsum Works
(Cotham)
Cotham
Blue Circle Wks.
(Kilvington)
Paul &
Sanders
Grain
Term.
Barkston East Junc.
Barkston South Junc.
Bottesford West
Junc.
LM
Aslockton
Bingham
ER
Elton &
Orston
Bottesford
Allington
Junc.
Peascliffe
Tun.
Gonerby
Tun.
Nottingham
Branch Junc.
Gds.
& C.S.
Grantham
Wks.
C
Grimston Tun.
Stoke Tun.
Stoke Summit
1
2
39
0
5
10
m.
(1:350,000)
0
5
10
15
km.

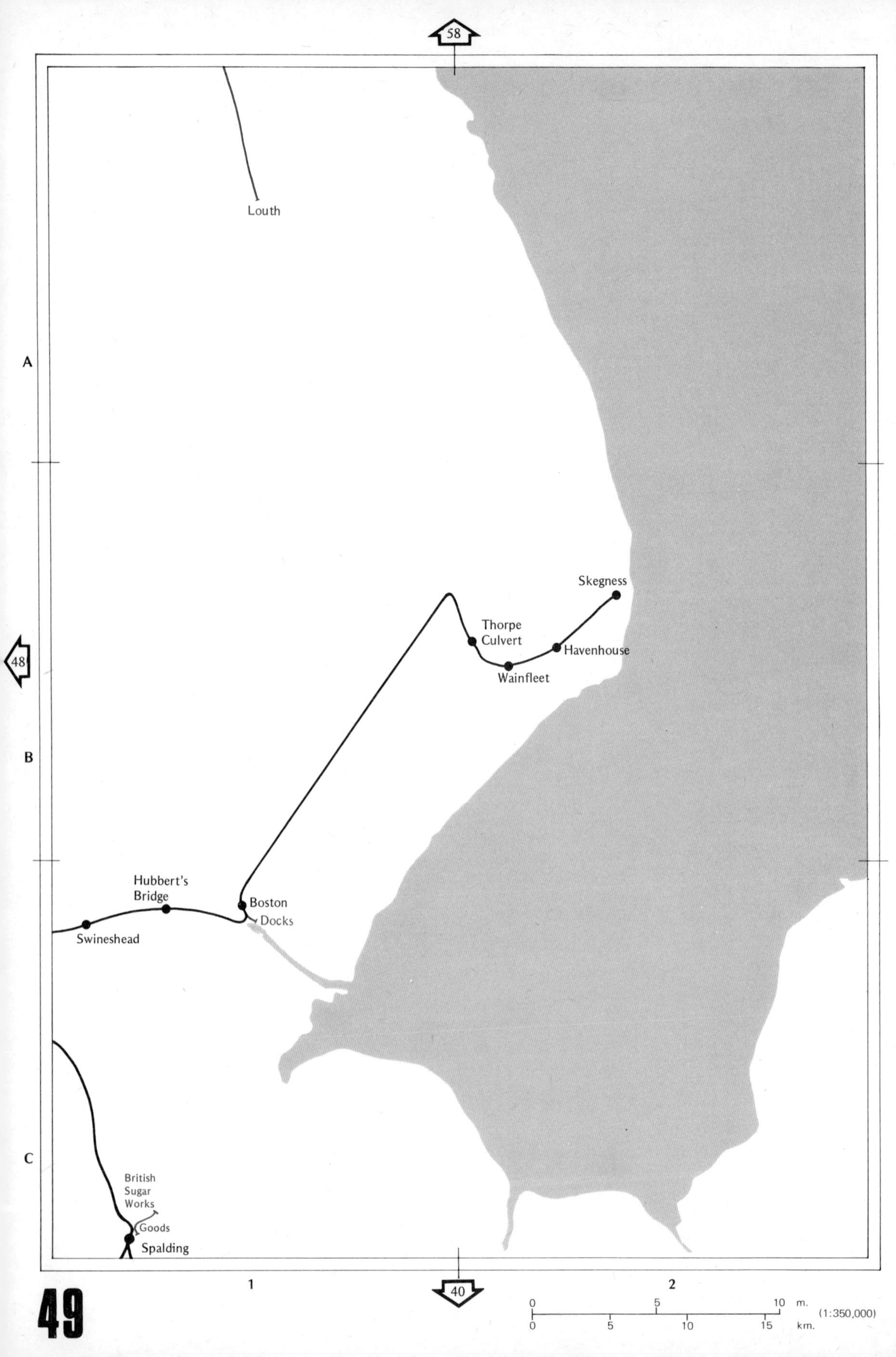
58
Louth
A
Skegness
Thorpe
Culvert
Havenhouse
Wainfleet
48
B
Hubbert's
Bridge
Boston
Docks
Swineshead
C
British
Sugar
Works
Goods
Spalding
1
40
2
0 5 10 m.
0 5 10 15 km.
(1:350,000)

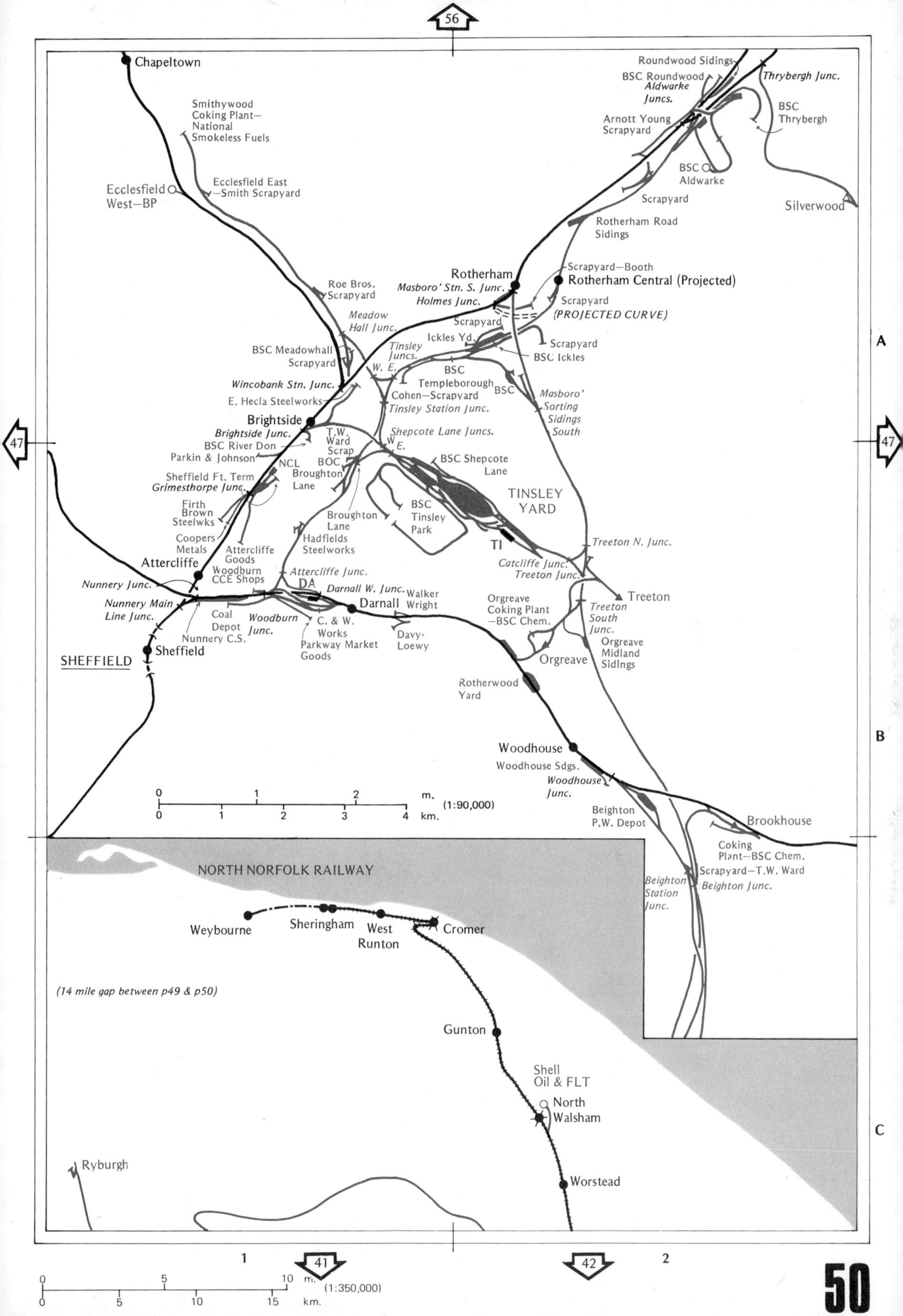

56

Chapeltown
Smithywood Coking Plant—National Smokeless Fuels
Ecclesfield West—BP
Ecclesfield East—Smith Scrapyard
Roundwood Sidings
BSC Roundwood
Aldwarke Juncs.
Thrybergh Junc.
BSC Thrybergh
Arnott Young Scrapyard
BSC Aldwarke
Scrapyard
Silverwood
Rotherham Road Sidings
Scrapyard—Booth
Rotherham
Rotherham Central (Projected)
Masboro' Stn. S. Junc.
Holmes Junc.
Scrapyard
(PROJECTED CURVE)
Roe Bros. Scrapyard
Meadow Hall Junc.
Scrapyard
Ickles Yd.
Scrapyard
BSC Ickles
BSC Meadowhall Scrapyard
Tinsley Juncs.
W. E.
BSC Templeborough
BSC
Masboro' Sorting Sidings South
Wincobank Stn. Junc.
E. Hecla Steelworks
Cohen—Scrapyard
Tinsley Station Junc.
Brightside
Brightside Junc.
BSC River Don
Parkin & Johnson
T.W. Ward Scrap
Shepcote Lane Juncs.
W E.
BSC Shepcote Lane
NCL
BOC
Broughton Lane
Sheffield Ft. Term
Grimesthorpe Junc.
Firth Brown Steelwks
BSC Tinsley Park
TINSLEY YARD
Broughton Lane
Coopers Metals
Attercliffe Goods
Hadfields Steelworks
TI
Treeton N. Junc.
Attercliffe
Woodburn CCE Shops
Attercliffe Junc.
Catcliffe Junc.
Treeton Junc.
Nunnery Junc.
DA
Darnall W. Junc.
Walker Wright
Treeton
Nunnery Main Line Junc.
Coal Depot
Nunnery C.S.
Woodburn Junc.
Darnall
C. & W. Works
Parkway Market Goods
Davy-Loewy
Orgreave Coking Plant—BSC Chem.
Treeton South Junc.
Orgreave
Orgreave Midland Sidings
Sheffield
SHEFFIELD
Rotherwood Yard
Woodhouse
Woodhouse Sdgs.
Woodhouse Junc.
Beighton P.W. Depot
Brookhouse
Coking Plant—BSC Chem.
Scrapyard—T.W. Ward
Beighton Junc.
Beighton Station Junc.

0 1 2 m.
0 1 2 3 4 km.
(1:90,000)

NORTH NORFOLK RAILWAY

Weybourne
Sheringham
West Runton
Cromer
(14 mile gap between p49 & p50)
Gunton
Shell Oil & FLT
North Walsham
Ryburgh
Worstead

A
B
C
1
2

47
47
41
42

0 5 10 m.
0 5 10 15 km.
(1:350,000)

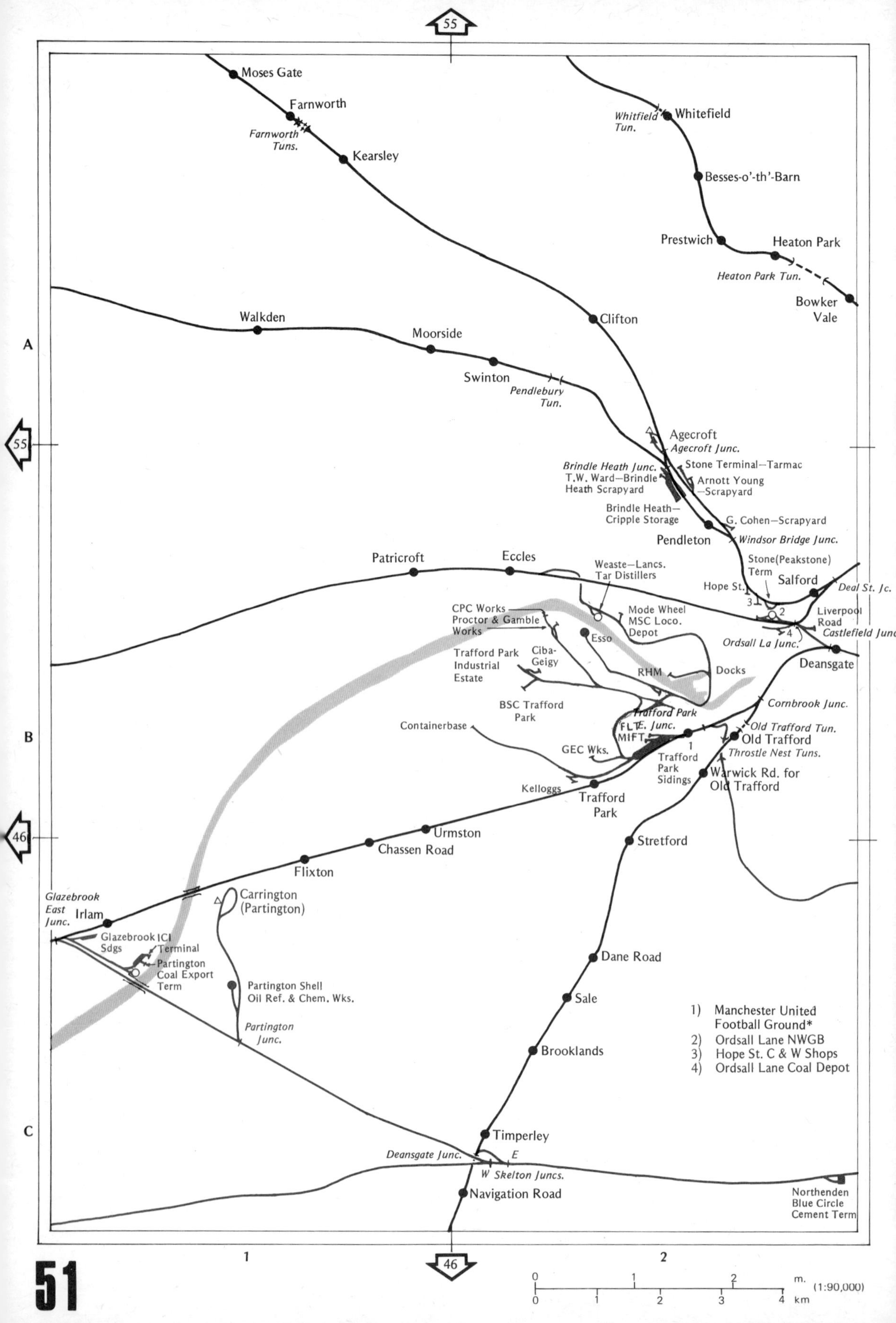
55
Moses Gate
Farnworth
Farnworth Tuns.
Kearsley
Whitfield Tun.
Whitefield
Besses-o'-th'-Barn
Prestwich
Heaton Park
Heaton Park Tun.
Bowker Vale
Walkden
Moorside
Swinton
Pendlebury Tun.
Clifton
A
55
Agecroft
Agecroft Junc.
Brindle Heath Junc.
Stone Terminal—Tarmac
T.W. Ward—Brindle Heath Scrapyard
Arnott Young —Scrapyard
Brindle Heath— Cripple Storage
G. Cohen—Scrapyard
Pendleton
Windsor Bridge Junc.
Patricroft
Eccles
Weaste—Lancs. Tar Distillers
Stone(Peakstone) Term
Salford
Hope St.
Deal St. Jc.
Liverpool Road
Castlefield Junc
Ordsall La Junc.
CPC Works
Proctor & Gamble Works
Mode Wheel MSC Loco. Depot
Esso
Trafford Park Industrial Estate
Ciba-Geigy
RHM
Docks
Deansgate
BSC Trafford Park
Cornbrook Junc.
Trafford Park E. Junc.
FLT
MIFT
Containerbase
Old Trafford Tun.
Old Trafford
Throstle Nest Tuns.
GEC Wks.
Trafford Park Sidings
Warwick Rd. for Old Trafford
Kelloggs
Trafford Park
B
46
Urmston
Chassen Road
Stretford
Flixton
Glazebrook East Junc.
Irlam
Carrington (Partington)
Glazebrook Sdgs
ICI Terminal
Partington Coal Export Term
Partington Shell Oil Ref. & Chem. Wks.
Partington Junc.
Dane Road
Sale
Brooklands
1) Manchester United Football Ground*
2) Ordsall Lane NWGB
3) Hope St. C & W Shops
4) Ordsall Lane Coal Depot
C
Timperley
Deansgate Junc.
E
W
Skelton Juncs.
Navigation Road
Northenden Blue Circle Cement Term
1
2
46
0 1 2 m.
0 1 2 3 4 km
(1:90,000)

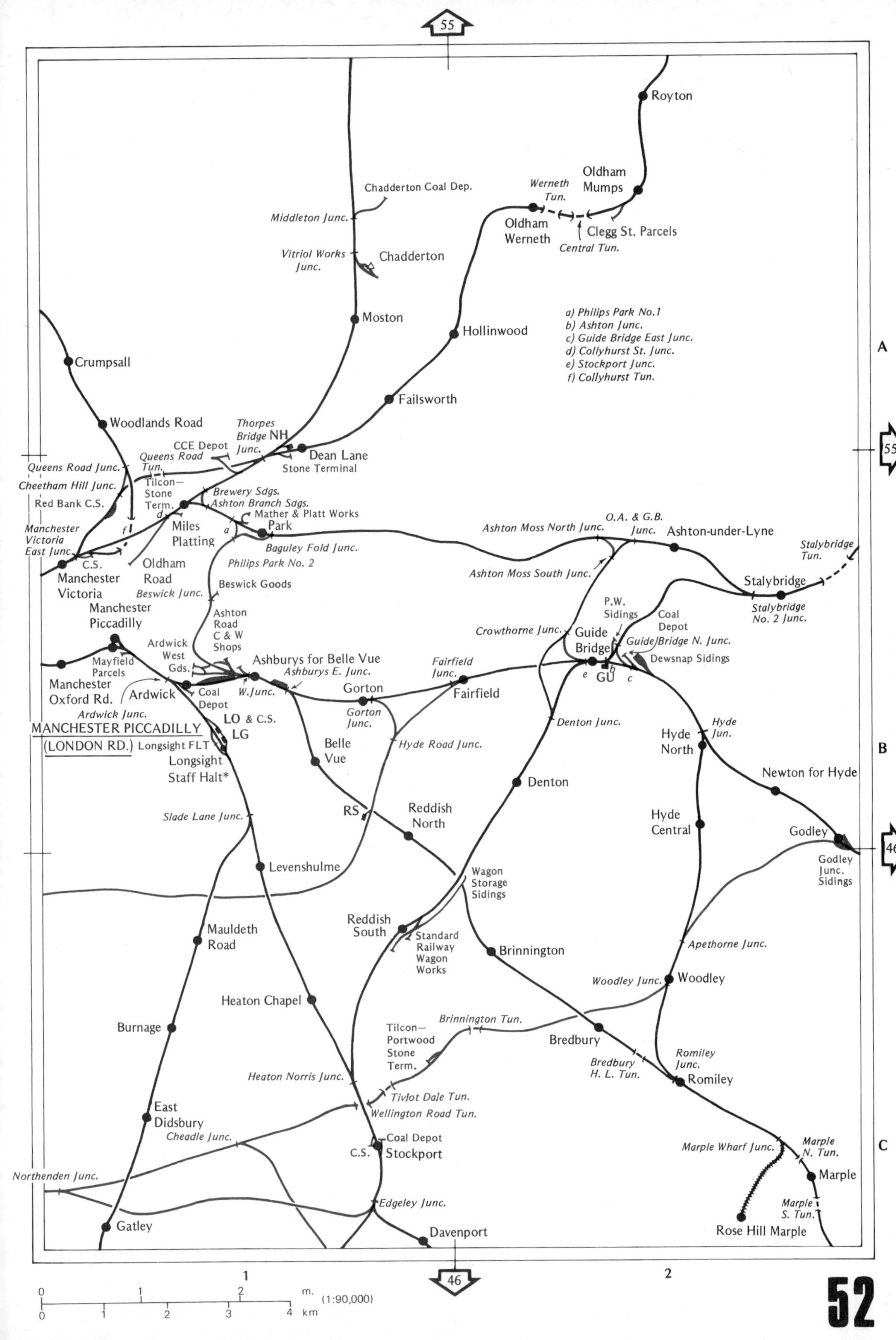
55
Royton
Oldham
Mumps
Werneth
Tun.
Chadderton Coal Dep.
Middleton Junc.
Oldham
Werneth
Clegg St. Parcels
Central Tun.
Vitriol Works
Junc.
Chadderton
Moston
Hollinwood
a) Philips Park No.1
b) Ashton Junc.
c) Guide Bridge East Junc.
d) Collyhurst St. Junc.
e) Stockport Junc.
f) Collyhurst Tun.
A
Crumpsall
Failsworth
Woodlands Road
Thorpes
Bridge NH
Junc.
CCE Depot
Queens Road
Tun.
Dean Lane
Stone Terminal
55
Queens Road Junc.
Cheetham Hill Junc.
Red Bank C.S.
Tilcon—
Stone
Term.
Brewery Sdgs.
Ashton Branch Sgs.
Mather & Platt Works
Manchester
Victoria
East Junc.
Miles
Platting
Park
O.A. & G.B.
Junc.
Ashton Moss North Junc.
Ashton-under-Lyne
Stalybridge
Tun.
Baguley Fold Junc.
C.S.
Manchester
Victoria
Oldham
Road
Philips Park No. 2
Beswick Goods
Ashton Moss South Junc.
Stalybridge
Beswick Junc.
Manchester
Piccadilly
Ashton
Road
C & W
Shops
P.W.
Sidings
Coal
Depot
Stalybridge
No. 2 Junc.
Crowthorne Junc.
Guide
Bridge
Guide Bridge N. Junc.
Dewsnap Sidings
Ardwick
West
Gds.
Mayfield
Parcels
Ashburys for Belle Vue
Ashburys E. Junc.
Fairfield
Junc.
GU
Manchester
Oxford Rd.
Ardwick
Coal
Depot
W.Junc.
Gorton
Fairfield
Ardwick Junc.
LO & C.S.
LG
Gorton
Junc.
Denton Junc.
Hyde
Jun.
Hyde
North
MANCHESTER PICCADILLY
(LONDON RD.)
Longsight FLT
Longsight
Staff Halt*
Belle
Vue
Hyde Road Junc.
B
Newton for Hyde
Denton
Reddish
North
RS
Slade Lane Junc.
Hyde
Central
Godley
46
Godley
Junc.
Sidings
Levenshulme
Wagon
Storage
Sidings
Mauldeth
Road
Reddish
South
Standard
Railway
Wagon
Works
Brinnington
Apethorne Junc.
Woodley Junc.
Woodley
Heaton Chapel
Brinnington Tun.
Burnage
Tilcon—
Portwood
Stone
Term.
Bredbury
Romiley
Junc.
Bredbury
H. L. Tun.
Romiley
Heaton Norris Junc.
Tiviot Dale Tun.
East
Didsbury
Wellington Road Tun.
Cheadle Junc.
Coal Depot
Marple
N. Tun.
C.S.
Stockport
Marple Wharf Junc.
C
Northenden Junc.
Marple
Edgeley Junc.
Marple
S. Tun.
Gatley
Davenport
Rose Hill Marple
46
1
2
0
1
2
m.
(1:90,000)
0
1
2
3
4
km

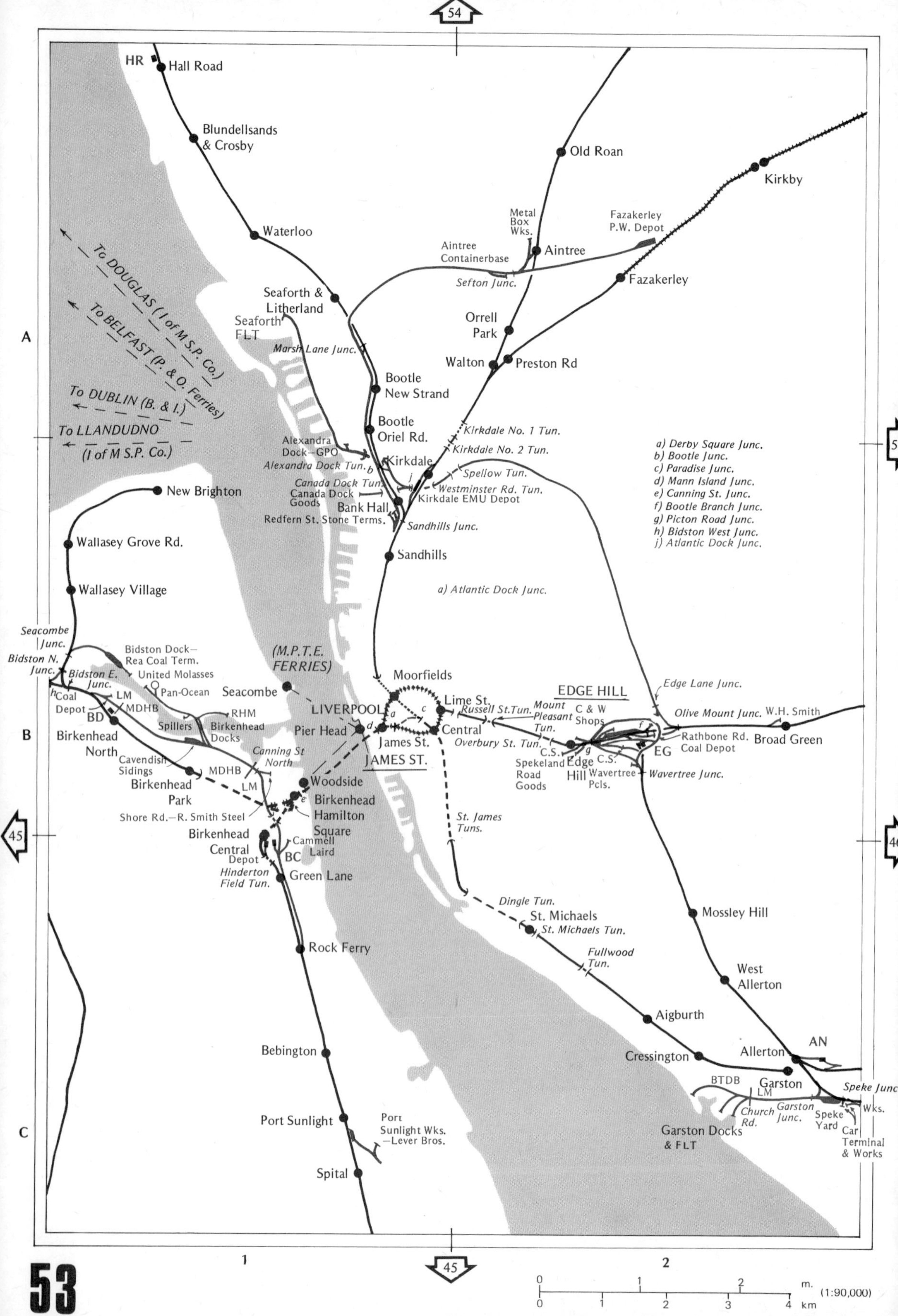
54
HR
Hall Road
Blundellsands
& Crosby
Old Roan
Kirkby
Waterloo
Metal
Box
Wks.
Fazakerley
P.W. Depot
Aintree
Containerbase
Aintree
To DOUGLAS (I of M S.P. Co.)
To BELFAST (P. & O. Ferries)
To DUBLIN (B. & I.)
To LLANDUDNO
(I of M S.P. Co.)
Sefton Junc.
Fazakerley
Seaforth &
Litherland
Seaforth
FLT
Orrell
Park
A
Marsh Lane Junc.
Walton
Preston Rd
Bootle
New Strand
Bootle
Oriel Rd.
Kirkdale No. 1 Tun.
Kirkdale No. 2 Tun.
Alexandra
Dock—GPO
Alexandra Dock Tun.
Kirkdale
Spellow Tun.
Canada Dock Tun.
Canada Dock
Goods
Westminster Rd. Tun.
Kirkdale EMU Depot
Bank Hall
Redfern St. Stone Terms.
Sandhills Junc.
New Brighton
a) Derby Square Junc.
b) Bootle Junc.
c) Paradise Junc.
d) Mann Island Junc.
e) Canning St. Junc.
f) Bootle Branch Junc.
g) Picton Road Junc.
h) Bidston West Junc.
j) Atlantic Dock Junc.
Wallasey Grove Rd.
Sandhills
Wallasey Village
a) Atlantic Dock Junc.
Seacombe
Junc.
Bidston N.
Junc.
Bidston Dock—
Rea Coal Term.
United Molasses
(M.P.T.E.
FERRIES)
Bidston E.
Junc.
Pan-Ocean
Seacombe
Moorfields
Edge Lane Junc.
EDGE HILL
Coal
Depot
LM
MDHB
RHM
LIVERPOOL
Lime St.
Russell St.Tun.
Mount
Pleasant
Tun.
C & W
Shops
Olive Mount Junc.
W.H. Smith
BD
Spillers
Birkenhead
Docks
Pier Head
James St.
Central
Overbury St. Tun.
Rathbone Rd.
Coal Depot
Broad Green
B
Birkenhead
North
EG
Canning St
North
JAMES ST.
C.S.
C.S.
Cavendish
Sidings
MDHB
Spekeland
Road
Goods
Edge
Hill
Wavertree
Pcls.
Wavertree Junc.
Birkenhead
Park
LM
Woodside
Birkenhead
Hamilton
Square
Shore Rd.—R. Smith Steel
St. James
Tuns.
45
46
Birkenhead
Central
Depot
Cammell
Laird
BC
Hinderton
Field Tun.
Green Lane
Dingle Tun.
St. Michaels
St. Michaels Tun.
Mossley Hill
Rock Ferry
Fullwood
Tun.
West
Allerton
Aigburth
AN
Bebington
Cressington
Allerton
BTDB
Garston
LM
Speke Junc.
Church
Rd.
Garston
Junc.
Speke
Yard
Wks.
Port Sunlight
Port
Sunlight Wks.
—Lever Bros.
C
Garston Docks
& FLT
Car
Terminal
& Works
Spital
1
45
2
m.
(1:90,000)
km

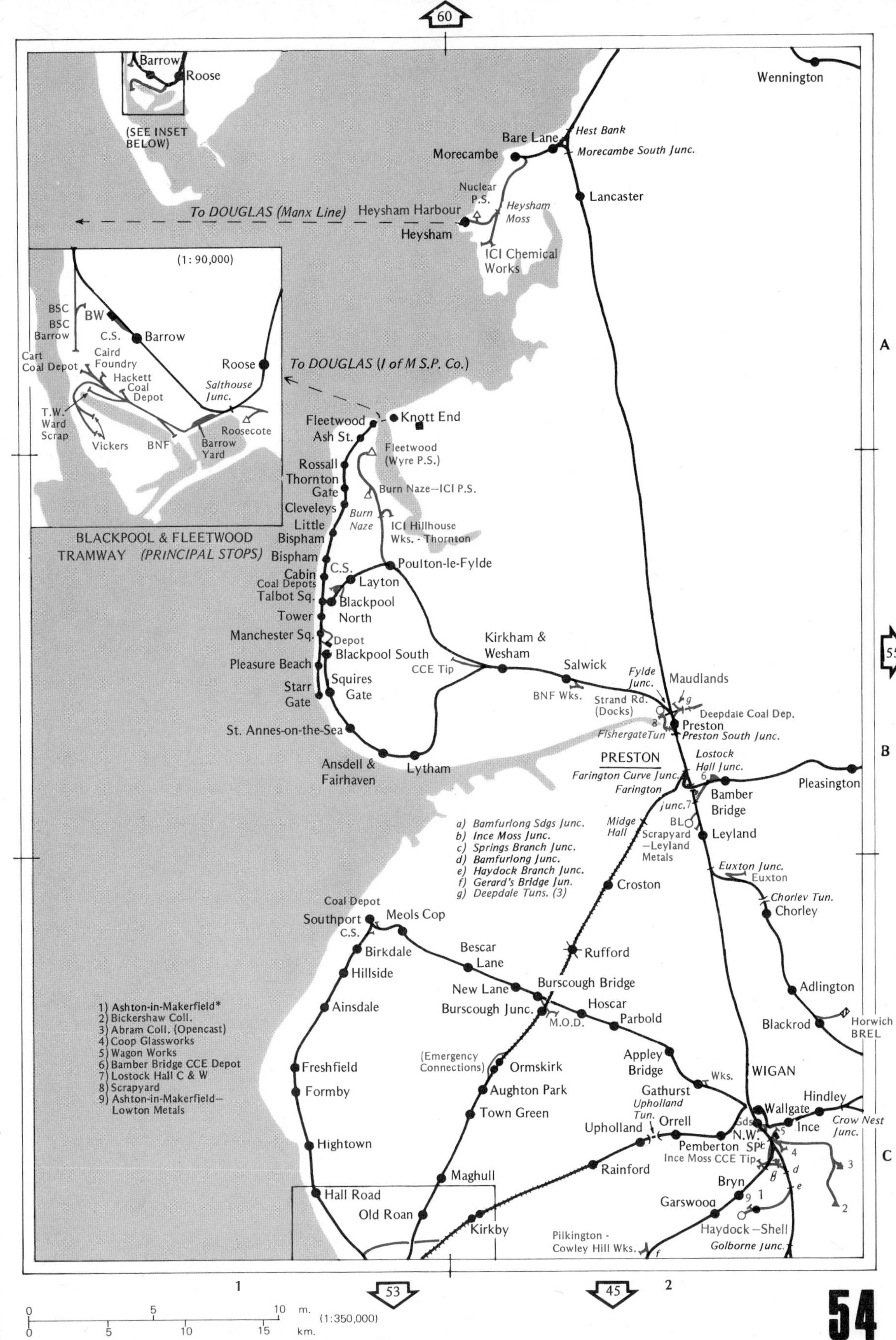

60
Barrow
Roose
(SEE INSET BELOW)
Wennington
Hest Bank
Bare Lane
Morecambe South Junc.
Morecambe
Lancaster
Nuclear P.S.
Heysham Moss
To DOUGLAS (Manx Line)
Heysham Harbour
Heysham
ICI Chemical Works
(1: 90,000)
BSC
BW
BSC Barrow
C.S.
Barrow
Cart Coal Depot
Caird Foundry
Hackett Coal Depot
Roose
Salthouse Junc.
T.W. Ward Scrap
Vickers
BNF
Barrow Yard
Roosecote
To DOUGLAS (I of M S.P. Co.)
A
Fleetwood
Knott End
Ash St.
Fleetwood (Wyre P.S.)
Rossall
Thornton Gate
Burn Naze–ICI P.S.
Cleveleys
Burn Naze
Little Bispham
ICI Hillhouse Wks. - Thornton
BLACKPOOL & FLEETWOOD TRAMWAY (PRINCIPAL STOPS)
Bispham
C.S.
Poulton-le-Fylde
Cabin
Coal Depots
Layton
Talbot Sq.
Blackpool North
Tower
Manchester Sq.
Depot
Kirkham & Wesham
Blackpool South
Pleasure Beach
Squires Gate
CCE Tip
Salwick
Starr Gate
BNF Wks.
Fylde Junc.
Maudlands
55
Strand Rd. (Docks)
g
Deepdale Coal Dep.
Preston
FishergateTun
Preston South Junc.
St. Annes-on-the-Sea
Lostock Hall Junc.
B
Ansdell & Fairhaven
Lytham
PRESTON
Farington Curve Junc.
Farington
Pleasington
Bamber Bridge
Junc.
BL
Leyland
Midge Hall
Scrapyard –Leyland Metals
a) Bamfurlong Sdgs Junc.
b) Ince Moss Junc.
c) Springs Branch Junc.
d) Bamfurlong Junc.
e) Haydock Branch Junc.
f) Gerard's Bridge Jun.
g) Deepdale Tuns. (3)
Euxton Junc.
Euxton
Croston
Chorley Tun.
Chorley
Coal Depot
Southport
Meols Cop
C.S.
Birkdale
Bescar Lane
Rufford
Hillside
New Lane
Burscough Bridge
Adlington
Burscough Junc.
Hoscar
Ainsdale
M.O.D.
Parbold
Horwich BREL
Blackrod
1) Ashton-in-Makerfield*
2) Bickershaw Coll.
3) Abram Coll. (Opencast)
4) Coop Glassworks
5) Wagon Works
6) Bamber Bridge CCE Depot
7) Lostock Hall C & W
8) Scrapyard
9) Ashton-in-Makerfield–Lowton Metals
(Emergency Connections)
Ormskirk
Appley Bridge
Freshfield
WIGAN
Wks.
Aughton Park
Gathurst
Formby
Upholland Tun.
Wallgate
Hindley
Town Green
Orrell
Upholland
Sdgs
N.W.
Ince
Crow Nest Junc.
Pemberton
SP
Hightown
Ince Moss CCE Tip
C
Maghull
Rainford
Bryn
Hall Road
Garswood
Old Roan
Haydock –Shell
Kirkby
Pilkington - Cowley Hill Wks.
Golborne Junc.
1
53
45
2
0 5 10 m.
0 5 10 15 km.
(1:350,000)

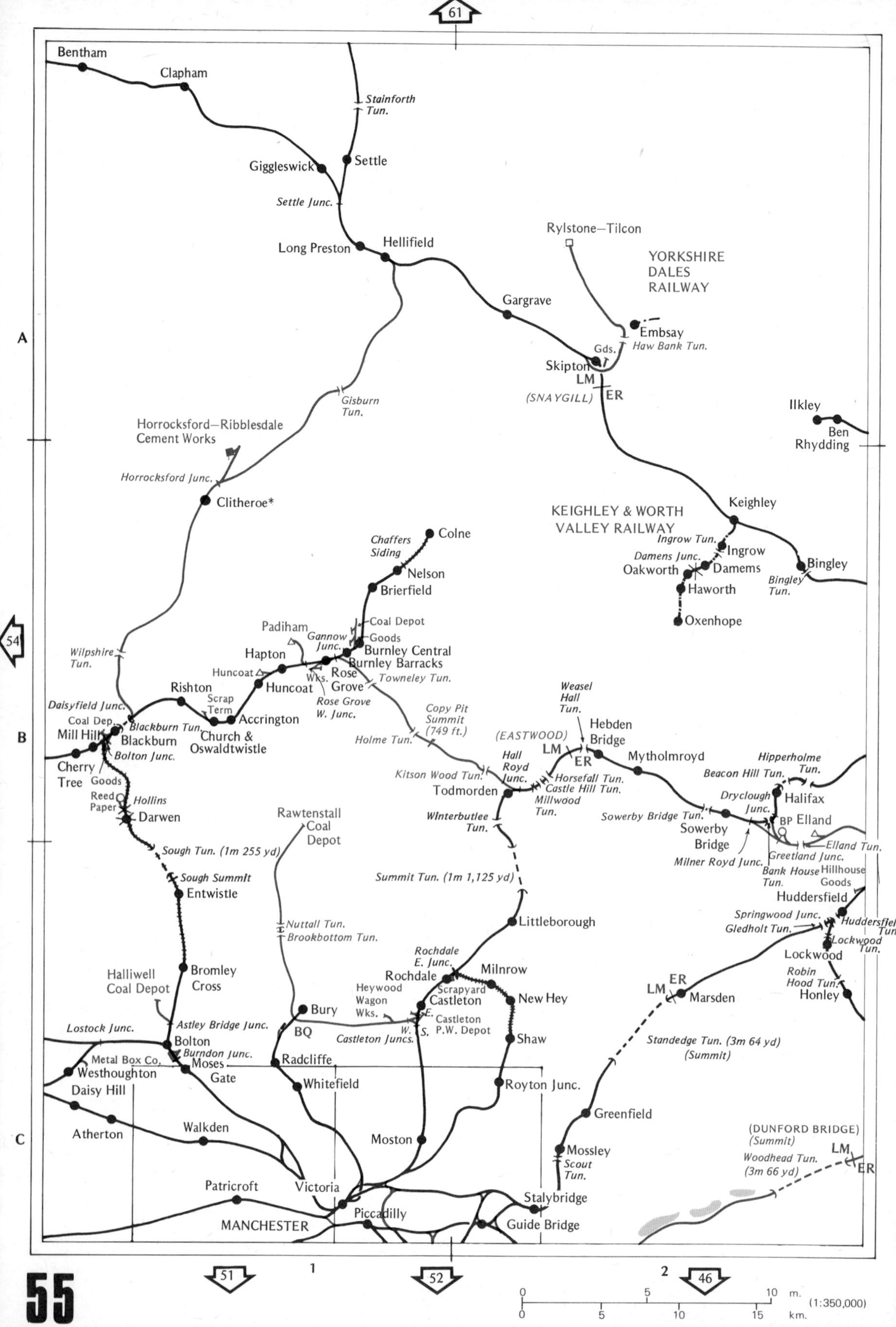
61
Bentham
Clapham
Stainforth Tun.
Giggleswick
Settle
Settle Junc.
Long Preston
Hellifield
Rylstone—Tilcon
YORKSHIRE DALES RAILWAY
Gargrave
Embsay
Haw Bank Tun.
Gds.
Skipton
LM
ER
(SNAYGILL)
A
Gisburn Tun.
Ilkley
Ben Rhydding
Horrocksford—Ribblesdale Cement Works
Horrocksford Junc.
Clitheroe*
Keighley
KEIGHLEY & WORTH VALLEY RAILWAY
Chaffers Siding
Colne
Ingrow Tun.
Ingrow
Damens Junc.
Oakworth
Damems
Bingley
Bingley Tun.
Nelson
Brierfield
Haworth
Oxenhope
Coal Depot
Padiham
Gannow Junc.
Goods
54
Wilpshire Tun.
Hapton
Burnley Central
Burnley Barracks
Huncoat
Rose Grove
Wks.
Towneley Tun.
Huncoat
Rishton
Rose Grove W. Junc.
Scrap Term
Weasel Hall Tun.
Daisyfield Junc.
Accrington
Copy Pit Summit (749 ft.)
Hebden Bridge
Coal Dep.
Blackburn Tun.
(EASTWOOD)
Mill Hill
Blackburn
Church & Oswaldtwistle
Holme Tun.
LM
ER
B
Bolton Junc.
Hall Royd Junc.
Mytholmroyd
Hipperholme Tun.
Cherry Tree
Goods
Kitson Wood Tun.
Horsefall Tun.
Castle Hill Tun.
Beacon Hill Tun.
Reed Paper
Hollins
Todmorden
Millwood Tun.
Dryclough Junc.
Halifax
Darwen
Rawtenstall Coal Depot
Winterbutlee Tun.
Sowerby Bridge Tun.
BP
Elland
Sowerby Bridge
Elland Tun.
Sough Tun. (1m 255 yd)
Greetland Junc.
Milner Royd Junc.
Bank House Tun.
Hillhouse Goods
Sough Summit
Summit Tun. (1m 1,125 yd)
Entwistle
Huddersfield
Springwood Junc.
Huddersfield Tuns.
Nuttall Tun.
Littleborough
Gledholt Tun.
Brookbottom Tun.
Lockwood Tun.
Rochdale E. Junc.
Lockwood
Halliwell Coal Depot
Bromley Cross
Milnrow
Robin Hood Tun.
Rochdale
ER
Heywood Wagon Wks.
Scrapyard
LM
Honley
Castleton
New Hey
Marsden
Bury
E.
Castleton P.W. Depot
Lostock Junc.
Astley Bridge Junc.
BQ
W.
S.
Standedge Tun. (3m 64 yd) (Summit)
Bolton
Castleton Juncs.
Shaw
Burndon Junc.
Metal Box Co.
Moses Gate
Radcliffe
Westhoughton
Whitefield
Royton Junc.
Daisy Hill
Greenfield
(DUNFORD BRIDGE) (Summit)
C
Atherton
Walkden
Moston
Mossley
LM
Scout Tun.
Woodhead Tun. (3m 66 yd)
ER
Patricroft
Victoria
Stalybridge
Piccadilly
MANCHESTER
Guide Bridge
51
1
52
2
46
0 5 10 m.
0 5 10 15 km.
(1:350,000)

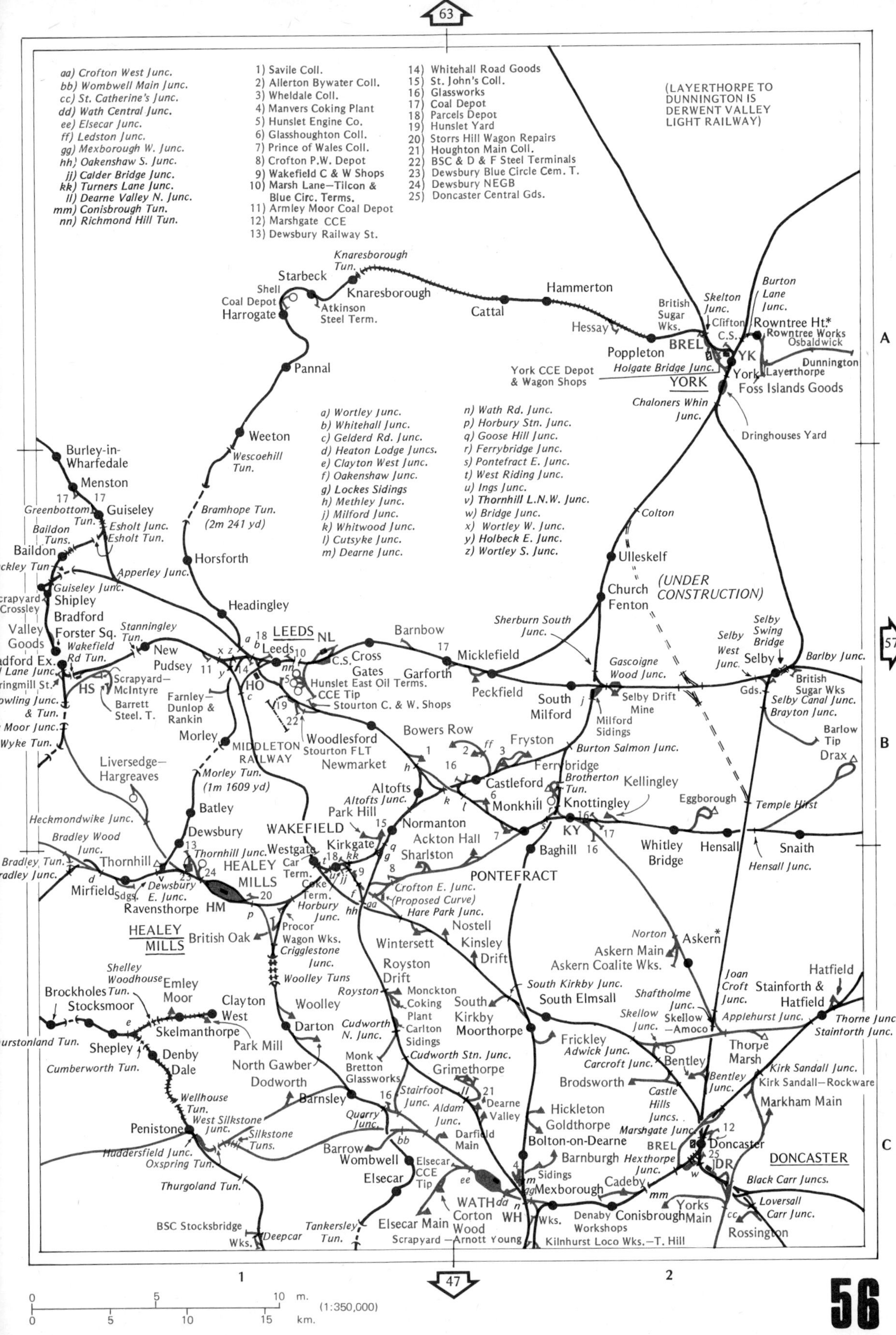
63
aa) Crofton West Junc.
bb) Wombwell Main Junc.
cc) St. Catherine's Junc.
dd) Wath Central Junc.
ee) Elsecar Junc.
ff) Ledston Junc.
gg) Mexborough W. Junc.
hh) Oakenshaw S. Junc.
jj) Calder Bridge Junc.
kk) Turners Lane Junc.
ll) Dearne Valley N. Junc.
mm) Conisbrough Tun.
nn) Richmond Hill Tun.
1) Savile Coll.
2) Allerton Bywater Coll.
3) Wheldale Coll.
4) Manvers Coking Plant
5) Hunslet Engine Co.
6) Glasshoughton Coll.
7) Prince of Wales Coll.
8) Crofton P.W. Depot
9) Wakefield C & W Shops
10) Marsh Lane—Tilcon & Blue Circ. Terms.
11) Armley Moor Coal Depot
12) Marshgate CCE
13) Dewsbury Railway St.
14) Whitehall Road Goods
15) St. John's Coll.
16) Glassworks
17) Coal Depot
18) Parcels Depot
19) Hunslet Yard
20) Storrs Hill Wagon Repairs
21) Houghton Main Coll.
22) BSC & D & F Steel Terminals
23) Dewsbury Blue Circle Cem. T.
24) Dewsbury NEGB
25) Doncaster Central Gds.
(LAYERTHORPE TO DUNNINGTON IS DERWENT VALLEY LIGHT RAILWAY)
a) Wortley Junc.
b) Whitehall Junc.
c) Gelderd Rd. Junc.
d) Heaton Lodge Juncs.
e) Clayton West Junc.
f) Oakenshaw Junc.
g) Lockes Sidings
h) Methley Junc.
j) Milford Junc.
k) Whitwood Junc.
l) Cutsyke Junc.
m) Dearne Junc.
n) Wath Rd. Junc.
p) Horbury Stn. Junc.
q) Goose Hill Junc.
r) Ferrybridge Junc.
s) Pontefract E. Junc.
t) West Riding Junc.
u) Ings Junc.
v) Thornhill L.N.W. Junc.
w) Bridge Junc.
x) Wortley W. Junc.
y) Holbeck E. Junc.
z) Wortley S. Junc.
Knaresborough Tun.
Starbeck
Shell Coal Depot
Harrogate
Knaresborough
Atkinson Steel Term.
Hammerton
Cattal
Hessay
British Sugar Wks.
Skelton Junc.
Clifton C.S.
Burton Lane Junc.
Rowntree Ht.*
Rowntree Works
Osbaldwick
Dunnington
Poppleton
BREL
YK
Holgate Bridge Junc.
York CCE Depot & Wagon Shops
York
Layerthorpe
YORK
Foss Islands Goods
Chaloners Whin Junc.
Dringhouses Yard
Pannal
Weeton
Wescoehill Tun.
Bramhope Tun. (2m 241 yd)
Burley-in-Wharfedale
Menston
Greenbottom Tun.
Guiseley
Esholt Junc.
Esholt Tun.
Baildon Tuns.
Baildon
Apperley Junc.
Guiseley Junc.
Shipley
Bradford Forster Sq.
Crossley
Valley Goods
Stanningley Tun.
Wakefield Rd Tun.
New Pudsey
Horsforth
Headingley
LEEDS
Leeds
NL
C.S.
Cross Gates
Barnbow
Micklefield
Garforth
Hunslet East Oil Terms.
CCE Tip
Stourton C. & W. Shops
HS
Scrapyard—McIntyre
Barrett Steel. T.
HO
Farnley—Dunlop & Rankin
Morley
MIDDLETON RAILWAY
Woodlesford
Stourton FLT
Newmarket
Bowers Row
Morley Tun. (1m 1609 yd)
Liversedge—Hargreaves
Colton
Ulleskelf
Church Fenton
(UNDER CONSTRUCTION)
Sherburn South Junc.
Selby West Junc.
Selby Swing Bridge
Selby
Barlby Junc.
British Sugar Wks
Selby Canal Junc.
Brayton Junc.
Barlow Tip
Drax
Gascoigne Wood Junc.
Selby Drift Mine
Peckfield
South Milford
Milford Sidings
Burton Salmon Junc.
Fryston
Ferrybridge
Brotherton Tun.
Kellingley
Castleford
Monkhill
Knottingley
KY
Eggborough
Temple Hirst
Whitley Bridge
Hensall
Snaith
Hensall Junc.
Altofts
Altofts Junc.
Park Hill
Normanton
Ackton Hall
Sharlston
PONTEFRACT
Baghill
Batley
Dewsbury
Heckmondwike Junc.
Bradley Wood Junc.
Thornhill
Thornhill Junc.
Bradley Tun.
Mirfield
Dewsbury E. Junc.
Ravensthorpe
HM
HEALEY MILLS
WAKEFIELD
Westgate
Kirkgate
Car Term.
Coke Term.
Horbury Junc.
Crofton E. Junc.
(Proposed Curve)
Hare Park Junc.
Nostell
Kinsley Drift
Wintersett
Royston Drift
Procor Wagon Wks.
Crigglestone Junc.
British Oak
Woolley Tuns
Royston
Monckton Coking Plant
Carlton Sidings
Woolley
Darton
Cudworth N. Junc.
Norton
Askern*
Askern Main
Askern Coalite Wks.
South Kirkby Junc.
South Elmsall
South Kirkby
Moorthorpe
Frickley
Adwick Junc.
Carcroft Junc.
Shaftholme Junc.
Skellow Junc.
Skellow—Amoco
Joan Croft Junc.
Applehurst Junc.
Stainforth & Hatfield
Hatfield
Thorne Junc.
Stainforth Junc.
Thorpe Marsh
Bentley
Bentley Junc.
Kirk Sandall Junc.
Kirk Sandall—Rockware
Markham Main
Shelley Woodhouse Tun.
Emley Moor
Brockholes
Stocksmoor
Clayton West
Skelmanthorpe
Park Mill
North Gawber
Dodworth
Shepley
Denby Dale
Cumberworth Tun.
Monk Bretton Glassworks
Cudworth Stn. Junc.
Grimethorpe
Barnsley
Stairfoot Junc.
Aldam Junc.
Dearne Valley
Quarry Junc.
Wellhouse Tun.
West Silkstone Junc.
Silkstone Tuns.
Penistone
Huddersfield Junc.
Oxspring Tun.
Thurgoland Tun.
Barrow
Wombwell
Elsecar
Elsecar CCE Tip
Darfield Main
Hickleton
Goldthorpe
Bolton-on-Dearne
Barnburgh
Brodsworth
Castle Hills Juncs.
Marshgate Junc.
BREL
Doncaster
DR
DONCASTER
Hexthorpe Junc.
Black Carr Juncs.
Sidings
Mexborough
Cadeby
Conisbrough
Yorks Main
Loversall Carr Junc.
Rossington
WATH
WH
Wks.
Denaby Workshops
Corton Wood
Elsecar Main
Tankersley Tun.
Scrapyard—Arnott Young
Kilnhurst Loco Wks.—T. Hill
BSC Stocksbridge Wks.
Deepcar
A
B
C
57
47
1
2
0 5 10 m.
0 5 10 15 km.
(1:350,000)

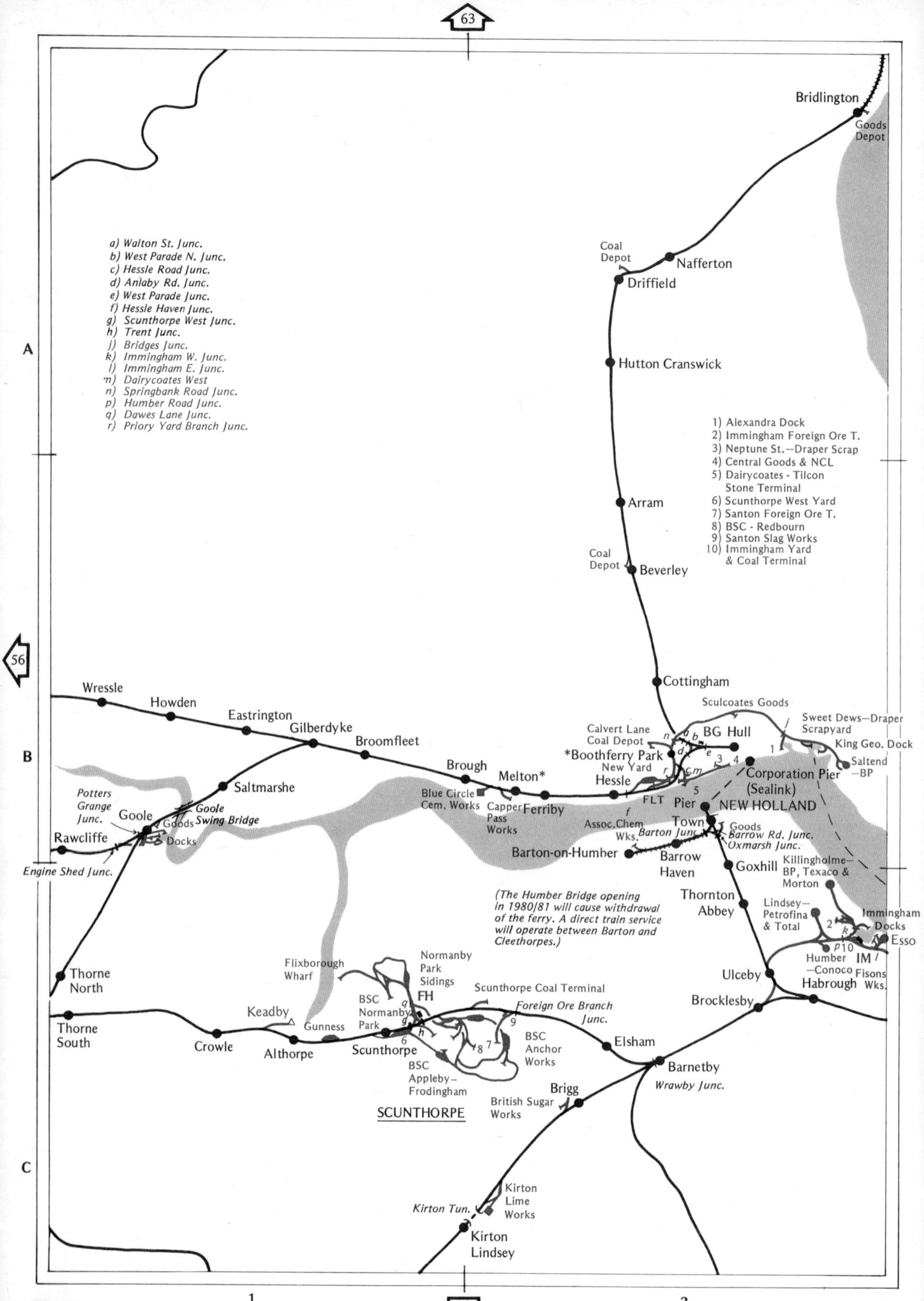

63

a) Walton St. Junc.
b) West Parade N. Junc.
c) Hessle Road Junc.
d) Anlaby Rd. Junc.
e) West Parade Junc.
f) Hessle Haven Junc.
g) Scunthorpe West Junc.
h) Trent Junc.
j) Bridges Junc.
k) Immingham W. Junc.
l) Immingham E. Junc.
m) Dairycoates West
n) Springbank Road Junc.
p) Humber Road Junc.
q) Dawes Lane Junc.
r) Priory Yard Branch Junc.

1) Alexandra Dock
2) Immingham Foreign Ore T.
3) Neptune St.—Draper Scrap
4) Central Goods & NCL
5) Dairycoates - Tilcon Stone Terminal
6) Scunthorpe West Yard
7) Santon Foreign Ore T.
8) BSC - Redbourn
9) Santon Slag Works
10) Immingham Yard & Coal Terminal

(The Humber Bridge opening in 1980/81 will cause withdrawal of the ferry. A direct train service will operate between Barton and Cleethorpes.)

A

B

C

Bridlington
Goods Depot
Coal Depot
Nafferton
Driffield
Hutton Cranswick
Arram
Coal Depot
Beverley
Cottingham
Sculcoates Goods
Sweet Dews—Draper Scrapyard
King Geo. Dock
Saltend —BP
Calvert Lane Coal Depot
BG Hull
*Boothferry Park
New Yard
Hessle
Corporation Pier (Sealink)
Pier
NEW HOLLAND
Town
FLT
Assoc.Chem Wks.
Barton Junc.
Goods
Barrow Rd. Junc.
Oxmarsh Junc.
Barton-on-Humber
Barrow Haven
Goxhill
Killingholme—BP, Texaco & Morton
Thornton Abbey
Lindsey—Petrofina & Total
Immingham Docks
Esso
Humber —Conoco
IM
Fisons Wks.
Ulceby
Habrough
Brocklesby
Wressle
Howden
Eastrington
Gilberdyke
Broomfleet
Brough
Melton*
Blue Circle Cem. Works
Capper Pass Works
Ferriby
Saltmarshe
Potters Grange Junc.
Goole
Goole Swing Bridge
Goods
Docks
Rawcliffe
Engine Shed Junc.
Thorne North
Thorne South
Crowle
Keadby
Althorpe
Gunness
Flixborough Wharf
Normanby Park Sidings
FH
BSC Normanby Park
Scunthorpe
Scunthorpe Coal Terminal
Foreign Ore Branch Junc.
BSC Anchor Works
BSC Appleby—Frodingham
SCUNTHORPE
Elsham
Barnetby
Wrawby Junc.
Brigg
British Sugar Works
Kirton Lime Works
Kirton Tun.
Kirton Lindsey

56

1 2

48

0 5 10 m.
0 5 10 15 km.
(1:350,000)

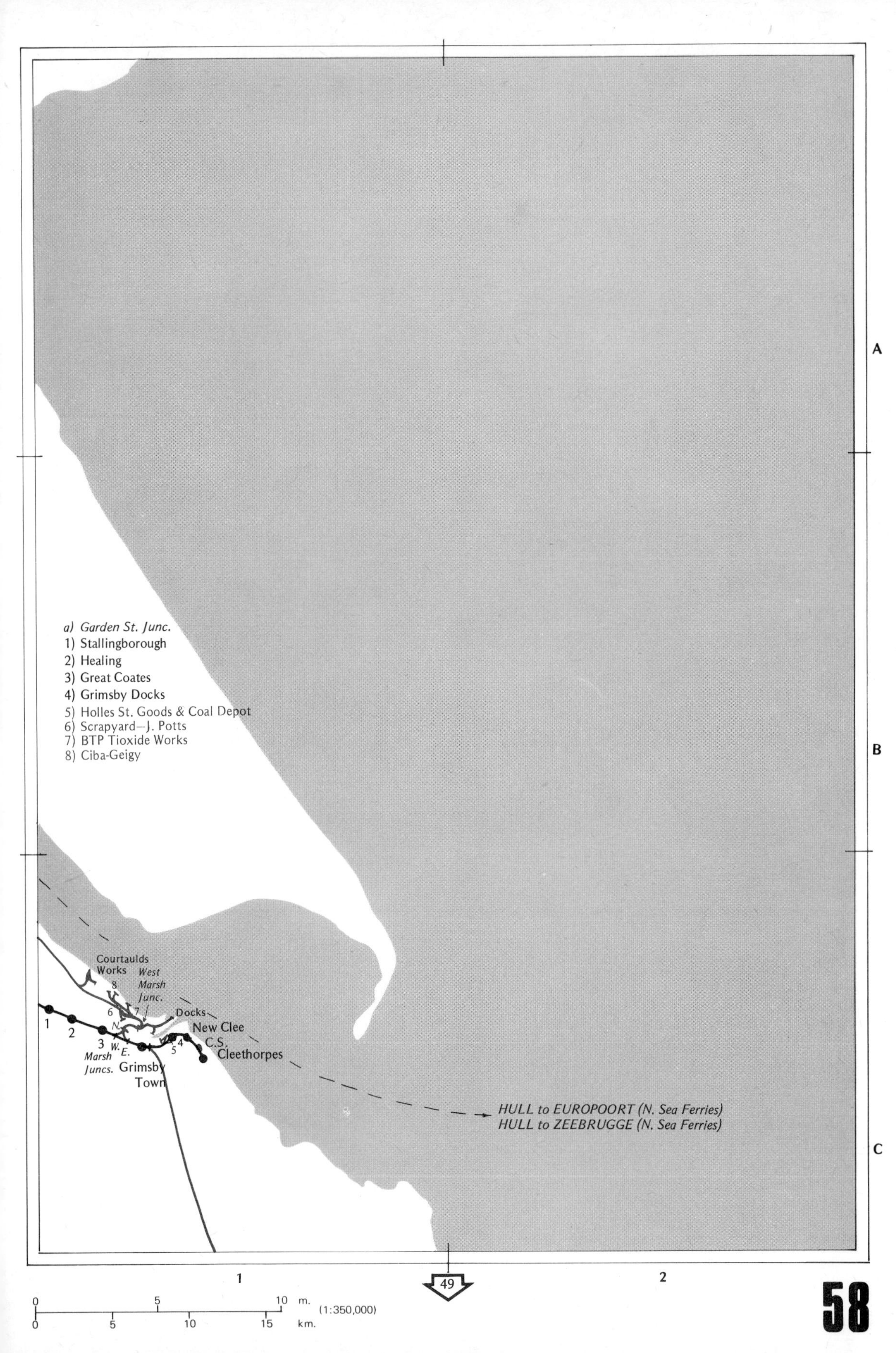
A
B
C
a) Garden St. Junc.
1) Stallingborough
2) Healing
3) Great Coates
4) Grimsby Docks
5) Holles St. Goods & Coal Depot
6) Scrapyard—J. Potts
7) BTP Tioxide Works
8) Ciba-Geigy
Courtaulds Works
West Marsh Junc.
Docks
New Clee
C.S.
Cleethorpes
N.
W.
E.
Marsh Juncs.
Grimsby Town
HULL to EUROPOORT (N. Sea Ferries)
HULL to ZEEBRUGGE (N. Sea Ferries)
1
2
49
0 5 10 m.
0 5 10 15 km.
(1:350,000)

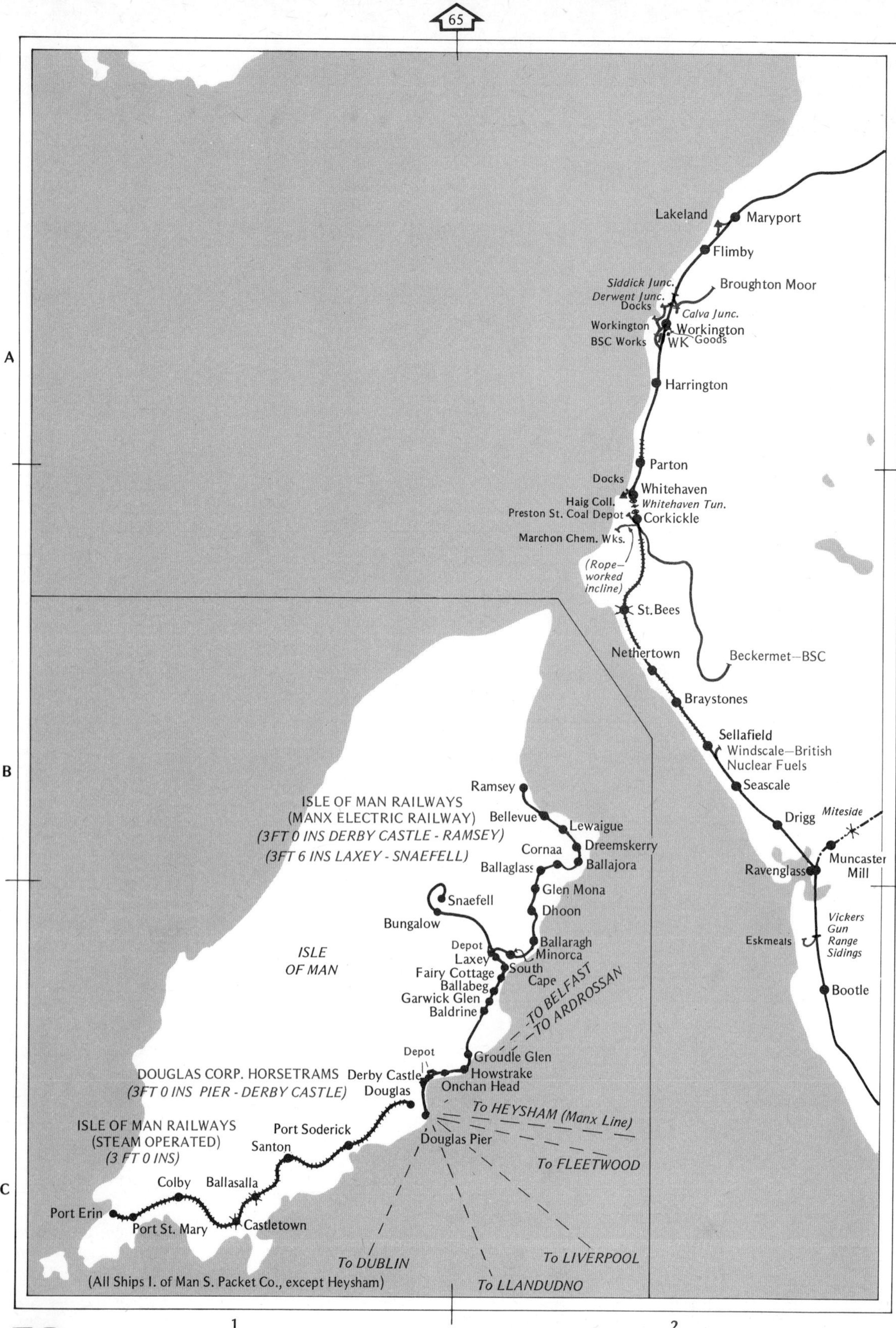

65

A

B

C

Lakeland
Maryport
Flimby
Siddick Junc.
Derwent Junc.
Docks
Broughton Moor
Calva Junc.
Workington
Workington
BSC Works
WK
Goods
Harrington
Parton
Docks
Whitehaven
Haig Coll.
Whitehaven Tun.
Preston St. Coal Depot
Corkickle
Marchon Chem. Wks.
(Rope–worked incline)
St. Bees
Nethertown
Beckermet–BSC
Braystones
Sellafield
Windscale–British Nuclear Fuels
Seascale
Drigg
Miteside
Muncaster Mill
Ravenglass
Eskmeals
Vickers Gun Range Sidings
Bootle

ISLE OF MAN RAILWAYS
(MANX ELECTRIC RAILWAY)
(3FT 0 INS DERBY CASTLE - RAMSEY)
(3FT 6 INS LAXEY - SNAEFELL)

Ramsey
Bellevue
Lewaigue
Dreemskerry
Cornaa
Ballaglass
Ballajora
Glen Mona
Snaefell
Dhoon
Bungalow
Ballaragh
Depot
Minorca
Laxey
South Cape
Fairy Cottage
Ballabeg
Garwick Glen
Baldrine

ISLE OF MAN

TO BELFAST
TO ARDROSSAN

Depot
Groudle Glen
Derby Castle
Howstrake
Onchan Head
Douglas

DOUGLAS CORP. HORSETRAMS
(3FT 0 INS PIER - DERBY CASTLE)

ISLE OF MAN RAILWAYS
(STEAM OPERATED)
(3 FT 0 INS)

Port Soderick
Santon
Colby
Ballasalla
Port Erin
Port St. Mary
Castletown
Douglas Pier

To HEYSHAM (Manx Line)
To FLEETWOOD
To DUBLIN
To LIVERPOOL
To LLANDUDNO

(All Ships I. of Man S. Packet Co., except Heysham)

1

2

0 5 10 m.
0 5 10 15 km.
(1:350,000)

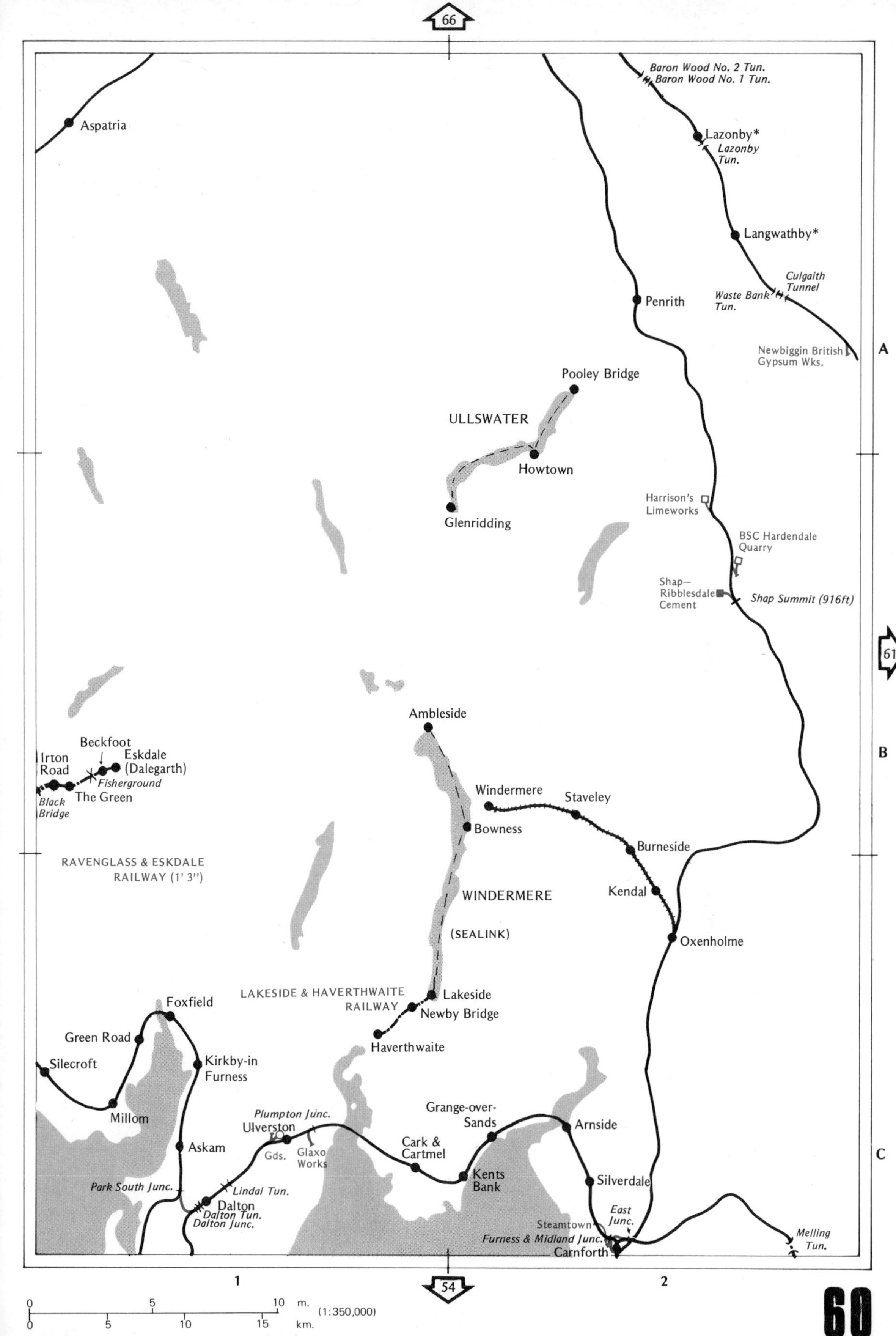

66
Aspatria
Baron Wood No. 2 Tun.
Baron Wood No. 1 Tun.
Lazonby*
Lazonby Tun.
Langwathby*
Culgaith Tunnel
Waste Bank Tun.
Penrith
Newbiggin British Gypsum Wks.
A
Pooley Bridge
ULLSWATER
Howtown
Glenridding
Harrison's Limeworks
BSC Hardendale Quarry
Shap—Ribblesdale Cement
Shap Summit (916ft)
61
Ambleside
B
Beckfoot
Irton Road
Eskdale (Dalegarth)
Fisherground
The Green
Black Bridge
Windermere
Staveley
Bowness
Burneside
RAVENGLASS & ESKDALE RAILWAY (1' 3")
Kendal
WINDERMERE
(SEALINK)
Oxenholme
LAKESIDE & HAVERTHWAITE RAILWAY
Lakeside
Newby Bridge
Haverthwaite
Foxfield
Green Road
Silecroft
Kirkby-in Furness
Millom
Plumpton Junc.
Ulverston
Gds.
Glaxo Works
Grange-over-Sands
Cark & Cartmel
Arnside
Askam
Kents Bank
Silverdale
C
Park South Junc.
Lindal Tun.
Dalton
Dalton Tun.
Dalton Junc.
East Junc.
Steamtown
Furness & Midland Junc.
Carnforth
Melling Tun.
1
54
2
0 5 10 m.
0 5 10 15 km.
(1:350,000)

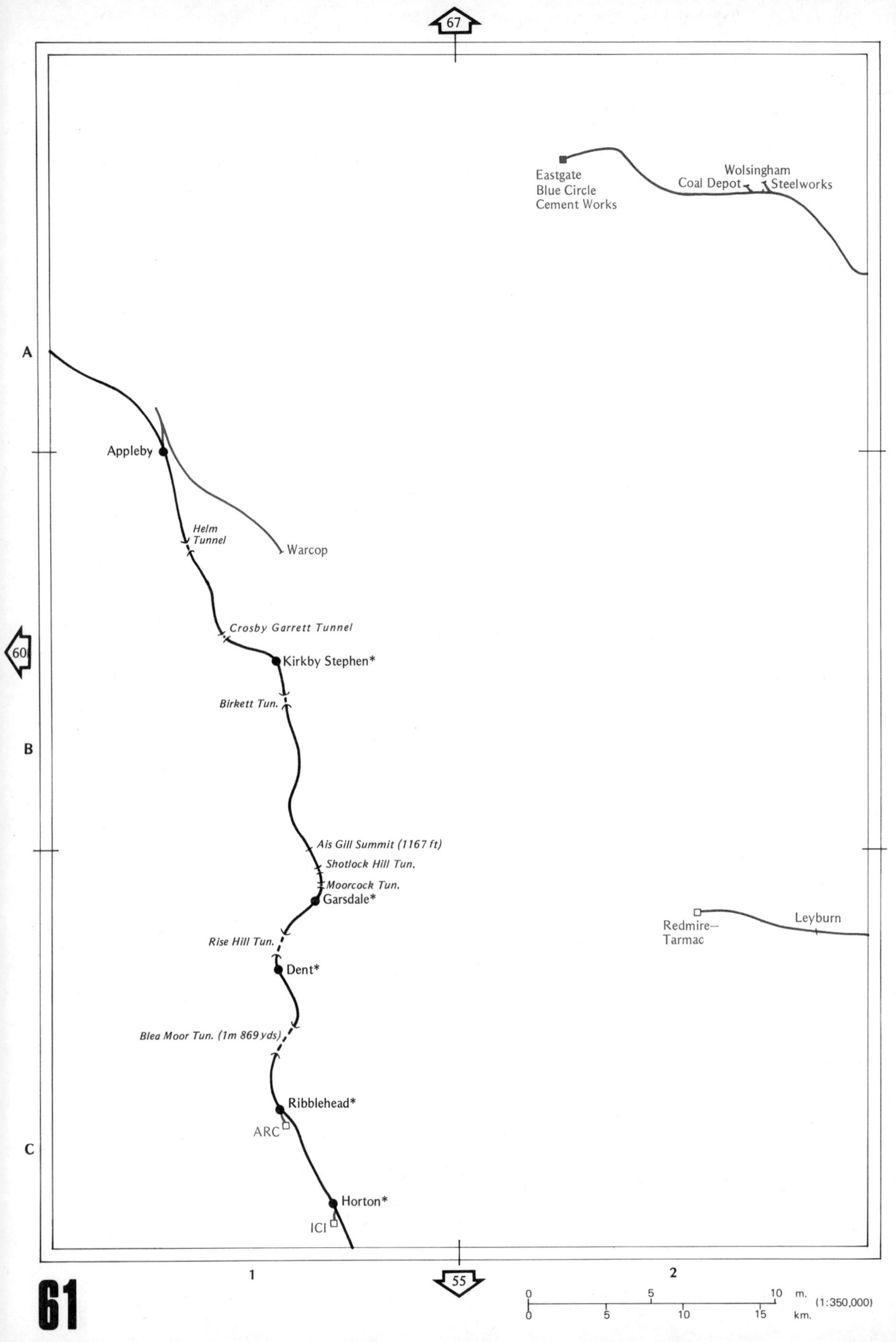
67
Eastgate
Blue Circle
Cement Works
Wolsingham
Coal Depot
Steelworks
A
Appleby
Helm
Tunnel
Warcop
Crosby Garrett Tunnel
60
Kirkby Stephen*
Birkett Tun.
B
Ais Gill Summit (1167 ft)
Shotlock Hill Tun.
Moorcock Tun.
Garsdale*
Redmire–
Tarmac
Leyburn
Rise Hill Tun.
Dent*
Blea Moor Tun. (1m 869 yds)
Ribblehead*
ARC
C
Horton*
ICI
1
55
2
0 5 10 m.
0 5 10 15 km.
(1:350,000)

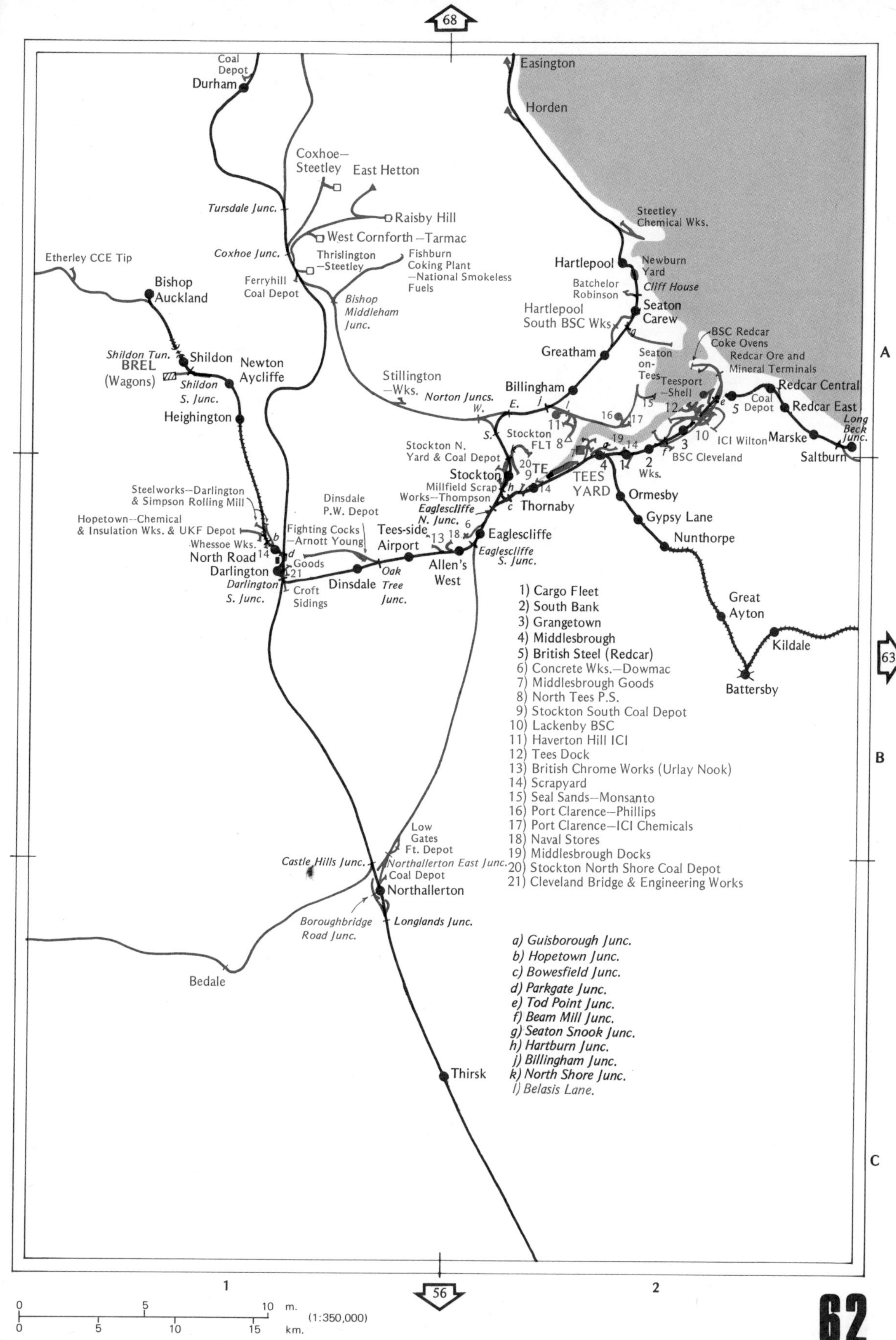
68
Coal Depot
Durham
Easington
Horden
Coxhoe—Steetley
East Hetton
Tursdale Junc.
Raisby Hill
West Cornforth—Tarmac
Coxhoe Junc.
Thrislington—Steetley
Fishburn Coking Plant—National Smokeless Fuels
Etherley CCE Tip
Bishop Auckland
Ferryhill Coal Depot
Bishop Middleham Junc.
Steetley Chemical Wks.
Hartlepool
Newburn Yard
Cliff House
Batchelor Robinson
Seaton Carew
Hartlepool South BSC Wks.
Greatham
Seaton on-Tees
BSC Redcar Coke Ovens
Redcar Ore and Mineral Terminals
Teesport—Shell
Redcar Central
Coal Depot
Redcar East
Long Beck Junc.
Marske
Saltburn
ICI Wilton
BSC Cleveland
Shildon Tun.
Shildon
BREL (Wagons)
Shildon S. Junc.
Newton Aycliffe
Heighington
Stillington—Wks.
Norton Juncs.
Billingham
Stockton FLT
Stockton N. Yard & Coal Depot
Stockton
Millfield Scrap Works—Thompson
TE
TEES YARD
Wks.
Ormesby
Gypsy Lane
Nunthorpe
Thornaby
Eaglescliffe N. Junc.
Eaglescliffe
Eaglescliffe S. Junc.
Steelworks—Darlington & Simpson Rolling Mill
Hopetown—Chemical & Insulation Wks. & UKF Depot
Whessoe Wks.
North Road
Darlington
Darlington S. Junc.
Goods
Croft Sidings
Dinsdale P.W. Depot
Fighting Cocks—Arnott Young
Tees-side Airport
Dinsdale
Oak Tree Junc.
Allen's West
Great Ayton
Kildale
Battersby
63
1) Cargo Fleet
2) South Bank
3) Grangetown
4) Middlesbrough
5) British Steel (Redcar)
6) Concrete Wks.—Dowmac
7) Middlesbrough Goods
8) North Tees P.S.
9) Stockton South Coal Depot
10) Lackenby BSC
11) Haverton Hill ICI
12) Tees Dock
13) British Chrome Works (Urlay Nook)
14) Scrapyard
15) Seal Sands—Monsanto
16) Port Clarence—Phillips
17) Port Clarence—ICI Chemicals
18) Naval Stores
19) Middlesbrough Docks
20) Stockton North Shore Coal Depot
21) Cleveland Bridge & Engineering Works
Low Gates Ft. Depot
Castle Hills Junc.
Northallerton East Junc.
Coal Depot
Northallerton
Boroughbridge Road Junc.
Longlands Junc.
Bedale
a) Guisborough Junc.
b) Hopetown Junc.
c) Bowesfield Junc.
d) Parkgate Junc.
e) Tod Point Junc.
f) Beam Mill Junc.
g) Seaton Snook Junc.
h) Hartburn Junc.
j) Billingham Junc.
k) North Shore Junc.
l) Belasis Lane.
Thirsk
A
B
C
1
2
56
0 5 10 m.
0 5 10 15 km.
(1:350,000)

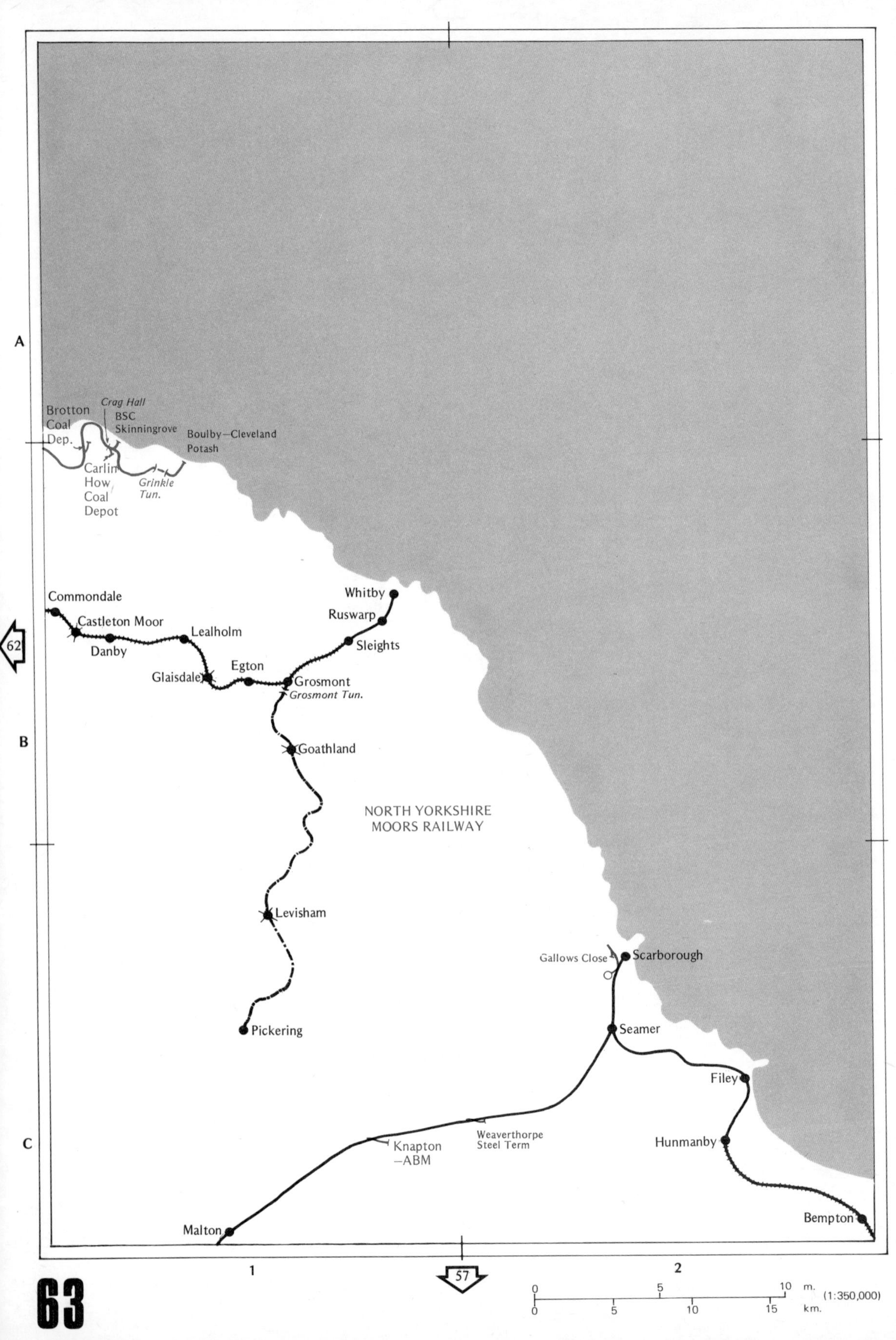
A
B
C
1
2
Brotton
Coal
Dep.
Crag Hall
BSC
Skinningrove
Boulby—Cleveland
Potash
Carlin
How
Coal
Depot
Grinkle
Tun.
Commondale
Castleton Moor
Danby
Lealholm
Glaisdale
Egton
Grosmont
Grosmont Tun.
Whitby
Ruswarp
Sleights
Goathland
NORTH YORKSHIRE
MOORS RAILWAY
Levisham
Pickering
Gallows Close
Scarborough
Seamer
Filey
Hunmanby
Bempton
Weaverthorpe
Steel Term
Knapton
—ABM
Malton
62
57
0 5 10 m.
0 5 10 15 km.
(1:350,000)

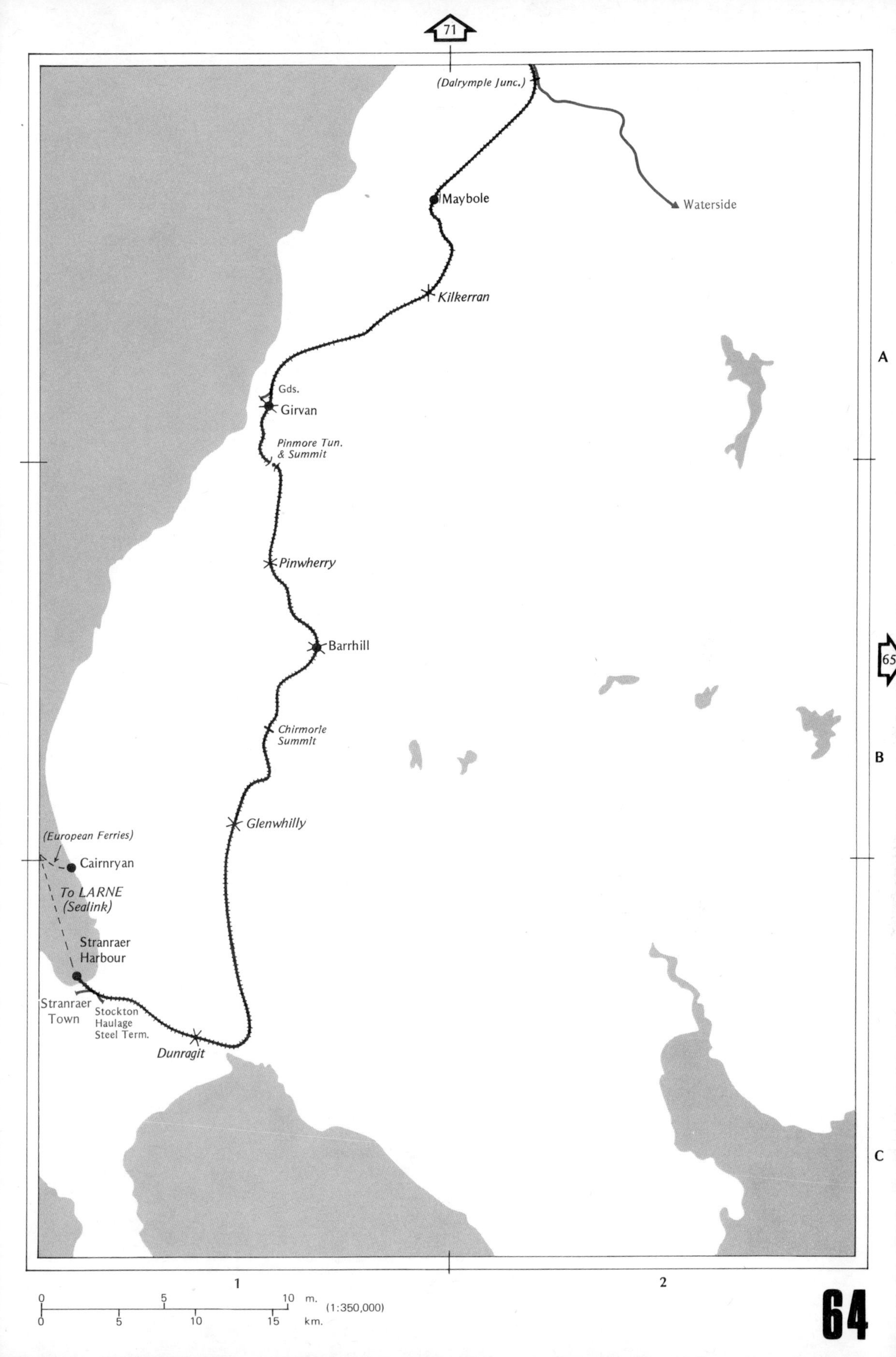
71
(Dalrymple Junc.)
Maybole
Waterside
Kilkerran
A
Gds.
Girvan
Pinmore Tun.
& Summit
Pinwherry
Barrhill
65
Chirmorle
Summit
B
Glenwhilly
(European Ferries)
Cairnryan
To LARNE
(Sealink)
Stranraer
Harbour
Stranraer
Town
Stockton
Haulage
Steel Term.
Dunragit
C
1
2
0
5
10
m.
(1:350,000)
0
5
10
15
km.

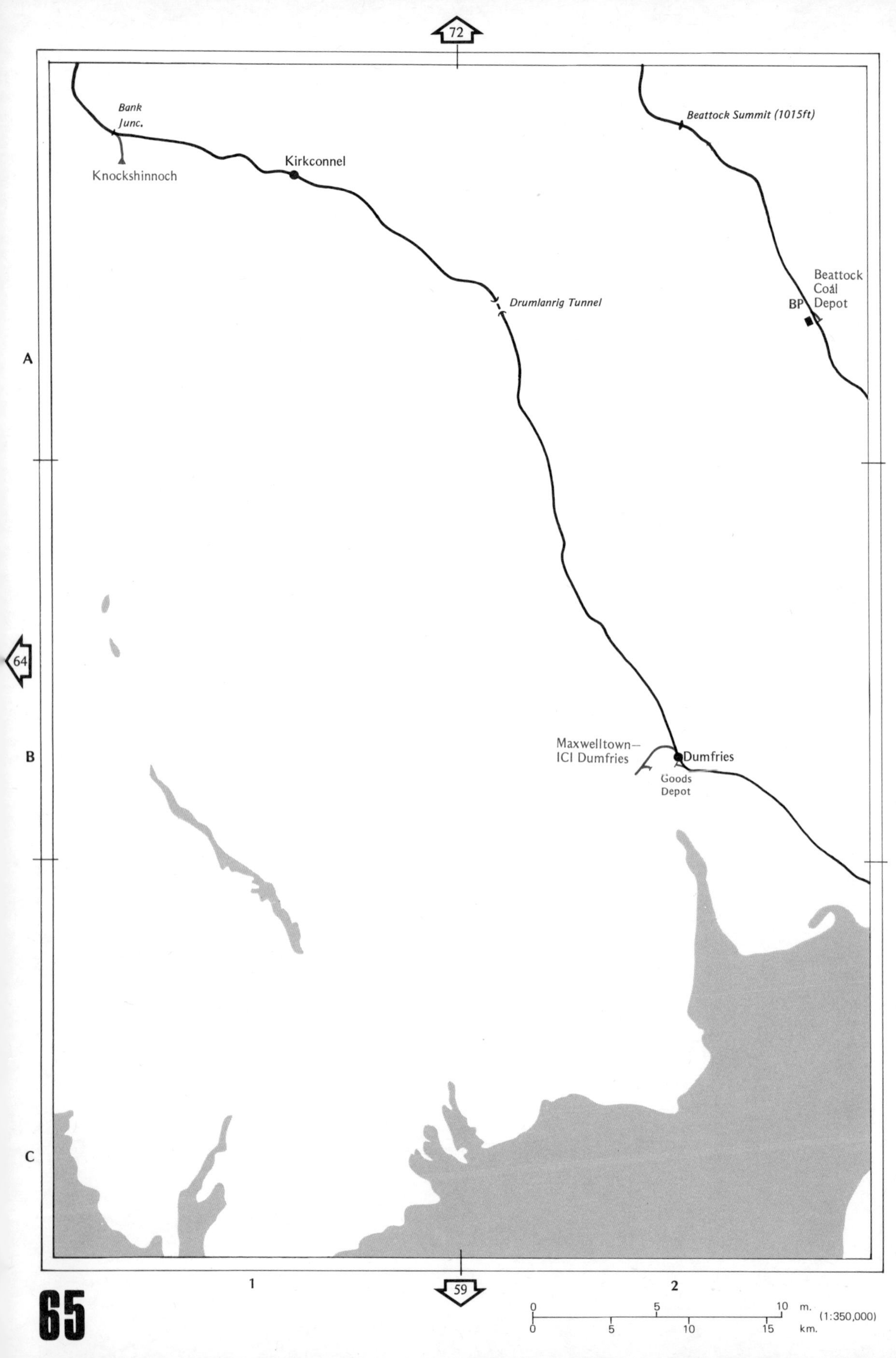
72
Bank
Junc.
Knockshinnoch
Kirkconnel
Beattock Summit (1015ft)
Drumlanrig Tunnel
Beattock
Coal
Depot
BP
A
64
B
Maxwelltown–
ICI Dumfries
Dumfries
Goods
Depot
C
1
59
2
0 5 10 m.
0 5 10 15 km.
(1:350,000)

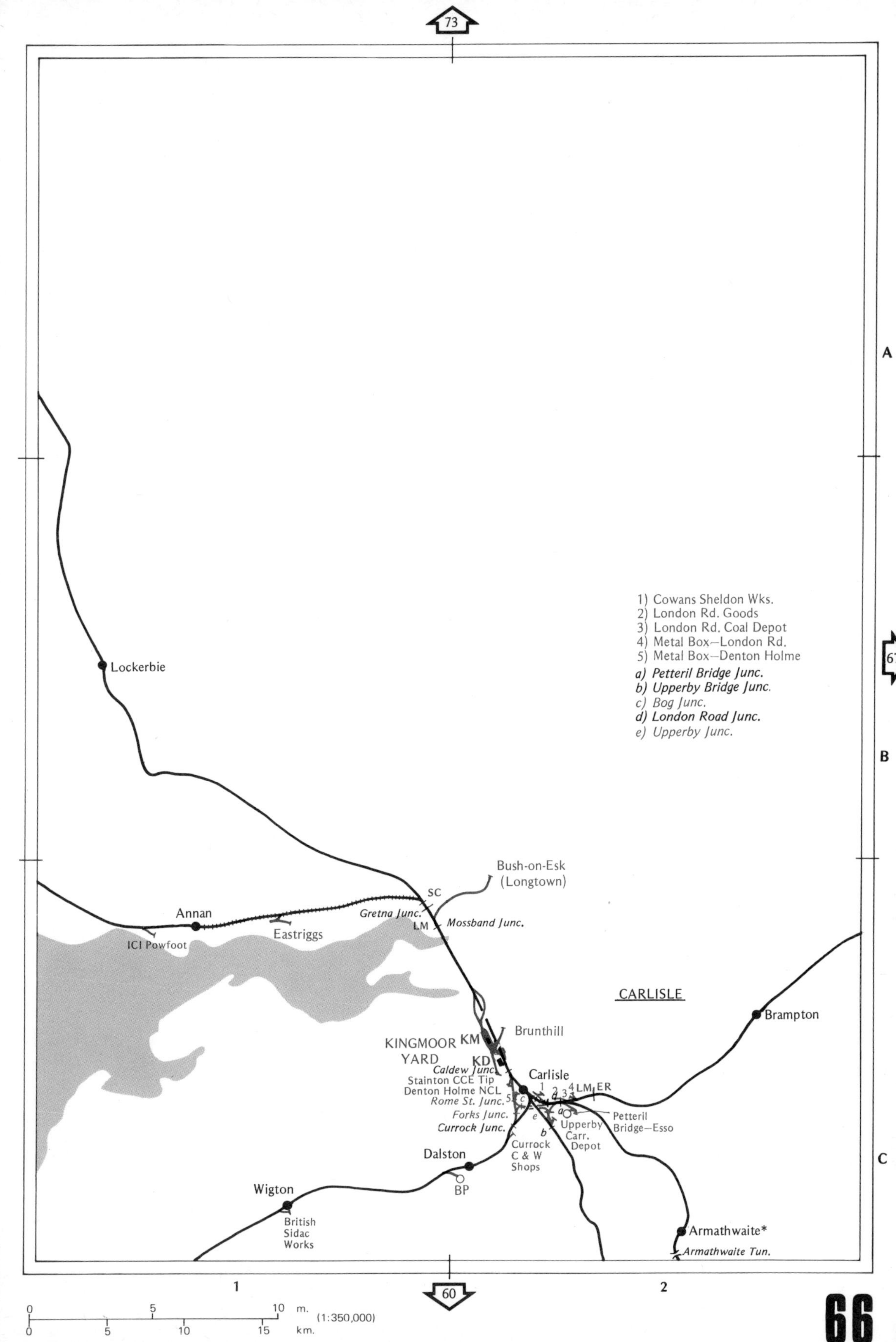
73
67
60
A
B
C
1
2
Lockerbie
Annan
ICI Powfoot
Eastriggs
Gretna Junc.
SC
LM
Mossband Junc.
Bush-on-Esk
(Longtown)
CARLISLE
Brampton
Brunthill
KINGMOOR
YARD
KM
KD
Caldew Junc.
Stainton CCE Tip
Denton Holme NCL
Rome St. Junc.
Forks Junc.
Currock Junc.
Carlisle
LM
ER
Petteril
Bridge–Esso
Upperby
Carr.
Depot
Currock
C & W
Shops
Dalston
BP
Wigton
British
Sidac
Works
Armathwaite*
Armathwaite Tun.
1) Cowans Sheldon Wks.
2) London Rd. Goods
3) London Rd. Coal Depot
4) Metal Box–London Rd.
5) Metal Box–Denton Holme
a) Petteril Bridge Junc.
b) Upperby Bridge Junc.
c) Bog Junc.
d) London Road Junc.
e) Upperby Junc.
0 5 10 m.
0 5 10 15 km.
(1:350,000)

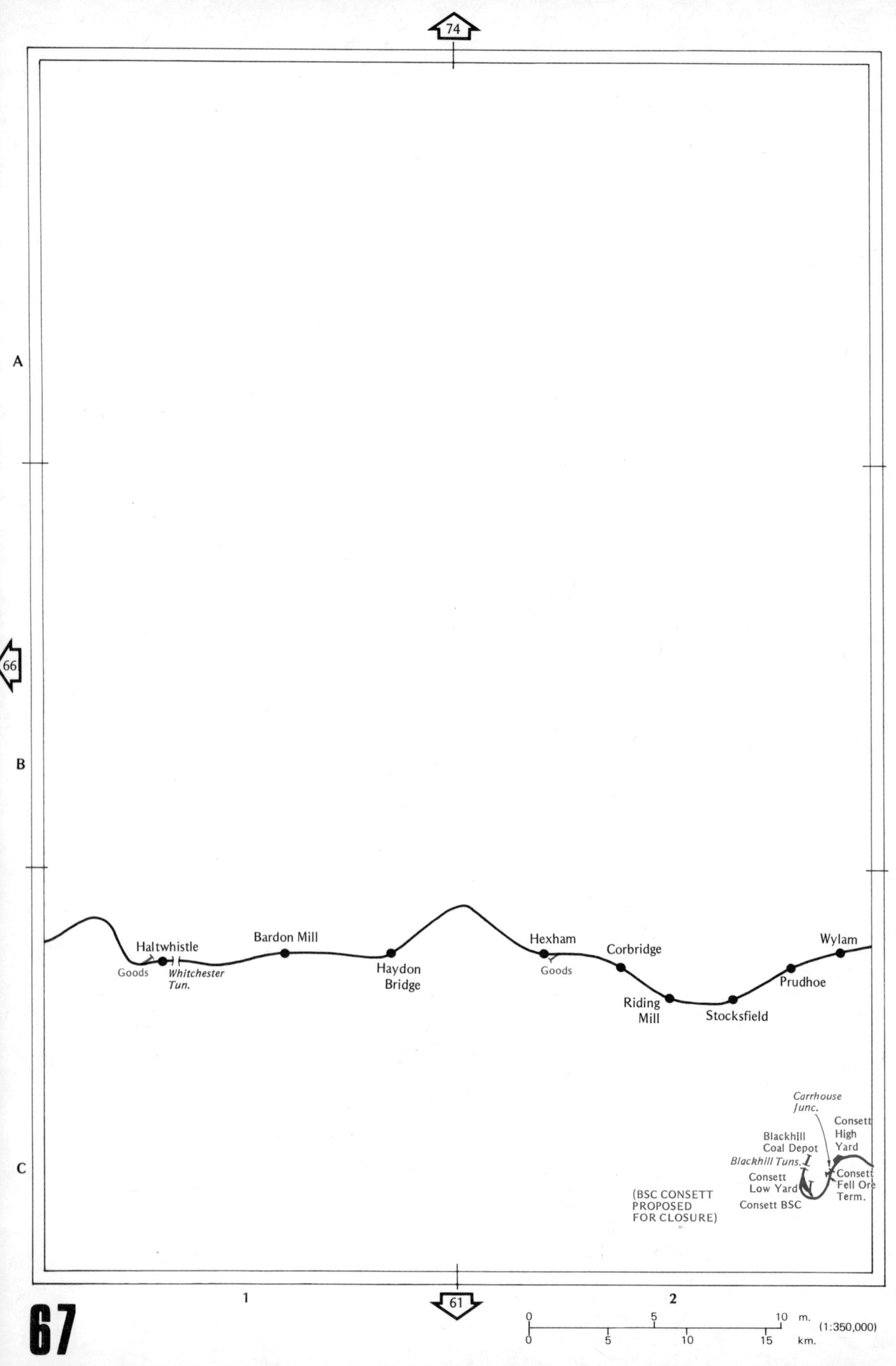
74
66
61
A
B
C
1
2
Haltwhistle
Goods
Whitchester Tun.
Bardon Mill
Haydon Bridge
Hexham
Goods
Corbridge
Riding Mill
Stocksfield
Prudhoe
Wylam
Carrhouse Junc.
Consett High Yard
Blackhill Coal Depot
Blackhill Tuns.
Consett Low Yard
Consett BSC
Consett Fell Ore Term.
(BSC CONSETT PROPOSED FOR CLOSURE)
0 5 10 m.
0 5 10 15 km.
(1:350,000)

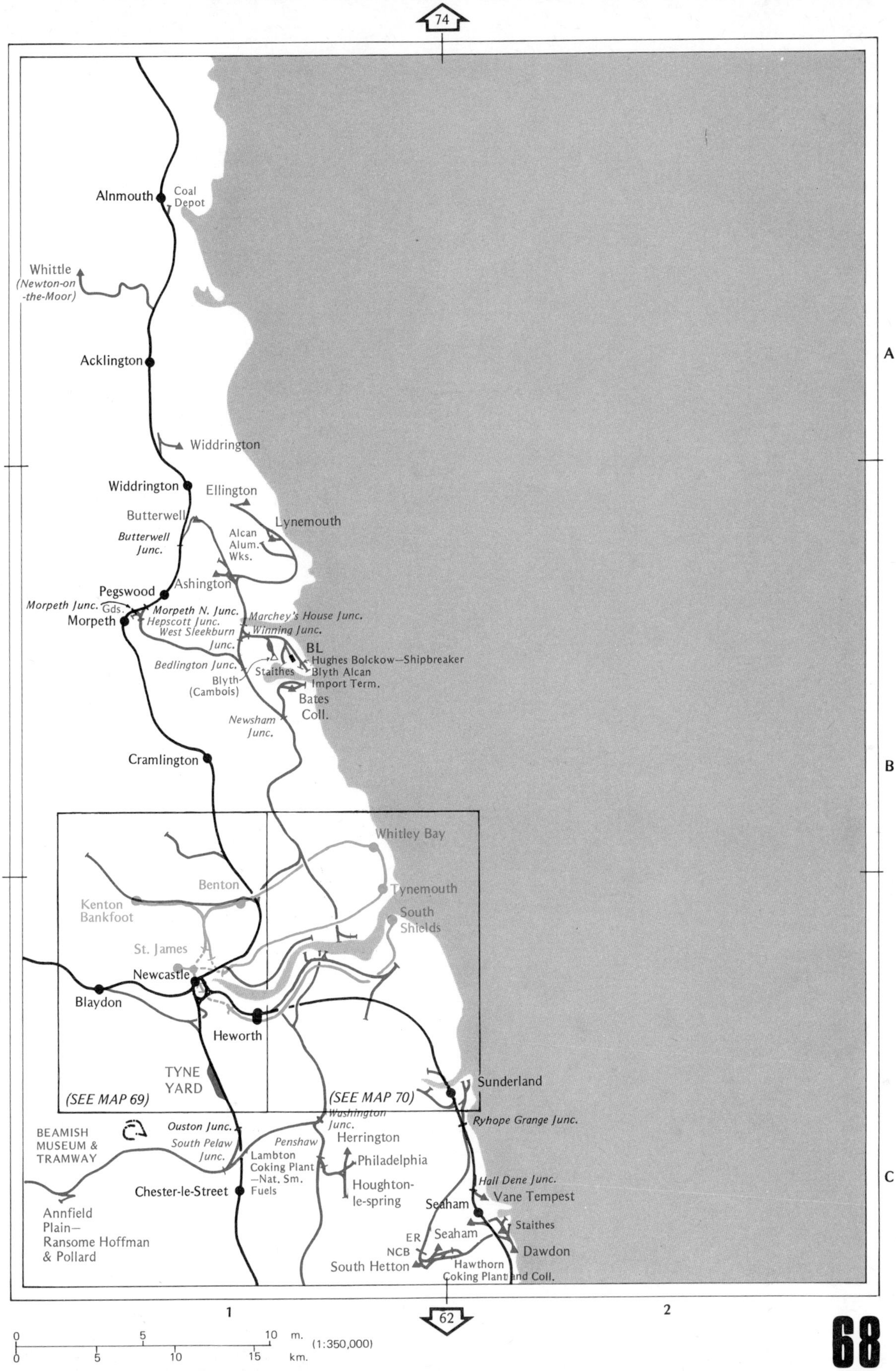

74

Alnmouth
Coal Depot
Whittle (Newton-on-the-Moor)
Acklington
Widdrington
Widdrington
Ellington
Butterwell
Lynemouth
Butterwell Junc.
Alcan Alum. Wks.
Ashington
Pegswood
Morpeth Junc.
Gds.
Morpeth N. Junc.
Morpeth
Hepscott Junc.
Marchey's House Junc.
West Sleekburn Junc.
Winning Junc.
BL
Hughes Bolckow—Shipbreaker
Bedlington Junc.
Staithes
Blyth Alcan Import Term.
Blyth (Cambois)
Bates Coll.
Newsham Junc.
Cramlington
Whitley Bay
Benton
Tynemouth
Kenton Bankfoot
South Shields
St. James
Newcastle
Blaydon
Heworth
TYNE YARD
Sunderland
(SEE MAP 69)
(SEE MAP 70)
Washington Junc.
Ryhope Grange Junc.
BEAMISH MUSEUM & TRAMWAY
Ouston Junc.
Herrington
South Pelaw Junc.
Penshaw
Lambton Coking Plant —Nat. Sm. Fuels
Philadelphia
Chester-le-Street
Houghton-le-spring
Hall Dene Junc.
Vane Tempest
Annfield Plain— Ransome Hoffman & Pollard
Seaham
Staithes
Seaham
ER
NCB
Dawdon
South Hetton
Hawthorn Coking Plant and Coll.

A
B
C
1
2

62

0 5 10 m. (1:350,000)
0 5 10 15 km.

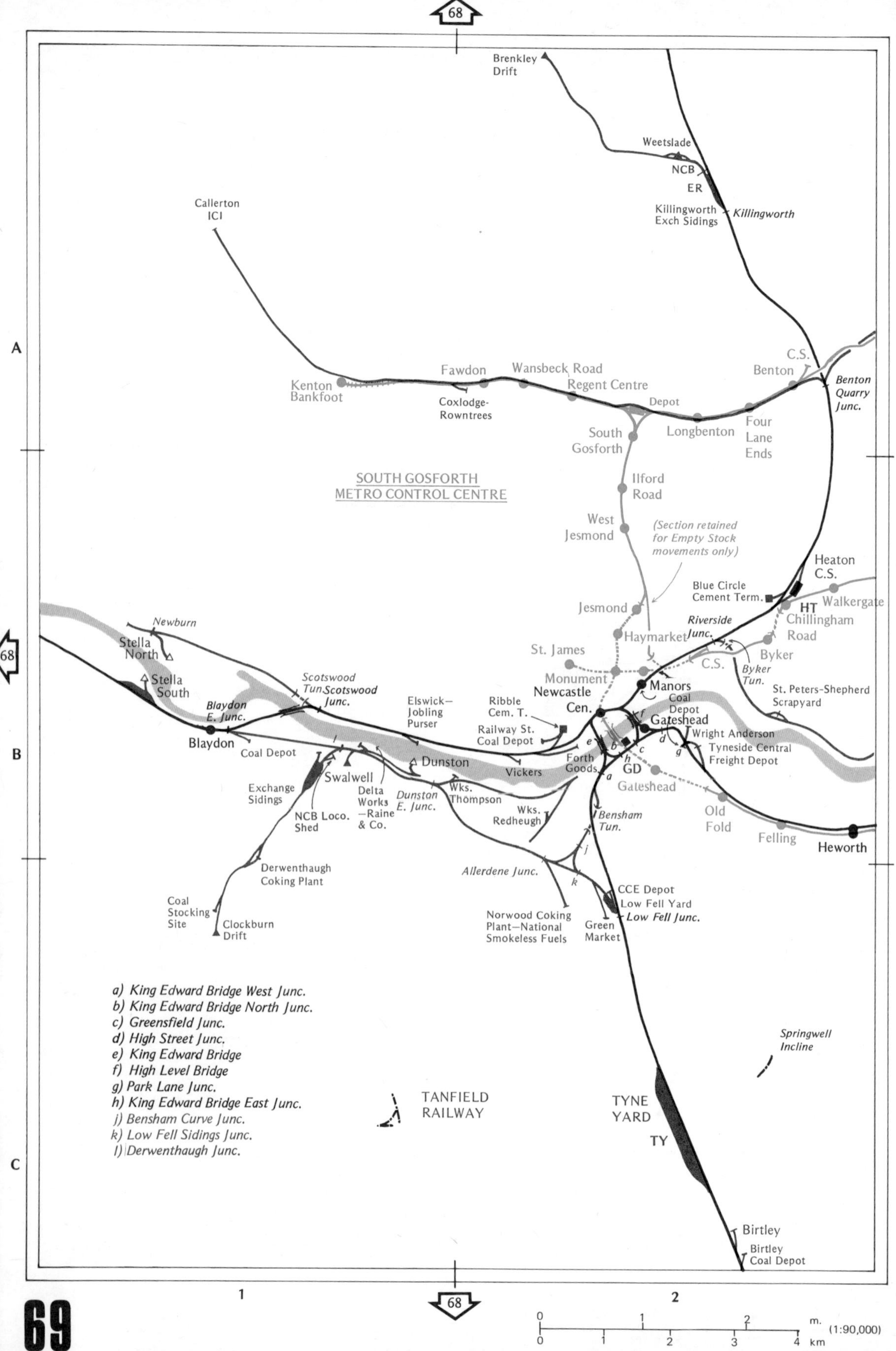

68
Brenkley Drift
Weetslade
NCB
ER
Killingworth Exch Sidings
Killingworth
Callerton ICI
A
Kenton Bankfoot
Fawdon
Coxlodge-Rowntrees
Wansbeck Road
Regent Centre
Depot
South Gosforth
Longbenton
Four Lane Ends
C.S.
Benton
Benton Quarry Junc.
SOUTH GOSFORTH METRO CONTROL CENTRE
Ilford Road
West Jesmond
(Section retained for Empty Stock movements only)
Heaton C.S.
Blue Circle Cement Term.
Walkergate
HT
Chillingham Road
Jesmond
Riverside Junc.
Haymarket
St. James
C.S.
Byker
Byker Tun.
Monument
Manors
St. Peters-Shepherd Scrapyard
Newburn
Stella North
Stella South
Scotswood Tun.
Scotswood Junc.
Blaydon E. Junc.
Blaydon
Coal Depot
Elswick—Jobling Purser
Ribble Cem. T.
Railway St. Coal Depot
Newcastle Cen.
Coal Depot
Gateshead
Wright Anderson
Tyneside Central Freight Depot
B
Swalwell
Dunston
Vickers
Forth Goods
GD
Gateshead
Exchange Sidings
NCB Loco. Shed
Delta Works —Raine & Co.
Dunston E. Junc.
Wks. Thompson
Wks. Redheugh
Bensham Tun.
Old Fold
Felling
Heworth
Derwenthaugh Coking Plant
Allerdene Junc.
CCE Depot
Low Fell Yard
Low Fell Junc.
Coal Stocking Site
Clockburn Drift
Norwood Coking Plant—National Smokeless Fuels
Green Market
a) King Edward Bridge West Junc.
b) King Edward Bridge North Junc.
c) Greensfield Junc.
d) High Street Junc.
e) King Edward Bridge
f) High Level Bridge
g) Park Lane Junc.
h) King Edward Bridge East Junc.
j) Bensham Curve Junc.
k) Low Fell Sidings Junc.
l) Derwenthaugh Junc.
TANFIELD RAILWAY
TYNE YARD
TY
Springwell Incline
C
Birtley
Birtley Coal Depot
1
2
0 1 2 m.
0 1 2 3 4 km
(1:90,000)

68
Holywell Junc. 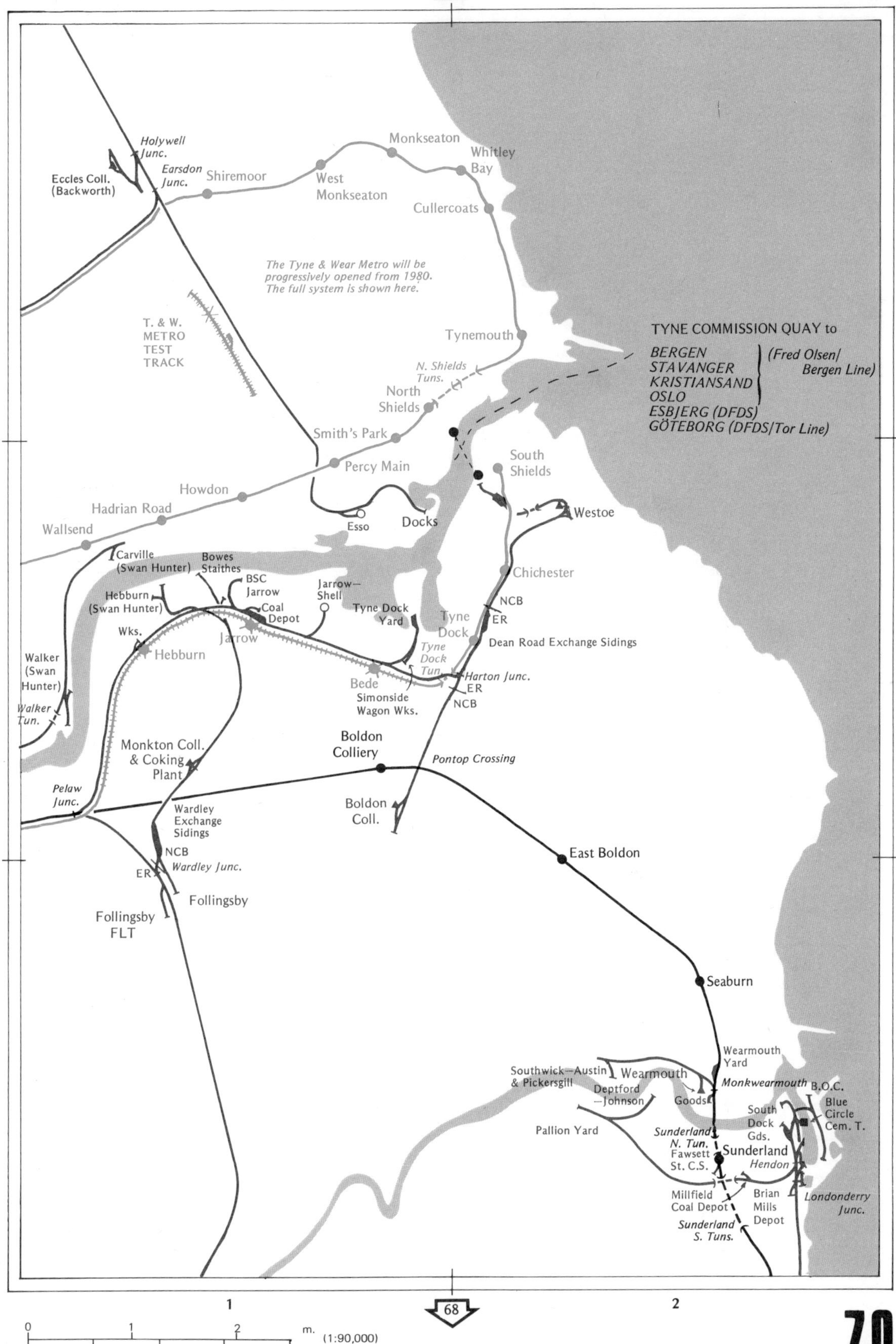
Eccles Coll. (Backworth)
Earsdon Junc.
Shiremoor
West Monkseaton
Monkseaton
Whitley Bay
Cullercoats
The Tyne & Wear Metro will be progressively opened from 1980. The full system is shown here.
T. & W. METRO TEST TRACK
Tynemouth
TYNE COMMISSION QUAY to
BERGEN
STAVANGER
KRISTIANSAND
OSLO
(Fred Olsen/ Bergen Line)
ESBJERG (DFDS)
GÖTEBORG (DFDS/Tor Line)
A
N. Shields Tuns.
North Shields
Smith's Park
Percy Main
South Shields
Howdon
Hadrian Road
Wallsend
Esso
Docks
Westoe
Carville (Swan Hunter)
Bowes Staithes
BSC Jarrow
Chichester
Hebburn (Swan Hunter)
Coal Depot
Jarrow—Shell
Tyne Dock Yard
Tyne Dock
NCB
ER
Wks.
Jarrow
Hebburn
Dean Road Exchange Sidings
68
Walker (Swan Hunter)
Walker Tun.
Tyne Dock Tun.
Harton Junc.
ER
NCB
Bede
Simonside Wagon Wks.
Monkton Coll. & Coking Plant
Boldon Colliery
Pontop Crossing
B
Pelaw Junc.
Wardley Exchange Sidings
Boldon Coll.
NCB
Wardley Junc.
ER
East Boldon
Follingsby
Follingsby FLT
Seaburn
Wearmouth Yard
Southwick—Austin & Pickersgill
Wearmouth
Monkwearmouth
B.O.C.
Deptford —Johnson
Goods
South Dock Gds.
Blue Circle Cem. T.
Pallion Yard
Sunderland N. Tun.
Fawsett St. C.S.
Sunderland
Hendon
C
Millfield Coal Depot
Brian Mills Depot
Londonderry Junc.
Sunderland S. Tuns.
1
68
2
0 1 2 m.
0 1 2 3 4 km
(1:90,000)

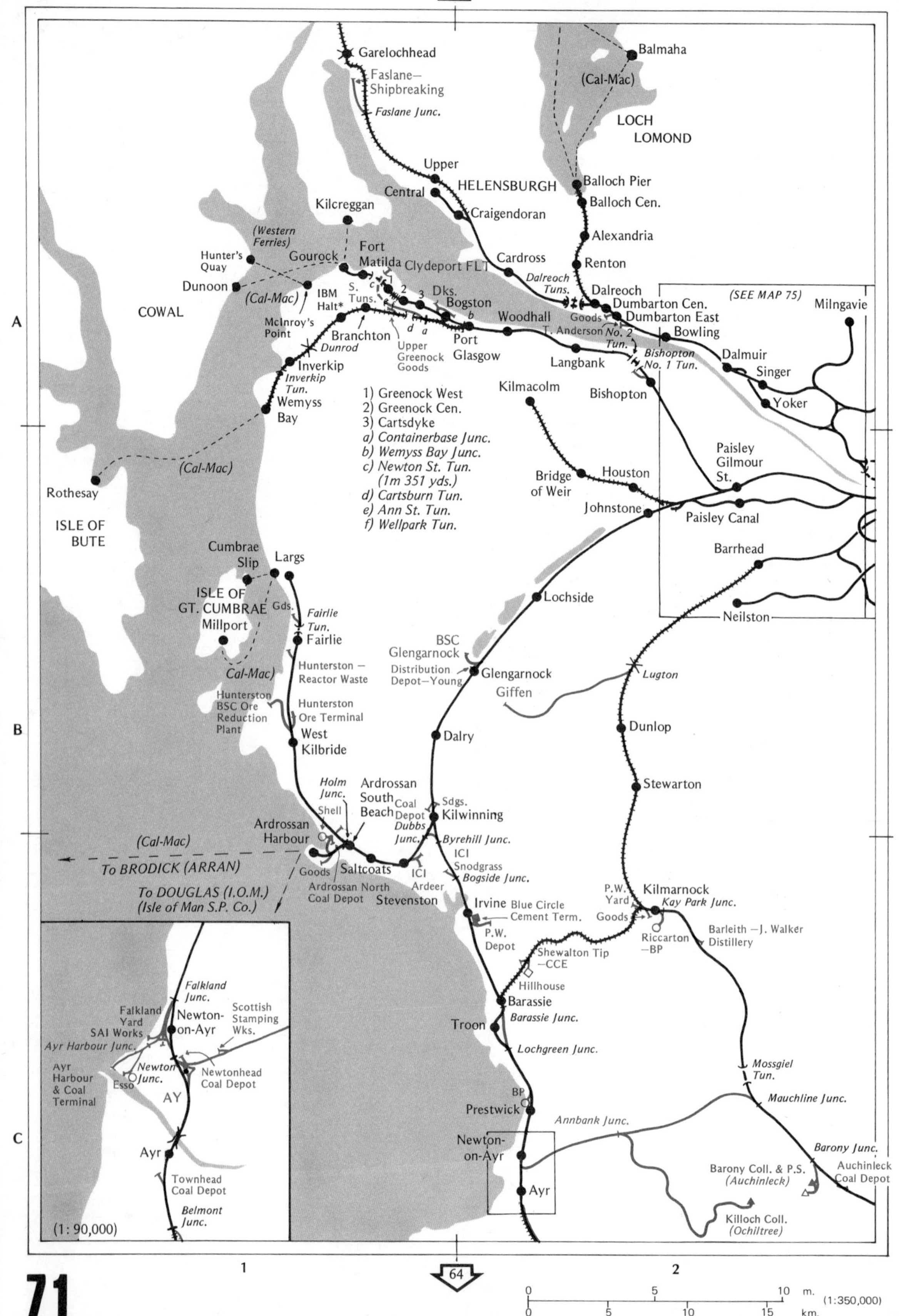

78
Garelochhead
Faslane—
Shipbreaking
Faslane Junc.
Balmaha
(Cal-Mac)
LOCH
LOMOND
Upper
Central
HELENSBURGH
Craigendoran
Balloch Pier
Balloch Cen.
Alexandria
Renton
Kilcreggan
(Western
Ferries)
Hunter's
Quay
Dunoon
Gourock
Fort
Matilda
Clydeport FLT
Cardross
Dalreoch
Tuns.
Dalreoch
Dumbarton Cen.
Dumbarton East
COWAL
(Cal-Mac)
IBM
Halt*
S.
Tuns.
Dks.
Bogston
Woodhall
Goods
T. Anderson
No. 2
Tun.
(SEE MAP 75)
Milngavie
Bowling
McInroy's
Point
Branchton
Dunrod
Upper
Greenock
Goods
Port
Glasgow
Langbank
Bishopton
No. 1 Tun.
Dalmuir
Singer
Yoker
Inverkip
Inverkip
Tun.
Wemyss
Bay
Kilmacolm
Bishopton
1) Greenock West
2) Greenock Cen.
3) Cartsdyke
a) Containerbase Junc.
b) Wemyss Bay Junc.
c) Newton St. Tun.
(1m 351 yds.)
d) Cartsburn Tun.
e) Ann St. Tun.
f) Wellpark Tun.
Paisley
Gilmour
St.
(Cal-Mac)
Rothesay
Bridge
of Weir
Houston
Johnstone
Paisley Canal
ISLE OF
BUTE
Cumbrae
Slip
Largs
ISLE OF
GT. CUMBRAE
Millport
Gds.
Fairlie
Tun.
Fairlie
Barrhead
Lochside
Neilston
Cal-Mac)
Hunterston —
Reactor Waste
BSC
Glengarnock
Distribution
Depot—Young
Glengarnock
Giffen
Lugton
Hunterston
BSC Ore
Reduction
Plant
Hunterston
Ore Terminal
West
Kilbride
Dalry
Dunlop
Holm
Junc.
Shell
Ardrossan
South
Beach
Coal
Depot
Dubbs
Junc.
Sdgs.
Kilwinning
Stewarton
Ardrossan
Harbour
(Cal-Mac)
To BRODICK (ARRAN)
Byrehill Junc.
ICI
Snodgrass
Bogside Junc.
Goods
Saltcoats
ICI
Ardeer
Ardrossan North
Coal Depot
Stevenston
To DOUGLAS (I.O.M.)
(Isle of Man S.P. Co.)
Irvine
Blue Circle
Cement Term.
P.W.
Depot
P.W.
Yard
Goods
Kilmarnock
Kay Park Junc.
Riccarton
—BP
Barleith —J. Walker
Distillery
Shewalton Tip
—CCE
Hillhouse
Barassie
Barassie Junc.
Troon
Lochgreen Junc.
Mossgiel
Tun.
Mauchline Junc.
Falkland
Junc.
Falkland
Yard
SAI Works
Newton-
on-Ayr
Scottish
Stamping
Wks.
Ayr Harbour Junc.
Ayr
Harbour
& Coal
Terminal
Esso
Newton
Junc.
Newtonhead
Coal Depot
AY
Ayr
Townhead
Coal Depot
Belmont
Junc.
(1: 90,000)
BP
Prestwick
Annbank Junc.
Newton-
on-Ayr
Ayr
Barony Junc.
Barony Coll. & P.S.
(Auchinleck)
Auchinleck
Coal Depot
Killoch Coll.
(Ochiltree)
A
B
C
1
2
64
0 5 10 m.
0 5 10 15 km.
(1:350,000)

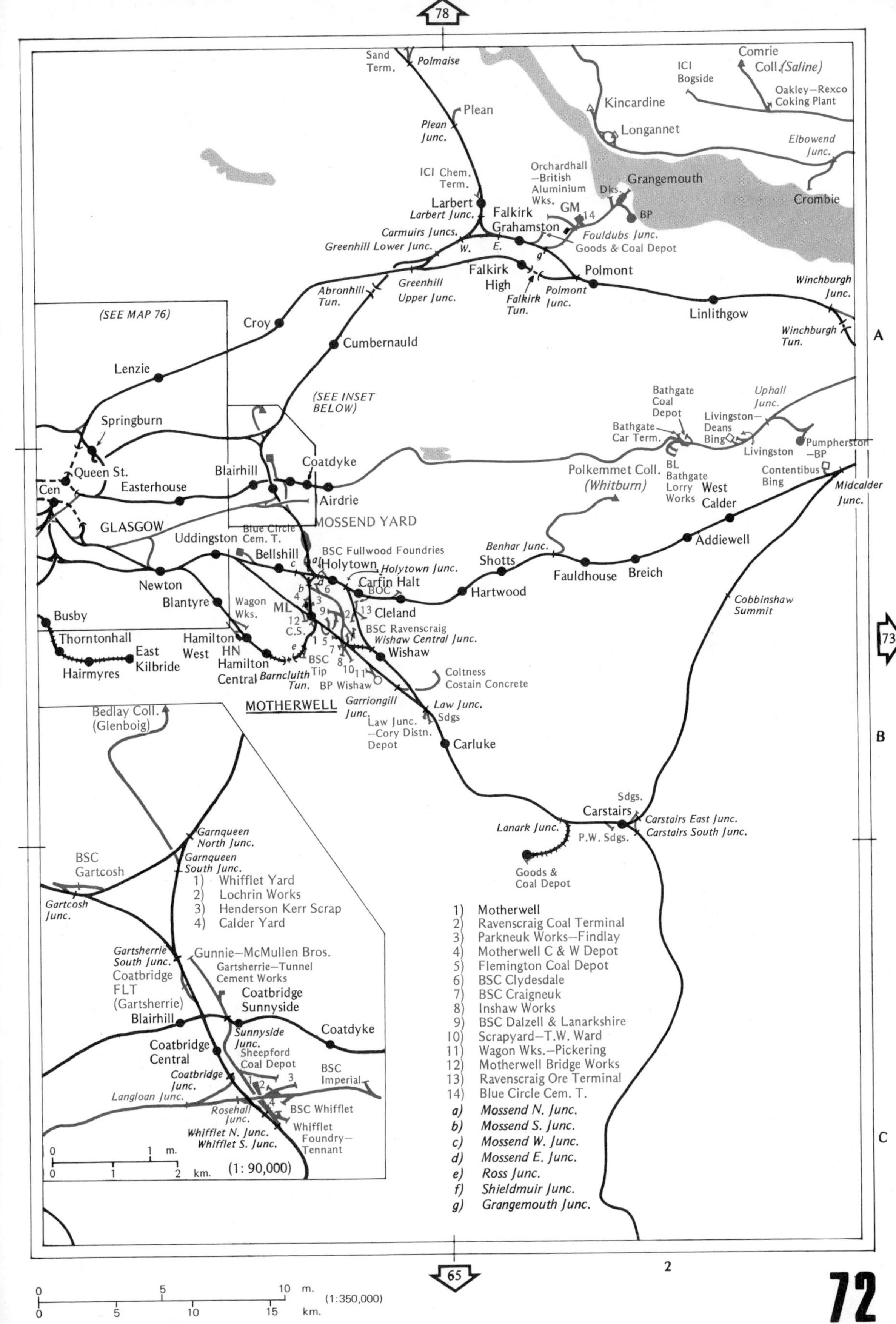

78
Sand Term.
Polmaise
Plean
Plean Junc.
ICI Chem. Term.
Larbert
Larbert Junc.
Carmuirs Juncs.
Greenhill Lower Junc.
Falkirk Grahamston
Falkirk High
Falkirk Tun.
Polmont Junc.
Polmont
Greenhill Upper Junc.
Abronhill Tun.
Croy
Cumbernauld
Lenzie
Springburn
Queen St.
Cen
Easterhouse
GLASGOW
Blairhill
Coatdyke
Airdrie
MOSSEND YARD
Uddingston
Blue Circle Cem. T.
Bellshill
BSC Fullwood Foundries
Holytown
Holytown Junc.
Carfin Halt
BOC
Cleland
BSC Ravenscraig
Wishaw Central Junc.
Wishaw
Newton
Blantyre
Wagon Wks.
ML
C.S.
Hamilton West
HN
Hamilton Central
Barncluith Tun.
BSC Tip
BP Wishaw
MOTHERWELL
Garriongill Junc.
Law Junc.
Sdgs
Law Junc. —Cory Distn. Depot
Coltness Costain Concrete
Carluke
Busby
Thorntonhall
Hairmyres
East Kilbride
(SEE MAP 76)
(SEE INSET BELOW)
Kincardine
Longannet
ICI Bogside
Comrie Coll. (Saline)
Oakley—Rexco Coking Plant
Elbowend Junc.
Crombie
Orchardhall —British Aluminium Wks.
GM
Dks.
Grangemouth
BP
Fouldubs Junc.
Goods & Coal Depot
Winchburgh Junc.
Winchburgh Tun.
Linlithgow
Bathgate Coal Depot
Bathgate Car Term.
Uphall Junc.
Livingston—Deans Bing
Livingston
Pumpherston —BP
Contentibus Bing
Polkemmet Coll. (Whitburn)
BL Bathgate Lorry Works
West Calder
Midcalder Junc.
Addiewell
Breich
Fauldhouse
Benhar Junc.
Shotts
Hartwood
Cobbinshaw Summit
73
Sdgs.
Carstairs
Carstairs East Junc.
Carstairs South Junc.
Lanark Junc.
P.W. Sdgs.
Goods & Coal Depot
A
B
C
Bedlay Coll. (Glenboig)
BSC Gartcosh
Gartcosh Junc.
Garnqueen North Junc.
Garnqueen South Junc.
1) Whifflet Yard
2) Lochrin Works
3) Henderson Kerr Scrap
4) Calder Yard
Gartsherrie South Junc.
Gunnie—McMullen Bros.
Gartsherrie—Tunnel Cement Works
Coatbridge FLT (Gartsherrie)
Coatbridge Sunnyside
Blairhill
Coatdyke
Sunnyside Junc.
Sheepford Coal Depot
Coatbridge Central
Coatbridge Junc.
BSC Imperial
Langloan Junc.
Rosehall Junc.
BSC Whifflet
Whifflet N. Junc.
Whifflet S. Junc.
Whifflet Foundry—Tennant
0 1 m.
0 1 2 km.
(1: 90,000)
1) Motherwell
2) Ravenscraig Coal Terminal
3) Parkneuk Works—Findlay
4) Motherwell C & W Depot
5) Flemington Coal Depot
6) BSC Clydesdale
7) BSC Craigneuk
8) Inshaw Works
9) BSC Dalzell & Lanarkshire
10) Scrapyard—T.W. Ward
11) Wagon Wks.—Pickering
12) Motherwell Bridge Works
13) Ravenscraig Ore Terminal
14) Blue Circle Cem. T.
a) Mossend N. Junc.
b) Mossend S. Junc.
c) Mossend W. Junc.
d) Mossend E. Junc.
e) Ross Junc.
f) Shieldmuir Junc.
g) Grangemouth Junc.
65
2
0 5 10 m.
0 5 10 15 km.
(1:350,000)

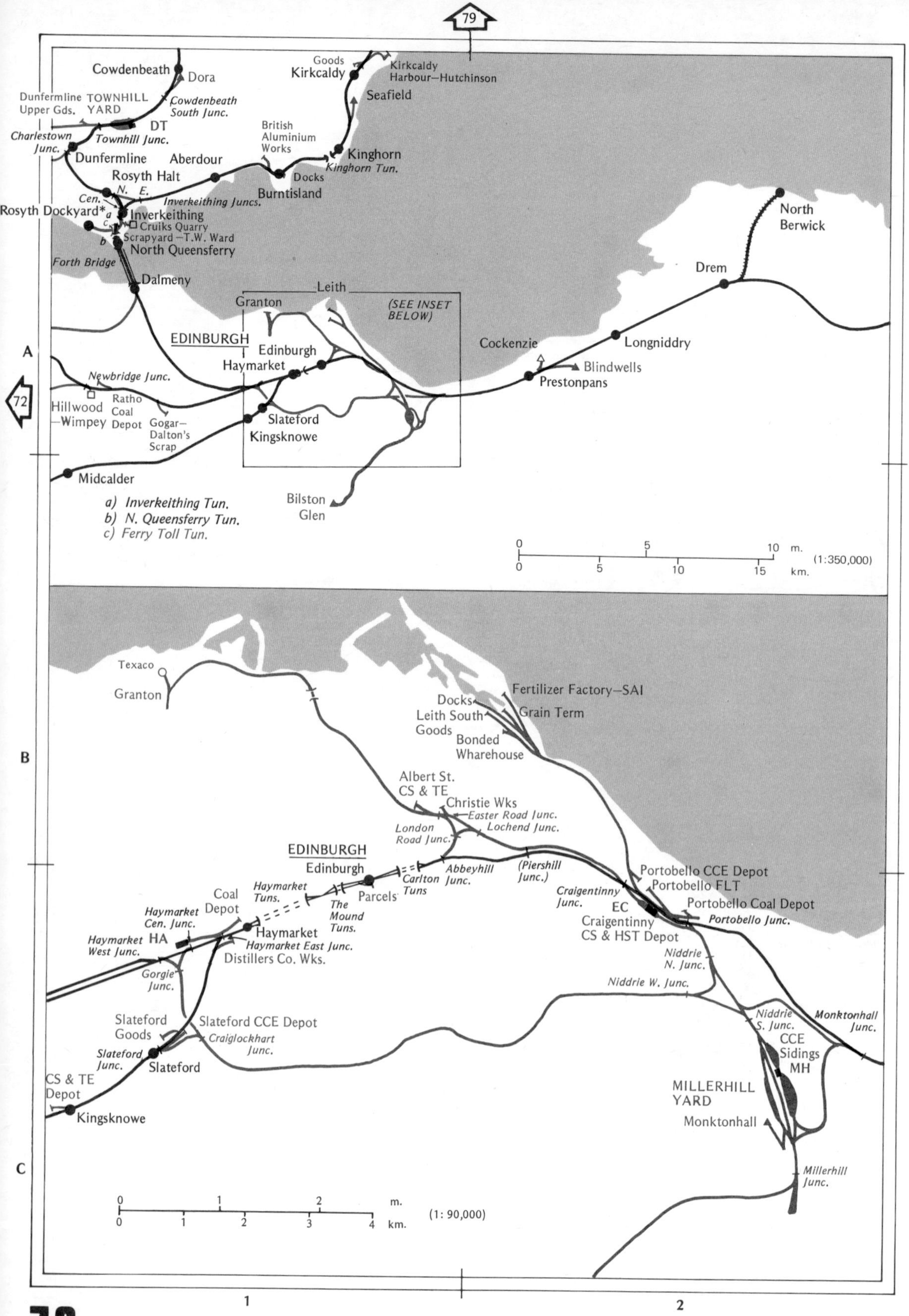
79
72
Cowdenbeath
Dora
Dunfermline Upper Gds.
TOWNHILL YARD
Cowdenbeath South Junc.
DT
Charlestown Junc.
Townhill Junc.
Dunfermline
Goods
Kirkcaldy
Kirkcaldy Harbour—Hutchinson
Seafield
British Aluminium Works
Kinghorn
Kinghorn Tun.
Aberdour
Docks
Burntisland
Rosyth Halt
Cen.
N.
E.
Inverkeithing Juncs.
Rosyth Dockyard*
Inverkeithing
Cruiks Quarry
Scrapyard—T.W. Ward
North Queensferry
Forth Bridge
Dalmeny
North Berwick
Drem
Leith
Granton
(SEE INSET BELOW)
EDINBURGH
Edinburgh
Haymarket
Cockenzie
Longniddry
Blindwells
Prestonpans
Newbridge Junc.
Hillwood—Wimpey
Ratho Coal Depot
Gogar—Dalton's Scrap
Slateford
Kingsknowe
Midcalder
Bilston Glen
a) Inverkeithing Tun.
b) N. Queensferry Tun.
c) Ferry Toll Tun.
0 5 10 m.
0 5 10 15 km.
(1:350,000)
Texaco
Granton
Fertilizer Factory—SAI
Docks
Leith South Goods
Grain Term
Bonded Wharehouse
Albert St. CS & TE
Christie Wks
Easter Road Junc.
Lochend Junc.
London Road Junc.
EDINBURGH
Edinburgh
Parcels
Carlton Tuns
Abbeyhill Junc.
(Piershill Junc.)
Haymarket Tuns.
The Mound Tuns.
Coal Depot
Haymarket Cen. Junc.
Haymarket West Junc.
HA
Haymarket
Haymarket East Junc.
Distillers Co. Wks.
Gorgie Junc.
Portobello CCE Depot
Portobello FLT
Portobello Coal Depot
Portobello Junc.
Craigentinny Junc.
EC
Craigentinny CS & HST Depot
Niddrie N. Junc.
Niddrie W. Junc.
Niddrie S. Junc.
Monktonhall Junc.
CCE Sidings
MH
MILLERHILL YARD
Monktonhall
Millerhill Junc.
Slateford Goods
Slateford CCE Depot
Craiglockhart Junc.
Slateford Junc.
Slateford
CS & TE Depot
Kingsknowe
0 1 2 m.
0 1 2 3 4 km.
(1: 90,000)

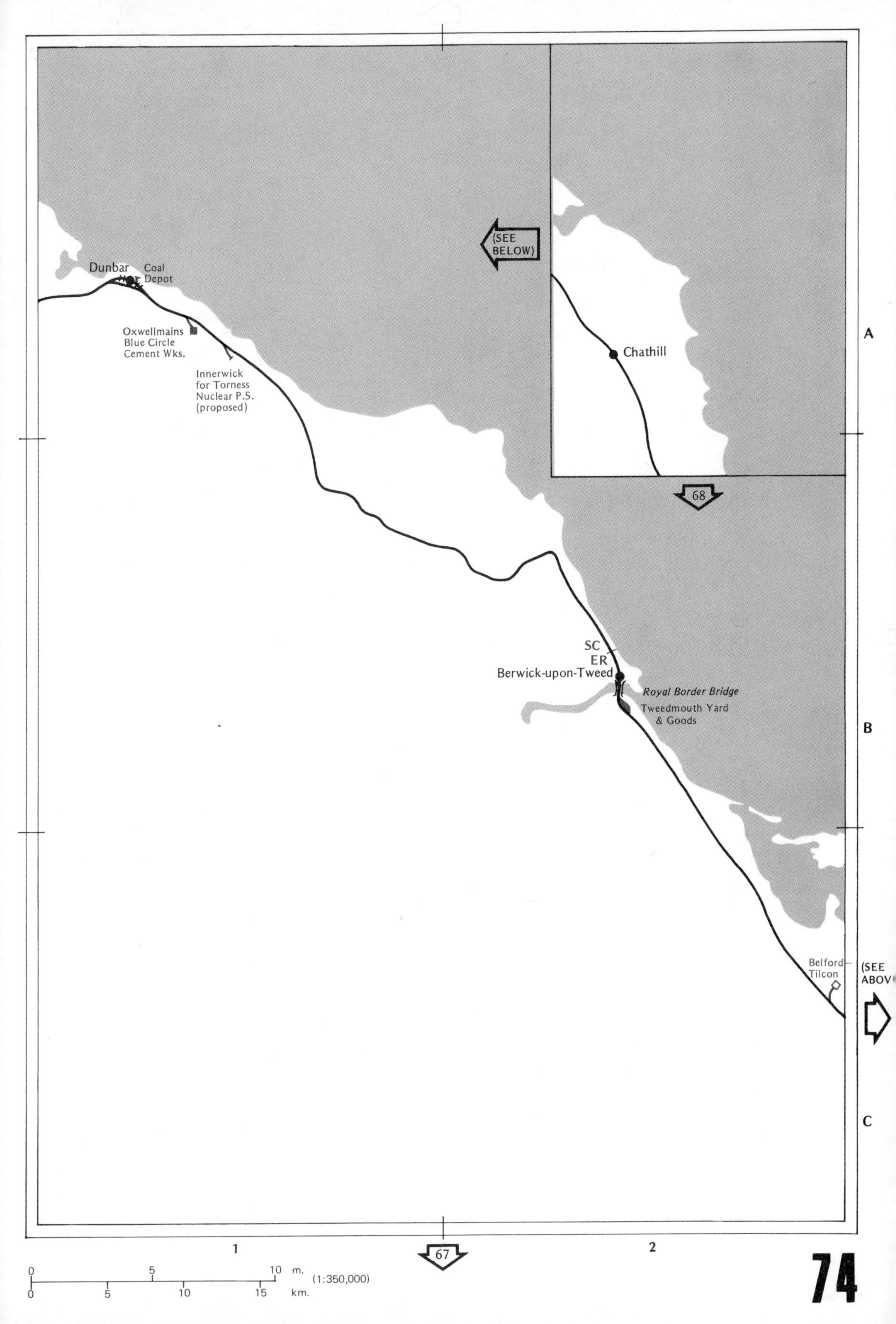

(SEE
BELOW)
Dunbar
Coal
Depot
Oxwellmains
Blue Circle
Cement Wks.
Innerwick
for Torness
Nuclear P.S.
(proposed)
Chathill
68
A
SC
ER
Berwick-upon-Tweed
Royal Border Bridge
Tweedmouth Yard
& Goods
B
Belford
Tilcon
(SEE
ABOV
C
1
2
67
0
5
10
m.
(1:350,000)
0
5
10
15
km.

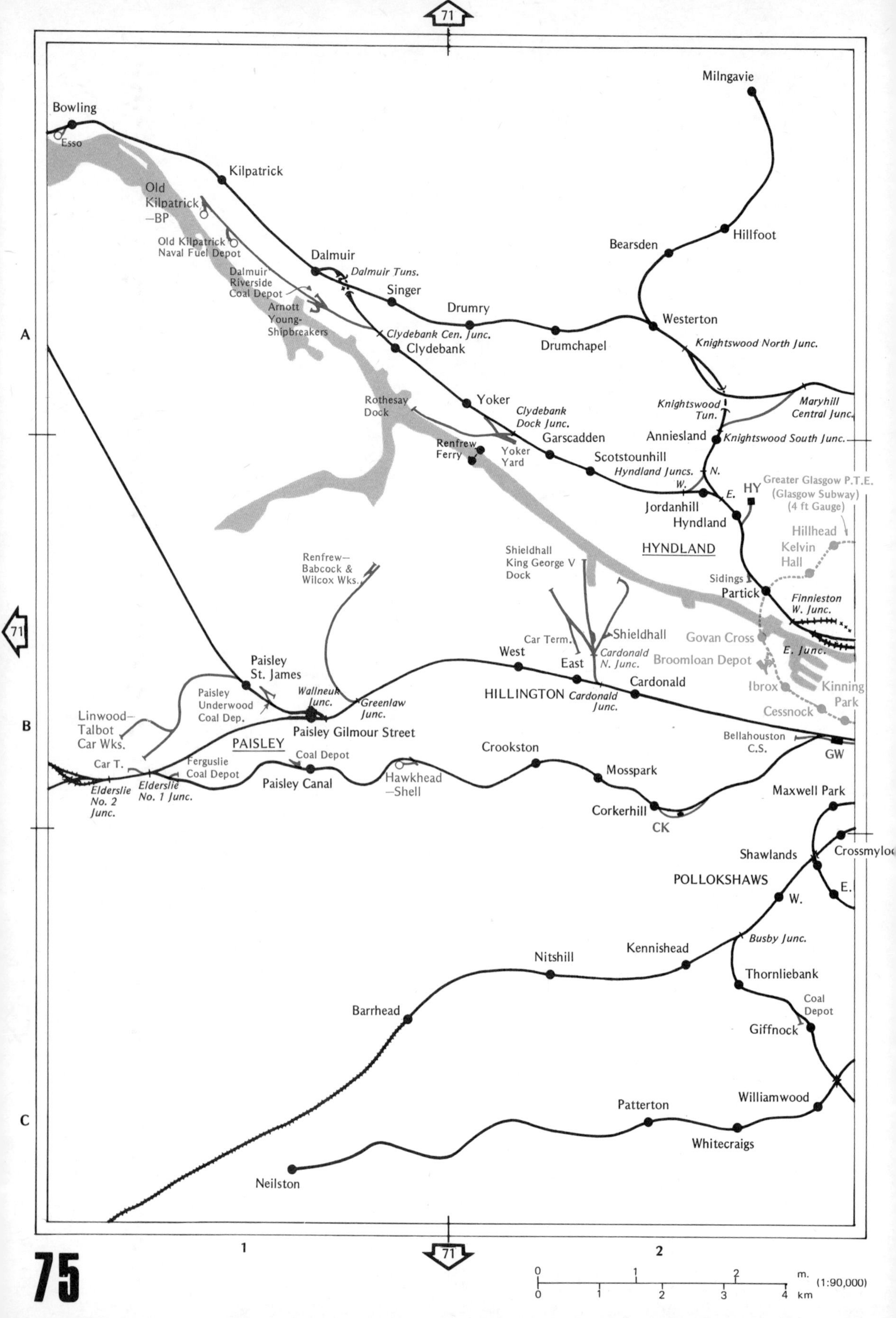
71
Milngavie
Bowling
Esso
Kilpatrick
Old Kilpatrick —BP
Hillfoot
Bearsden
Old Kilpatrick Naval Fuel Depot
Dalmuir
Dalmuir Tuns.
Dalmuir Riverside Coal Depot
Singer
Arnott Young-Shipbreakers
Drumry
Westerton
Clydebank Cen. Junc.
Clydebank
Drumchapel
Knightswood North Junc.
A
Yoker
Knightswood Tun.
Maryhill Central Junc.
Rothesay Dock
Clydebank Dock Junc.
Garscadden
Anniesland
Knightswood South Junc.
Renfrew Ferry
Yoker Yard
Scotstounhill
Hyndland Juncs.
N.
W.
E.
HY
Greater Glasgow P.T.E. (Glasgow Subway) (4 ft Gauge)
Jordanhill
Hyndland
Hillhead
HYNDLAND
Kelvin Hall
Renfrew—Babcock & Wilcox Wks.
Shieldhall King George V Dock
Sidings
Partick
Finnieston W. Junc.
71
Shieldhall
Govan Cross
Car Term.
E. Junc.
West
East
Cardonald N. Junc.
Broomloan Depot
Paisley St. James
Cardonald
Ibrox
Kinning Park
Paisley Underwood Coal Dep.
Wallneuk Junc.
Greenlaw Junc.
HILLINGTON
Cardonald Junc.
Cessnock
Linwood—Talbot Car Wks.
B
Paisley Gilmour Street
Bellahouston C.S.
PAISLEY
GW
Car T.
Ferguslie Coal Depot
Coal Depot
Crookston
Mosspark
Elderslie No. 2 Junc.
Elderslie No. 1 Junc.
Paisley Canal
Hawkhead —Shell
Maxwell Park
Corkerhill
CK
Crossmyloo
Shawlands
POLLOKSHAWS
E.
W.
Busby Junc.
Kennishead
Nitshill
Thornliebank
Coal Depot
Barrhead
Giffnock
Williamwood
Patterton
C
Whitecraigs
Neilston
1
71
2
0 1 2 m.
0 1 2 3 4 km
(1:90,000)

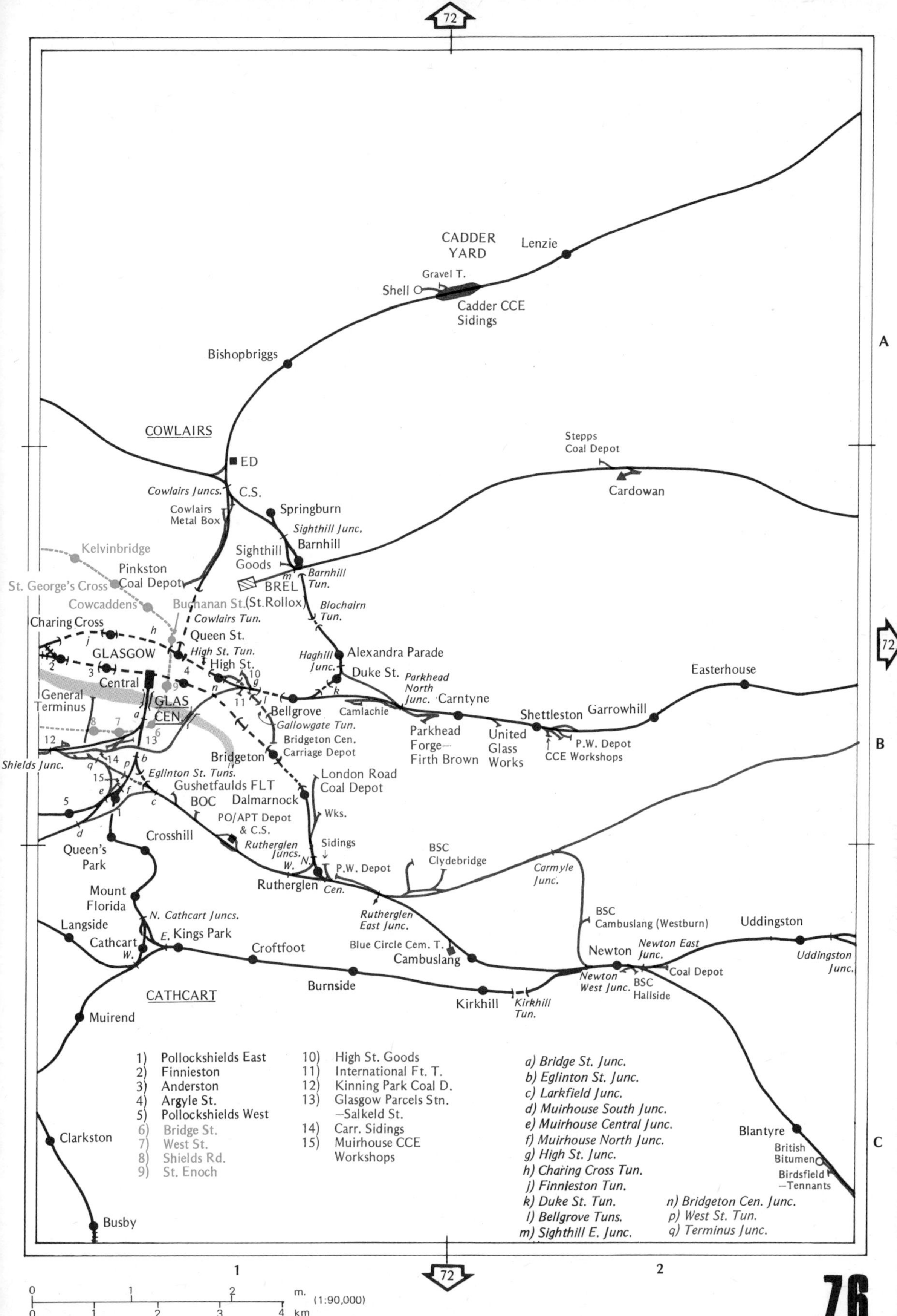

72
CADDER
YARD
Lenzie
Gravel T.
Shell
Cadder CCE
Sidings
A
Bishopbriggs
COWLAIRS
ED
Stepps
Coal Depot
Cardowan
Cowlairs Juncs.
C.S.
Cowlairs
Metal Box
Springburn
Sighthill Junc.
Barnhill
Kelvinbridge
Sighthill
Goods
Pinkston
Coal Depot
St. George's Cross
BREL
Barnhill
Tun.
Cowcaddens
Buchanan St.
(St.Rollox)
Blochairn
Tun.
Charing Cross
Cowlairs Tun.
Queen St.
High St. Tun.
Haghill
Junc.
Alexandra Parade
GLASGOW
High St.
Central
Duke St.
Parkhead
North
Junc.
Carntyne
Easterhouse
General
Terminus
GLAS
CEN.
Bellgrove
Camlachie
Shettleston
Garrowhill
Gallowgate Tun.
Parkhead
Forge—
Firth Brown
United
Glass
Works
P.W. Depot
CCE Workshops
B
Bridgeton Cen.
Carriage Depot
Bridgeton
Shields Junc.
London Road
Coal Depot
Eglinton St. Tuns.
Gushetfaulds FLT
BOC
Dalmarnock
Wks.
PO/APT Depot
& C.S.
Crosshill
Sidings
BSC
Clydebridge
Queen's
Park
Rutherglen
Juncs.
P.W. Depot
Carmyle
Junc.
Rutherglen
Cen.
Mount
Florida
Rutherglen
East Junc.
BSC
Cambuslang (Westburn)
Uddingston
N. Cathcart Juncs.
Langside
Kings Park
Cathcart
Croftfoot
Blue Circle Cem. T.
Cambuslang
Newton
Newton East
Junc.
Uddingston
Junc.
Coal Depot
Newton
West Junc.
BSC
Hallside
Burnside
Kirkhill
Kirkhill
Tun.
CATHCART
Muirend
1) Pollockshields East
2) Finnieston
3) Anderston
4) Argyle St.
5) Pollockshields West
6) Bridge St.
7) West St.
8) Shields Rd.
9) St. Enoch
10) High St. Goods
11) International Ft. T.
12) Kinning Park Coal D.
13) Glasgow Parcels Stn. —Salkeld St.
14) Carr. Sidings
15) Muirhouse CCE Workshops
a) Bridge St. Junc.
b) Eglinton St. Junc.
c) Larkfield Junc.
d) Muirhouse South Junc.
e) Muirhouse Central Junc.
f) Muirhouse North Junc.
g) High St. Junc.
h) Charing Cross Tun.
j) Finnieston Tun.
k) Duke St. Tun.
l) Bellgrove Tuns.
m) Sighthill E. Junc.
n) Bridgeton Cen. Junc.
p) West St. Tun.
q) Terminus Junc.
Blantyre
British
Bitumen
Birdsfield
—Tennants
C
Clarkston
Busby
1
2
72
m.
km
(1:90,000)

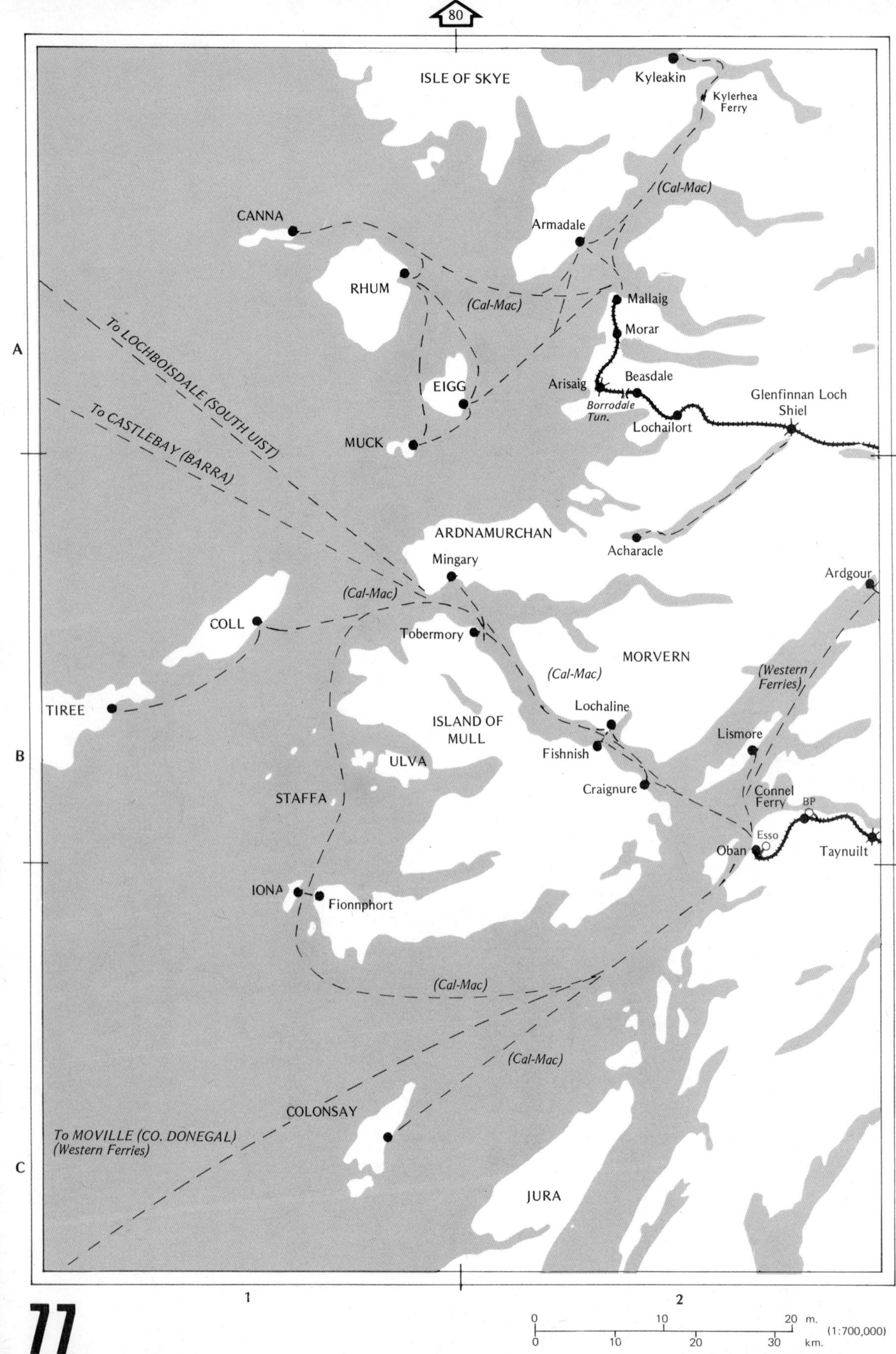
80
ISLE OF SKYE
Kyleakin
Kylerhea Ferry
(Cal-Mac)
CANNA
Armadale
RHUM
(Cal-Mac)
Mallaig
Morar
To LOCHBOISDALE (SOUTH UIST)
To CASTLEBAY (BARRA)
EIGG
Arisaig
Beasdale
Borrodale Tun.
Lochailort
Glenfinnan Loch Shiel
MUCK
ARDNAMURCHAN
Acharacle
Mingary
Ardgour
(Cal-Mac)
COLL
Tobermory
MORVERN
(Cal-Mac)
(Western Ferries)
TIREE
ISLAND OF MULL
Lochaline
Fishnish
Lismore
ULVA
STAFFA
Craignure
Connel Ferry
BP
Esso
Oban
Taynuilt
IONA
Fionnphort
(Cal-Mac)
(Cal-Mac)
COLONSAY
To MOVILLE (CO. DONEGAL) (Western Ferries)
JURA
A
B
C
1
2
77
0 10 20 m.
0 10 20 30 km.
(1:700,000)

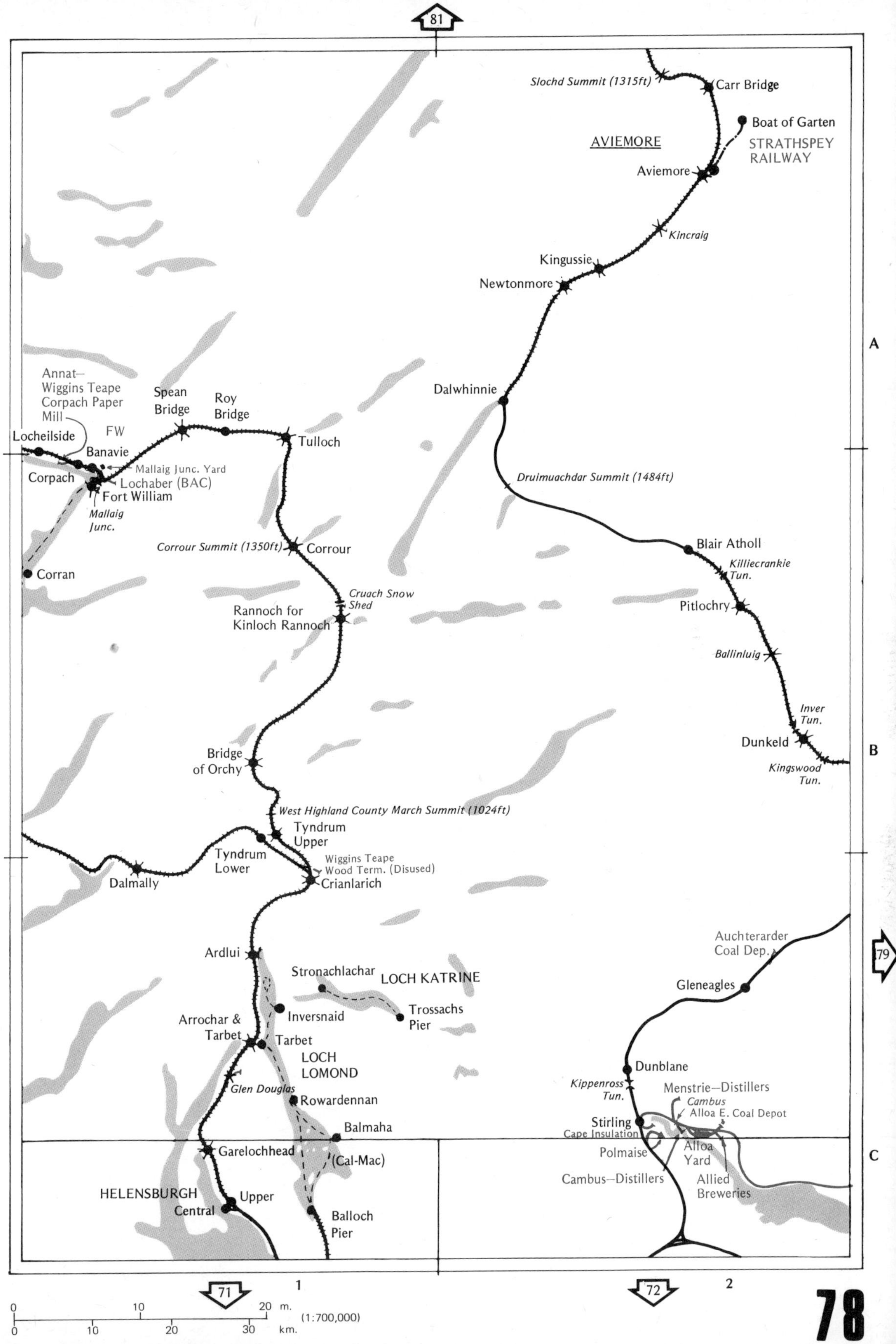

81

Slochd Summit (1315ft)
Carr Bridge
Boat of Garten
AVIEMORE
STRATHSPEY RAILWAY
Aviemore
Kincraig
Kingussie
Newtonmore
A
Dalwhinnie
Druimuachdar Summit (1484ft)
Blair Atholl
Killiecrankie Tun.
Pitlochry
Ballinluig
Inver Tun.
Dunkeld
Kingswood Tun.
B

Annat–Wiggins Teape Corpach Paper Mill
Spean Bridge
Roy Bridge
FW
Locheilside
Banavie
Tulloch
Mallaig Junc. Yard
Corpach
Lochaber (BAC)
Fort William
Mallaig Junc.
Corrour Summit (1350ft)
Corrour
Corran
Cruach Snow Shed
Rannoch for Kinloch Rannoch
Bridge of Orchy
West Highland County March Summit (1024ft)
Tyndrum Upper
Tyndrum Lower
Dalmally
Wiggins Teape Wood Term. (Disused)
Crianlarich
Ardlui
Stronachlachar
LOCH KATRINE
Inversnaid
Trossachs Pier
Arrochar & Tarbet
Tarbet
LOCH LOMOND
Glen Douglas
Rowardennan
Balmaha
Garelochhead
(Cal-Mac)
HELENSBURGH
Upper
Central
Balloch Pier
C

Auchterarder Coal Dep.
Gleneagles
Dunblane
Kippenross Tun.
Menstrie–Distillers
Cambus
Alloa E. Coal Depot
Stirling
Cape Insulation
Polmaise
Alloa Yard
Cambus–Distillers
Allied Breweries

79
71
1
72
2

0 10 20 m.
0 10 20 30 km.
(1:700,000)

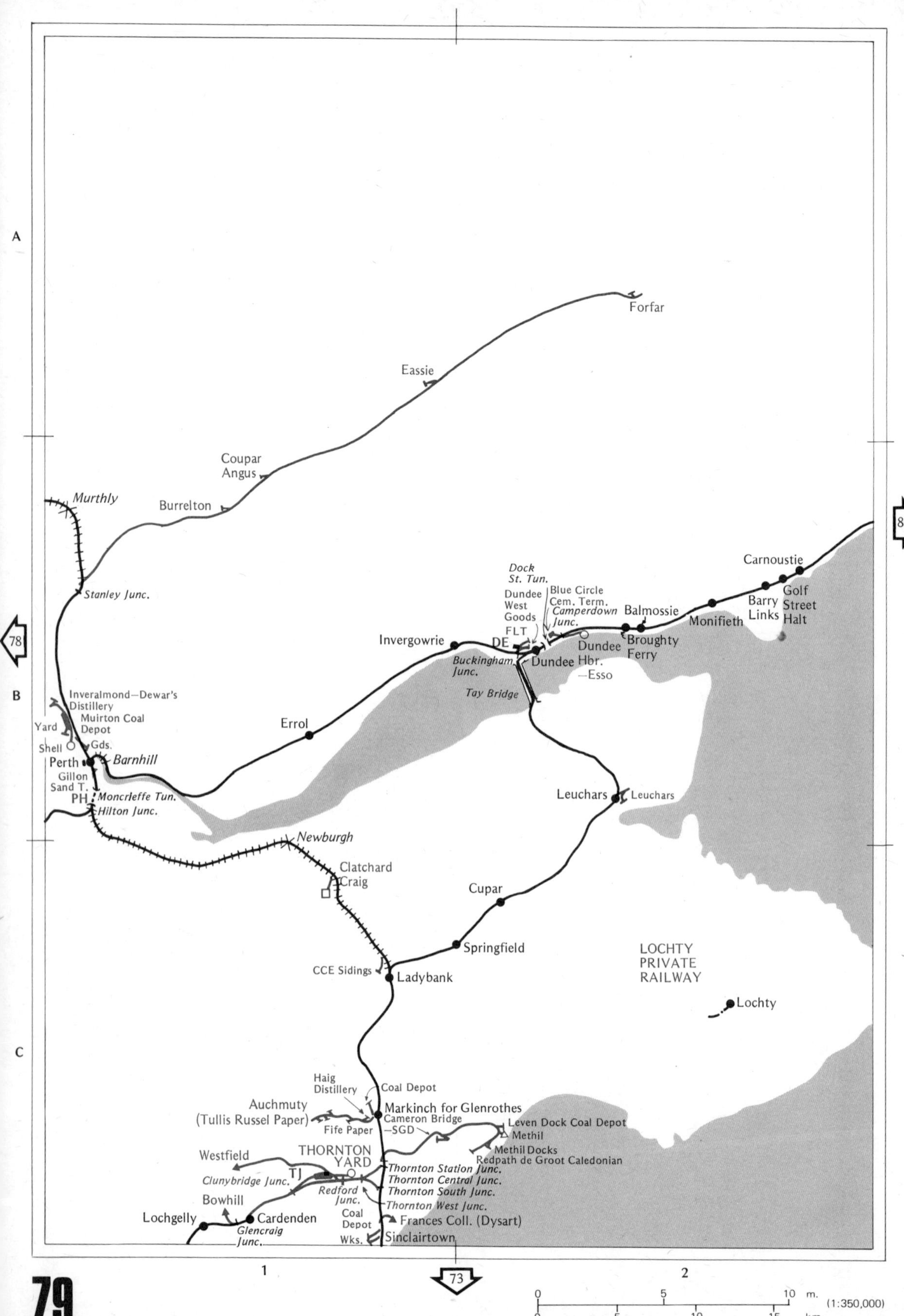

A
B
C
1
2
Forfar
Eassie
Coupar
Angus
Burrelton
Murthly
Stanley Junc.
78
80
Carnoustie
Golf
Street
Halt
Barry
Links
Monifieth
Balmossie
Broughty
Ferry
Dock
St. Tun.
Dundee
West
Goods
FLT
Blue Circle
Cem. Term.
Camperdown
Junc.
Dundee
Hbr.
—Esso
Invergowrie
DE
Dundee
Buckingham
Junc.
Tay Bridge
Inveralmond—Dewar's
Distillery
Muirton Coal
Depot
Yard
Shell
Gds.
Perth
Barnhill
Gillon
Sand T.
PH
Moncrieffe Tun.
Hilton Junc.
Errol
Leuchars
Leuchars
Newburgh
Clatchard
Craig
Cupar
Springfield
CCE Sidings
Ladybank
LOCHTY
PRIVATE
RAILWAY
Lochty
Haig
Distillery
Coal Depot
Markinch for Glenrothes
Auchmuty
(Tullis Russel Paper)
Fife Paper
Cameron Bridge
—SGD
Leven Dock Coal Depot
Methil
Methil Docks
Redpath de Groot Caledonian
Westfield
THORNTON
YARD
Thornton Station Junc.
Thornton Central Junc.
Thornton South Junc.
Thornton West Junc.
Clunybridge Junc.
TJ
Redford
Junc.
Bowhill
Lochgelly
Cardenden
Glencraig
Junc.
Coal
Depot
Frances Coll. (Dysart)
Wks.
Sinclairtown
73
0 5 10 m.
0 5 10 15 km.
(1:350,000)

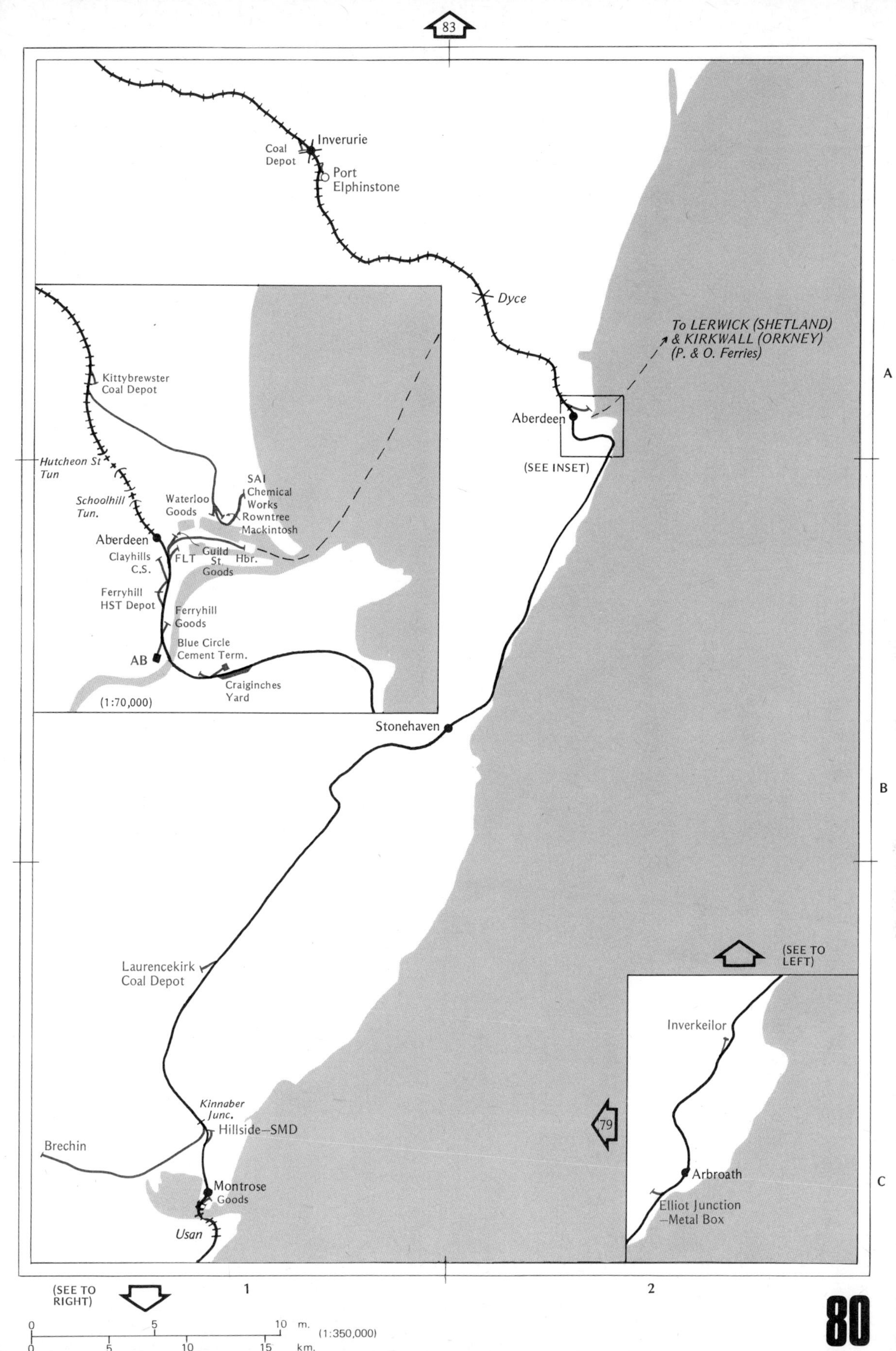
83
Inverurie
Coal Depot
Port Elphinstone
Dyce
To LERWICK (SHETLAND) & KIRKWALL (ORKNEY) (P. & O. Ferries)
A
Aberdeen
(SEE INSET)
Kittybrewster Coal Depot
Hutcheon St Tun
Schoolhill Tun.
Waterloo Goods
SAI Chemical Works
Rowntree Mackintosh
Aberdeen
Clayhills C.S.
FLT
Guild St. Goods
Hbr.
Ferryhill HST Depot
Ferryhill Goods
Blue Circle Cement Term.
AB
Craiginches Yard
(1:70,000)
Stonehaven
B
(SEE TO LEFT)
Laurencekirk Coal Depot
Inverkeilor
79
Kinnaber Junc.
Hillside–SMD
Brechin
Arbroath
C
Montrose Goods
Elliot Junction –Metal Box
Usan
(SEE TO RIGHT)
1
2
0 5 10 m.
0 5 10 15 km.
(1:350,000)

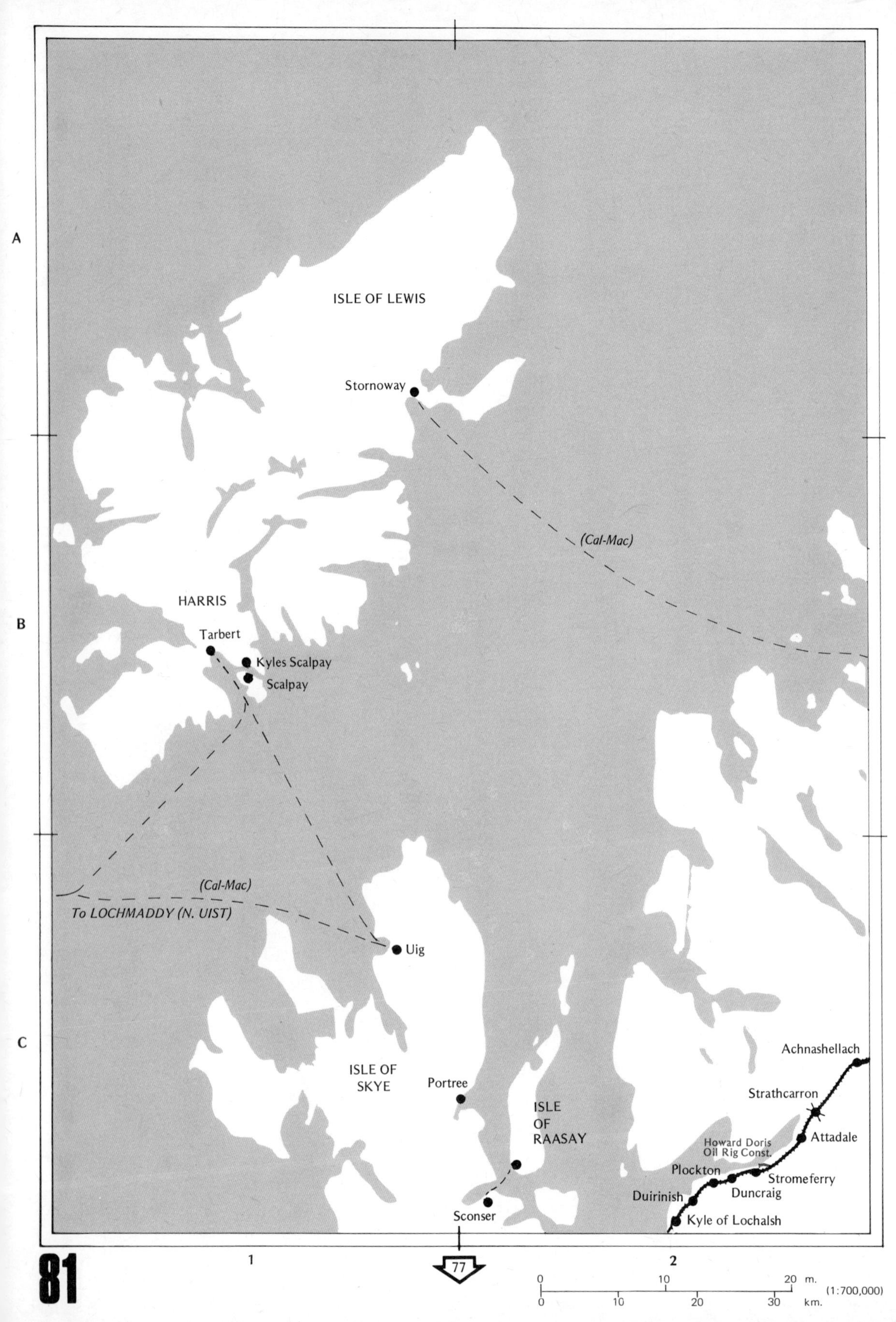
A
B
C
ISLE OF LEWIS
Stornoway
(Cal-Mac)
HARRIS
Tarbert
Kyles Scalpay
Scalpay
(Cal-Mac)
To LOCHMADDY (N. UIST)
Uig
ISLE OF SKYE
Portree
ISLE OF RAASAY
Sconser
Achnashellach
Strathcarron
Attadale
Howard Doris Oil Rig Const.
Plockton
Stromeferry
Duncraig
Duirinish
Kyle of Lochalsh
1
2
77
0 10 20 m.
0 10 20 30 km.
(1:700,000)

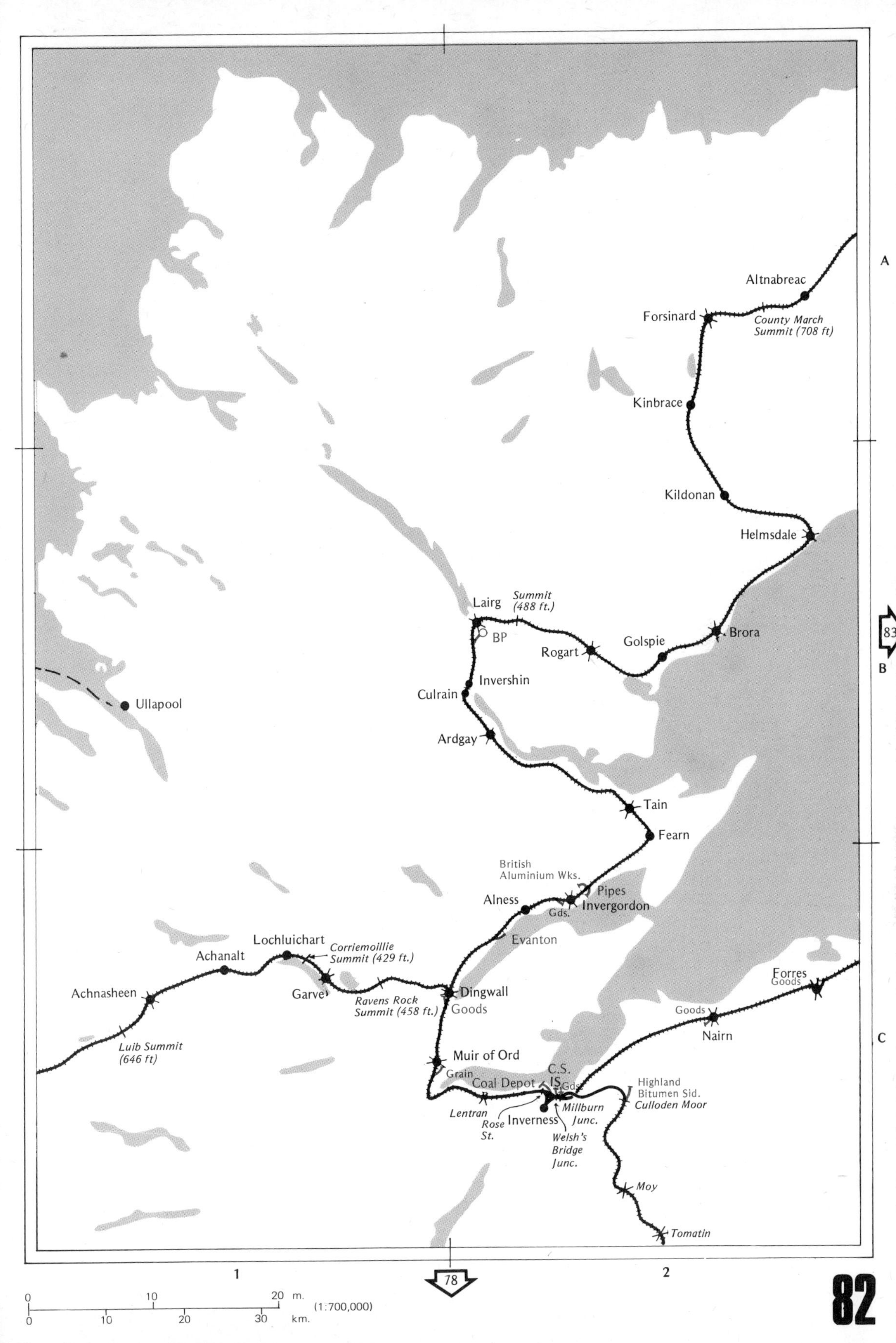

Altnabreac
Forsinard
County March Summit (708 ft)
Kinbrace
Kildonan
Helmsdale
Brora
Golspie
Rogart
Lairg
Summit (488 ft.)
BP
Invershin
Culrain
Ullapool
Ardgay
Tain
Fearn
British Aluminium Wks.
Pipes
Invergordon
Gds.
Alness
Evanton
Lochluichart
Corriemoillie Summit (429 ft.)
Achanalt
Achnasheen
Garve
Ravens Rock Summit (458 ft.)
Dingwall
Goods
Luib Summit (646 ft)
Forres
Goods
Goods
Nairn
Muir of Ord
Grain
Coal Depot
C.S.
IS
Gds
Highland Bitumen Sid.
Culloden Moor
Lentran
Rose St.
Inverness
Millburn Junc.
Welsh's Bridge Junc.
Moy
Tomatin
A
B
C
1
2
83
78
0 10 20 m.
0 10 20 30 km.
(1:700,000)

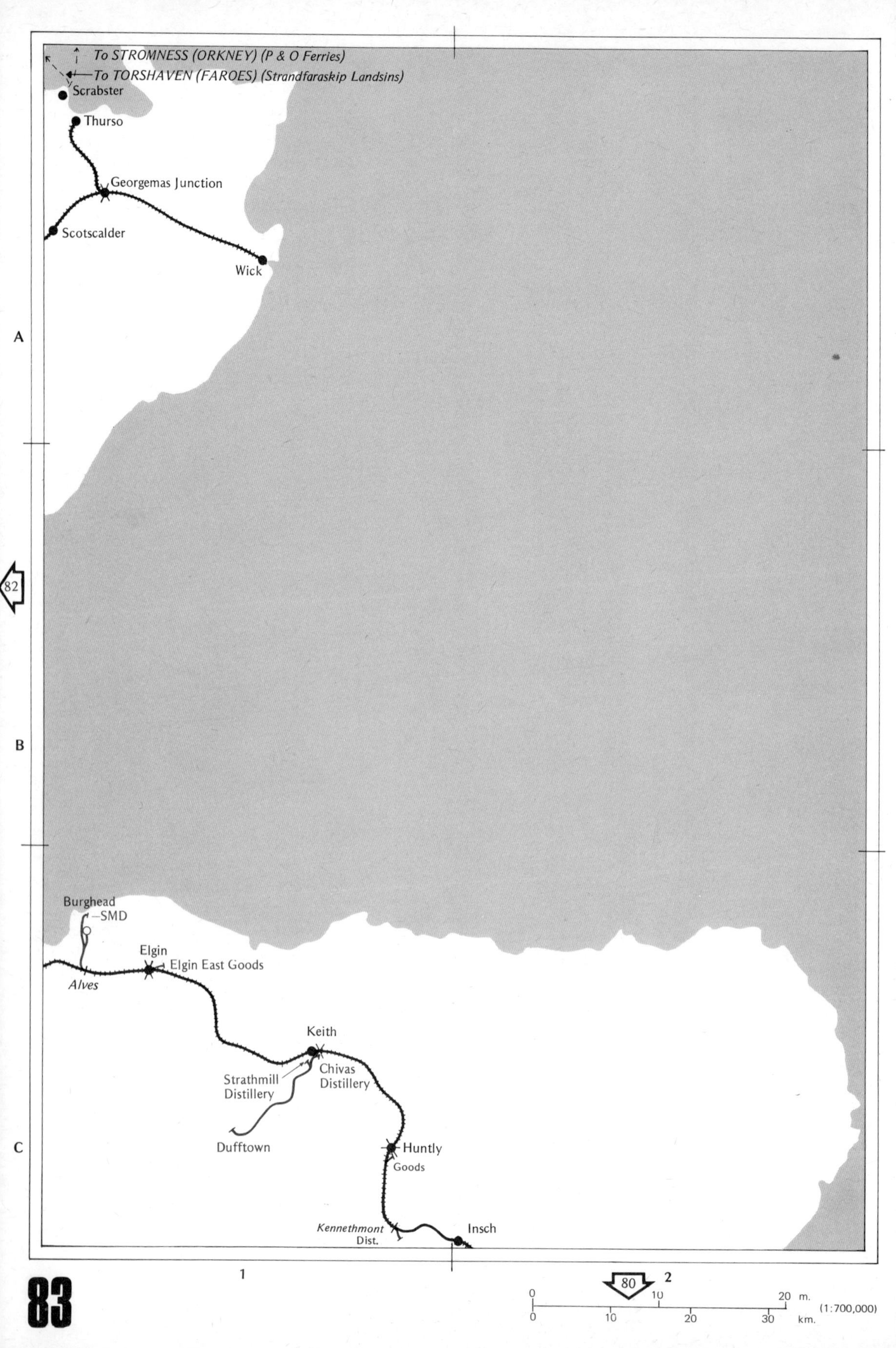
To STROMNESS (ORKNEY) (P & O Ferries)
To TORSHAVEN (FAROES) (Strandfaraskip Landsins)
Scrabster
Thurso
Georgemas Junction
Scotscalder
Wick
A
82
B
Burghead
SMD
Elgin
Elgin East Goods
Alves
Keith
Strathmill Distillery
Chivas Distillery
Dufftown
C
Huntly
Goods
Kennethmont Dist.
Insch
1
80
2
0
10
20 m.
0
10
20
30
km.
(1:700,000)

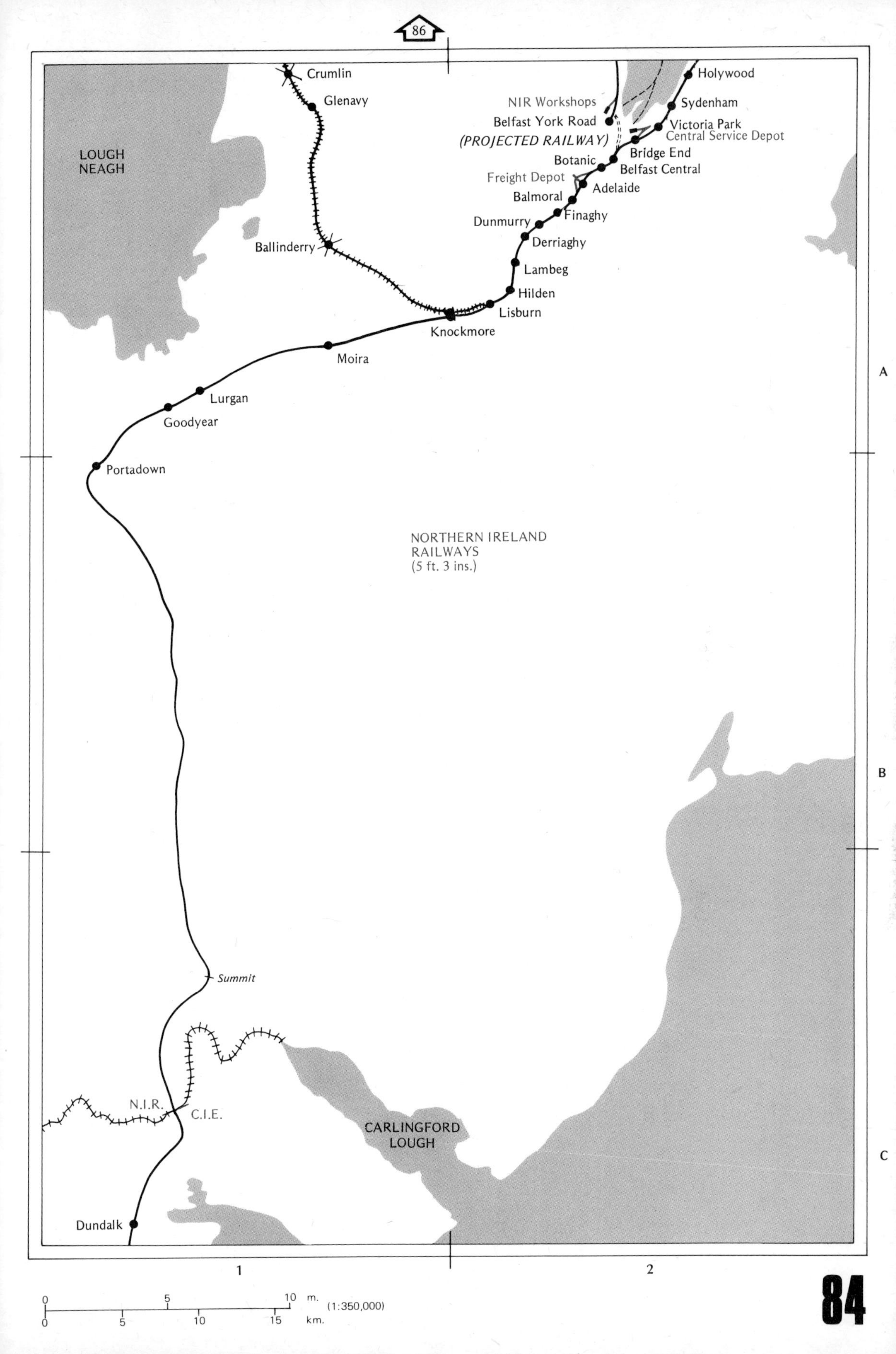
86
Crumlin
Glenavy
LOUGH
NEAGH
Ballinderry
NIR Workshops
Belfast York Road
(PROJECTED RAILWAY)
Holywood
Sydenham
Victoria Park
Central Service Depot
Bridge End
Botanic
Belfast Central
Freight Depot
Adelaide
Balmoral
Finaghy
Dunmurry
Derriaghy
Lambeg
Hilden
Lisburn
Knockmore
Moira
Lurgan
Goodyear
Portadown
NORTHERN IRELAND
RAILWAYS
(5 ft. 3 ins.)
Summit
N.I.R.
C.I.E.
CARLINGFORD
LOUGH
Dundalk
A
B
C
1
2
0 5 10 m.
0 5 10 15 km.
(1:350,000)

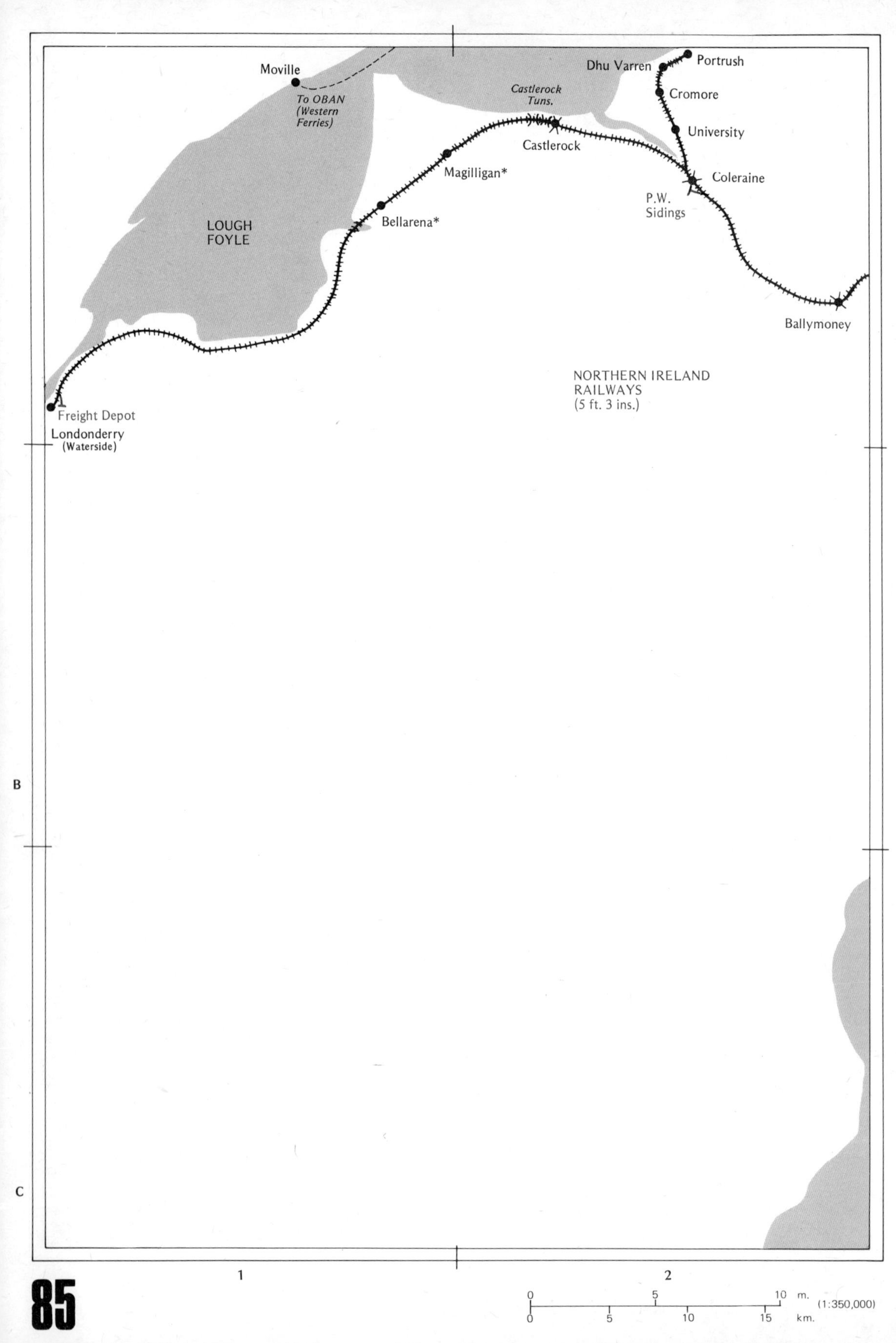
Moville
To OBAN
(Western
Ferries)
Castlerock
Tuns.
Dhu Varren
Portrush
Cromore
University
Castlerock
Magilligan*
Coleraine
P.W.
Sidings
Bellarena*
LOUGH
FOYLE
Ballymoney
NORTHERN IRELAND
RAILWAYS
(5 ft. 3 ins.)
Freight Depot
Londonderry
(Waterside)
B
C
1
2
0 5 10 m.
0 5 10 15 km.
(1:350,000)

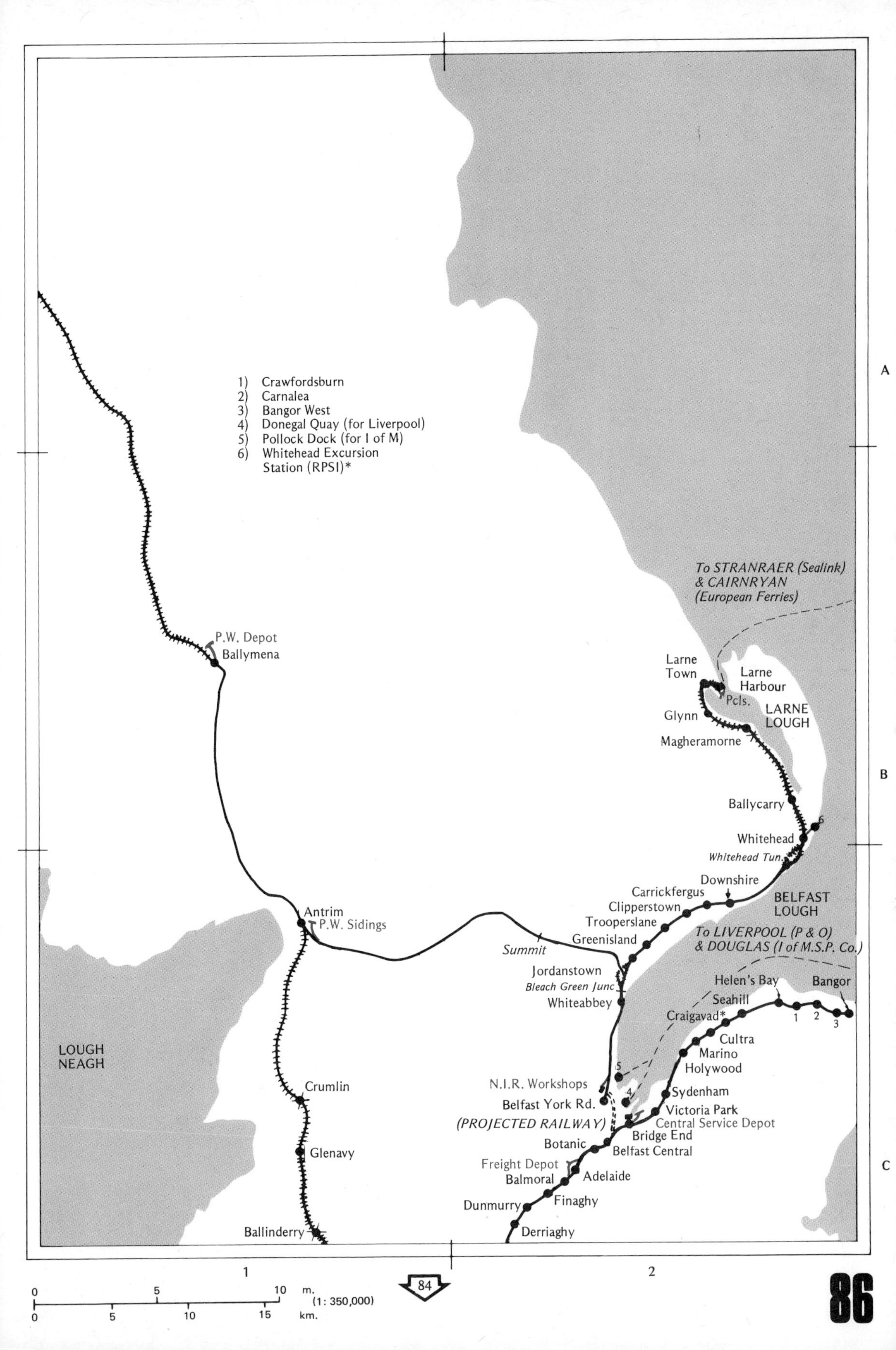
1) Crawfordsburn
2) Carnalea
3) Bangor West
4) Donegal Quay (for Liverpool)
5) Pollock Dock (for I of M)
6) Whitehead Excursion Station (RPSI)*
To STRANRAER (Sealink) & CAIRNRYAN (European Ferries)
P.W. Depot
Ballymena
Larne Town
Larne Harbour
Pcls.
LARNE LOUGH
Glynn
Magheramorne
Ballycarry
Whitehead
Whitehead Tun.
Downshire
Carrickfergus
Clipperstown
Trooperslane
Greenisland
BELFAST LOUGH
To LIVERPOOL (P & O) & DOUGLAS (I of M.S.P. Co.)
Antrim
P.W. Sidings
Summit
Jordanstown
Bleach Green Junc.
Whiteabbey
Helen's Bay
Bangor
Seahill
Craigavad*
Cultra
Marino
Holywood
LOUGH NEAGH
Crumlin
N.I.R. Workshops
Belfast York Rd.
Sydenham
Victoria Park
(PROJECTED RAILWAY)
Central Service Depot
Bridge End
Botanic
Belfast Central
Glenavy
Freight Depot
Balmoral
Adelaide
Finaghy
Dunmurry
Derriaghy
Ballinderry
A
B
C
1
2
0 5 10 m.
(1: 350,000)
0 5 10 15 km.
84

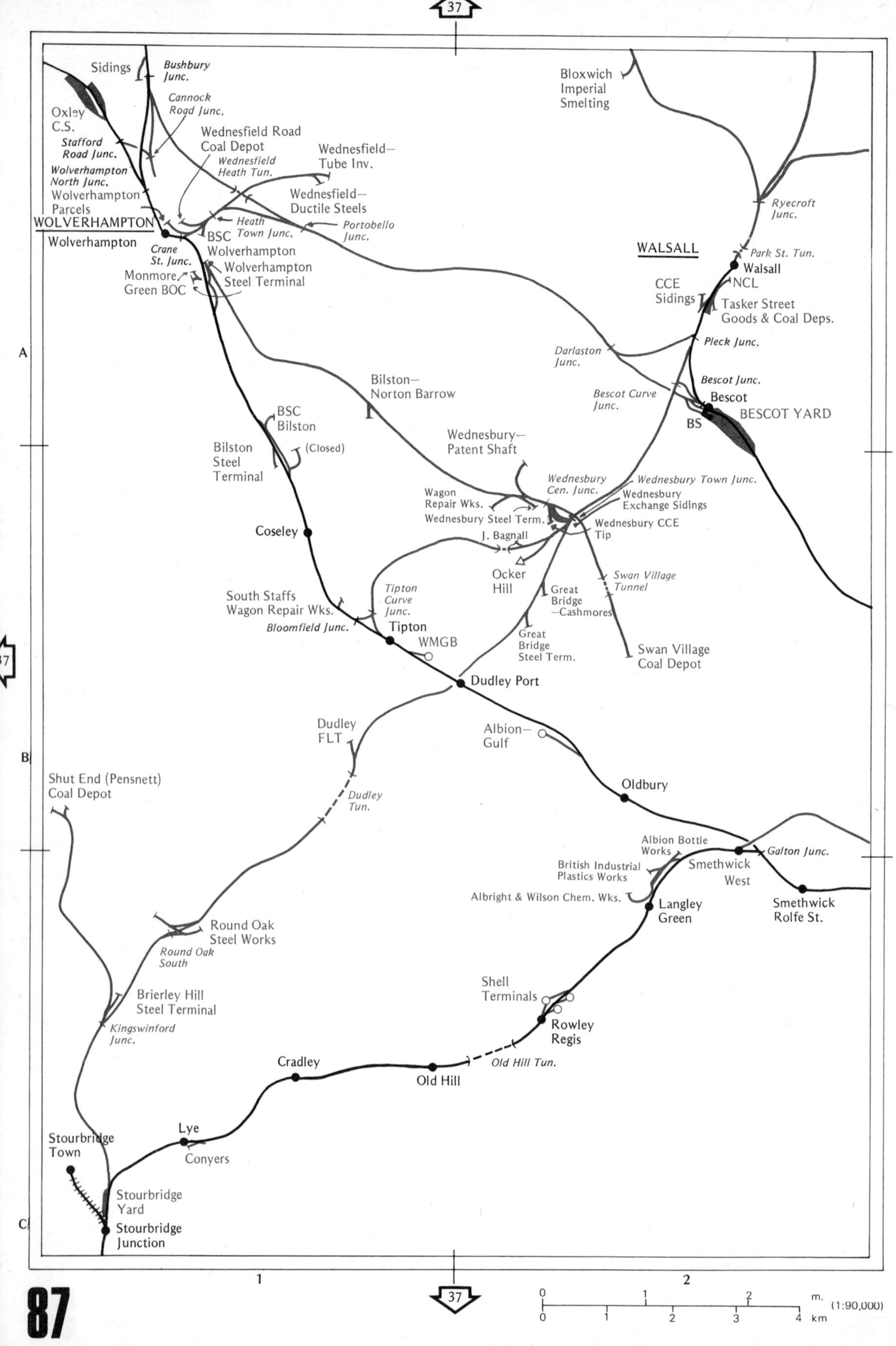
37
Sidings
Bushbury Junc.
Oxley C.S.
Cannock Road Junc.
Stafford Road Junc.
Wolverhampton North Junc.
Wolverhampton Parcels
WOLVERHAMPTON
Wolverhampton
Wednesfield Road Coal Depot
Wednesfield Heath Tun.
Wednesfield—Tube Inv.
Wednesfield—Ductile Steels
Heath Town Junc.
Portobello Junc.
BSC Wolverhampton
Crane St. Junc.
Monmore Green BOC
Wolverhampton Steel Terminal
Bloxwich Imperial Smelting
Ryecroft Junc.
WALSALL
Park St. Tun.
Walsall
NCL
CCE Sidings
Tasker Street Goods & Coal Deps.
Pleck Junc.
Darlaston Junc.
Bescot Junc.
Bescot Curve Junc.
Bescot
BESCOT YARD
BS
Bilston—Norton Barrow
BSC Bilston
Bilston Steel Terminal
(Closed)
Wednesbury—Patent Shaft
Wednesbury Cen. Junc.
Wednesbury Town Junc.
Wagon Repair Wks.
Wednesbury Exchange Sidings
Wednesbury Steel Term.
Wednesbury CCE Tip
J. Bagnall
Coseley
Ocker Hill
Swan Village Tunnel
Great Bridge —Cashmores
South Staffs Wagon Repair Wks.
Tipton Curve Junc.
Bloomfield Junc.
Tipton
WMGB
Great Bridge Steel Term.
Swan Village Coal Depot
Dudley Port
Dudley FLT
Albion—Gulf
Dudley Tun.
Shut End (Pensnett) Coal Depot
Oldbury
Albion Bottle Works
British Industrial Plastics Works
Smethwick West
Galton Junc.
Albright & Wilson Chem. Wks.
Langley Green
Smethwick Rolfe St.
Round Oak Steel Works
Round Oak South
Brierley Hill Steel Terminal
Kingswinford Junc.
Shell Terminals
Rowley Regis
Old Hill Tun.
Cradley
Old Hill
Lye
Conyers
Stourbridge Town
Stourbridge Yard
Stourbridge Junction
A
B
C
1
2
37
0 1 2 m.
0 1 2 3 4 km
(1:90,000)

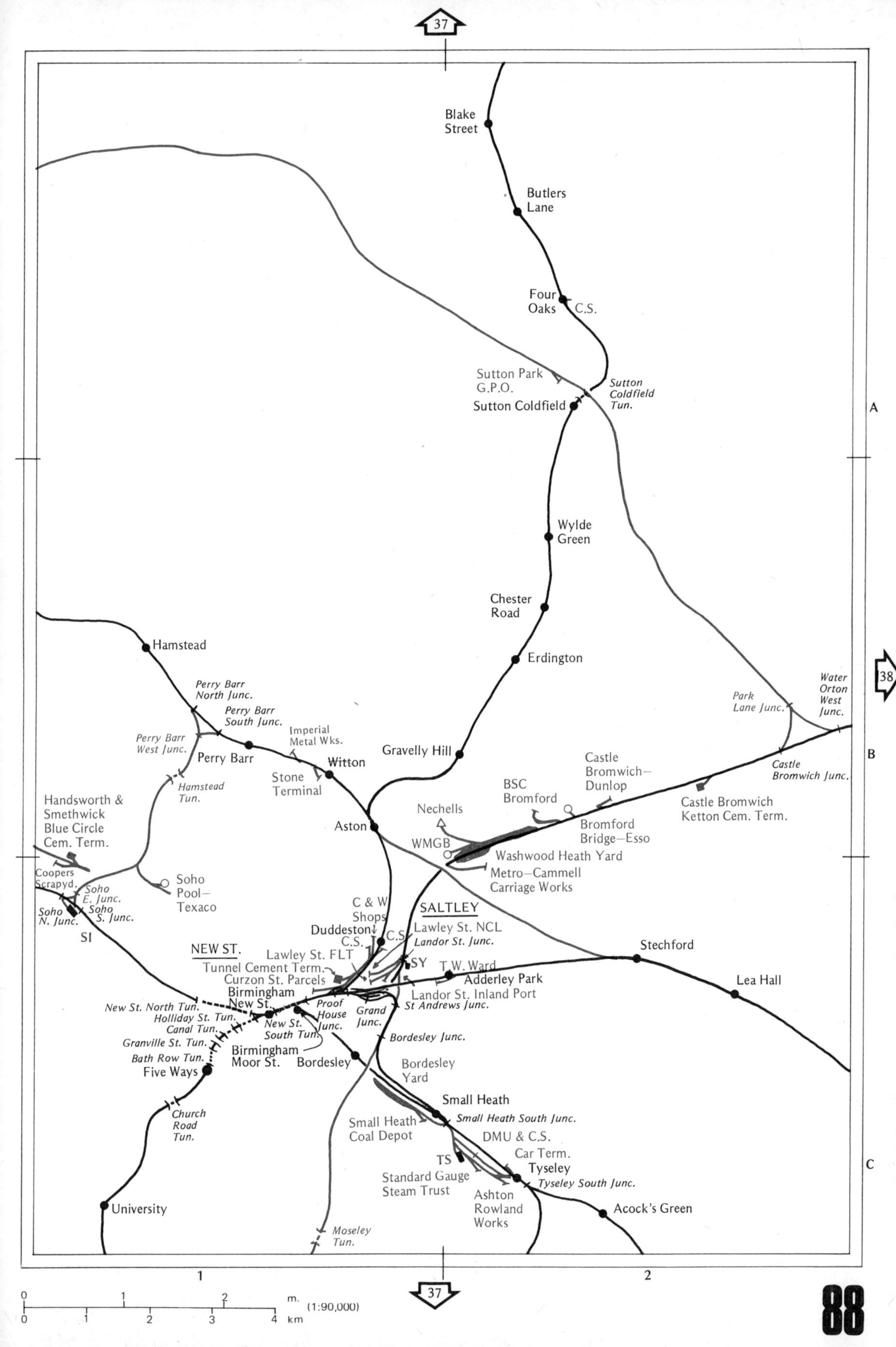

37
Blake Street
Butlers Lane
Four Oaks
C.S.
Sutton Park G.P.O.
Sutton Coldfield
Sutton Coldfield Tun.
A
Wylde Green
Chester Road
Erdington
Hamstead
38
Water Orton West Junc.
Park Lane Junc.
Perry Barr North Junc.
Perry Barr South Junc.
Perry Barr West Junc.
Perry Barr
Imperial Metal Wks.
Witton
Gravelly Hill
Castle Bromwich–Dunlop
Castle Bromwich Junc.
B
Hamstead Tun.
Stone Terminal
BSC Bromford
Castle Bromwich Ketton Cem. Term.
Handsworth & Smethwick Blue Circle Cem. Term.
Aston
Nechells
Bromford Bridge–Esso
WMGB
Washwood Heath Yard
Coopers Scrapyd.
Soho Pool–Texaco
Metro–Cammell Carriage Works
Soho E. Junc.
Soho N. Junc.
Soho S. Junc.
SI
C & W Shops
SALTLEY
Lawley St. NCL
Duddeston
C.S.
C.S.
Landor St. Junc.
NEW ST.
Lawley St. FLT
SY
Stechford
Tunnel Cement Term.
T.W. Ward
Curzon St. Parcels
Adderley Park
Lea Hall
Birmingham New St.
Landor St. Inland Port
St Andrews Junc.
New St. North Tun.
Proof House Junc.
Grand Junc.
Holliday St. Tun.
New St. South Tun.
Canal Tun.
Bordesley Junc.
Granville St. Tun.
Birmingham Moor St.
Bath Row Tun.
Bordesley
Bordesley Yard
Five Ways
Small Heath
Church Road Tun.
Small Heath South Junc.
Small Heath Coal Depot
DMU & C.S.
Car Term.
C
TS
Tyseley
Standard Gauge Steam Trust
Tyseley South Junc.
Ashton Rowland Works
Acock's Green
University
Moseley Tun.
1
2
37
0 1 2 m.
0 1 2 3 4 km
(1:90,000)

INDEX TO PASSENGER STATIONS

For list of abbreviations see end of Passenger Station Index
(*Indicates unadvertised or excursion station)

NAME	RAILWAY CODE	PAGE NO.	PAGE REF.
Abbey Wood	SO	32	C2
Aber	WR	28	C1
Abercynon	WR	27	C2
Aberdare*	WR	27	B2
Aberdeen	SC	80	B1
Aberdour	SC	73	A1
Aberdovey	LM	34	B2
Abererch	LM	43	C2
Aberffrwd	LM	34	B2
Abergavenny	WR	28	B1
Abergele & Pensarn	LM	44	A2
Abergynolwyn	TL	34	A2
Abertafol	LM	34	B2
Aberystwyth	LM	34	B2
Accrington	LM	55	B1
Achanalt	SC	82	C1
Achnasheen	SC	82	C1
Achnashellach	SC	81	C2
Acklington	ER	68	A1
Acle	ER	42	A1
Acock's Green	LM	88	C2
Acton Bridge	LM	45	A2
Acton Central	LM	20	B2
Acton Main Line	WR	20	B2
Acton Town	LT	20	C2
Adderley Park	LM	88	C2
Addiewell	SC	72	B2
Addiscombe	SO	17	B2
Addlestone	SO	15	C1
Adelaide	NI	84	A2
Adisham	SO	13	A2
Adlington (Cheshire)	LM	46	A2
Adlington (Lancs.)	LM	54	C2
Aigburth	LM	53	C2
Ainsdale	LM	54	C1
Aintree	LM	53	A2
Airdrie	SC	72	B1
Albany Park	SO	32	C2
Albrighton	LM	37	A1
Alderley Edge	LM	46	A1
Aldermaston	WR	10	A2
Aldershot	SO	11	A1
Aldgate	LT	21	B2
Aldgate East	LT	21	B2
Aldrington	SO	12	C1
Aldwych	LT	21	B2
Alexandra Parade	SC	76	B1
Alexandria	SC	71	A2
Alfreton & Mansfield Parkway	LM	47	B2
Allen's West	ER	62	B2
Allerton	LM	53	C2
Alness	SC	82	C2
Alnmouth	ER	68	A1
Alperton	LT	20	B1
Alresford (Essex)	ER	33	B2
Alresford (Hants.)	MH	10	B2
Alsager	LM	46	B2
Althorne	ER	33	B1
Althorpe	ER	57	C1
Altnabreac	SC	82	A2
Altofts	ER	56	B1
Alton	SO	11	B1
Altrincham	LM	46	A1
Alvechurch	LM	37	B2
Ambergate	LM	47	B1
Amberley	SO	11	C2
Amersham	LM/LT	31	C2
Ammanford	WR	27	B1
Ancaster	ER	48	C2
Anderston	SC	76	B1
Andover	SO	10	B1
Anerley	SO	18	A1
Angel	LT	21	B2
Angel Road	ER	24	C1
Angmering	SO	11	C2
Annan	SC	66	C1
Anniesland	SC	75	B2
Ansdell & Fairhaven	LM	54	B1
Antrim	NI	86	C1

NAME	RAILWAY CODE	PAGE NO.	PAGE REF.
Appleby	LM	61	A1
Appledore	SO	13	B1
Appleford	WR	30	C2
Appley Bridge	LM	54	C2
Apsley	LM	31	B2
Arbroath	SC	80	C2
Archway	LT	21	A2
Ardgay	SC	82	B2
Ardlui	SC	78	C1
Ardrossan Harbour	SC	71	C1
Ardrossan South Beach	SC	71	C1
Ardwick	LM	52	B1
Argyle Street	SC	76	B1
Arisaig	SC	77	A2
Arley	SV	37	B1
Armathwaite*	LM	66	C2
Arnos Grove	LT	23	C2
Arnside	LM	60	C2
Arram	ER	57	B2
Arrochar & Tarbet	SC	78	C1
Arsenal	LT	21	A2
Arundel	SO	11	C2
Ascot	SO	11	A1
Ascott-under-Wychwood	WR	30	B1
Ash	SO	11	A1
Ashburys for Belle Vue	LM	52	B1
Ashford (Kent)	SO	13	B2
Ashford (Middlesex)	SO	15	A1
Ashley	LM	46	A1
Ash Street	BF	54	A1
Ashtead	SO	11	A2
Ashton-under-Lyne	LM	52	B2
Ashton-in-Makerfield*	LM	54	C2
Ashton Gate*	WR	8	B1
Ashurst	SO	12	B2
Ash Vale	SO	11	A1
Ashwell & Morden	ER	32	A1
Askam	LM	60	C1
Askern*	ER	56	C2
Aslockton	ER	48	C1
Aspatria	LM	60	A1
Aspley Guise	LM	31	A1
Aston	LM	88	B1
Atherstone	LM	38	A1
Atherton	LM	55	C1
Attadale	SC	81	A2
Attenborough	LM	47	C2
Attercliffe	ER	50	B1
Attleborough	ER	41	B2
Audley End	ER	32	A2
Aughton Park	LM	54	C2
Aviemore	SC/SY	78	A2
Avoncliff	WR	9	A1
Avonmouth	WR	28	C2
Axminster	WR	4	A1
Axmouth	ST	4	A1
Aylesbury	LM	31	B1
Aylesford	SO	12	A2
Aylesham	SO	13	A2
Ayr	SC	71	C1
Bagshot	SO	11	A1
Baildon	ER	56	B1
Baker Street	LT	21	B1
Bala	BA	44	C2
Balcombe	SO	12	B1
Baldock	ER	32	A1
Baldrine	ME	59	C2
Balham	SO/LT	17	A1
Ballabeg*	ME	59	C2
Ballaglass	ME	59	B2
Ballajura	ME	59	B2
Ballaragh	ME	59	C2
Ballasalla	ME	59	C1
Ballinderry	NI	86	C1
Balloch Central	SC	71	A2
Balloch Pier	SC	71	A2
Ballycarry	NI	86	B2
Ballymena	NI	86	B1
Ballymoney	NI	85	A2

Balmoral	NI	84	A2
Balmossie	SC	79	B2
Bamber Bridge	LM	54	B2
Bamford	LM	47	A1
Banavie	SC	78	B1
Banbury	LM	30	A2
Bangor (Co. Down)	NI	86	C2
Bangor (Gwynedd)	LM	43	A2
Bangor West	NI	86	C2
Bank	SO/LT	21	B2
Bank Hall	LM	53	B1
Bank Foot	TW	69	A1
Banstead	SO	17	C1
Barassie	SC	71	C2
Barbican	LM/LT	21	B2
Bardon Mill	ER	67	C1
Bare Lane	LM	54	A2
Bargoed	WR	28	B1
Barking	ER/LT	22	B2
Barkingside	LT	22	A2
Barlaston	LM	46	C1
Barming	SO	13	A1
Barmouth	LM	34	A2
Barmouth Ferry	FB	34	A2
Barnehurst	SO	32	C2
Barnes	SO	20	C2
Barnes Bridge	SO	20	C2
Barnetby	ER	57	C2
Barnham	SO	11	C2
Barnhill	SC	76	B1
Barnsley	ER	56	C1
Barnstaple	WR	6	B2
Barnt Green	LM	37	B2
Barons Court	LT	21	C1
Barrhead	SC	75	C1
Barrhill	SC	64	B1
Barrow Haven	ER	57	B2
Barrow-in-Furness	LM	54	A1
Barry	WR	7	A1
Barry Docks	WR	7	A1
Barry Island	WR	7	A1
Barry Links	SC	79	B2
Barton-on-Humber	ER	57	B2
Basildon	ER	32	C2
Basingstoke	SO	10	A2
Bat & Ball	SO	12	A2
Bath Spa	WR	9	A1
Batley	ER	56	B1
Battersby	ER	62	B2
Battersea Park	SO	21	C1
Battle	SO	13	C1
Battlesbridge	ER	33	C1
Bayford	ER	32	B1
Bayswater	LT	21	B1
Beaconsfield	LM	31	C1
Bearley	LM	38	C1
Bearsden	SC	75	A2
Bearsted	SO	13	A1
Beasdale	SC	77	A2
Beaulieu Road	SO	10	C1
Bebington	LM	53	C1
Beccles	ER	42	B1
Beckenham Hill	SO	18	A1
Beckenham Junction	SO	18	A1
Beckfoot	RE	60	B1
Becontree	LT	32	C1
Beddington Lane	SO	17	B2
Bede	TW	70	B1
Bedford Midland	LM	39	C2
Bedford St. John's	LM	39	C2
Bedhampton	SO	11	C1
Bedminster	WR	8	B2
Bedwyn	WR	10	A1
Beeston	LM	47	C2
Bekesbourne	SO	13	A2
Belfast Central	NI	84	A2
Belfast York Road	NI	86	C2
Bellarena*	NI	85	A1
Bellevue	ME	59	B2
Belle Vue	LM	52	B1
Bellgrove	SC	76	B1
Bellingham	SO	18	A1

Bellshill	SC	72	B1
Belmont	SO	17	C1
Belper	LM	47	C1
Belsize Park	LT	21	A1
Beltring	SO	12	A2
Belvedere	SO	32	C2
Bempton	ER	63	C2
Benfleet for Canvey I.	ER	33	C1
Ben Rhydding	ER	55	A2
Bentham	LM	55	A1
Bentley	SO	11	B1
Benton	TW	69	A2
Bere Alston	WR	2	B2
Bere Ferrers	WR	2	B2
Berkhamsted	LM	31	B2
Berkswell	LM	38	B1
Berney Arms	ER	42	A1
Berrylands	SO	16	B2
Berwick (Sussex)	SO	12	C2
Berwick-upon-Tweed	ER	74	B2
Bescar Lane	LM	54	C2
Bescot	LM	87	A2
Besses-o'-th'-Barn	LM	51	A2
Betchworth	SO	11	A2
Bethnal Green	ER/LT	22	B1
Betws-y-Coed	LM	44	B1
Beverley	ER	57	B2
Bewdley	SV	37	B1
Bexhill	SO	13	C1
Bexley	SO	32	C2
Bexleyheath	SO	32	C2
Bicester	LM	30	A2
Bickley	SO	18	B2
Bideford*	WR	6	B2
Bidston	LM	45	A1
Biggleswade	ER	31	A2
Bilbrook	LM	37	A1
Billericay	ER	32	C2
Billingham	ER	62	A2
Billingshurst	SO	11	B2
Bingham	LM	48	C1
Bingham Road	SO	17	B2
Bingley	ER	55	B2
Birchgrove	WR	28	C1
Birchington-on-Sea	SO	14	A1
Birchwood	LM	46	A1
Birkbeck	SO	18	B1
Birkdale	LM	54	C1
Birkenhead Central	LM	53	C1
Birkenhead Hamilton Square	LM	53	B1
Birkenhead North	LM	53	B1
Birkenhead Park	LM	53	B1
Birmingham International	LM	38	B1
Birmingham Moor Street	LM	88	C1
Birminham New Street	LM	88	C1
Bishop Auckland	ER	62	A1
Bishopbriggs	SC	76	A1
Bishops Lydeard	WS	8	B7
Bishops Stortford	ER	32	B2
Bishopstone	SO	12	C2
Bishopton	SC	71	A2
Bispham	BF	54	B1
Blackburn	LM	55	B1
Blackfriars	SO/LT	21	B2
Blackheath	SO	22	C1
Black Horse Road	ER/LT	22	A1
Blackpool North	LM	54	B1
Blackpool South	LM	54	B1
Blackrod	LM	54	C2
Blackwater	SO	11	A1
Blaenau Ffestiniog	LM/FR	44	C1
Blair Atholl	SC	78	B2
Blairhill	SC	72	C1
Blakedown	LM	37	B1
Blake Hall	LT	32	B2
Blake Street	LM	88	A2
Blantyre	SC	76	C2
Blaydon	ER	69	B1
Bleasby	LM	48	B1
Bletchley	LM	31	A1
Blue Anchor	WS	7	B2
Blundellsands & Crosby	LM	53	A1

Blythe Bridge	LM	46	C2
Boat of Garten	SY	78	A2
Bodmin Road	WR	2	B1
Bodorgan	LM	43	B2
Bognor Regis	SO	11	C1
Bogston	SC	71	A1
Boldon Colliery	ER	70	B1
Bolton	LM	55	C1
Bolton-on-Dearne	ER	56	C2
Bond Street	LT	21	B1
Bookham	SO	11	A2
Boothferry Park*	ER	57	B2
Bootle (Cumbria)	LM	59	C2
Bootle New Strand	LM	53	A1
Bootle Oriel Road	LM	53	A1
Bordesley	LM	88	C1
Borough	LT	21	B2
Borough Green & Wrotham	SO	12	A2
Borth	LM	34	B2
Bosham	SO	11	C1
Boston	ER	49	C1
Boston Lodge	FR	43	C2
Boston Manor	LT	20	C1
Botley	SO	10	C2
Bottesford	ER	48	C1
Bounds Green	LT	23	C2
Bourne End	WR	31	C1
Bournemouth	SO	5	A2
Bournville	LM	37	B2
Bow Brickhill	LM	31	A1
Bowes Park	ER	23	C2
Bowker Vale	LM	51	A2
Bowling	SC	75	A1
Bow Road	LT	22	B1
Boxhill & Westhumble	SO	11	A2
Bracknell	SO	11	A1
Bradford Exchange	ER	56	B1
Bradford Forster Square	ER	56	B1
Bradford-on-Avon	WR	8	A1
Brading	SO	6	A2
Braintree	ER	33	A1
Bramhall	LM	46	A1
Bramley	SO	10	A2
Brampton (Cumbria)	ER	66	C2
Brampton (Suffolk)	ER	42	B1
Branchton	SC	71	A1
Brandon	ER	41	B1
Branksome	SO	5	A2
Braystones	LM	59	B2
Bredbury	LM	52	C2
Breich	SC	72	B2
Brent Cross	LT	20	A2
Brentford	SO	20	C1
Brentwood	ER	32	C2
Bricket Wood	LM	31	B2
Bridge End	NI	86	C2
Bridgend	WR	27	C2
Bridge of Orchy	SC	78	B1
Bridge of Weir	SC	71	B2
Bridge Street	GG	76	B1
Bridgeton	SC	76	B1
Bridgnorth	WR	8	B1
Bridgwater	SV	37	B1
Bridlington	ER	57	A2
Brierfield	LM	55	B1
Brigg	ER	57	C2
Brighton	SO	12	C1
Brightside	ER	50	A1
Brimsdown	ER	24	B1
Brinnington	LM	52	C2
Bristol Parkway	WR	28	C2
Bristol Temple Meads	WR	8	B2
Brithdir	WR	28	B1
British Steel (Redcar)	ER	62	A2
Brixton	SO/LT	21	C2
Broadbottom	LM	46	A2
Broad Green	LM	53	B2
Broadstairs	SO	14	A1
Broad Street	LM	21	B2
Brockenhurst	SO	10	C1
Brockholes	ER	56	C1
Brocklesby	ER	57	C2
Brockley	SO	22	C1
Bromborough	LM	45	A1
Bromley-by-Bow	LT	22	B1
Bromley Cross	LM	55	C1
Bromley North	SO	18	B2
Bromley South	SO	18	B2
Bromsgrove	WR	37	C2
Brondesbury	LM	21	B1
Brondesbury Park	LM	21	B1
Bronwydd Arms	GW	62	A2
Brooklands	LM	51	C2
Brookman's Park	ER	32	B1
Brookwood	SO	11	A2
Broome	WR	36	B2
Broomfleet	ER	57	B1
Brora	SC	82	B2
Brough	ER	57	B2
Broughty Ferry	SC	79	B2
Broxbourne	ER	32	B1
Bruce Grove	ER	23	C2
Brundall	ER	42	A1
Brundall Gardens	ER	42	A1
Brunton	WR	9	B1
Bryn	LM	54	C2
Brynglas	TL	34	A2
Buchanan Street	GG	76	B1
Buckenham	ER	42	A1
Buckfastleigh	DV	3	B1
Buckhurst Hill	LT	24	C2
Buckley	LM	45	B1
Bucknell	WR	36	B1
Bugle	WR	1	B2
Builth Road	LM	35	C2
Bungalow	ME	59	C1
Bures	ER	33	A1
Burgess Hill	SO	12	C1
Burley-in-Wharfdale	ER	56	A1
Burmash Road Halt*	RH	13	B2
Burnage	LM	52	C1
Burneside	LM	60	C2
Burnham	WR	31	C1
Burnham-on-Crouch	ER	33	C1
Burnley Barracks	LM	55	B1
Burnley Central	LM	55	B1
Burnside	SC	76	C1
Burntisland	SC	73	A1
Burnt Oak	LT	31	C2
Burscough Bridge	LM	54	C2
Burscough Junction	LM	54	C2
Bursledon	SO	10	C2
Burton Joyce	LM	47	C2
Burton-on-Trent	LM	47	C1
Bury	LM	55	C1
Bury St. Edmunds	ER	41	C1
Busby	SC	76	C1
Bushey	LM/LT	31	C2
Bush Hill Park	ER	23	B2
Butlers Lane	LM	88	A2
Buxted	SO	12	B2
Buxton	LM	46	A2
Byfleet & New Haw	SO	15	C1
Byker	TW	69	B2
Bynea	WR	26	B2
Cabin	BF	54	B1
Cadoxton	WR	7	A1
Caergwrle	LM	45	B1
Caerphilly	WR	28	C1
Caersws	LM	35	B2
Caldicot	WR	28	C2
Caledonian Road	LT	21	A2
Caledonian Road & Barnsbury	LM	21	B2
Calstock	WR	2	B2
Camberley	SO	11	A1
Camborne	WR	1	C1
Cambridge	ER	40	C1
Cambridge Heath	ER	22	B1
Cambuslang	SC	76	C2
Camden Road	LM	21	B1
Camden Town	LT	21	B1
Canley	LM	38	B1
Canning Town	ER	22	B1
Cannon Street	SO/LT	21	B2

Canonbury	LM	21	A2
Canons Park	LT	31	C2
Canterbury East	SO	13	A2
Canterbury West	SO	13	A2
Cantley	ER	42	A1
Capel Bangor	LM	33	B2
Capenhurst	LM	45	A1
Carbis Bay	WR	1	A1
Cardendon	SC	79	C1
Cardiff Bute Road	WR	28	A1
Cardiff Central	WR	28	A1
Cardiff Queen Street	WR	28	A1
Cardonald	SC	75	B2
Cardross	SC	71	A2
Carfin Halt	SC	72	B1
Cargo Fleet	ER	62	B2
Cark & Cartmel	LM	60	C1
Carlisle	LM	66	C2
Carlton	LM	47	C2
Carluke	SC	72	B2
Carmarthen	WR	26	B2
Carnalea	NI	86	B2
Carnforth	LM	60	C2
Carnoustie	SC	79	B2
Carntyne	SC	76	B2
Carpenders Park	LM/LT	31	C2
Carr Bridge	SC	78	A2
Carrickfergus	NI	86	C2
Carshalton	SO	17	B1
Carshalton Beeches	SO	17	C1
Carstairs	SC	72	B2
Cartsdyke	SC	71	A1
Castle Bar Park	WR	20	B1
Castle Caereinion	WL	36	A1
Castle Cary	WR	8	B2
Castleford	ER	56	B2
Castlerock	NI	85	A2
Castleton	LM	55	C1
Castleton Moor	ER	63	B1
Castletown	ME	59	C1
Caterham	SO	12	A1
Catford	SO	18	A1
Catford Bridge	SO	18	A1
Cathcart	SC	76	C1
Cattal	ER	56	A2
Causeland	WR	2	B1
Cefn-Onn	WR	28	C1
Cefn-y-Bedd	LM	45	B1
Cei Llydan	LL	43	B2
Cessnock	GG	75	B2
Chadwell Heath	ER	32	C2
Chalfont & Latimer	LM/LT	31	C2
Chalk Farm	LT	21	B1
Chalkwell	ER	33	C1
Chancery Lane	LT	21	B2
Chapel-en-le-Frith	LM	46	A2
Chapelton	WR	6	B2
Chapeltown	ER	50	A1
Chappel & Wakes Colne	ER	33	A1
Charing	SO	13	A1
Charing Cross (Glasgow)	SC	76	B1
Charing Cross (London)	SO/LT	21	B2
Charlbury	WR	30	B1
Charlton	SO	22	C2
Chartham	SO	13	A2
Chassen Road	LM	51	C1
Chatham	SO	13	A1
Chathill	SC	74	A2
Cheadle Hulme	LM	46	A1
Cheam	SO	17	C1
Cheddington	LM	31	B1
Chelford	LM	46	A1
Chelmsford	ER	32	B2
Chelsfield	SO	12	A1
Cheltenham Spa	WR	29	A2
Chepstow	WR	28	C2
Cherry Tree	LM	55	B1
Chertsey	SO	15	B1
Chesham	LT	31	B2
Cheshunt	ER	24	A1
Chessington North	SO	16	C1
Chessington South	SO	16	C1
Chester	LM	45	B2
Chester-le-Street	ER	68	C1
Chesterfield	ER	47	B1
Chester Road	LM	88	B2
Chestfield & Swalecliffe	SO	13	A2
Chetnole	WR	8	C2
Chichester (Sussex)	SO	11	C1
Chichester (Tyne & Wear)	TW	70	B2
Chigwell	LT	24	C2
Chilham	SO	13	A2
Chillingham Road	TW	69	B2
Chilworth	SO	11	B2
Chingford	ER	24	C1
Chinley	LM	46	A2
Chippenham	WR	29	C2
Chipstead	SO	12	A1
Chirk	LM	45	C1
Chislehurst	SO	18	B2
Chiswick	SO	20	C2
Chiswick Park	LT	20	C2
Cholsey	WR	30	C2
Chorley	LM	54	C2
Chorley Wood	LM/LT	31	C2
Christ's Hospital	SO	11	B2
Christchurch	SU	5	A2
Church & Oswaldtwistle	LM	55	B1
Church Fenton	ER	56	B2
Church Stretton	LM	36	B2
Churston	TD	3	B2
Cilmeri	LM	35	C2
Clacton	ER	33	B2
Clandon	SO	11	A2
Clapham	SO	21	C2
Clapham (Yorks.)	LM	55	A1
Clapham Common	LT	21	C2
Clapham Junction	SO	21	C1
Clapham North	LT	21	C2
Clapham South	LT	17	A1
Clapton	ER	22	A1
Clarbeston Road	WR	25	A2
Clarkston	SC	76	C1
Claverdon	LM	38	C1
Claygate	SO	16	C1
Clayton West	ER	56	C1
Cleethorpes	ER	58	C1
Cleland	SC	72	B1
Cleveleys	BF	54	B1
Clifton	LM	51	A2
Clifton Down	WR	8	A2
Clipperstown	NI	86	C2
Clitheroe*	LM	55	B1
Clock House	SO	18	B1
Clogwyn	SM	43	B2
Clunderwen	WR	26	B1
Clydebank	SC	75	A1
Coatbridge Central	SC	72	C1
Coatbridge Sunnyside	SC	72	C1
Coatdyke	SC	72	C1
Cobham & Stoke d'Abernon	SO	11	A2
Cockfosters	LT	23	B1
Codsall	LM	37	A1
Cogan	WR	28	B1
Colby	ME	59	C1
Colchester	ER	33	A1
Coleraine	NI	85	A2
Colindale	LT	31	C2
Collier's Wood	LT	17	A1
Collingham	ER	48	B1
Collington	SO	12	C2
Colne	LM	55	B1
Colwall	WR	29	A1
Colwyn Bay	LM	44	A1
Colyford	ST	4	A1
Colyton	ST	4	A1
Combe (Oxon)	WR	30	B1
Commondale	ER	63	B1
Congleton	LM	46	B1
Conisbrough	ER	56	C2
Connel Ferry	SC	77	B2
Cooden Beach	SO	12	C2
Cookham	WR	31	C1
Cooksbridge	SO	12	C1

Station	Region	Map	Grid
Coombe (Cornwall)	WR	2	B1
Coombe Road	SO	17	C2
Copplestone	WR	7	C1
Corbridge	ER	67	C2
Corkerhill	SC	75	B2
Corkickle	LM	59	B2
Cornaa	ME	59	B2
Corpach	SC	78	B1
Corrour	SC	78	B1
Coryton	WR	28	C1
Coseley	LM	87	B1
Cosford	LM	37	A1
Cosham	SO	10	C2
Cottingham	ER	57	B2
Coulsdon North	SO	12	A1
Coulsdon South	SO	12	A1
Covent Garden	LT	21	B2
Coventry	LM	38	B1
Cowcaddens	GG	76	B1
Cowden	SO	12	B2
Cowdenbeath	SC	73	A1
Cradley	LM	87	C1
Craigavad*	NI	86	C2
Craigendoran	SC	71	A1
Cramlington	ER	68	B1
Craven Arms	WR	36	B2
Crawfordsburn	NI	86	C2
Crawley	SO	12	B1
Crayford	SO	32	C2
Crediton	WR	3	A1
Cressing	ER	33	B1
Cressington	LM	53	C2
Crewe	LM	46	B1
Crewkerne	WR	8	C2
Crews Hill	ER	23	A2
Crianlarich	SC	78	C1
Criccieth	LM	43	C2
Cricklewood	LM	20	A2
Croftfoot	SC	76	C1
Crofton Park	SO	18	A1
Cromer	ER	50	C1
Cromford	LM	47	B1
Cromore	NI	85	A2
Crookston	SC	75	B2
Cross Gates	ER	56	B1
Crosshill	SC	76	C1
Crossmyloof	SC	75	C2
Croston	LM	54	C2
Crouch Hill	ER	21	A2
Crowborough	SO	12	B2
Crowcombe	WS	8	B1
Crowle	ER	57	C1
Crowthorne	SO	11	A1
Croxley	LT	31	C2
Croxley Green	LM	31	C2
Croy	SC	72	A1
Crumlin	NI	86	C1
Crumpsall	LM	52	A1
Crystal Palace	SO	17	A2
Cuddington	LM	45	A2
Cuffley	ER	23	A2
Culham	WR	30	C2
Cullercoats	TW	70	A2
Culrain	SC	82	B2
Cultra	NI	86	C2
Cumbernauld	SC	72	A1
Cupar	SC	79	C2
Custom House Victoria Dock	ER	22	B2
Cuxton	SO	12	A2
Cwmdwyfran	GW	26	A2
Cyfronydd	WL	36	A1
Cynghordy	WR	27	A1
Dagenham Dock	ER	32	C2
Dagenham East	LT	32	C2
Dagenham Heathway	LT	32	C2
Daisy Hill	LM	55	C1
Dalmally	SC	78	C1
Dalmarnock	SC	76	B1
Dalmeny	SC	73	A1
Dalmuir	SC	75	A1
Dalreoch	SC	71	A2
Dalry	SC	71	B1
Dalston (Cumbria)	LM	66	C2
Dalston (Proposed)	LM	21	A2
Dalston Junction	LM	21	A2
Dalton	LM	60	C1
Dalwhinnie	SC	78	A2
Damems	KW	55	B2
Danby	ER	63	B1
Dane Road	LM	51	C2
Danzey	LM	37	C2
Darlington	ER	62	B1
Darnall	ER	50	B1
Darsham	ER	42	C1
Dartford	SO	32	C2
Dartmouth Ferry & Kingswear	TD	3	B2
Darton	ER	56	C1
Darwen	LM	55	B1
Datchet	SO	31	C2
Davenport	LM	52	C1
Dawlish	WR	3	A2
Dawlish Warren	WR	3	A2
Dduallt	FR	44	C1
Deal	SO	14	A1
Dean	SO	10	B1
Dean Lane	LM	52	A1
Deansgate	LM	51	B2
Debden	LT	24	B2
Deepdene	SO	11	A2
Deganwy	LM	44	A1
Delamere	LM	45	B2
Denby Dale	ER	56	C1
Denham	LM	19	A1
Denham Golf Club	LM	31	C2
Denmark Hill	SO	21	C2
Dent*	LM	61	C1
Denton	LM	52	B2
Deptford	SO	22	C1
Derby	LM	47	C1
Derby Castle (Douglas)	ME	59	C1
Derby Road (Ipswich)	ER	33	A2
Dereham*	ER	41	A1
Derriaghy	NI	84	A2
Devil's Bridge	LM	34	B2
Devonport	WR	2	B2
Dewsbury	ER	56	B1
Dhoon	ME	59	C2
Dhu Varren	NI	85	A2
Didcot	WR	30	C2
Dilton Marsh	WR	9	A1
Dinas Powys	WR	8	A1
Dinas	WR	27	C2
Dingle Road	WR	28	B1
Dingwall	SC	82	C2
Dinsdale	ER	62	B1
Dinting	LM	46	A2
Disley	LM	46	A2
Diss	ER	41	B2
Ditton	LM	45	A2
Dockyard	WR	2	B2
Dolau	WR	36	C1
Doleham	SO	13	C1
Dolgarrog	LM	44	B1
Dolgoch Falls	TL	34	A2
Dollis Hill	LT	20	A2
Dolwyddelan	LM	44	B1
Doncaster	ER	56	C2
Dorchester South	SO	5	A1
Dorchester West	SO	5	A1
Dore	ER	47	A1
Dorking	SO	11	A2
Dorking Town	SO	11	A2
Dormans	SO	12	B1
Dorridge	LM	38	B1
Douglas	ME	59	C1
Dove Holes	LM	46	A2
Dovercourt	ER	33	A2
Dover Priory	SO	14	B1
Dover Western Docks	SO	14	B1
Dovey Junction	LM	34	A2
Downham	ER	40	A2
Downshire	NI	86	C2
Drayton Green	WR	20	B1
Drayton Park	ER	21	A2

Dreemskerrie	ME	59	B2
Drem	SC	73	A2
Driffield	ER	57	A2
Drigg	LM	59	B2
Droitwich Spa	WR	37	C1
Dronfield	ER	47	A1
Drumchapel	SC	75	A2
Drumry	SC	75	A2
Duddeston	LM	88	C1
Dudley Port	LM	87	B2
Duffield	LM	47	C1
Duirinish	SC	81	C2
Duke Street	SC	76	B1
Dullingham	ER	40	C2
Dumbarton Central	SC	71	A2
Dumbarton East	SC	71	A2
Dumfries	SC	63	B2
Dumpton Park	SO	14	A1
Dunbar	SC	74	A1
Dunblane	SC	78	C2
Dunbridge	SO	10	B1
Duncraig	SC	81	C2
Dundee	SC	79	B2
Dunfermline	SC	73	A1
Dungeness	RH	13	C2
Dunkeld	SC	78	B2
Dunlop	SC	71	B2
Dunmurry	NI	84	A2
Dunster	WS	7	B2
Dunton Green	SO	12	A2
Durham	ER	62	A1
Durrington-on-Sea	SO	11	C2
Dyffryn Ardudwy	LM	43	C2
Dymchurch	RH	13	B2
Eaglescliffe	ER	62	B2
Ealing Broadway	WR/LT	20	B1
Ealing Common	LT	20	B2
Eardington	SV	37	B1
Earl's Court	LT	21	C1
Earlestown	LM	45	A2
Earley	SO	11	A1
Earlsfield	SO	17	A1
Earlswood (Surrey)	SO	12	A1
Earlswood (West Midlands)	LM	37	B2
East Acton	LT	20	B2
East Boldon	ER	70	C2
Eastbourne	SO	12	C2
Eastcote	LT	19	A2
East Croydon	SO	17	B2
East Didsbury	LM	52	C1
East Dulwich	SO	21	C2
Easterhouse	SC	76	B2
East Farleigh	SO	13	A1
East Finchley	LT	21	A1
East Grinstead	SO	12	B1
East Ham	LT	22	B2
East Kilbride	SC	72	B1
Eastleigh	SO	10	C2
East Malling	SO	12	A2
East Putney	LT	21	C1
Eastrington	ER	57	B1
East Tilbury	ER	32	C2
East Worthing	SO	11	C2
Eccles	LM	51	B2
Eccles Road	ER	41	B2
Eccleston Park	LM	45	A2
Edale	LM	46	A2
Edenbridge	SO	12	A1
Edenbridge Town	SO	12	B1
Eden Park	SO	18	B1
Edge Hill	LM	53	B2
Edgware	LT	31	C2
Edgware Road	LT	21	B1
Edinburgh	SC	73	C1
Effingham Junction	SO	11	A2
Eggesford	WR	7	C1
Egham	SO	11	A2
Egton	ER	63	B1
Elephant & Castle	SO/LT	21	C2
Elgin	SC	83	C1
Ellesmere Port	LM	45	A2
Elmers End	SO	18	B1
Elm Park	LT	32	C2
Elmstead Woods	SO	18	A2
Elmswell	ER	41	C1
Elsecar	ER	56	C1
Elsenham	ER	32	A2
Elsham	ER	57	C2
Elstree	LM	31	C2
Eltham Park	SO	22	C2
Eltham Well Hall	SO	22	C2
Elton & Orston	ER	48	C1
Ely	ER	40	B2
Embankment	LT	21	B2
Emerson Park	ER	32	C2
Emsworth	SO	11	C1
Enfield Chase	ER	23	B2
Enfield Lock	ER	24	B1
Enfield Town	ER	23	B2
Entwistle	LM	55	C1
Epping	LT	32	B1
Epsom	SO	16	C2
Epsom Downs	SO	12	A1
Erdington	LM	88	B2
Eridge	SO	12	B2
Erith	SO	32	C2
Errol	SC	79	B1
Esher	SO	16	B1
Eskdale (Dalegarth)	RE	60	B1
Essex Road	ER	21	B2
Etchingham	SO	12	B2
Etruria	LM	46	C1
Euston	LM/LT	21	B2
Euston Square	LT	21	B2
Evesham	WR	29	A2
Ewell East	SO	16	C2
Ewell West	SO	16	C2
Exeter Central	WR	3	A2
Exeter St. David's	WR	3	A2
Exeter St. Thomas	WR	3	A2
Exmouth	WR	3	A2
Exton	WR	3	A2
Eynsford	SO	12	A2
Failsworth	LM	52	A1
Fairbourne	LM/FB	34	A2
Fairfield	LM	52	B2
Fairlie	SC	71	B1
Fairlop	LT	24	C2
Fairy Cottage	ME	59	C2
Falconwood	SO	22	C2
Falkirk Grahamston	SC	72	A2
Falkirk High	SC	72	A2
Falmer	SO	12	C1
Falmouth	WR	1	C2
Fambridge	ER	33	B1
Fareham	SO	10	C2
Farnborough (Main)	SO	11	A1
Farnborough North	SO	11	A1
Farncombe	SO	11	B2
Farnham	SO	11	B1
Farningham Road & Sutton-at-Hone	SO	12	A2
Farnworth	LM	51	A1
Farringdon	LM/LT	21	B2
Fauldhouse	SC	72	B2
Faversham	SO	13	A2
Fawdon	TW	69	A2
Faygate	SO	12	B1
Fazakerley	LM	53	A2
Fearn	SC	82	B2
Felixstowe	ER	34	A1
Felling	TW	69	B2
Feltham	SO	15	A2
Fenchurch Street	ER	21	B2
Feniton	WR	3	A2
Fenny Stratford	LM	31	A1
Ferriby	ER	57	B2
Ferry Meadows	NV	39	A2
Ferryside	WR	26	B2
Ffairfach	WR	27	B1
Filey	ER	63	C2
Filton	WR	28	C2
Finaghy	NI	84	A2
Finchley Central	LT	23	C1

Finchley Road	LT	21	A1
Finchley Road & Frognal	LM	21	A1
Finnieston	SC	76	B1
Finsbury Park	ER/LT	21	A2
Finstock	WR	30	B1
Fishbourne	SO	11	C1
Fishersgate	SO	12	C1
Fishguard Harbour	WR	25	A2
Fiskerton	LM	48	B1
Five Ways	LM	88	C1
Fleet	SO	11	A1
Fleetwood	BF	54	A1
Flimby	LM	59	A2
Flint	LM	45	A1
Flitwick	LM	31	A2
Flixton	LM	51	C1
Folkestone Central	SO	13	B2
Folkestone East*	SO	13	B2
Folkestone Harbour	SO	13	B2
Folkestone Warren*	SO	13	B2
Folkestone West	SO	13	B2
Ford	SO	11	C2
Forest Gate	ER	22	A2
Forest Hill	SO	18	A1
Formby	LM	54	C1
Forres	SC	82	C2
Forsinard	SC	82	A2
Fort Matilda	SC	71	A1
Fort William	SC	78	B1
Four Oaks	LM	88	A2
Foxfield	LM	60	C1
Foxton	ER	40	C1
Frant	SO	12	B2
Fratton	SO	10	C2
Freshfield (Mersyside)	LM	54	C1
Freshfield Halt (Sussex)	BL	12	B1
Freshford	WR	9	A1
Frimley	SO	11	A1
Frinton	ER	33	B2
Frodsham	LM	45	A2
Frome	WR	9	B1
Fulham Broadway	LT	21	C1
Fulwell	SO	16	A1
Furness Vale	LM	46	A2
Furze Platt	WR	31	C1
Gainsborough Central	ER	48	A1
Gainsborough Lea Road	ER	48	A1
Gants Hill	LT	22	A2
Garelochhead	SC	71	A1
Garforth	ER	56	B2
Gargrave	LM	55	A2
Garrowhill	SC	76	B2
Garscadden	SC	75	B2
Garsdale*	LM	61	C1
Garston (Herts.)	LM	31	B2
Garston (Merseyside)	LM	53	C2
Garswood	LM	54	C2
Garth	LM	35	C2
Garve	SC	82	C1
Garwick Glen	ME	59	C2
Gateshead	TW	69	B2
Gathurst	LM	54	C2
Gatley	LM	52	C1
Gatwick Airport	SO	12	B1
Georgemas Junction	SC	83	A1
Gerrards Cross	LM	31	C2
Giffnock	SC	75	C2
Giggleswick	LM	55	A1
Gilberdyke	ER	57	B1
Gilfach Ddu (Llanberis)	LL	43	B2
Gilfach Fargoed	WR	28	B1
Gillingham (Dorset)	SO	9	B1
Gillingham (Kent)	SO	13	A1
Gipsy Hill	SO	17	A2
Girvan	SC	64	A1
Glaisdale	ER	63	B1
Glan Conwy	LM	44	A1
Glanrafon	LM	33	B2
Glasgow Central	SC	76	B1
Glasgow Queen Street	SC	76	B1
Glazebrook	LM	46	A1
Glenavy	NI	86	C1
Glen Mona	ME	59	C2
Gleneagles	SC	78	C2
Glenfinnan Loch Shiel	SC	77	A2
Glengarnock	SC	71	B2
Glossop	LM	46	A2
Gloucester	WR	29	B1
Gloucester Road	LT	21	C1
Glynde	SO	12	C1
Glynn	NI	86	B2
Goathland	NY	63	B1
Gobowen	LM	45	C1
Godalming	SO	11	B2
Godley	LM	52	B2
Godstone	SO	12	A1
Gogarth	LM	34	A2
Golders Green	LT	21	A1
Goldhawk Road	LT	20	C2
Golf Street Halt	SC	79	B2
Golfa	WL	36	A1
Golspie	SC	82	B2
Gomshall	SO	11	A2
Goodge Street	LT	21	B2
Goodmayes	ER	32	C1
Goodrington Sands	TD	3	B2
Goodyear	NI	84	A1
Goole	ER	57	B1
Goostrey	LM	46	B1
Gordon Hill	ER	23	B2
Goring & Streatley	WR	30	C2
Goring-by-Sea	SO	11	C2
Gorton	LM	52	B1
Gospel Oak	LM	21	A1
Gourock	SC	71	A1
Govan Cross	GG	75	B2
Gowerton	WR	26	C2
Goxhill	ER	57	B2
Grange-over-Sands	LM	60	C2
Grange Hill	LT	24	C2
Grange Park	ER	23	B2
Grangetown (Cleveland)	ER	62	A2
Grangetown (S. Glam.)	WR	28	A1
Grantham	ER	48	C1
Grateley	SO	10	B1
Gravelly Hill	LM	88	B2
Gravesend	SO	32	C2
Grays	ER	32	C2
Great Ayton	ER	62	B2
Great Bentley	ER	33	B2
Great Chesterford	ER	32	A2
Great Coates	ER	58	C1
Greatham	ER	62	A2
Great Malvern	WR	29	A1
Great Missenden	LM	31	B1
Great Orme	GO	44	A1
Great Portland Street	LT	21	B1
Greatstone	RH	13	B2
Greenbank	LM	46	A1
Greenfield	LM	55	C2
Greenford	WR/LT	20	B1
Greenhithe	SO	32	C2
Greenisland	NI	86	C2
Green Lane	LM	53	C1
Greenock Central	SC	71	A1
Greenock West	SC	71	A1
Green Park	LT	21	B1
Green Road	LM	60	C1
Greenwich	SO	22	C1
Grimsby Docks	ER	58	C1
Grimsby Town	ER	58	C1
Grindleford	LM	47	A1
Groombridge	SO	12	B2
Grosmont	ER/NY	63	B1
Groudle Glen	ME	59	C2
Grove Park	SO	18	A2
Guide Bridge	LM	52	B2
Guildford	SO	11	A2
Guiseley	ER	56	B1
Gunnersbury	SO/LT	20	C2
Gunnislake	WR	2	B2
Gunton	ER	50	C2
Gwersyllt	LM	45	B1
Gypsy Lane	ER	62	B2

Station			
Habrough	ER	57	C2
Hackbridge	SO	17	B1
Hackney Central	ER	22	A1
Hackney Downs	ER	22	A1
Hackney Wick	ER	22	B1
Haddiscoe	ER	42	A1
Hadfield	LM	46	A2
Hadley Wood	ER	23	B1
Hadrian Road	TW	70	B1
Hagley	LM	37	B1
Hainault	LT	24	C2
Hairmyres	SC	72	B1
Hale	LM	46	A1
Halesworth	ER	42	B1
Halfway (Great Orme)	GO	44	A1
Halfway (Snowdon)	SM	43	B2
Halifax	ER	55	B2
Hall Green	LM	37	B2
Halling	SO	12	A2
Hall Road	LM	53	A1
Haltwhistle	ER	67	C1
Hamble	SO	10	C2
Hamilton Central	SC	72	B1
Hamilton West	SC	72	B1
Hammersmith	LT	20	C2
Hammerton	ER	56	A2
Hampden Park	SO	12	C2
Hampstead	LT	21	A1
Hampstead Heath	LM	21	A1
Hampton	SO	15	B2
Hampton-in-Arden	LM	38	B1
Hampton Court	SO	16	B1
Hampton Loade	SV	37	B1
Hampton Wick	SO	16	B1
Hamstead	LM	88	B1
Ham Street	SO	13	B2
Hamworthy	SO	5	A2
Handborough	WR	30	B2
Handforth	LM	46	A1
Hanger Lane	LT	20	B1
Hanwell	WR	20	B1
Hapton	LM	55	B1
Harlech	LM	43	C2
Harlesden	LM/LT	20	B2
Harling Road	ER	41	B1
Harlington	LM	31	A2
Harlow Mill	ER	32	B2
Harlow Town	ER	32	B1
Harold Wood	ER	32	C2
Harpenden	LM	31	B2
Harrietsham	SO	13	A1
Harringay	ER	21	A2
Harringay Stadium	ER	21	A2
Harrington	LM	59	A2
Harrogate	ER	56	A1
Harrow & Wealdstone	LM/LT	20	A1
Harrow-on-Hill	LM/LT	20	A1
Hartford	LM	45	B2
Hartlebury	LM	37	C1
Hartlepool	ER	62	A2
Hartwood	SC	72	B2
Harwich Parkeston Quay	ER	33	A2
Harwich Town	ER	33	A2
Haslemere	SO	11	B1
Hassocks	SO	12	C1
Hastings	SO	13	C1
Hatch End	LM/LT	31	C2
Hatfield	ER	32	B1
Hatfield Peverel	ER	33	B1
Hathersage	LM	47	A1
Hattersley	LM	46	A2
Hatton	LM	38	C1
Hatton Cross	LT	19	C2
Havant	SO	11	C1
Havenhouse	ER	49	B2
Havenstreet	IW	6	A2
Haverfordwest	WR	25	B2
Haverthwaite	LH	60	C1
Hawarden	LM	45	B1
Hawarden Bridge	LM	45	B1
Haworth	KW	55	B2
Haydon Bridge	ER	67	C1
Haydons Road	SO	17	A1
Hayes (Kent)	SO	18	B2
Hayes & Harlington	WR	19	C2
Hayle	WR	1	A1
Haymarket (Edinburgh)	SC	73	C1
Haymarket (Newcastle)	TW	69	B2
Haywards Heath	SO	12	B1
Hazel Grove	LM	46	B2
Headcorn	SO	13	B1
Headingley	ER	56	B1
Headstone Lane	LM/LT	31	C2
Heald Green	LM	46	A1
Healing	ER	58	C1
Heath High Level	WR	28	C1
Heath Low Level	WR	28	C1
Heathrow Central	LT	19	C1
Heaton Chapel	LM	52	C1
Heaton Park	LM	51	A2
Hebburn	TW	70	B1
Hebden Bridge	ER	55	B2
Hebron	SM	43	B2
Heckington	ER	48	C2
Heighington	ER	62	A1
Helen's Bay	NI	86	C2
Helensburgh Central	SC	71	A1
Helensburgh Upper	SC	71	A1
Hellifield	LM	55	A1
Helmsdale	SC	82	B2
Helsby	LM	45	A2
Hemel Hempstead	LM	31	B2
Hendon	LM	20	A2
Hendon Central	LT	20	A2
Hengoed	WR	28	C1
Heniarth	WL	35	A2
Henley-in-Arden	LM	37	C2
Henley-on-Thames	WR	31	C1
Hensall	ER	56	B2
Hereford	WR	28	A2
Herne Bay	SO	13	A2
Herne Hill	SO	17	A2
Hersham	SO	15	B2
Hertford East	ER	32	B1
Hertford North	ER	32	B1
Hessle	ER	57	B2
Heswall	LM	45	A1
Hever	SO	12	B1
Heworth	ER/TW	69	B2
Hexham	ER	67	C2
Heyford	WR	30	A2
Higham	SO	32	C2
Highams Park	ER	24	C1
High Barnet	LT	23	B1
Highbridge	WR	8	B1
High Brooms	SO	12	B2
Highbury & Islington	ER/LT	21	A2
Highgate	LT	21	A1
Highley	SV	37	B1
High Shields	ER	70	B2
High Street (Glasgow)	SC	76	B1
High Street, Kensington	LT	21	C1
Hightown	LM	54	C1
High Wycombe	LM	31	C1
Hilden	NI	84	A2
Hidenborough	SO	12	A2
Hillfoot	SC	75	A2
Hillhead	GG	75	B2
Hillingdon	LT	19	A1
Hillington East	SC	75	B2
Hillington West	SC	75	B2
Hillside	LM	54	C1
Hilsea	SO	10	C2
Hinchley Wood	SO	16	B1
Hinckley	LM	38	B2
Hindley	LM	54	C2
Hinton Admiral	SO	6	A1
Hitchin	ER	31	A2
Hither Green	SO	18	A1
Hockley	ER	33	C1
Holborn	LT	21	B2
Holborn Viaduct	SO	21	B2
Holland Park	LT	21	B1
Hollingbourne	SO	13	A1

Hollinwood	LM	52	A1
Holloway Road	LT	21	A2
Holmes Chapel	LM	46	B1
Holmwood	SO	11	B2
Holton Heath	SO	5	A2
Holyhead	LM	43	A1
Holytown	SC	72	B1
Holywood	NI	86	C2
Homerton	ER	22	A1
Honiton	WR	8	C1
Honley	ER	55	C2
Honor Oak Park	SO	18	A1
Hook	SO	11	A1
Hoo Staff Halt*	SO	32	C2
Hooton	LM	45	A1
Hope (Clwyd)	LM	45	B1
Hope (Derbyshire)	LM	47	A1
Hopton Heath	WR	36	B1
Horley	SO	12	B1
Hornchurch	LT	32	C2
Hornsey	ER	21	A2
Horsforth	ER	56	B1
Horsham	SO	11	B2
Horsley	SO	11	A2
Horsted Keynes	BL	12	B1
Horton*	LM	61	C1
Hoscar	LM	54	C2
Hough Green	LM	45	A2
Hounslow	SO	20	C1
Hounslow Central	LT	19	C2
Hounslow East	LT	20	C1
Hounslow West	LT	19	C2
Howdon	TW	70	B1
Hove	SO	12	C1
Howden	ER	57	B1
Howstrake	ME	59	C2
Hoylake	LM	45	A1
Hubbert's Bridge	ER	49	C1
Huddersfield	ER	55	C2
Hull	ER	57	B2
Huncoat	LM	55	B1
Hungerford	WR	10	A1
Hunmanby	ER	63	C2
Huntingdon	ER	40	C1
Huntly	SC	83	C1
Hunt's Cross	LM	45	A2
Hurst Green	SO	12	A1
Hutton Cranswick	ER	57	A2
Huyton	LM	45	A2
Hyde Central	LM	52	B2
Hyde North	LM	52	B2
Hyde Park Corner	LT	21	B1
Hykeham	ER	48	B2
Hyndland	SC	75	B2
Hythe (Essex)	ER	33	A2
Hythe (Kent)	RH	13	B2
IBM Halt*	SC	71	A1
Ibrox	GG	75	B2
Ickenham	LT	19	A1
Ifield	SO	12	B1
Ilford	ER	22	A2
Ilford Road	TW	69	B2
Ilkley	ER	55	A2
Ince (Greater Manchester)	LM	54	C2
Ince & Elton	LM	45	A2
Ingatestone	ER	32	B2
Ingrow	KW	55	B2
Insch	SC	83	C2
Invergordon	SC	82	C2
Invergowrie	SC	79	B2
Inverkeithing	SC	73	A1
Inverkip	SC	71	A1
Inverness	SC	82	C2
Invershin	SC	82	B2
Inverurie	SC	80	A1
Ipswich	ER	33	A2
Irlam	LM	51	C1
Irton Road	RE	60	B1
Irvine	SC	71	C2
Isleworth	SO	20	C1
Iver	WR	19	B1
Jarrow	TW	70	B1
Jesmond	TW	69	B2
Johnston (Dyfed)	WR	25	B2
Johnstone	SC	71	B2
Jordanhill	SC	75	B2
Jordanstown	NI	86	C2
Kearsley	LM	51	A1
Kearsney	SO	14	B1
Keighley	ER/KW	55	B2
Keith	SC	83	C1
Kelvedon	ER	33	B1
Kelvinbridge	GG	76	B1
Kelvin Hall	GG	75	B2
Kemble	WR	29	C2
Kempston Hardwick	LM	31	A2
Kempton Park*	SO	15	A2
Kemsing	SO	12	A2
Kemsley	SO	13	A1
Kemsley Down	SK	13	A1
Kendal	LM	60	C2
Kenley	SO	17	C2
Kennett	ER	40	C2
Kennington	LT	21	C2
Kennishead	SC	75	C2
Kensal Green	LM/LT	20	B2
Kensal Rise	LM	20	B2
Kensington Olympia	LM/LT	21	C1
Kent House	SO	18	A1
Kentish Town	LM	21	A1
Kentish Town West	LM	21	B1
Kenton	LM/LT	20	A1
Kenton Bank Foot	TW	69	A1
Kents Bank	LM	60	C2
Kettering for Corby	LM	39	B1
Kew Bridge	SO	20	C2
Kew Gardens	SO/LT	20	C2
Keyham	WR	2	B2
Keynsham	WR	9	A1
Kidbrooke	SO	22	C2
Kidderminster	LM	37	B1
Kidgrove	LM	46	B2
Kidwelly	WR	26	B2
Kilburn	LT	21	A1
Kilburn High Road	LM	21	B1
Kilburn Park	LT	21	B1
Kildale	ER	62	B2
Kildonan	SC	82	B2
Kilgetty	WR	26	B1
Kilmacolm	SC	71	A2
Kilmarnock	SC	71	C2
Kilpatrick	SC	75	A1
Kilwinning	SC	71	B1
Kinbrace	SC	82	A2
King's Cross	ER/LT	21	B2
King's Langley	LM	31	B2
King's Lynn	ER	40	A2
King's Norton	LM	37	B2
King's Nympton	WR	7	C1
King's Park	SC	76	C1
King's Sutton	LM	30	A2
Kingham	WR	30	B1
Kinghorn	SC	73	A1
Kinsbury	LT	20	A2
Kingsknowe	SC	73	C1
Kingston	SO	16	B1
Kingswood	SO	12	A1
Kingussie	SC	78	A2
Kinning Park	GG	75	B2
Kintbury	WR	10	A1
Kirby Cross	ER	33	B2
Kirkby (Merseyside)	LM	53	A2
Kirkby-in-Furness	LM	60	C1
Kirkby Stephen*	LM	61	B1
Kirkcaldy	SC	73	A1
Kirkconnel	SC	63	A1
Kirkdale	LM	53	B1
Kirkham & Wesham	LM	54	B2
Kirkhill	SC	76	C2
Kirton Lindsey	ER	57	C2
Kiveton Bridge	ER	47	A2
Kiveton Park	ER	47	A2
Knaresborough	ER	56	A1
Knebworth	ER	32	B1

Knighton	WR	36	C1
Knightsbridge	LT	21	C1
Knockholt	SO	12	A2
Knockmore	NI	84	A2
Knottingley	ER	56	B2
Knucklas	WR	36	B1
Knutsford	LM	46	A1
Kyle of Lochalsh	SC	80	C2
Ladbroke Grove	LT	21	B1
Lade Halt	RH	13	C2
Ladybank	SC	79	C1
Ladywell	SO	22	C1
Laindon	ER	32	C2
Lairg	SC	82	B2
Lakenheath	ER	40	B2
Lakeside	LH	60	C1
Lambeg	NI	84	A2
Lambeth North	LT	21	C2
Lamphey	WR	25	B2
Lanark	SC	72	C2
Lancaster	LM	54	A2
Lancaster Gate	LT	21	B1
Lancing	SO	11	C2
Langbank	SC	71	A2
Langley	WR	31	C2
Langley Green	LM	87	C2
Langside	SC	76	C1
Langwathby*	LM	60	A2
Lapford	WR	7	C1
Lapworth	LM	38	C1
Larbert	SC	72	A2
Largs	SC	71	B1
Larne Harbour	NI	86	B2
Larne Town	NI	86	B2
Latimer Road	LT	20	B2
Lawrence Hill	WR	8	A2
Laxey	ME	59	C2
Layton	LM	54	B1
Lazonby*	LM	60	A2
Lea Bridge	ER	22	A1
Leagrave	LM	31	A2
Lea Hall	LM	88	C2
Lealholm	ER	63	B1
Leamington Spa	LM	38	C1
Leasowe	LM	45	A1
Leatherhead	SO	11	A2
Ledbury	WR	29	A1
Lee	SO	18	A2
Leeds	ER	56	B1
Leicester	LM	38	A2
Leicester Square	LT	21	B2
Leigh	SO	12	B2
Leigh-on-Sea	ER	33	C1
Leighton Buzzard	LM	31	A1
Lelant	WR	1	A1
Lelant Saltings	WR	1	A1
Lenham	SO	13	A1
Lenzie	SC	76	A2
Leominster	WR	36	C2
Letchworth	ER	32	A1
Leuchars	SC	79	B2
Levenshulme	LM	52	C1
Levisham	NY	63	C1
Lewaigue	ME	59	B2
Lewes	SO	12	C1
Lewisham	SO	22	C1
Leyland	LM	54	B2
Leyton	LT	22	A1
Leyton Midland Road	ER	22	A1
Leytonstone	LT	22	A1
Leytonstone High Road	ER	22	A1
Lichfield City	LM	37	A2
Lichfield Trent Valley	LM	37	A2
Lidlington	LM	31	A2
Lincoln Central	ER	48	B2
Lincoln St. Marks	ER	48	B2
Lingfield	SO	12	B1
Linlithgow	SC	72	A2
Liphook	SO	11	B1
Lisburn	NI	84	A2
Liskeard	WR	2	B1
Liss	SO	11	B1

Little Bispham	BF	54	B1
Littleborough	LM	55	C2
Littlehampton	SO	11	C2
Littlehaven	SO	11	B2
Little Kimble	LM	31	B1
Littleport	ER	40	B2
Little Sutton	LM	45	A1
Liverpool Central	LM	53	B1
Liverpool James Street	LM	53	B1
Liverpool Lime Street	LM	53	B1
Liverpool Moorfields	LM	53	B1
Liverpool Street (London)	ER/LT	21	B2
Llanaber	LM	34	A2
Llanbadarn	LM	34	B2
Llanbedr	LM	43	C2
Llanberis	SM	43	B2
Llanbister Road	WR	36	C1
Llanbradach	WR	28	C1
Llandaf	WR	28	C1
Llandanwg	LM	43	C2
Llandecwyn	LM	44	C1
Llandeilo	WR	27	A1
Llandovery	WR	27	A1
Llandrindod	LM	35	C2
Llandudno	LM	44	A1
Llandudno Junction	LM	44	A1
Llandudno Victoria	GO	44	A1
Llandybie	WR	27	B1
Llanelli	WR	26	B2
Llanfair Caereinion	WL	35	A2
Llanfairfechan	LM	44	A1
Llanfairpwll	LM	43	A2
Llangadog	WR	27	A1
Llangammarch	WR	27	A2
Llangelynin	LM	33	A2
Llangennech	WR	26	B2
Llangower	BA	44	C2
Llangynllo	WR	36	B1
Llanishen	WR	28	C1
Llanuwchllyn	BA	44	C2
Llanrwst	LM	44	B1
Llanwrda	WR	27	A1
Llanwrtyd	WR	27	A2
Llwyngwril	LM	34	A2
Llwynpia	WR	27	C2
Lochailort	SC	77	A2
Locheilside	SC	78	A1
Lochgelly	SC	79	C1
Lochluichart	SC	82	C1
Lochside	SC	71	B2
Lochty	LY	79	C2
Lockerbie	SC	66	B1
Lockwood	ER	55	C2
London Bridge	SO/LT	21	B2
Londonderry	NI	85	A1
London Fields	ER	22	B1
London Road (Brighton)	SO	12	C1
London Road (Guildford)	SO	11	A2
Longbenton	TW	69	A2
Longbridge	LM	37	B2
Long Buckby	LM	38	C2
Longcross	SO	11	A2
Long Eaton	LM	47	C2
Longfield	SO	12	A2
Longniddry	SC	73	A2
Longport	LM	46	B1
Long Preston	LM	55	A1
Longsight Staff Halt*	LM	52	B1
Longton	LM	46	C2
Looe	WR	2	B1
Lostock Gralam	LM	46	A1
Lostwithiel	WR	2	B1
Loughborough	LM	38	A2
Loughborough Central	ML	38	A2
Loughborough Junction	SO	21	C2
Loughton	LT	24	B2
Lowdham	LM	47	C2
Lower Edmonton	ER	23	C2
Lower Sydenham	SO	18	A1
Lowestoft	ER	42	B2
Ludgershall*	SO	10	A1
Ludlow	WR	36	B2

Lurgan	NI	84	A1
Luton	LM	31	B2
Luxulyan	WR	1	B2
Lydney	WR	28	B2
Lye	LM	87	C1
Lymington Pier	SO	6	A1
Lymington Town	SO	6	A1
Lympstone	WR	3	A2
Lympstone Commando	WR	3	A2
Lyndhurst Road	SO	10	C1
Lytham	LM	54	B1
Macclesfield	LM	46	A2
Machynlleth	LM	34	A2
Maddieson's Camp	RH	13	C2
Magdalen Road	ER	40	A2
Magheramore	NI	86	B2
Maghull	LM	54	C2
Magilligan*	NI	85	A1
Maida Vale	LT	21	B1
Maidenhead	WR	31	C1
Maiden Newton	WR	4	A2
Maidstone Barracks	SO	13	A1
Maidstone East	SO	13	A1
Maidstone West	SO	13	A1
Malden Manor	SO	16	B2
Mallaig	SC	77	A2
Malton	ER	63	C1
Malvern Link	WR	37	C1
Manchester Oxford Road	LM	52	B1
Manchester Piccadilly	LM	52	B1
Manchester Square	BF	54	B1
Manchester United Football Ground*	LM	51	B2
Manchester Victoria	LM	52	B1
Manea	ER	40	B2
Manningtree	ER	33	A2
Manorbier	WR	25	B2
Manor House	LT	21	A2
Manor Park	ER	22	A2
Manor Road	LM	45	A1
Manors	ER/TW	69	B2
Mansion House	LT	21	B2
Marble Arch	LT	21	B1
March	ER	40	B1
Marden	SO	13	B1
Margate	SO	14	A1
Marino	NI	86	C2
Market Bosworth	SH	38	A1
Market Harborough	LM	39	B1
Market Rasen	ER	48	A2
Markinch for Glenrothes	SC	79	C1
Marks Tey	ER	33	A1
Marlow	WR	31	C1
Marple	LM	52	C2
Marsden	ER	55	C2
Marske	ER	62	A2
Marston Green	LM	38	B1
Martin Mill	SO	14	B1
Maryland	ER	22	A1
Marylebone	LM/LT	21	B1
Maryport	LM	59	A2
Matlock	LM	47	B1
Matlock Bath	LM	47	B1
Mauldeth Road	LM	52	C1
Maxwell Park	SC	75	B2
Maybole	SC	64	A1
Maze Hill	SO	22	C1
Meldreth	ER	32	A1
Melton*	ER	57	B2
Melton Mowbray	LM	39	A1
Menheniot	WR	2	B1
Menston	ER	56	B1
Meols	LM	45	A1
Meols Cop	LM	54	C1
Meopham	SO	12	A2
Merstham	SO	12	A1
Merthyr Tydfil	WR	27	B2
Merthyr Vale	WR	27	B2
Merton Park	SO	17	A1
Metheringham	ER	48	B2
Mexborough	ER	56	C2
Micheldever	SO	10	B2
Micklefield	ER	56	B2
Midcalder	SC	73	B1
Middlesbrough	ER	62	B2
Middlewood	LM	46	A2
Midgham	WR	10	A2
Mile End	LT	22	B1
Miles Platting	LM	52	B1
Milford (Surrey)	SO	11	B2
Milford Haven	WR	25	B2
Millbrook (Beds.)	LM	31	A2
Millbrook (Hants.)	SO	10	C1
Mill Hill (Lancs.)	LM	55	B1
Mill Hill Broadway	LM	31	C2
Mill Hill East	LT	23	C1
Millom	LM	60	C1
Milngavie	SC	75	A2
Milnrow	LM	55	C2
Milton Keynes	LM	31	A1
Minehead	WS	7	B2
Minffordd	LM/FR	43	C2
Minorca	ME	59	C2
Minster	SO	14	A1
Mirfield	ER	56	C1
Mistley	ER	33	A2
Mitcham	SO	17	B1
Mitcham Junction	SO	17	B1
Mobberley	LM	46	A1
Moira	NI	85	A1
Monifieth	SC	79	B2
Monkseaton	TW	70	A1
Monks Risborough	LM	31	B1
Montpelier	WR	8	A2
Montrose	SC	80	C1
Monument (London)	LT	21	B2
Monument (Newcastle)	TW	69	B2
Moorgate	ER/LT	21	B2
Moor Park	LM/LT	31	C2
Moorside	LM	51	A1
Moorthorpe	ER	56	C2
Morar	SC	77	A2
Morchard Road	WR	7	C1
Morden	LT	17	B1
Morden Road	SO	17	B1
Morden South	SO	17	B1
Morecambe	LM	54	A2
Moreton (Dorset)	SO	5	A1
Moreton (Merseyside)	LM	45	A1
Moreton-in-Marsh	WR	30	A1
Morfa Mawddach	LM	34	A2
Morley	ER	56	B1
Mornington Crescent	LT	21	B1
Morpeth	ER	68	B1
Mortimer	SO	10	A2
Mortlake	SO	20	C2
Moses Gate	LM	51	A1
Mossley	LM	55	C2
Mossley Hill	LM	53	C2
Mosspark	SC	75	B2
Moston	LM	52	A1
Motherwell	SC	72	B1
Motspur Park	SO	16	B2
Mottingham	SO	18	A2
Mottram Staff Halt*	LM	46	A2
Mouldsworth	LM	45	B2
Moulsecoomb	SO	12	C1
Mount Florida	SC	76	C1
Mountain Ash*	WR	27	B2
Muirend	SC	76	C1
Muir of Ord	SC	82	C1
Muncaster Mill	RE	59	B2
Mytholmroyd	ER	55	B2
Nafferton	ER	57	A2
Nailsea and Backwell	WR	8	A2
Nairn	SC	82	C2
Nant Gwernol	TL	34	A2
Nantwich	LM	46	B2
Nantyronen	LM	34	B2
Narberth	WR	26	B1
Narborough	LM	38	A2
Navigation Road	LM	51	C2
Neasden	LT	20	A2
Neath	WR	27	C1

Needham Market	ER	41	C2
Neilston	SC	75	C1
Nelson	LM	55	B1
Neston	LM	45	A1
Netherfield	LM	47	C2
Netherton	LM	59	B2
Netley	SO	10	C2
Newark Castle	ER	48	B1
Newark Northgate	ER	48	B1
New Barnet	ER	23	B1
New Beckenham	SO	18	A1
New Brighton	LM	53	B1
Newbury	WR	10	A2
Newbury Park	Lt	22	A2
Newbury Racecourse*	WR	10	A2
Newby Bridge	LH	60	C1
Newcastle (Central)	ER/TW	69	B2
New Clee	ER	58	C1
New Cross	SO/LT	22	C1
New Cross Gate	SO/LT	22	C1
New Eltham	SO	18	A2
New Hadley	LM	37	A1
Newhaven Harbour	SO	12	C1
Newhaven Town	SO	12	C1
New Hey	LM	55	C2
New Holland Pier	ER	57	B2
New Holland Town	ER	57	B2
New Hythe	SO	12	A2
Newington	SO	13	A1
New Lane	LM	54	C2
New Malden	SO	16	B2
Newmarket	ER	40	C2
New Mills Central	LM	46	A2
New Mills Newtown	LM	46	A2
New Milton	SO	6	A1
Newport (Essex)	ER	32	A2
Newport (Gwent)	WR	28	A2
New Pudsey	ER	56	B1
Newquay	WR	1	B2
New Romney	RH	13	B2
New Southgate	ER	23	C1
Newton (Greater Glasgow)	SC	76	C2
Newton (Greater Manchester)	LM	52	B2
Newton Abbot	WR	3	B2
Newton Aycliffe	ER	62	A1
Newton-le-Willows	LM	45	A2
Newtonmore	SC	78	A2
Newton-on-Ayr	SC	71	C1
Newton St. Cyres	WR	3	A1
Newtown	LM	35	B2
Ninian Park*	WR	28	A1
Nitshill	SC	75	C2
Norbiton	SO	16	B2
Norbury	SO	17	B2
Norman's Bay	SO	12	C2
Normanton	ER	56	B1
North Acton	LT	20	B2
Northallerton	ER	62	C1
Northampton	LM	39	C1
North Berwick	SC	73	A2
North Camp	SO	11	A1
North Dulwich	SO	17	A2
North Ealing	LT	20	B2
Northfield	LM	37	B2
Northfields	LT	20	C1
North Filton Platform*	WR	28	C2
Northfleet	SO	32	C2
North Harrow	LT	19	A2
Northolt	LT	19	B2
Northolt Park	LM	20	A1
North Queensferry	SC	73	A1
North Road	ER	62	B1
North Sheen	SO	20	C2
North Shields	TW	70	A1
Northumberland Park	ER	24	C1
North Walsham	ER	50	C2
North Weald	LT	32	B2
North Wembley	LM/LT	20	A1
Northwich	LM	46	A1
Northwick Park	LT	20	A1
Northwood (Greater London)	LT	31	C2
Northwood (Worcs.)	SV	37	B1
Northwood Hills	LT	31	C2
North Woolwich	ER	22	B2
Norton Bridge	LM	46	C1
Norwich	ER	41	A2
Norwood Junction	SO	17	B2
Nottingham	LM	47	C2
Notting Hill Gate	LT	21	B1
Nuneaton	LM	38	B1
Nunhead	SO	22	C1
Nunthorpe	ER	62	B2
Nutbourne	SO	11	C1
Nutfield	SO	12	A1
Oakengates	LM	37	A1
Oakham	LM	39	A1
Oakleigh Park	ER	23	B1
Oakwood	LT	23	B2
Oakworth	KW	55	B2
Oban	SC	77	B2
Ockendon	ER	32	C2
Ockley	SO	11	B2
Okehampton*	WR	3	A1
Oldbury	LM	87	B2
Oldfield Park	WR	9	A1
Oldham Mumps	LM	52	A2
Oldham Werneth	LM	52	A2
Old Fold	TW	69	B2
Old Hill	LM	87	C1
Old Roan	LM	53	A2
Old Street	ER/LT	21	B2
Old Trafford	LM	51	B2
Olton	LM	37	B2
Onchan Head	ME	59	C1
Ongar	LT	32	B2
Ore	SO	13	C1
Ormesby	ER	62	B2
Ormskirk	LM	54	C2
Orpington	SO	12	A1
Orrell	LM	54	C2
Orrell Park	LM	53	A2
Orton Mere	NV	39	A2
Osterley	LT	20	C1
Otford	SO	12	A2
Oulton Broad North	ER	42	B2
Oulton Broad South	ER	42	B2
Oval	LT	21	C2
Overton	SO	10	A2
Oxenholme	LM	60	C2
Oxenhope	KW	55	B2
Oxford	WR	30	B2
Oxford Circus	LT	21	B1
Oxshott	SO	16	C1
Oxted	SO	12	A1
Paddington	WR/LT	21	B1
Paddock Wood	SO	12	B2
Padgate	LM	45	A2
Paignton	WR	3	B2
Paignton (Queen's Park)	TD	3	B2
Paisley Canal	SC	75	B1
Paisley Gilmour Street	SC	75	B1
Paisley St. James	SC	75	B1
Palmers Green	ER	23	C2
Pangbourne	WR	30	C2
Pannal	ER	56	A1
Pantyffynon	WR	27	B1
Par	WR	2	B1
Parbold	LM	54	C2
Park	LM	52	B1
Park Royal	LT	20	B2
Parkstone	SO	5	A2
Park Street	LM	31	B2
Parsons Green	LT	21	C1
Parson Street	WR	8	B2
Partick	SC/GG	75	B2
Parton	LM	59	B2
Patchway	WR	28	C2
Patricroft	LM	51	B1
Patterton	SC	75	C2
Peartree	LM	47	C1
Peckham Rye	SO	21	C2
Pegswood	ER	68	B1
Pemberton	LM	54	C2
Pembrey & Burry Port	WR	26	B2

Station	Region	Map	Ref
Pembroke	WR	25	B2
Pembroke Dock	WR	25	B2
Penally	WR	26	B1
Penarth	WR	28	B1
Pendleton	LM	51	B2
Pengam	WR	28	C1
Penge East	SO	18	A1
Penge West	SO	18	A1
Penhelig	LM	34	B2
Penistone	ER	56	C1
Penkridge	LM	37	A2
Penmaenmawr	LM	44	A1
Penmere	WR	1	C1
Penrhiwceiber*	WR	27	B2
Penrhyn (Gwynedd)	FR	44	C1
Penrhyndeudraeth	LM	44	C1
Penrith	LM	60	A2
Penryn (Cornwall)	WE	1	C1
Pensarn (Gwynedd)	LM	43	C2
Penshurst	SO	12	B2
Pentre-bach	WR	27	B2
Pen-y-Bont	LM	35	C2
Penybont	GW	26	A2
Penychain	LM	43	C2
Penyffordd	LM	45	B1
Penzance	WR	1	A1
Percy Main	TW	70	B1
Perivale	LT	20	B1
Perranwell	WR	1	C1
Perry Barr	LM	88	B1
Pershore	WR	37	C2
Perth	SC	79	B1
Peterborough	ER	39	A2
Petersfield	SO	11	B1
Petts Wood	SO	18	B2
Pevensey & Westham	SO	12	C2
Pevensey Bay	SO	12	C2
Pewsey	WR	9	A2
Piccadilly Circus	LT	21	B2
Pickering	NY	63	C1
Pilning	WR	28	C2
Pimlico	LT	21	C2
Pinner	LT	19	A2
Pitlochry	SC	78	B2
Pitsea	ER	33	C1
Plaistow	LT	22	B2
Pleasington	LM	54	B2
Pleasure Beach	BF	54	B1
Plockton	SC	81	A2
Pluckley	SO	13	B1
Plumley	LM	46	A1
Plumpton	SO	12	C1
Plumstead	SO	22	C2
Plymouth	WR	2	B2
Pokesdown	SO	5	A2
Polegate	SO	12	C2
Polesworth	LM	38	A1
Pollokshaws East	SC	75	C2
Pollokshaws West	SC	75	C2
Pollokshields East	SC	76	B1
Pollokshields West	SC	76	B1
Polmont	SC	72	A2
Polsloe Bridge	WR	3	A2
Ponders End	ER	24	B1
Pontarddulais	WR	26	B2
Pontefract Baghill	ER	56	B2
Pontefract Monkhill	ER	56	B2
Pontlottyn	WR	27	B2
Pont-y-Pant	LM	44	B1
Pontypool	WR	28	B1
Pontypridd	WR	27	C2
Poole	SO	5	A2
Poppleton	ER	56	A2
Portadown	NI	84	A1
Portchester	SO	10	C2
Port Erin	ME	59	C1
Port Glasgow	SC	71	A2
Porth	WR	27	C2
Porthmadog	LM/FR	43	C2
Portrush	NI	85	A2
Portslade	SO	12	C1
Portsmouth & Southsea	SO	10	C2
Portsmouth Arms	WR	7	C1
Portsmouth Harbour	SO	10	C2
Port Soderick	ME	59	C1
Port St. Mary	ME	59	C1
Port Sunlight	LM	53	C1
Port Talbot	WR	27	C1
Potters Bar	ER	23	A1
Poulton-le-Fylde	LM	54	B1
Poynton	LM	46	A2
Prees	LM	45	C2
Prescot	LM	45	A2
Prestatyn	LM	44	A2
Prestbury	LM	46	A2
Preston	LM	54	B2
Prestonpans	SC	73	A2
Preston Park	SO	12	C1
Preston Road (Greater London)	LT	20	A1
Preston Road (Merseyside)	LM	53	A2
Prestwich	LM	51	A2
Prestwick	SC	71	C2
Primrose Hill	LM	21	B1
Princes Risborough	LM	31	B1
Prittlewell	ER	33	C1
Prudhoe	ER	67	C2
Pulborough	SO	11	C2
Purfleet	ER	32	C2
Purley	SO	17	C2
Purley Oaks	SO	17	C2
Putney	SO	20	C2
Putney Bridge	LT	21	C1
Pwllheli	LM	43	C2
Quainton Road*	LM	31	B1
Quaker's Yard	WR	27	C2
Queenborough	SO	33	C1
Queen's Park (Glasgow)	SC	76	C1
Queen's Park (London)	LM/LT	21	B1
Queen's Road, Peckham	SO	22	C1
Queenstown Rd. (Battersea)	SO	21	C1
Queensbury	LT	31	C2
Queensway	LT	21	B1
Quintrel Downs	WR	1	B2
Quorn & Woodhouse	ML	38	A2
Radcliffe (Greater Manchester)	LM	55	C1
Radcliffe (Notts.)	LM	47	C2
Radipole	SO	5	A1
Radlett	LM	31	B2
Radley	WR	30	B2
Radyr	WR	28	C1
Rainford	LM	54	C2
Rainham (Essex)	ER	32	C2
Rainham (Kent)	SO	13	A1
Rainhill	LM	45	A2
Ramsey	ME	59	B2
Ramsgate	SO	14	A1
Rannoch	SC	78	B1
Rauceby	ER	48	C2
Ravenglass	LM/RE	59	C2
Ravensbourne	SO	18	A1
Ravenscourt Park	LT	20	C2
Ravensthorpe	ER	56	C1
Rawcliffe	ER	57	B1
Rayleigh	ER	33	C1
Rayners Lane	LT	19	A2
Rayners Park	SO	16	B2
Reading	WR	31	C1
Reading West	WR	31	C1
Rectory Road	ER	21	A2
Redbridge (Greater London)	LT	22	A2
Redbridge (Hants.)	SO	10	C1
Redcar Central	ER	62	A2
Redcar East	ER	62	A2
Reddish North	LM	52	B1
Reddish South	LM	52	C1
Redditch	LM	37	C2
Redhill	SO	12	A1
Redland	WR	8	A2
Redruth	WR	1	C1
Reedham (Norfolk)	ER	42	A1
Reedham (Surrey)	SO	17	C2
Regent Centre	TW	69	A2
Regent's Park	LT	21	B1
Reigate	SO	12	A1

Renton	SC	71	A2
Retford	ER	48	A1
Rheidol Falls	LM	34	B2
Rhiwbina	WR	28	C1
Rhiwfron	LM	34	B2
Rhosneigr	LM	43	A1
Rhydyronen	TL	34	A2
Rhyl	LM	44	A2
Rhymney	WR	27	B2
Ribblehead*	LM	61	C1
Richmond	SO/LT	20	C1
Rickmansworth	LM/LT	31	C2
Riddlesdown	SO	17	C2
Ridgmont	LM	31	A2
Riding Mill	ER	67	C2
Rishton	LM	55	B1
Robertsbridge	SO	13	B1
Roby	LM	45	A2
Rochdale	LM	55	C1
Roche	WR	1	B2
Rochester	SO	13	A1
Rochford	ER	33	C1
Rock Ferry	LM	53	C1
Roding Valley	LT	24	C2
Rogart	SC	82	B2
Rolleston	LM	48	B1
Rolvenden	KS	13	B1
Roman Bridge	LM	44	B1
Romford	ER	32	C2
Romiley	LM	52	C2
Romsey	SO	10	C1
Roose	LM	54	A1
Ropley	MH	10	B2
Rose Grove	LM	55	B1
Rose Hill (Marple)	LM	52	C2
Rossall	BF	54	B1
Rosyth Halt	SC	73	A1
Rosyth Dockyard*	SC	73	A1
Rotherham	ER	50	A2
Rotherham Central (Proj.)	ER	50	A2
Rotherhithe	LT	22	C1
Rothley	ML	38	A2
Rowland's Castle	SO	11	C1
Rowley Regis	LM	37	B2
Rowntree Halt*	ER	56	A2
Royal Oak	LT	21	B1
Roy Bridge	SC	78	A1
Roydon	ER	32	B1
Royston	ER	32	A1
Royton	LM	52	A2
Ruabon	LM	45	C1
Rufford	LM	54	C2
Rugby	LM	38	B2
Rugeley	LM	37	A2
Ruislip	LT	19	A2
Ruislip Gardens	LT	19	A2
Ruislip Manor	LT	19	A2
Runcorn	LM	45	A2
Ruskington	ER	48	B2
Russell Square	LT	21	B2
Ruswarp	ER	63	B1
Rutherglen	SC	76	C1
Ryde Esplanade	SO	6	A2
Ryde Pier Head	SO	6	A2
Ryde St. John's Road	SO	6	A2
Rye	SO	13	C1
Rye House	ER	32	B1
St. Albans Abbey	LM	31	B2
St. Albans City	LM	31	B2
St. Andrews Road	WR	28	C2
St. Annes-on-the-Sea	LM	54	B1
St. Austell	WR	1	B2
St. Bees	LM	59	B2
St. Botolphs	ER	33	A2
St. Budeaux (Ferry Road)	WR	2	B2
St. Budeaux (Victoria Road)	WR	2	B2
St. Columb Road	WR	1	B2
St. Denys	SO	10	C1
St. Enoch	GG	76	B1
St. Erth	WR	1	A1
St. George's Cross	GG	76	B1
St. Germans	WR	2	B2
St. Helens Junction	LM	45	A2
St. Helens Shaw Street	LM	45	A2
St. Helier	SO	17	B1
St. Ives	WR	1	A1
St. James' Park (London)	LT	3	A2
St. James' Park (Newcastle)	TW	69	B2
St. James' Street, Walthamstow	ER	22	A1
St. John's	SO	22	C1
St. John's Wood	LT	21	B1
St. Keyne	WR	2	B1
St. Leonards Warrior Square	SO	13	C1
St. Margaret's (Herts.)	ER	32	B1
St. Margaret's (Middlesex)	SO	16	A1
St. Mary Cray	SO	12	A1
St. Mary's Bay	RH	13	B2
St. Michaels	LM	53	C2
St. Neots	ER	39	C2
St. Pancras	LM	21	B2
St. Paul's	LT	21	B2
Sale	LM	51	C2
Salford	LM	51	B2
Salfords	SO	12	B1
Salhouse	ER	42	A1
Salisbury	SO	9	B2
Saltash	WR	2	B2
Saltburn	ER	62	A2
Saltcoats	SC	71	C1
Saltmarshe	ER	57	B1
Salwick	LM	54	B2
Sandbach	LM	46	B1
Sanderstead	SO	17	C2
Sandhills	LM	53	B1
Sandhurst	SO	11	A1
Sandling	SO	13	B2
Sandown	SO	6	A2
Sandplace	WR	2	B1
Sandwich	SO	14	A1
Sandy	ER	39	C2
Sankey for Penketh	LM	45	A2
Santon	ME	59	C1
Saundersfoot	WR	26	B1
Saunderton	LM	31	C1
Sawbridgeworth	ER	32	B2
Saxilby	ER	48	A1
Saxmundham	ER	42	C1
Scarborough	ER	63	C2
Scotscalder	SC	83	A1
Scotstounhill	SC	75	B2
Scunthorpe	ER	57	C1
Seaburn	ER	70	C2
Seaford	SO	12	C2
Seaforth & Litherland	LM	53	A1
Seaham	ER	68	C2
Seahill	NI	86	C2
Seamer	ER	63	C2
Sea Mills	WR	28	C2
Seascale	LM	59	B2
Seaton	ST	4	A1
Seaton Carew	ER	62	A2
Seer Green	LM	31	C2
Selby	ER	56	B2
Selhurst	SO	17	B2
Sellafield	LM	59	B2
Selling	SO	13	A2
Selly Oak	LM	37	B2
Selsdon	SO	17	C2
Settle	LM	55	A1
Seven Kings	ER	32	C1
Sevenoaks	SO	12	A2
Seven Sisters	ER/LT	21	A2
Severn Beach	WR	28	C2
Severn Tunnel Junction	WR	28	C2
Shackerstone	SH	38	A1
Shadwell	LT	22	B1
Shakespeare Staff Halt*	SO	14	B1
Shalford	SO	11	B2
Shanklin	SO	6	A2
Shaw	LM	55	C2
Shawford	SO	10	B2
Shawlands	SC	75	C2
Sheerness-on-Sea	SO	33	C1
Sheffield	ER	50	B1

Sheffield Park	BL	12	B1
Shelford	ER	40	C1
Shenfield	ER	32	C2
Shenstone	LM	37	A2
Shepherd's Bush	LT	20	B2
Shepherd's Well	SO	14	A1
Shepley	ER	56	C1
Shepperton	SO	15	B1
Shepreth	ER	40	C1
Sherborne	SO	8	C2
Sheringham	ER/NN	50	C1
Shettleston	SC	76	B2
Shields Road	GG	76	B1
Shifnal	LM	37	A1
Shildon	ER	62	A1
Shiplake	WR	31	C1
Shipley	ER	56	B1
Shippea Hill	ER	40	B2
Shipton	WR	30	B1
Shirehampton	WR	28	C2
Shiremoor	TW	70	A1
Shireoaks	ER	47	A2
Shirley	LM	37	B2
Shoeburyness	ER	33	C1
Sholing	SO	10	C2
Shoreditch	LT	21	B2
Shoreham (Kent)	SO	12	A2
Shoreham-by-Sea	SO	12	C1
Shortlands	SO	18	B1
Shotton	LM	45	B1
Shrewsbury	LM	36	A2
Sidcup	SO	32	C1
Silecroft	LM	60	C1
Silverdale	LM	60	C2
Silver Street	ER	23	C2
Silvertown	ER	22	B2
Sinfin Central	LM	47	C1
Sinfin North	LM	47	C1
Singer	SC	75	A1
Sittingbourne	SO/SK	13	A1
Skegness	ER	49	B2
Skelmanthorpe	ER	56	C1
Skipton	LM	55	A2
Slade Green	SO	32	C2
Slateford	SC	73	C1
Sleaford	ER	48	C2
Sleights	ER	63	B1
Sloane Square	LT	21	C1
Slough	WR	31	C2
Small Heath	LM	88	C2
Smethwick Rolfe Street	LM	87	C2
Smethwick West	LM	87	B2
Smitham	SO	12	A1
Smith's Park	TW	70	A1
Snaefell	ME	59	C1
Snaith	ER	56	B2
Snaresbrook	LT	22	A2
Snodland	SO	12	A2
Snowdon Summit	SM	43	B2
Snowdown	SO	13	A2
Sole Street	SO	12	A2
Solihull	LM	37	B2
Somerleyton	ER	42	B1
South Acton	LM	20	C2
Southall	WR	19	C2
Southampton	SO	10	C1
Southampton Airport	SO	10	C2
Southampton Docks	SO	10	C1
South Bank	ER	62	A2
South Bermondsey	SO	22	C1
Southbourne	SO	11	C1
Southbury	ER	24	B1
South Cape	ME	59	C2
South Croydon	SO	17	C2
South Ealing	LT	20	C1
Southease	SO	12	C1
South Elmsall	ER	56	C2
Southend Central	ER	33	C1
Southend East	ER	33	C1
Southend Victoria	ER	33	C1
Southfields	LT	17	A1
Southgate	LT	23	C2

South Gosforth	TW	69	A2
South Greenford	WR	20	B1
South Hampstead	LM	21	B1
South Harrow	LT	20	A1
South Kensington	LT	21	C1
South Kenton	LM/LT	20	A1
South Merton	SO	17	B1
South Milford	ER	56	A2
Southminster	ER	33	B1
Southport	LM	54	C1
South Ruislip	LM/LT	19	A2
South Shields	TW	70	B2
South Tottenham	ER	21	A2
Southwick	SO	12	C1
South Wimbledon	LT	17	A1
South Woodford	LT	24	C2
Sowerby Bridge	ER	55	B2
Spalding	ER	49	C1
Spean Bridge	SC	78	A1
Spital	LM	53	C1
Spondon	LM	47	C1
Spooner Row	ER	41	B2
Springburn	SC	76	B1
Springfield	SC	79	C2
Spring Road	LM	37	B2
Squires Gate	LM	54	B1
Stafford	LM	46	C2
Staines	SO	15	A1
Stainforth & Hatfield	ER	56	C2
Stallingborough	ER	58	C1
Stalybridge	LM	52	B2
Stamford	ER	39	A2
Stamford Brook	LT	20	C2
Stamford Hill	ER	21	A2
Stanford-le-Hope	ER	32	C2
Stanlow & Thornton	LM	45	A2
Stanmore	LT	31	C2
Stansted	ER	32	A2
Staplehurst	SO	13	B1
Stapleton Road	WR	8	A2
Starbeck	ER	56	A1
Starcross	WR	3	A2
Starr Gate	BF	54	B1
Staveley	LM	60	B2
Staverton Bridge	DV	3	B1
Stechford	LM	88	C2
Stepney East	ER	22	B1
Stepney Green	LT	22	B1
Stevenage	ER	32	A1
Stevenston	SC	71	C1
Stewartby	LM	31	A2
Stewarton	SC	71	B2
Stirling	SC	78	C2
Stockport	LM	52	C1
Stocksfield	ER	67	C2
Stocksmoor	ER	56	C1
Stockton	ER	62	B2
Stockwell	LT	21	C2
Stogumber	WS	7	B2
Stoke-on-Trent	LM	46	C1
Stoke Mandeville	LM	31	B1
Stoke Newington	ER	21	A2
Stone	LM	46	C1
Stonebridge Park	LM/lt	20	B2
Stone Crossing	SO	32	C2
Stonegate	SO	12	B2
Stonehaven	SC	80	B2
Stonehouse	WR	28	B1
Stoneleigh	SO	16	C2
Stourbridge Junction	LM	87	C1
Stourbridge Town	LM	87	C1
Stowmarket	ER	41	C2
Stranraer Harbour	SC	64	C1
Stratford	ER/LT	22	B1
Stratford-upon-Avon	LM	38	C1
Strathcarron	SC	81	A2
Strawberry Hill	SO	16	A1
Streatham	SO	17	A2
Streatham Common	SO	17	A2
Streatham Hill	SO	17	A2
Stretford	LM	51	C2
Strines	LM	46	A2

Stromeferry	SC	81	A2
Strood	SO	13	A1
Stroud	WR	29	B1
Sturry	SO	13	A2
Styal	LM	46	A1
Sudbury (Suffolk)	ER	33	A1
Sudbury & Harrow Road	LM	20	A1
Sudbury Hill	LT	20	A1
Sudbury Hill, Harrow	LM	20	A1
Sudbury Town	LT	20	A1
Sunbury	SO	15	A2
Sunderland	ER	20	C2
Sundridge Park	SO	18	A2
Sunningdale	SO	11	A1
Sunnymeads	SO	31	C2
Surbiton	SO	16	B1
Surrey Docks	LT	22	C1
Sutton	SO	17	C1
Sutton Coldfield	LM	88	A2
Sutton Common	SO	17	B1
Swale	SO	13	A1
Swanley	SO	12	A2
Swanscombe	SO	32	C2
Swansea	WR	27	C1
Swanwick	SO	10	C2
Sway	SO	10	C1
Swaythling	SO	10	C1
Swinderby	ER	48	B1
Swindon	WR	29	C2
Swineshead	ER	49	C1
Swinton	LM	51	A2
Swiss Cottage	LT	21	B1
Sydenham (Belfast)	NI	86	C2
Sydenham (Greater London)	SO	18	A1
Sydenham Hill	SO	17	A2
Sylfaen	WL	36	A1
Syon Lane	SO	20	C1
Tackley	WR	30	B2
Tadworth	SO	12	A1
Taffs Well	WR	28	C1
Tain	SC	82	B2
Talbot Square	BF	54	B1
Talsarnau	LM	43	C2
Talybont	LM	33	A2
Tal-y-Cafn	LM	44	A1
Tamworth	LM	37	A1
Tan-y-Bwlch	FR	44	C1
Tan-y-Grisiau	FR	44	C1
Taplow	WR	31	C1
Tattenham Corner	SO	12	A1
Taunton	WR	8	B1
Taynuilt	SC	77	B2
Teddington	SO	16	A1
Tees-side Airport	ER	62	B1
Teignmouth	WR	3	B2
Temple	LT	21	B2
Tenby	WR	26	B1
Tenterden Town	KS	13	B1
Teynham	SO	13	A1
Thames Ditton	SO	16	B1
Thatcham	WR	10	A2
Thatto Heath	LM	45	A2
Theale	WR	10	A2
The Dell (Falmouth)	WR	1	C1
The Green	RE	60	B1
The Lakes	LM	37	B2
Theobalds Grove	ER	24	A1
The Pilot Halt	RH	13	C2
Thetford	ER	41	B1
Theydon Bois	LT	32	B1
Thirsk	ER	62	C2
Thornaby	ER	62	B2
Thorne North	ER	57	C1
Thorne South	ER	57	C1
Thornford	WR	8	C2
Thornliebank	SC	75	C2
Thornton Abbey	ER	57	C2
Thornton Gate	BF	54	B1
Thorntonhall	SC	72	B1
Thornton Heath	SO	17	B2
Thorpe Bay	ER	33	C1
Thorpe Culvert	ER	49	B2
Thorpe-le-Soken	ER	33	B2
Three Bridges	SO	12	B1
Three Oaks	SO	13	C1
Thurgarton	LM	48	B1
Thurso	SC	83	A1
Thurston	ER	41	C1
Tilbury Riverside	ER	32	C2
Tilbury Town	ER	32	C2
Tile Hill	LM	38	B1
Tilehurst	WR	30	C2
Timperley	LM	51	C2
Tipton	LM	87	B1
Tir-phil	WR	28	B1
Tisbury	SO	9	B2
Tiverton Junction	WR	7	C2
Todmorden	LM	55	B2
Tolworth	SO	16	B2
Tonbridge	SO	12	B2
Tonfanau	LM	33	A2
Tonypandy	WR	27	C2
Tooting	SO	17	A1
Tooting Bec	LT	17	A1
Tooting Broadway	LT	17	A1
Topsham	WR	3	A2
Torquay	WR	3	B2
Torre	WR	3	B2
Torrington*	WR	6	C2
Totnes	WR	3	B1
Totnes Riverside	DV	3	B1
Tottenham Court Road	LT	21	B2
Tottenham Hale	ER/LT	21	A2
Totteridge & Whetstone	LT	23	C1
Totton	SO	10	C1
Tower	BF	54	B1
Tower Hill	LT	21	B2
Town Green	LM	54	C2
Trafford Park	LM	51	B2
Trefforest	WR	27	C2
Trefforest Estate	WR	27	C2
Trehafod	WR	27	C2
Treherbert	WR	27	B2
Treorchy	WR	27	C2
Trimley	ER	34	A1
Tring	LM	31	B1
Troed-y-Rhiw	WR	27	B2
Troon	SC	71	C2
Trooperslane	NI	86	C2
Trowbridge	WR	9	A1
Truro	WR	1	C2
Tufnell Park	LT	21	A1
Tulloch	SC	78	A1
Tulse Hill	SO	17	A2
Tunbridge Wells Central	SO	12	B2
Tunbridge Wells West	SO	12	B2
Turkey Street	ER	24	B1
Turnham Green	LT	20	C2
Turnpike Lane	LT	23	C2
Twickenham	SO	16	A1
Twyford	WR	31	C1
Ty Croes	LM	43	A1
Tygwyn	LM	43	C2
Tyndrum Lower	SC	78	B1
Tyndrum Upper	SC	78	B1
Tyne Dock	TW	70	B2
Tynemouth	TW	88	C2
Tyseley	LM	37	B2
Tywyn	LM	34	A2
Tywyn Pendre	TL	34	A2
Tywyn Wharf	TL	34	A2
Uckfield	SO	12	C2
Uddington	SC	76	C2
Ulceby	ER	57	C2
Ulleskelf	ER	56	B2
Ulverston	LM	60	C1
Umberleigh	WR	7	C1
University (Birmingham)	LM	88	C1
University (Coleraine)	NI	85	A2
Upholland	LM	54	C2
Upminster	ER/LT	32	C2
Upminster Bridge	LT	32	C2
Upney	LT	32	C1
Upper Halliford	SO	15	B2

Upper Holloway	LM	21	A2
Upper Warlingham	SO	12	A1
Upton	LM	45	A1
Upton-by-Chester	LM	45	B2
Upton Park	LT	22	B2
Upwey	SO	5	A1
Urmston	LM	51	C1
Uttoxeter	LM	46	C2
Uxbridge	LT	19	B1
Vauxhall	SO/LT	21	C2
Victoria	SO/LT	21	C1
Victoria Park	NI	86	C2
Virginia Water	SO	11	A2
Waddon	SO	17	C2
Waddon Marsh	SO	17	B2
Wadhurst	SO	12	B2
Wadsley Bridge*	ER	47	A1
Wainfleet	ER	49	B2
Wakefield Kirkgate	ER	56	C1
Wakefield Westgate	ER	56	C1
Walkden	LM	51	A1
Walkergate	TW	69	B2
Wallasey Grove Road	LM	53	B1
Wallasey Village	LM	53	B1
Wallington	SO	17	C1
Wallsend	TW	70	B1
Walmer	SO	14	A1
Walsall	LM	87	A2
Waltham Cross	ER	24	A1
Walthamstow Central	ER/LT	22	A1
Walthamstow Queen's Road	ER	22	A1
Walton (Merseyside)	LM	53	A2
Walton-on-Naze	ER	33	B2
Walton-on-Thames	SO	15	C2
Wanborough	SO	11	A1
Wandsworth Common	SO	17	A1
Wandsworth Road	SO	21	C2
Wandsworth Town	SO	21	C1
Wansbeck Road	TW	69	A2
Wansford	NV	39	A2
Wanstead	LT	22	A2
Wanstead Park	ER	22	A2
Wapping	LT	22	B1
Warblington	SO	11	C1
Ware	ER	32	B1
Wareham	SO	5	A2
Wargrave	WR	31	C1
Warminster	WR	9	B1
Warnham	SO	11	B2
Warren Street	LT	21	B2
Warrington Bank Quay	LM	45	A2
Warrington Central	LM	45	A2
Warwick	LM	38	C1
Warwick Avenue	LT	21	B1
Warwick Road	LM	51	B2
Washford Halt	WS	7	B2
Watchet	WS	7	B2
Wateringbury	SO	12	A2
Waterloo (London)	SO/LT	21	B2
Waterloo (Merseyside)	LM	53	A1
Water Orton	LM	38	B1
Watford	LT	31	C2
Watford High Street	LM/LT	31	C2
Watford Junction	LM/LT	31	C2
Watford North	LM	31	B2
Watford West	LM	31	C2
Wedgwood	LM	46	C1
Weeley	ER	33	B2
Weeton	ER	56	A1
Welling	SO	32	C1
Wellingborough	LM	39	C1
Wellington	LM	37	A1
Wellworthy Ampress Works Halt*	SO	6	A1
Welshpool	LM	36	A1
Welshpool Raven Square (Under Constr.)	WL	36	A1
Welwyn Garden City	ER	32	B1
Welwyn North	ER	32	B1
Wem	LM	45	C2
Wembley Central	LM/LT	20	A1
Wembley Complex	LM	20	A2
Wembley Park	LT	20	A2
Wemyss Bay	SC	71	A1
Wendover	LM	31	B1
Wennington	LM	54	A2
West Acton	LT	20	B2
West Allerton	LM	53	C2
Westbourne Park	WR/LT	21	B1
West Brompton	LT	21	B1
Westbury	WR	9	A1
West Byfleet	SO	15	C1
West Calder	SC	72	B2
Westcliff	ER	33	C1
Westcombe Park	SO	22	C2
West Croydon	SO	17	B2
West Drayton	WR	19	B1
West Dulwich	SO	17	A2
West Ealing	WR	20	B1
Westenhanger	SO	13	B2
Westerfield	ER	33	A2
Westerton	SC	75	A2
West Finchley	LT	23	C1
Westgate-on-Sea	SO	14	A1
West Ham	ER/LT	22	B1
West Hampstead	LM/LT	21	A1
West Hampstead Midland	LM	21	A1
West Harrow	LT	20	A1
West Horndon	ER	32	C2
Westhoughton	LM	55	C1
West Jesmond	TW	69	B2
West Kensington	LT	21	C1
West Kilbride	SC	71	B1
West Kirby	LM	45	A1
West Malling	SO	12	A2
Westminster	LT	21	B2
West Monkseaton	TW	70	A1
West Norwood	SO	17	A2
Weston Milton	WR	8	A1
Weston-super-Mare	WR	8	A1
West Ruislip	LM/LT	19	A2
West Runton	ER	50	C1
West St. Leonards	SO	13	C1
West Street	GG	76	B1
West Sutton	SO	17	C1
West Wickham	SO	18	B1
West Worthing	SO	11	C2
Weybourne	NN	50	C1
Weybridge	SO	15	C1
Weymouth	SO	5	A1
Weymouth Quay	SO	5	A1
Whaley Bridge	LM	46	A2
Whatstandwell	LM	47	B1
Whimple	WR	3	A2
Whitby	ER	63	B1
Whitchurch (Hants.)	SO	10	A2
Whitchurch (Salop)	LM	45	C2
Whitchurch (South Glam.)	WR	28	C1
Whiteabbey	NI	86	C2
Whitechapel	LT	22	B1
White City	LT	20	B2
Whitecraigs	SC	75	C2
Whitefield	LM	51	A2
White Hart Lane	ER	23	C2
Whitehaven	LM	59	B2
Whitehead	NI	86	C2
Whitehead Excn. Stn.*	NI	86	C2
White Notley	ER	33	B1
Whitland	WR	26	B1
Whitley Bay	TW	70	A2
Whitley Bridge	ER	56	B2
Whitlock's End	LM	37	B2
Whitstable	SO	13	A2
Whittlesea	ER	40	B1
Whittlesford	ER	32	A2
Whitton	SO	16	A1
Whyteleafe	SO	12	A1
Whyteleafe South	SO	12	A1
Wick	SC	83	A1
Wickford	ER	33	C1
Wickham Market	ER	42	C1
Widdrington	ER	68	B1
Widnes	LM	45	A2
Widney Manor	LM	37	B2

Wigan North Western	LM	54	C2
Wigan Wallgate	LM	54	C2
Wigton	LM	66	C1
Willesden Green	LT	20	A2
Willesden Junction	LM/LT	20	B2
Williamwood	SC	75	C2
Williton	WS	7	B2
Wilmcote	LM	38	C1
Wilmslow	LM	46	A1
Wilnecote	LM	38	A1
Wimbledon	SO/LT	17	A1
Wimbledon Chase	SO	17	B1
Wimbledon Park	LT	17	A1
Wimbledon Staff Halt*	SO	17	A1
Winchelsea	SO	13	C1
Winchester	SO	10	B2
Winchfield	SO	11	A1
Winchmore Hill	ER	23	C2
Windermere	LM	60	B2
Windsor & Eton Central	WR	31	C2
Windsor & Eton Riverside	SO	31	C2
Winnersh	SO	11	A1
Winsford	LM	46	B1
Wisbech*	ER	40	A1
Wishaw	SC	72	B1
Wistaston Road (Crewe Wks.)*	LM	46	C1
Witham	ER	33	B1
Witley	SO	11	B2
Wittersham Road	KS	13	B1
Witton	LM	88	B1
Wivelsfield	SO	12	C1
Wivenhoe	ER	33	B2
Woburn Sands	LM	31	A1
Woking	SO	11	A2
Wokingham	SO	11	A1
Woldingham	SO	12	A1
Wolverhampton	LM	87	A1
Wolverton	LM	31	A1
Wombwell	ER	56	C1
Woodbridge	ER	42	C1
Wood End	LM	37	C2
Woodford	LT	24	C2
Woodgrange Park	ER	22	A2
Wood Green	ER/LT	23	C2
Woodhall	SC	71	A2
Woodham Ferrers	ER	33	B1
Woodhouse	ER	50	B2
Woodlands Road	LM	52	A1
Woodlesford	ER	56	B1
Woodley	LM	52	C2
Woodmansterne	SO	12	A1
Woodside	SO	18	B1
Woodside Park	LT	23	C1
Wood Street Walthamstow	ER	22	A1
Wool	SO	5	A1
Woolston	SO	10	C2
Woolwich Arsenal	SO	22	C2
Woolwich Dockyard	SO	22	C2
Wootton	IW	6	A2
Wootton Wawen	LM	37	C2
Worcester Foregate Street	WR	37	C1
Worcester Park	SO	16	B2
Worcester Shrub Hill	WR	37	C1
Workington	LM	59	A2
Worksop	ER	47	A2
Worplesden	SO	11	A2
Worstead	ER	50	C2
Worthing	SO	11	C2
Wrabness	ER	33	A2
Wraysbury	SO	31	C2
Wrenbury	LM	45	B2
Wressle	ER	57	B1
Wrexham Central	LM	45	B1
Wrexham Exchange	LM	45	B1
Wrexham General	LM	45	B1
Wroxham	ER	42	A1
Wye	SO	13	A2
Wylam	ER	67	C2
Wylde Green	LM	88	B2
Wymondham	ER	41	A2
Wythall	LM	37	B2
Yalding	SO	12	A2
Yardley Wood	LM	37	B2
Yarmouth	ER	42	A2
Yatton	WR	8	A2
Yeoford	WR	3	A1
Yeovil Junction	WR	8	C2
Yeovil Pen Mill	WR	8	C2
Yetminster	WR	8	C2
Yoker	SC	75	A2
York	ER	56	A2
Yorton	LM	45	C2
Ystrad Mynach	WR	28	C1
Ystrad Rhondda	WR	27	C2

KEY TO RAILWAY CODES

CODE	NAME
BA	Bala Lake Railway
BF	Blackpool & Fleetwood Tramway
BL	Bluebell Railway
DV	Dart Valley Railway
ER	British Rail—Eastern
FB	Fairbourne Railway
FR	Festiniog Railway
GG	Greater Glasgow P.T.E.
GO	Great Orme Tramway
GW	Gwili Railway
IW	Isle of Wight Railway
KW	Keighley & Worth Valley Railway
KS	Kent & East Sussex Railway
LH	Lakeside & Haverthwaite Railway
LL	Llanberis Lake Railway
LM	British Rail—London Midland
LT	London Transport
LY	Lochty Railway
ME	Isle of Man Railway
MH	Mid-Hants Railway
ML	Main Line Steam Trust
NI	Northern Ireland Railways
NN	North Norfolk Railway
NV	Nene Valley Railway
NY	North Yorkshire Moors Railway
RE	Ravenglass & Eskdale Railway
RH	Romney, Hythe & Dymchurch Railway
SC	British Rail—Scottish
SH	Shackerstone Railway
SK	Sittingbourne and Kemsley Railway
SM	Snowdon Moutain Railway
SO	British Rail—Southern
ST	Seaton Tramway
SV	Severn Valley Railway
SY	Strathspey Railway
TD	Torbay and Dartmouth Railway
TL	Talyllyn Railway
TW	Tyne & Wear Metro
WL	Welshpool & Llanfair Railway
WR	British Rail—Western
WS	West Somerset Railway

INDEX TO BRITISH RAIL DEPOTS AND STABLING POINTS

CODE	NAME	PAGE No.	MAP REF.
AB	Aberdeen (Ferryhill)	80	B1
AF	Ashford (Chart Leacon)	13	B2
AN	Allerton, Liverpool	53	C2
AY	Ayr	71	C1
BC	Birkenhead Mollington Street	53	C1
BD	Birkenhead North	53	B1
BE	Bedford Midland	39	C2
BG	Botanic Gardens, Hull	57	B2
BH	Barrow Hill	47	A1
BI	Brighton	12	C1
BJ	Bristol Marsh Junction	8	B2
BL	Blyth	68	B1
BM	Bournemouth	5	A2
BN	Bounds Green (HST)	23	C2
BQ	Bury	55	C1
BR	Bristol Bath Road	8	B2
BS	Bescot	87	A2
BU	Burton	47	C1
BW	Barrow	54	A1
BX	Buxton	46	A2
BY	Bletchley	31	A1
BZ	St. Blazey	1	B2
CA	Cambridge	40	C1
CC	Clacton	33	B2
CD	Crewe Diesel Depot	46	C1
CE	Crewe Electric Depot	46	C1
CF	Cardiff (Canton)	28	A1
CG	Croxley Green	31	C2
CH	Chester	45	B2
CJ	Clapham Junction	21	C1
CK	Corkerhill	75	B2
CP	Crewe Carriage Shed	46	C1
CR	Colchester	33	A1
CW	Cricklewood	20	A2
DA	Darnall	50	B1
DE	Dundee	79	B2
DN	Darlington	62	B1
DR	Doncaster	56	C2
DT	Dunfermline (Townhill)	73	A1
DY	Derby Etches Park	47	C1
EC	Edinburgh Craigentinny (HST)	73	C2
ED	Eastfield	76	B1
EG	Edge Hill	53	B2
EH	Eastleigh	10	C2
EJ	Ebbw Junction, Newport	28	B2
EM	East Ham	22	A2
EU	Euston Station	21	B2
EX	Exeter St. Davids	3	A1
FH	Frodingham, Scunthorpe	57	C1
FP	Finsbury Park	21	A2
FR	Fratton, Portsmouth	10	C2
FW	Fort William	78	B1
GD	Gateshead	69	B2
GI	Gillingham	13	A1
GL	Gloucester	29	B1
GM	Grangemouth	72	A2
GU	Guide Bridge	52	B2
GW	Glasgow (Shields Road)	75	B2
HA	Haymarket	73	C1
HD	Holyhead	43	A1
HE	Hornsey	21	A2
HF	Hereford	28	A2
HG	Hither Green	18	A1
HI	Hitchin	31	A2
HM	Healey Mills	56	C1
HN	Hamilton	72	B1
HO	Holbeck	56	B1
HR	Hall Road	53	A1
HS	Hammerton Street, Bradford	56	B1
HT	Heaton (HST)	69	B2
HY	Hyndland	75	B2
IL	Ilford	22	A2
IM	Immingham	57	C2
IP	Ipswich Station	33	A2
IS	Inverness	82	C2
KD	Carlisle (Kingmoor)	66	C2
KM	Carlisle Yard	66	C2
KX	King's Cross	21	B2
KY	Knottingley	56	B2
LA	Laira	2	B2
LE	Landore, Swansea	27	C1
LG	Longsight Electric Depot	52	B1
LJ	Llandudno Junction	44	A1
LN	Lincoln	48	B2
LO	Longsight Diesel Depot	52	B1
LR	Leicester	38	A2
LV	Liverpool Street	21	B2
ME	Marylebone	21	B1
MG	Margam	27	C1
MH	Millerhill	73	C2
ML	Motherwell	72	B1
MN	Machynlleth	34	A2
MR	March	40	A1
NA	Newton Abbot	3	B2
NH	Newton Heath	52	A1
NL	Neville Hill	56	B1
NM	Nottingham (Carr. Sidings)	47	C2
NR	Norwich	41	A2
NW	Northwich	46	A1
OC	Old Oak Common (Loco.)	20	B2
ON	Orpington	12	A1
OO	Old Oak Common (HST)	20	B2
OX	Oxford	30	B2
PA	St. Pancras	21	B2
PB	Peterborough	39	A2
PH	Perth Station	79	B1
PM	Bristol St. Philip's Marsh (HST)	8	B2
PO	Polmadie	76	B1
PZ	Penzance	1	A1
RB	Ranelagh Bridge, Paddington	21	B1
RE	Ramsgate	14	A1
RG	Reading	31	C1
RL	Ripple Lane	32	C2
RS	Reddish	52	B1
RY	Ryde	6	A2
SB	Shirebrook	47	B2
SE	St. Leonards	13	C1
SF	Stratford	22	A1
SG	Slade Green	32	C2
SI	Soho	88	C1
SL	Stewarts Lane	21	C1
SP	Wigan (Springs Branch)	54	C2
SR	Stratford Repair Depot	22	A1
ST	Severn Tunnel Junction	28	C2
SU	Selhurst	17	B2
SW	Swindon	29	C2
SY	Saltley	88	C1
SZ	Southall	19	B2
TE	Thornaby	62	B2
TI	Tinsley	50	B2
TJ	Thornton Junction	79	C1
TO	Toton	47	C2
TS	Tyseley	88	C2
TW	Tunbridge Wells West	12	B2
TY	Tyne Yard	69	C2
VR	Vale of Rheidol Railway	34	B2
WC	Waterloo & City	21	B2
WD	Wimbledon	17	A1
WH	Wath	56	C2
WJ	Watford Junction	31	B2
WK	Workington	59	A2
WN	Willesden	20	B2
WO	Wellingborough	39	C1
WS	Worcester	37	C1
WT	Westhouses	47	B2
WY	Westbury	9	A1
YK	York	56	A2

INDEX TO FREIGHT TERMINALS AND YARDS

NAME	PAGE NO.	PAGE REF.
Abbey (Norfolk)	40	A2
Abbey–BSC	27	C1
Abbey (Shrewsbury)	36	A2
Abbey Foregate C.S.	36	A2
Abenbury Sidings (Wrexham)	45	B1
Abercwmboi Phurnacite	27	B2
Aberdare	27	B2
Abernant Colliery	27	B1
Aberpergwm Colliery	27	B2
Aberthaw P.S.	7	B2
Abingdon	30	C2
Abram Colliery	54	C2
Ackton Hall Colliery	56	C2
Acton Lane P.S.	20	B2
Acton Yard	20	B2
Agecroft Colliery & P.S.	51	A2
Aintree Containerbase	53	A2
Akeman St.	31	B1
Albion	87	B2
Aldwarke–BSC	50	A2
Alexandra Dock (Hull)	57	B2
Alexandra Dock (Liverpool)	53	B1
Alexandra Dock Junc. Yards	28	B2
Allerton Bywater Colliery	56	B2
Allington	13	A1
Alloa	78	C2
Allscott–British Sugar	36	A2
Amlwch	43	A2
Anchor–BSC (Scunthorpe)	57	C2
Angerstein Wharf	22	C2
Annat	78	B1
Annfield Plain	68	C1
Appleby Frodingham–BSC	57	C1
Ardeer–ICI	71	C1
Ardingly	12	B1
Ardrossan North Coal Depot	71	C1
Ardwick West	52	B1
Arkwright Colliery	47	B2
Armley Moor	56	B1
Arncott	30	B2
Ashburton Grove	21	A2
Ashington Colliery	68	B1
Ashton-in-Makerfield	54	C2
Askern Coalite	56	C2
Askern Main Colliery	56	C2
Attercliffe Goods	50	B1
Auchinleck	71	C2
Auchmuty	79	C1
Auchterarder	78	C2
Avenue Carbonisation	47	B1
Avenue (Leamington Spa)	38	C1
Avonside Wharf	8	B2
Ayr Harbour	71	C1
Babbington Colliery	47	C2
Baddesley Colliery	38	A1
Baglan Bay	27	C1
Bagworth Colliery	38	A2
Bamber Bridge CCE Depot	54	B2
Banbury Road (Oxford)	30	B2
Banwen Colliery	27	B2
Bardney	48	B2
Bardon Hill	38	A2
Bargoed Colliery	28	B1
Barking P.S.	32	C1
Barleith	71	C2
Barlow Tip	56	B2
Barnbow	56	B1
Barnburgh Colliery	56	C2
Barnwell	40	C1
Barnwood (Gloucester)	29	B1
Barony Colliery & P.S.	71	C2
Barrington Cem. Wks.	40	C1
Barrow–BSC	54	A1
Barrow Cart Coal Depot	54	A1
Barrow Collliery	56	C1
Barrow Hill Yard	47	A1
Barrow–Vickers	54	A1
Barrow Yard	54	A1
Barton Hill Wagon Shops	8	A2
Barton Mill C.S.	10	A2
Basford Hall Yard	46	C1
Bates Colliery	68	B1
Bathgate	72	A2
Battersea Wharf	21	C1
Bayston Hill Quarry	36	A2
Beattock Coal Depot	65	A2
Beckermet Quarry–BSC	59	B2
Becket St. (Oxford)	30	B2
Bedale	62	C1
Bedenham	10	C2
Bedlay Colliery (Glenboig)	72	B1
Bedwas Colliery	28	C1
Bedworth	38	B1
Beechgrove	9	B1
Beeding Cem. Wks.	12	C1
Beeston	47	C2
Beeston Castle Coal Depot	45	B2
Beighton P.W. Depot	50	B2
Belford Quarry	74	C2
Bellahouston C.S.	75	B2
Bennerley Colliery	47	C2
Bentinck Colliery	47	B2
Bentley Colliery	56	C2
Berkeley Nuclear P.S.	29	B1
Berry Hill	47	B2
Bersham Colliery	45	B1
Bescot Yard	87	A2
Bestwood Park Sidings	47	B2
Beswick	52	B1
Betteshanger Colliery	14	A1
Betws Drift Mine	27	B1
Bevercotes Colliery	48	A1
Bevois Park (Southampton)	10	C1
Bicester London Road	30	B2
Bickershaw Colliery	54	C2
Bidston Coal Terminal	53	B1
Bilthorpe Colliery	47	B2
Bilston	87	A1
Bilston Glen Colliery	73	B1
Birch Coppice Colliery	38	A1
Birdsfield	76	C2
Birkenhead Docks	53	B1
Birtley	69	C2
Blackhill Coal Depot	67	C2
Blackwell Sidings	47	B2
Blaenant Colliery	27	B1
Bletchington Cem. Wks.	30	B2
Blidworth Colliery	47	B2
Blindwells Colliery	73	A2
Blodwell Quarry	45	C1
Bloxwich	87	A2
Blyth P.S. & Docks	68	B1
Bodmin General	2	B1
Bogside–ICI	72	A2
Bold Colliery	45	A2
Boldon Colliery	70	B1
Bolsover Coalite & Colliery	47	B2
Bordesley Yard	88	C1
Boulby	63	B1
Bow Creek	22	B1
Bow Goods	22	B1
Bowers Row Colliery	56	B1
Bowes Staithes	70	B1
Bowhill Colliery	79	C1
Bradwell Nuclear P.S.	33	B1
Branthams Sdgs. (Manningtree)	33	A2
Braunstone Gate	38	A2
Brechin	80	C1
Brenkley Colliery	69	A2
Brent	20	A2
Brentfords Goods	20	C1
Brian Mills Depot (Sunderland)	70	C2
Bricklayer's Arms	21	C2
Bridge Street (Northampton)	39	C1
Bridgeton Central Carr. Dep.	76	B1
Brierley Hill Steel Term.	87	C1
Briggs Sidings	46	B2
Brindle Heath	51	B2

Bristol East Depot	8	B2
Bristol West Depot	8	B2
British Oak Colliery	56	C1
Briton Ferry	27	C1
Brodsworth Colliery	56	C2
Bromford Bridge	88	B2
Brookhouse Coll. & Coking Pl.	50	B2
Brooklands Avenue (Cambridge)	40	C1
Broomloan GGPTE Depot	75	B2
Brotton Coal Depot	63	B1
Broughton Lane	50	B1
Broughton Moor	59	A2
Brownhills	37	A2
Brunthill	66	C2
Brymbo Steelworks–GKN	45	B1
Brynlliw Colliery	26	B2
BSC Abbey	27	C1
BSC Aldwarke	50	A2
BSC Anchor	57	C2
BSC Appleby–Frodingham	57	C1
BSC Barrow	54	A1
BSC Beckermet Quarry	59	B2
BSC Bilston (Closed)	87	A1
BSC Bromford	88	B2
BSC Cambuslang (Westburn)	76	C2
BSC Cleveland	62	A2
BSC Clydebridge	76	C1
BSC Clydesdale	72	B1
BSC Consett	67	C2
BSC Corby	39	B1
BSC Craigneuk	72	B1
BSC Dalzell	72	B1
BSC Ebbw Vale	28	B1
BSC Frodingham	57	C1
BSC Fullwood Foundry	72	B1
BSC Gartcosh	72	C1
BSC Glendon East Quarry	39	B1
BSC Glengarnock	71	B2
BSC Hallside	76	C2
BSC Hardendale Quarry	60	A2
BSC Hartlepool South	62	A2
BSC Hunterston	71	B1
BSC Ickles	50	A2
BSC Imperial	72	C1
BSC Jarrow	70	B1
BSC Lackenby	62	A2
BSC Lanarkshire	72	B1
BSC Lancashire	45	A2
BSC Landore	27	C1
BSC Llanwern	28	C2
BSC Margam	27	C1
BSC Meadowhall	50	A1
BSC Monkshall	45	A2
BSC Normanby Park	57	C1
BSC Orb	28	B2
BSC Panteg	28	B1
BSC Ravenscraig	72	B1
BSC Redbourn (Scunthorpe)	57	C2
BSC Redcar	62	A2
BSC River Don	50	B1
BSC Roundwood	50	A2
BSC Shelton	46	B1
BSC Shepcote Lane	50	B1
BSC Shotton	45	B1
BSC Skinningrove	63	B1
BSC Stanton	47	C2
BSC Staveley	47	A1
BSC Stocksbridge	56	C1
BSC Templeborough	50	A2
BSC Thrybergh	50	A2
BSC Tinsley Park	50	B1
BSC Trafford Park	51	B2
BSC Trostre	26	B2
BSC Velindre	27	B1
BSC Whifflet	72	C1
BSC Whitehead	28	A2
BSC Wolverhampton	87	A1
BSC Workington	59	A2
Bull Point	2	B2
Bulmer's Works (Hereford)	28	A2
Bulwark Street (Dover)	14	B1
Burghead	83	C1
Burn Naze–ICI P.S.	54	B1
Burngullow	1	B2
Burrelton	79	B1
Burrows Sidings (Swansea)	27	C1
Burtonwood	45	A2
Bush-on-Esk (Longtown)	66	C2
Butterwell Colliery	68	B1
Buxton South Goods	46	A2
Cadder Yard	76	A2
Cadeby Colliery	56	C2
Cadley Hill Colliery	38	A1
Caerwent	28	C2
Calder Yard	72	C1
Caldon Low Quarry	46	B2
Callerton–ICI	69	A1
Calvert Lane Coal Depot (Hull)	57	B2
Calverton Colliery	47	B2
Cambois (Blyth)	68	B1
Cambus	78	C2
Cambuslang–BSC	76	C2
Cameron Bridge	79	C1
Camlachie	76	B1
Cannock Colliery	37	A2
Canton	28	A1
Carbis Wharf	1	B2
Cardowan Colliery (Stepps)	76	B2
Carlton Sidings (Cudworth)	56	C1
Carmarthen Bay P.S.	26	B2
Carne Point	2	B1
Carrington P.S. (Partington)	51	C1
Carville	70	B1
Castle Bromwich	88	B2
Castle Donington P.S.	47	C2
Castle Foregate (Shrewsbury)	36	A2
Castle Works–GKN (Cardiff)	78	A1
Castleton P.W. Depot	55	C1
Cattewater	2	B2
Cavendish Sidings	53	B1
Celynen North Colliery	28	C1
Celynen South Colliery	28	C1
Chacewater	1	C1
Chadderton P.S.	52	A1
Chaddesden	47	C1
Channelsea Sidings	22	B1
Chatham Docks	13	A1
Cheadle	46	C2
Chelsea Basin	21	C1
Chesterton P.W. Depot	40	C1
Chettisham	40	B2
Chilmark	9	B2
Chilwell	47	C2
Chinnor Cem. Wks.	31	B1
Chipping Sodbury	29	C1
City Basin (Exeter)	3	A2
Clatchard Craig Quarry	79	C1
Claydon Cem. Wks.	41	C2
Clayhills C.S. (Aberdeen)	80	B1
Clegg Street (Oldham)	52	A2
Cleveland–BSC	62	A2
Cliffe	32	C2
Cliffe Hill	38	A2
Clifton C.S. (York)	56	A2
Clipstone Colliery	47	B2
Clockburn Colliery	69	C1
Clydach-on-Tawe	27	B1
Clydebridge–BSC	76	C1
Clydeport FLT	71	A1
Clydesdale–BSC	72	B1
Coalfield Farm Colliery	38	A2
Coalfields Goods (Cambridge)	40	C1
Coalville	38	A1
Coatbridge FLT (Gartsherrie)	72	C1
Cockenzie P.S.	73	A2
Cockshute Sidings	46	C1
Codnor Park Sidings	47	B2
Coed Bach Washery	26	B2
Coed Ely Colliery	27	C2
Cofton Hackett–BL	37	B2
Coity Goods (Bridgend)	27	C2
Coldham Lane (Cambridge)	40	C1
Coleham (Shrewsbury)	36	A2
Coleshill	38	B1

Colnbrook	19	C1
Colthrop	10	A2
Coltness	72	B1
Colwick Industrial Estate	47	C2
Comrie Colliery (Saline)	72	A2
Connah's Quay P.S.	45	B1
Connington South CCE Tip	39	B2
Consett	67	C2
Contentibus Bing	72	B2
Corby	39	B1
Corton Wood Colliery	56	C1
Coryton Oil Ref.	33	C1
Cotgrave Colliery	47	C2
Cotham	48	C1
Coton Hill Yard	36	A2
Cottam P.S.	48	A1
Coundon Road (Coventry)	38	B1
Coupar Angus	79	B1
Courthouse Green (Coventry)–BL	38	B1
Coventry Colliery & Homefire	38	B1
Cowlairs	76	B1
Cowley Hill Wks.–Pilkingtons	54	C2
Coxes Lock Mill	15	C1
Coxhoe	62	A1
Coxlodge	69	A2
Coypool	2	B2
Crag Hall Coal Depot	63	B1
Craig-y-Nos Quarry	27	B1
Craigentinny C.S.	73	C2
Craiginches Yard (Aberdeen)	80	B1
Craigneuk–BSC	72	B1
Cranmore	9	B1
Cransley	39	B1
Crawley New Yard	12	B1
Creswell Colliery	47	A2
Cricklewood Recess Sidings	20	A2
Croes Newydd Yard	45	B1
Croft Quarry	38	A2
Croft Sidings (Darlington)	62	B1
Crofton P.W. Depot	56	C1
Crombie	72	A2
Cronton Colliery	45	A2
Croxley Mill	31	C2
Croydon 'B' P.S.	17	B2
Cruiks Quarry	73	A1
Culloden Moor	82	C2
Currock C. & W. Shops	66	C2
Curzon Street Parcels	88	C1
Cuxton	12	A2
Cwm Bargoed	27	B2
Cwm Colliery	27	C2
Cwmawr Colliery	26	B2
Cwmparc	27	C2
Cynheidre Colliery	26	B2
Dairycoates	57	B2
Dalmuir Riverside	75	A1
Dalzell–BSC	72	B1
Danygraig FLT	27	C1
Darfield Main Colliery	56	C2
Daw Mill Colliery (Whitacre)	38	B1
Dawdon Colliery	68	C2
Dean Hill	10	B1
Dean Road	70	B2
Dearne Valley Colliery	56	C2
Deep Duffryn Colliery	27	B2
Deep Navigation Colliery	27	B2
Deepdale Coal Depot	54	B2
Denaby NCB Workshops	56	C2
Denby Colliery	47	B1
Denton Holme NCL	66	C2
Deptford	70	C2
Dereham	41	A1
Derwenthaugh Coking Plant	69	B1
Desford Colliery	38	A2
Dewsbury Railway Street	56	C1
Dewsnap Sidings	52	B2
Dibles Wharf	10	C1
Didcot Distribution Centre	30	C2
Didcot P.S.	30	C2
Dinnington Colliery	47	A2
Dinsdale P.W. Depot	62	B1
Dinton	9	B2
Dock Street (Newport)	28	A2
Dodworth Colliery	56	C1
Doe Hill	47	B2
Dolcoath	1	C1
Doncaster Central Goods	56	C2
Donisthorpe Colliery	38	A1
Donnington	37	A1
Dora Colliery	73	A1
Dowlais	27	B2
Dowlow	46	B2
Drakelow P.S.	38	A1
Drax P.S.	56	B2
Draycott	47	C2
Drayton Gravel Terminal	11	C1
Dringhouses Yard (York)	56	A2
Drinnick Mill	1	B2
Dudley FLT	87	B1
Dufftown	83	C1
Dundee Harbour	79	B2
Dundee West	79	B2
Dunfermline Upper Goods	73	A1
Dungeness Nuclear P.S.	13	C2
Dunnington	56	A2
Dunstable	31	A2
Dunston P.S.	69	B1
Duxford	32	A2
Earles Sidings (Hope)	47	A1
Earley P.S.	31	C1
Easington Colliery	62	A2
Eassie	79	A1
East Depot (Bristol)	8	B2
East Grimstead	10	B1
East Hecla Steelworks	50	A1
East Hetton Colliery	62	A1
East Leake	47	C2
East Usk Yard	28	A2
Eastgate	61	A2
Eastriggs	66	C1
Ebbw Vale–BSC	28	B1
Eccles Colliery	70	A1
Ecclesfield East & West	50	A1
Edwalton	47	C2
Eggborough P.S.	56	B2
Eight Ash Green	33	A1
Eling Wharf	10	C1
Elland P.S.	55	B2
Ellington Colliery	68	B1
Elliot Junction	80	C2
Elsecar CCE Tip	56	C2
Elsecar Main Colliery	56	C1
Elswick	69	B1
Ely (Cardiff)	28	A1
Emley Moor Colliery	56	C1
Ernesettle	2	B2
Eskmeals	59	C2
Etherley CCE Tip	62	A1
Euxton	54	C2
Evanton	82	C2
Exeter City Basin	3	A2
Exeter Riverside Yard	3	A2
Exmouth Junction	3	A2
Fairwater CCE Depot	8	B1
Falkland Yard	71	C1
Far Cotton	39	A1
Farnley	56	B1
Farnworth	45	A2
Faslane	71	A1
Fawcett Street (Sunderland)	70	C2
Fawley Oil Ref.	10	C2
Fazakerley P.W. Depot	53	A2
Felixstowe Docks & FLT	34	A1
Fen Drayton	40	C1
Ferguslie Coal Depot	75	B1
Ferrybridge P.S.	56	B2
Ferryhill Coal Depot	62	A1
Ferryhill Goods (Aberdeen)	80	B1
Ferry Road (Grangetown)	28	B1
Fiddlers Ferry P.S.	45	A2
Fighting Cocks	62	B1
Fishburn Coking Plant	62	A1
Flax Bourton	8	A2
Fleetwood (Wyre P.S.)	54	B1

Location	Map	Grid
Flemington Coal Depot	72	B1
Fletton	39	A2
Flixborough	57	C1
Florence Colliery	46	C2
Foley Park–British Sugar	37	B1
Follingsby FLT	70	C1
Folly Lane	45	A2
Forders Sidings	31	A2
Forfar	79	A2
Forth Goods (Newcastle)	69	B2
Foss Island Goods (York)	56	A2
Four Ashes	37	A2
Fowey	2	B1
Frances Colliery (Dysart)	79	C1
Fremington Quay	6	B2
Friary Goods (Plymouth)	2	B2
Frickley Colliery	56	C2
Frodingham–BSC	57	C1
Fryston Colliery	56	B2
Fulbourne Cem. Wks.	40	C2
Fullwood Foundry–BSC	72	B1
Furzebrook	5	A2
Gabalfa Coal Depot (Cardiff)	28	A1
Galley Hill	13	C1
Gallows Close	63	C2
Garston Docks & FLT	53	C2
Gartcosh–BSC	72	C1
Gartsherrie Cem. Wks.	72	C1
Gartsherrie (Coatbridge FLT)	72	C1
Garw Colliery	27	C2
Gatewen Colliery	45	B1
Gedling Colliery	47	C2
General Terminus (Glasgow)	76	B1
Giffen	71	B2
Glascoed	28	B1
Glasgow International Ft. Tml.	76	B1
Glasshoughton Colliery	56	B2
Glazebrook	51	C1
Glen Douglas	78	C1
Glendon East–BSC Quarries	39	B1
Glengarnock–BSC	71	B2
Godfrey Road (Newport)	28	A2
Godley Junction	52	B2
Gogar	73	A1
Goldthorpe Colliery	56	C2
Gorseinon	26	B2
Gosford Green	38	B1
Grain Oil Ref.	33	C1
Grangemouth	72	A2
Granton	73	B2
Great Bridge	87	B2
Green Market (Low Fell)	69	C2
Greetland	55	B2
Gresty Lane (Crewe)	46	C1
Gresty Road (Crewe)	46	C1
Griffin Wharf & FLT	33	A2
Grimethorpe Colliery	56	C2
Grimsargh	54	B2
Grosvenor EMU Depot	21	C1
Guild Street FLT (Aberdeen)	80	B1
Gunness	57	C1
Gunnie	72	C1
Gushetfaulds FLT	76	B1
Gwaun-cae-Gurwen Colliery	27	B1
Hackney Yard (Newton Abbot)	3	B2
Hafod Goods (Swansea)	27	C1
Haig Colliery	59	B2
Halewood	45	A2
Halling Cem. Wks.	12	A2
Halliwell Coal Depot	55	C1
Hallside–BSC	76	C2
Hamble Oil Ref.	10	C2
Hams Hall P.S.	38	B1
Hamworthy Goods & FLT	5	A2
Handsworth & Smethwick	88	C1
Harbury Cem. Wks.	38	C1
Hardendale Quarry	60	B2
Harrison's Limeworks (Shap)	60	B2
Hartshill Quarry	38	B1
Harworth Colliery	47	A2
Harworth Glassworks	47	A2
Hartlepool South–BSC	62	A2
Hatfield Colliery	56	C2
Haverton Hill–ICI	62	A2
Hawkesbury Lane	38	B1
Hawkhead	75	B1
Hawthorn Coll. & Coking Pl.	68	C2
Haydock	54	C2
Hayle Wharf	1	A1
Healey Mills Yard	56	C1
Heathfield	3	B1
Heaton Cement Term.	69	B2
Hele & Bradninch	7	C2
Hem Heath Colliery	46	C1
Hendon–Brian Mills Depot	70	C2
Herbrandston Oil Ref.	25	B2
Herrington Colliery	68	C1
Hessay	56	A2
Hethersett	41	A2
Heysham Harbour	54	A2
Heysham Nuclear P.S.	54	A2
Heywood	55	C1
Hickleton Colliery	56	C2
High Marnham P.S.	48	B1
High St. Goods (Glasgow)	76	B1
Highgate L.T. Depot	21	A1
Highgate Wood L.T. Sidings	21	A1
Hillhouse Gds. (Huddersfield)	55	C2
Hillhouse ICI Works	54	B1
Hillhouse Quarry	71	C2
Hillside Distillery	80	C1
Hillwood Quarry	73	A1
Hilton	47	C1
Hindlow	46	B2
Hinksey Yard (Oxford)	30	B2
Histon	40	C1
Hither Green Yard	18	A1
Holborough Cem. Wks.	12	A2
Holditch Colliery	46	B1
Holles Street (Grimsby)	58	C1
Holmes Yard (Lincoln)	48	B2
Holmethorpe	12	A1
Holyhead Breakwater	43	A1
Holywell Junction	45	A1
Honeybourne	29	A2
Hookagate P.W. Depot	36	A2
Hope (Earles Sidings) Cem. Wks.	47	A1
Hope Street (Manchester)	51	B2
Hopetown	62	B1
Hopton Heath Coll. (Proposed)	46	C2
Horbury–Procor Works	56	C1
Horden Colliery	62	A2
Horrocksford Cem. Wks.	55	B1
Horsehay & Dawley	37	A1
Hotchley Hill	47	C2
Hothfield	13	B1
Houghton-le-Spring	68	C1
Houghton Main Colliery	56	C2
Hucknall Colliery	47	C2
Hull Central Goods	57	B2
Hull New Yard	57	B2
Hullavington	29	C1
Humber Oil Ref.	57	C2
Humberstone Road (Leicester)	38	A2
Huncoat P.S.	55	B1
Hunslet East	56	B1
Hunslet Engine Co.	56	B1
Hunslet Yard	56	B1
Hunterston	71	B1
Huntspill	8	B1
ICI Ardeer	71	C1
ICI Bogside	72	A2
ICI Castner–Keller	45	A2
ICI Haverton Hill	62	A2
ICI Hillhouse	54	B1
ICI Over & Wharton	46	B1
ICI Powfoot	66	C1
ICI Rocksavage	45	A2
ICI Severnside	28	C2
ICI Snodgrass	71	C1
ICI Tunstead	46	A2
ICI Weston	45	A2
ICI Wilton	62	A2
ICI Winnington	46	A1

Ickles Yard (Rotherham)	50	A2
Ilford Milk Depot	22	A2
Immingham	57	C2
Ince Marshes– Shellstar	45	A2
Ince Moss CCE Tip	54	C2
Innerwick (Torness)	74	A1
Inshaw Works	72	B1
Inveralmond	79	B1
Inverkeilor	80	C2
Ironbridge P.S.	37	A1
Ivybridge	3	B1
Jarrow–BSC	70	B1
Jersey Marine	27	C1
Keadby P.S.	57	C1
Kellingley Colliery	56	B2
Kennethmont	83	C1
Keresley	38	B1
Ketton Cem. Wks.	39	A2
Killingholme Oil Ref.	57	C2
Killingworth Exchange Sidings	69	A2
Killoch Colliery	71	C2
Kilvington	48	C1
Kincardine P.S.	72	A2
Kineton	38	C1
King George Dock (Hull)	57	B2
Kingmoor Yard	66	C2
Kingsbury	38	B1
Kingsland Road Goods (Bristol)	8	B2
Kinning Park Coal Depot	76	B1
Kinsley Drift Mine	56	C2
Kirk Sandall	56	C2
Kirkcaldy Harbour	73	A1
Kirkdale EMU Depot	53	B1
Kittybrewster Coal Depot	80	A1
Kiveton Park Colliery	47	A2
Knapton	63	C1
Knighton CCE Depot	38	A2
Knockshinnoch Colliery	65	A1
Lackenby–BSC	62	A2
Lady Windsor Colliery	27	C2
Lakeland Colliery	59	A2
Lamberts Colliery (Proposed)	26	B2
Lambton Coking Plant	68	C1
Lanarkshire–BSC	72	B1
Lancashire–BSC (Warrington)	45	A2
Landor Street Inland Port	88	C1
Landore–BSC	27	C1
Laurencekirk Coal Depot	80	C1
Lavant	11	C1
Law Junction	72	B1
Lawley St.–FLT & NCL	88	C1
Layerthorpe	56	A2
Lea Hall Colliery	37	A2
Leiston Coal Depot	42	C1
Leith South & Docks	73	B2
Lenton P.W. Depot	47	C2
Lenwade	41	A2
Letchworth P.S.	32	A1
Leven Dock Coal Depot	79	C2
Leyburn	61	C2
Lidlington CCE Tip	31	A2
Lillie Bridge LT P.W. Depot	21	C1
Limbury Road (Luton)	31	A2
Linby Colliery	47	B2
Lindsey Oil Ref.	57	C2
Linwood–Talbot	75	B1
Littlemore	30	B2
Littleton Colliery	37	A2
Liverpool Rd. (Manchester)	51	B2
Liversedge	56	B1
Livingston	72	A2
Llandarcy Oil Ref.	27	C1
Llandeilo Junction Yard	26	B2
Llanharan Colliery	27	C2
Llantony (Gloucester)	29	B1
Llantrisant	27	C2
Llanwern–BSC	28	C2
Lochaber Aluminium Works	78	B1
Lochrin Works	72	C1
London Int. Ft. Term. (LIFT)	22	A1
London Road (Carlisle)	66	C2
London Road (Glasgow)	76	B1
London Road LT Depot	21	C2
Long Eaton	47	C2
Long Marston	29	A2
Longannet P.S.	72	A2
Longbridge–BL	37	B2
Longsight FLT	52	B1
Longtown	66	C2
Lostock Hall	54	B2
Louth	49	A1
Low Fell	69	C2
Low Gates	62	C1
Ludgershall	10	A1
Lydney	28	B2
Lynemouth Colliery	68	B1
Machen Quarry	28	C1
Maerdy Colliery	27	B2
Maesglas CCE Tip	28	A2
Maesteg Colliery	27	C1
Maindee CCE Depot	28	A2
Maindy	28	A1
Malago Vale C.S.	8	B2
Mallaig Junction Yard	78	B1
Maltby Main Colliery	47	A2
Manchester Int. Ft. T. (MIFT)	51	B2
Mansfield Colliery	47	B2
Mansfield Concentration Sdgs.	47	B2
Mantle Lane (Coalville)	38	A1
Manton Wood Colliery	47	A2
Manvers Coking Plant	56	C2
Marchon Chem. Wks.	59	B2
Marchwood	10	C1
Margam Yard	27	C1
Marine Colliery	28	B1
Maritime FLT (Southampton)	10	C1
Markham Colliery	47	B2
Markham Main Colliery	56	C2
Marland	6	C2
Marsh Lane (Leeds)	56	B1
Marsh Mills	2	B2
Marsh Pond	8	B2
Marshgate (Doncaster)	56	C2
Marshmoor	32	B1
Maudlands (Preston)	54	B2
Maxwelltown	65	B2
Mayfield Parcels (Manchester)	52	B1
Meadowhall–BSC	50	A1
Meaford P.S.	46	C1
Measham Colliery	38	A1
Meeth	6	C2
Meldon	2	A2
Meledor Mill	1	B2
Melksham	9	A1
Melton	42	C1
Menstrie	78	C2
Merehead Quarry	9	B1
Merthyr Vale Colliery	27	B2
Methil Docks & P.S.	79	C2
Metro–Cammell (Birmingham)	88	C2
Mickleover Test Centre	47	C1
Middlesbrough Docks	62	A2
Middlesbrough Goods	62	A2
Middleton Towers	40	A2
Middlewich	46	B1
Mile End Stone Terminal	22	B1
Milford Sidings	56	B2
Mill Pit Colliery	27	C1
Millbrook FLT	10	C1
Millerhill Yard	73	C2
Millfield Coal Depot	70	C2
Millfield (Stockton)	62	A2
Misterton	48	A1
Mode Wheel	51	B2
Mold	45	B1
Mold Junction Sidings	45	B1
Monckton Coking Plant	56	C1
Monk Bretton	56	C1
Monkshall–BSC	45	A2
Monksmoor	3	B1
Monkton Colliery & Coking Pt.	70	B1
Monktonhall Colliery	73	C2
Monkwearmouth Goods	70	C2
Monmore Green	87	A1

Moor Greeen Colliery	47	B2
Moorfield P.S.	28	A2
Moorswater	2	B1
Moreton-on-Lugg	36	C2
Morris Cowley	30	B2
Morriston	27	C1
Mossend Yard	72	B1
Mostyn	45	A1
Mountain Ash Colliery	27	B2
Mountfield	12	C2
Mountsorrel Quarry	38	A2
Muirhouse CCE Workshops	76	B1
Muirton (Perth)	79	B1
Nantgarw Colliery	27	C2
Neath Canalside	27	C1
Nechells P.S.	88	B2
Neptune Street (Hull)	57	B2
New Bilton Cem. Wks.	38	B2
New Hucknall Colliery	47	B2
New Yard (Hull)	57	B2
Newbiggin	60	A2
Newbridge	28	C1
Newburn Yard (Hartlepool)	62	A2
Newcourt	3	A2
Newdigate Colliery	38	B1
Newland P.W. Depot	37	C1
Newstead Colliery	47	B2
Newtonhead Coal Depot	71	C1
Normanby Park—BSC	57	C1
North Elmham	41	A1
North Gawber Colliery	56	C1
North Tees P.S.	62	A2
North Wilford P.S.	47	C2
Northam Yard (Southampton)	10	C1
Northenden	51	C2
Northfleet Cem. Wks.	32	C2
Norton Junction	37	A2
Norwich P.S.	41	A2
Norwich (Victoria)	41	A2
Norwood Coking Plant	69	C2
Norwood Yard	17	B2
Nostell Colliery	56	C1
Nunnery C.S.	50	B1
Oakamoor	46	C2
Oakdale Colliery	28	B1
Oakley	72	A2
Ocker Hill P.S.	87	B2
Offord	40	C1
Ogmore Valley Washery	27	C2
Old Kilpatrick	75	A1
Oldham Road (Manchester)	52	B1
Ollerton Colliery	47	B2
Onllwyn Colliery	27	B1
Orb Works (Newport)—BSC	28	B2
Orchardhall	72	A2
Ordsall Lane	51	B2
Orgreave Colliery & Coking Plant	50	B2
Osbaldwick	56	A2
Oughtibridge	47	A1
Over & Wharton—ICI	46	B1
Overseal Sidings	38	A1
Oxcroft Colliery	47	A2
Oxley C.S.	87	A1
Oxwellmains Cem. Wks.	74	A1
Padiham P.S.	55	B1
Padworth	10	A2
Paisley Underwood	75	B1
Palace Gates Coal Depot	23	C2
Pallion	70	C2
Panteg—BSC	28	B1
Par Harbour	2	B1
Park Hill Colliery	56	B1
Park Mill Coliery	56	C1
Park Royal	20	B2
Parkandillack	1	B2
Parkend	28	B2
Parkhead Forge	76	B1
Parkneuk Works	72	B1
Parkside Colliery	45	A2
Parkway Market	50	B1
Partington Coal Terminal	51	C1
Partington Oil Ref. & Chem. Wks.	51	C1
Peak Forest	46	A2
Peckfield Colliery	56	B2
Penallta Colliery	28	C1
Penallta Junction Tip	27	C2
Penarth Curve Sidings	28	A1
Penderyn Quarry	27	B2
Pengam FLT	28	A1
Penrhiwceiber Colliery	27	B2
Pensnett (Shut End) Coal Depot	87	B1
Penyfford Cem. Wks.	45	B1
Petteril Bridge	66	C2
Philadelphia	68	C1
Piddington	39	B1
Pig's Bay	33	C1
Pinhoe	3	A2
Pinkston Coal Depot	76	B1
Pitstone Cem. Wks.	31	B1
Plaistow & West Ham	22	B1
Plean	72	A2
Pleasley Colliery	47	B2
Plymstock	2	B2
Point of Ayr Colliery	44	A2
Polkemmet Colliery (Whitburn)	72	B2
Polmaise Colliery	78	C2
Ponsandane C.S. & HST Depot	1	A1
Pontarddulais Stocking Site	26	B2
Pontsmill	1	B2
Poplar Docks	22	B1
Port Clarence	62	A2
Port Elphinstone	80	A1
Port Sunlight	53	C1
Port Tennant	27	C1
Portfield	11	C1
Portishead	28	C2
Portobello FLT & CCE & Coal Depot	73	C2
Portwood	52	C1
Powfoot—ICI	66	C1
Prescot	45	A2
Preston Street (Whitehaven)	59	B2
Prince of Wales Colliery	56	B2
Pumpherston	72	B2
Puriton	8	B1
Pye Hill Colliery	47	B2
Pylle Hill	8	B2
Quedgeley	29	B1
Queen Alexandra Dock	28	A1
Quidhampton	9	B2
Radstock	9	A1
Radway Green	46	B1
Radyr Yard	28	C1
Raglan Colliery	27	C2
Railway Street (Dewsbury)	56	C1
Railway Street (Newcastle)	69	B2
Railway Technical Centre	47	C1
Raisby Hill Quarry	62	A1
Ratcliffe-on-Soar P.S.	47	C2
Rathbone Road Coal Depot	53	B2
Ratho Coal Depot	73	A1
Ravenhead	45	A2
Ravenscraig—BSC	72	B1
Rawdon Colliery	38	A1
Rawtenstall Coal Depot	55	B1
Reading Central	11	A1
Red Bank C.S.	52	B1
Redbourne (Scunthorpe)—BSC	57	C2
Redbridge CCE Depot	10	C1
Redcar Ore & Mineral Terminal	62	A2
Redfern Street (Sandhills)	53	B1
Redmire	61	C2
Renfrew	75	B1
Renishaw Park Colliery	47	A2
Rewley Road (Oxford)	30	B2
Rhoose Cem. Wks.	7	A2
Riccarton	71	C2
Richborough P.S.	14	A1
Ridham Docks	13	A1
Ripple Lane Yard	32	C2
River Don (Brightside)—BSC	50	B1
Roath Branch Cripple Sidings	28	A1
Roath Dock & Goods	28	A1
Robeston Oil Ref.	25	B2
Rochester Docks	13	A1

Location	Map	Grid
Rogerstone P.S.	28	C1
Roosecote P.S.	54	A1
Rose Heyworth Colliery	28	B1
Roskear	1	C1
Ross Junction Tip	72	B1
Rossington Colliery	56	C2
Rotherham Road	50	A2
Rotherwood Yard	50	B2
Rothesay Dock (Glasgow)	75	A1
Round Oak Steelworks	87	C1
Roundwood–BSC	50	A2
Royston Drift Mine	56	C1
Ruddington	47	C2
Rufford Colliery	47	B2
Rugeley P.S.	37	A2
Ryburgh	50	C1
Rye House P.S.	32	B1
Rylstone	55	A2
Saffron Lane P.S.	38	A2
St. Blazey Yard	1	B2
St. Dennis CCE Tip	1	B2
St. James Sidings (New Cross)	22	C1
St. Johns Colliery	56	B1
St. Johns Goods (Bedford)	39	C2
St. Mary's Yard (Derby)	47	C1
Salkeld Street Parcels	76	B1
Saltend	57	B2
Santon Foreign Ore Terminal	57	C2
Savile Colliery	56	B1
Sculcoates	57	B2
Scunthorpe Coal Terminal	57	C2
Scunthorpe West Yard	57	C1
Seafield Colliery	73	A1
Seaforth FLT	53	A1
Seaham Colliery	68	C1
Seal Sands	62	A2
Seaton-on-Tees	62	A2
Selby Drift Mine	56	B2
Severn Tunnel Junction Yard	28	C2
Severnside–ICI	28	C2
Seymour Yard	47	A2
Shap	60	B2
Sharlston Colliery	56	C1
Sharpness	29	B1
Sheepbridge	47	A1
Sheepford	72	C1
Sheerness Steelworks	33	C1
Sheffield Freight Terminal	50	B1
Shelton–BSC	46	B1
Shelton Wharf	46	C1
Shepcote Lane–BSC	50	B1
Sherwood Colliery	47	B2
Shewalton Tip	71	C2
Shieldhall	75	B2
Shirebrook Colliery	47	B2
Shireoaks Colliery	47	A2
Shore Road (Birkenhead)	53	B1
Shotton–BSC	45	B1
Shut End Coal Depot	87	B1
Sighthill Goods	76	B1
Silverdale Colliery	46	B1
Silverhill Colliery	47	B2
Silvertown Tramway	22	B2
Silverwood Colliery	50	A2
Simonside Wagon Works	70	B1
Sinclairtown	79	C1
Sizewell Nuclear P.S.	42	C1
Skellow	56	C2
Skinningrove–BSC	63	B1
Slateford CCE & Goods	73	C1
Small Heath Coal Depot	88	C1
Smithywood Coking Plant	50	A1
Snailwell	40	C2
Snibston Colliery	38	A1
Snodgrass–ICI	71	C1
Snowdown Colliery	13	A2
Soho Pool	88	C1
South Hetton Colliery	68	C1
South Kirkby Colliery	56	C2
South Lambeth	21	C1
South Lynn	40	A2
Southam Cem. Wks.	38	C1
Southerham Cem. Wks.	12	C1
Southwark EMU Depot	21	B2
Southwick	70	C2
Speke Yard	53	C2
Spekeland Road Goods (Liverpool)	53	B2
Spondon P.S.	47	C1
Springmill Street (Bradford)	56	B1
Sproughton	33	A2
Staines West	15	A1
Stainton CCE Tip	66	C2
Standard Gauge Steam Trust	88	C2
Stanlow Oil Ref.	45	A2
Stanton–BSC	47	C2
Staunton	48	C1
Staveley–BSC	47	A1
Staythorpe P.S.	46	B1
Steamtown (Carnforth)	60	C2
Steetley Colliery	47	A2
Stella North P.S.	69	B1
Stella South P.S.	69	B1
Stepps Coal Depot	76	B2
Stillington	62	A1
Stocksbridge–BSC	56	C1
Stockton FLT	62	B2
Stockton North Shore	62	B2
Stockton South Coal Depot	62	B2
Stoneycombe Quarry	3	B2
Storrs Hill	56	C1
Stourport P.S.	37	C1
Stourton C. & W. and FLT	56	B1
Stow Park	48	A1
Strand Road (Preston)	54	B2
Stranraer Town	64	C1
Stratford FLT	22	A1
Stratford Market	22	B1
Sudbrook	28	C2
Sunderland South Dock	70	C2
Sutton Colliery	47	B2
Sutton-in-Ashfield	47	B2
Sutton Manor Colliery	45	A2
Sutton Park	88	A2
Swains Park Colliery	37	A1
Swalwell Colliery	69	B1
Swan Village Coal Depot	87	B2
Swanscombe Cem. Wks.	32	C2
Swansea East Coal Depot	27	C1
Sweet Dews	57	B2
Syston	38	A2
Taff Merthyr Colliery	27	B2
Tallington	39	A2
Tanhouse Lane	45	A2
Tavistock Junction Yard	2	B2
Taylors Lane P.S.	20	B2
Tees Dock	62	A2
Tees Yard	62	B2
Teesport	62	A2
Teignbridge	3	B1
Temple Mills Yard	22	A1
Thame	31	B1
Thames Haven Oil Ref.	33	C1
Thames Wharf	22	B1
Thoresby Colliery	47	B2
Thorney Mill	19	C1
Thornhill P.S.	56	C1
Thornton Fields C.S.	22	B1
Thornton Yard	79	C1
Thorpe Marsh P.S.	56	C2
Three Bridges P.W. Depot	12	B1
Thrislington	62	A1
Thrybergh–BSC	50	A2
Thurcroft Colliery	47	A2
Tibshelf Sidings	47	B2
Tickhill	47	A2
Tidal Yard (Cardiff)	28	A1
Tidenham Quarry	28	C2
Tilmanstone Quarry	14	A1
Tinsley Park–BSC	50	B1
Tinsley Yard	50	B1
Tintern Quarry	28	B2
Tondu	27	C2
Topley Pike Quarry	46	A2
Torksey	48	A1

Torrington	6	C2
Toton Yard	47	C2
Tower Colliery	27	B2
Townhead Coal Depot	71	C1
Townhill Yard	73	A1
Trafford Park Sidings & FLT	51	B2
Trawsfynydd Nuclear P.S.	44	C1
Trecwn	25	A2
Tredomen NCB Works	28	C1
Treeton Colliery	50	B2
Treforgan Colliery (Proposed)	27	B1
Trelewis Drift Mine	27	B2
Tremorfa Steelworks—GKN	28	A1
Trentham Sidings	46	C1
Trostre—BSC	26	B2
Trowse (Norwich)	41	A2
Tunstead Quarry—ICI	46	A2
Tutbury	47	C1
Tuxford	48	B1
Tweedmouth	74	B2
Tymawr Colliery	27	C2
Tyndall Field Goods (Cardiff)	28	A1
Tyne Dock	70	B1
Tyne Yard	69	C2
Tyneside Central Freight Dep.	69	B2
Tytherington Quarry	29	C1
Valley	43	A1
Valley Goods (Bradford)	56	B1
Vane Tempest Colliery	68	C2
Velindre—BSC	27	B1
Victoria Coal Depot (Norwich)	41	A2
Virgil St. Coal Depot	28	A1
Upper Greenock	71	A1
Upperby Carriage Depot	66	C2
Upton Park Coal Depot	22	B2
Urlay Nook	62	B1
Wakefield C. & W. Shops	56	C1
Walker	70	B1
Wallerscote—ICI	46	A1
Wallingford	30	C2
Wandsworth Road	21	C1
Wapping Wharf	8	B2
Warcop	61	B1
Wardley	70	B1
Warsop	47	B2
Warsop Main Colliery	47	B2
Washwood Heath Yard	88	B2
Waterloo Goods (Aberdeen)	80	B1
Waterside Colliery	64	A2
Waterston Oil Ref.	25	B2
Watery Road Goods (Wrexham)	45	B1
Watford Cardiff Road P.S.	31	C2
Wath Main Colliery	56	C2
Wath Yard	56	C2
Watton-at-Stone	32	B1
Wavertree Parcels	53	B2
Wearmouth Colliery	70	C2
Weaste	51	B2
Weaverthorpe	63	C2
Wednesbury	87	B2
Wednesfield	87	A1
Wednesfield Road Coal Depot	87	A1
Weetslade Washery	69	A2
Welbeck Colliery	47	B2
Wenford Bridge	2	B1
Wensum (Norwich)	41	A2
Wern Tarw	27	C2
Wernos Washery	27	B1
West Burton P.S.	48	A1
West Cornforth Quarry	62	A1
West Depot (Bristol)	8	B2
West Hallam Colliery	47	C2
West Somerset Quarry	9	B1
West Yard (Lincoln)	48	B2
Westfield Colliery	79	C1
Westoe Colliery	70	B2
Westthorpe Colliery	47	A2
Whatley Quarry	9	B1
Wheldale Colliery	56	B2
Whifflet Foundry	72	C1
Whifflet Yard	72	C1
Whitacre (Daw Mill Colliery)	38	B1
Whitehall Road Goods (Leeds)	56	B1
Whitehead—BSC	28	A2
Whitemoor Yard	40	A1
Whitlingham	42	A1
Whittington	45	C1
Whittle Colliery	68	A1
Whitwell Colliery & Quarry	47	A2
Whitwick Sidings	38	A1
Widdrington Colliery	68	A1
Wigston	38	A2
Willesden Yards & FLT	20	B2
Willington P.S.	47	C1
Wilton—ICI	62	A2
Windscale	59	B2
Winfrith	5	A1
Winnington—ICI	46	A1
Wintersett Colliery	56	C1
Wirksworth Quarry	47	B1
Wisbech	40	A1
Wissington	40	A2
Wolsingham	61	A2
Wolstanton Colliery	46	B1
Wolverhamton Steel Terminal	87	A1
Wood Lane	20	B2
Woodburn CCE Shops	50	B1
Woodston	39	A2
Woodville Colliery	38	A1
Woolley Colliery	56	C1
Wootton Bassett	29	C2
Worksop Yard	47	A2
Wrangaton	3	B1
Wyndham Colliery	27	C2
Yardley Chase (Piddington)	39	A1
Ynysarwed Colliery	27	B1
Yoker Yard	75	B2
Yorkshire Main Colliery	56	C2

INDEX TO BRITISH RAIL ENGINEERING LTD. WORKS

NAME	PAGE NO.	PAGE REF.
Ashford	13	B2
Crewe	46	C1
Derby Litchurch Lane	47	C1
Derby Locomotive Works	47	C1
Doncaster	56	C2
Eastleigh	10	C2
Glasgow	76	B1
Horwich	54	C2
Shildon	62	A1
Swindon	29	C2
Temple Mills	22	A1
Wolverton	31	A1
York	56	A2

INDEX TO MINOR RAILWAYS

NAME	PAGE NO.	PAGE REF.
Beamish Museum & Tramway	68	C1
Brecon Mountain Railway	27	B2
Chasewater Railway	37	A2
Derwent Valley Light Railway	56	A2
Foxfield Railway	46	C2
Middleton Railway	56	B1
Midland Railway Company	47	B1
Springwell—Incline	69	C2
Tanfield Railway	69	C1
Tramway Museum Society	47	B1
Yorkshire Dales Railway	55	A2